THE BRITISH FOLK REVIVAL

To the two women in my life: Chris and Steph

The British Folk Revival

1944–2002

MICHAEL BROCKEN
Liverpool Hope University College, UK

ASHGATE

Published by
Ashgate Publishing Limited
Gower House
Croft Road
Aldershot
Hants GU11 3HR
England

Ashgate Publishing Company
Suite 420
101 Cherry Street
Burlington, VT 05401-4405
USA

Ashgate website: http://www.ashgate.com

British Library Cataloguing in Publication Data
Brocken, Michael
    The British folk revival. – (Ashgate popular and folk music series)
    1. Folk music – Great Britain – History and criticism 2. Folk music – Great Britain – Analysis, appreciation – History – 20th century
    I. Title
    781.6'221

Library of Congress Cataloging-in-Publication Data
Brocken, Michael.
    The British folk revival / Michael Brocken.
        p. cm. – (Ashgate popular and folk music series)
    Includes bibliographical references and discography and index.
    ISBN 0-7546-3281-4 (alk. paper) – ISBN 0-7546-3282-2 (pbk.: alk. paper)
        1. Folk music–Great Britain–History and criticism. 2. Popular music–Great Britain–20th century–History and criticism. I. Title. II. Series.

    ML3650.B76 2003
    781.62'21–dc21

                                                                            2002043960

ISBN 0 7546 3281 4 (Hbk)
ISBN 0 7546 3282 2 (Pbk)

Typeset by Manton Typesetters, Louth, Lincolnshire, UK.
Printed and bound in Great Britain by MPG Books Ltd, Bodmin, Cornwall.

Contents

General Editor's Preface

The upheaval that occurred in musicology during the last two decades of the twentieth century has created a new urgency for the study of popular music alongside the development of new critical and theoretical models. A relativistic outlook has replaced the universal perspective of modernism (the international ambitions of the 12-note style); the grand narrative of the evolution and dissolution of tonality has been challenged, and emphasis has shifted to cultural context, reception and subject position. Together, these have conspired to eat away at the status of canonical composers and categories of high and low in music. A need has arisen, also, to recognise and address the emergence of crossovers, mixed and new genres, to engage in debates concerning the vexed problem of what constitutes authenticity in music and to offer a critique of musical practice as the product of free, individual expression.

Popular musicology is now a vital and exciting area of scholarship, and the Ashgate Popular and Folk Music series aims to present the best research in the field. Authors will be concerned with locating musical practices, values and meanings in cultural context, and may draw upon methodologies and theories developed in cultural studies, semiotics, post-structuralism, psychology and sociology. The series will focus on popular musics of the twentieth and twenty-first centuries. It is designed to embrace the world's popular musics from Acid Jazz to Zydeco, whether high-tech or low-tech, commercial or non-commercial, contemporary or traditional.

Professor Derek B. Scott
Chair of Music
University of Salford

Preface

Like many British youngsters in the 1960s, I was first drawn towards folk music by Americans, for example, Dylan singing 'It Ain't Me, Babe', the Byrds' 'Turn, Turn, Turn' and Baez singing Ochs's 'There but for Fortune'. I can still remember the first time I heard the last of these three songs. It was Bob-a-Job week and I was a member of the Cubs. I was washing dishes for a young mother when the plaintive melody drifted into her kitchen from the radio in the parlour ('mmm … almost as good as the Beatles', I thought).

A few years later I was attracted to the beatnik, 'alternative' culture of the British folk revival when a local folk group (I forget their name) visited my school – West Derby Comprehensive in Liverpool – and performed a folk concert in the school hall. As I remember, they mostly sang shanties but also included a couple of Tom Paxton and Ewan MacColl songs. These they described as 'protest' songs and they portrayed them as 'serious'. This appealed to my teenage angst, I suppose, although I now realise that Paxton's superb melodies were also very important.

By this time (1968) the folk revival was booming. But it almost immediately appeared to me to be divided into two distinct camps, those who followed and applauded contemporary folk songs such as myself, and those who wished everything to remain 'traditional'. I was somewhat confused. Nevertheless, I could see that the revival was a musical and social force to be reckoned with. Ordinary people seemed to be playing an important social, political and musical role by cleaving to the revival. It was less about 'crack' (i.e. the fun of playing) then, and more about using music to bring about long overdue change – however naïve that might now seem. By the time I was 16 I had already visited – illegally, I might add – the Spinners Club at Gregson's Well and Jacquie and Bridie's club. By the age of 17, Oily Joe's was my spiritual home, with intermittent visits to Frank McCall's club – at the Criterion, I think – and the various clubs run by the Crofters.

I must admit, however, that I was always somewhat wayward as a folkie. I did not subscribe to Communism, for a start (which wasn't always a help in Liverpool folk clubs!), and, if I were brutally honest, it was the magnificent Byrds who had introduced me to the verities of (what one could do with) 'traditional' material. They also led me to an encounter with Jefferson Airplane and Love – for which I shall remain eternally grateful.

The upshot of this unconventional route into folk music was my taking into account as much value in the work of Kantner as Carthy and Arthur Lee as A.L. Lloyd. Indeed, my popular music perspective always ran the rule over any performance, for everything – literally everything – was measured by the attainments of the Beatles.

This perspective began to get me into trouble. In 1971, at both the Black Diamond and the Bothy folk clubs, I found myself at odds with self-appointed, all-pervading musical-cum-social hierarchies. Yet, after reading Richard Mabey's *The Pop Process* (1969) and Nik Cohn's *Awopbopaloobopalopbamboom* (1970) that same year, I realised that at least I was not alone in finding value and quality in the popular. Furthermore, the seminal writings of Gillett and Frith in the *Rock File* series of readers (together with Pete Frame and John Tobler's articles in *Zig Zag* magazine) revealed to me that there was an evolving popular music tradition.

Greil Marcus's *Mystery Train* (1976), too, was a revelation; his essay on Elvis – 'Elvis: Presliad' – was an inspiration dealing, as it did, with the myth of Presley in a passionate, yet serious (perhaps even academic) manner. The collective effort of the writers involved with *The Electric Muse* (1975) – Dallas, Denselow, Laing, Shelton (perhaps still the only work up to this moment to analyse the folk revivals in the UK and the USA from a popular music point of view) – was also highly efficacious. I also remember reading Fred Woods's (1979) history of the folk revival and wondering, firstly, why he had bothered and secondly, why such folklorists had not appeared to expand their theoretical bases as much as those writing in popular music. I drew the conclusion that they were still hidebound by political theory.

By the late 1980s I had given up on Thatcher's Britain for full-time study and it was while at Chester College that I came across two works – one from the popular music sphere of writing, the other from the folk world – that made me realise just how little theoretic development had taken place within the British folk revival up until that time. Firstly, I was fascinated by the work of Richard Middleton. Despite seemingly having been written in Ancient Sanskrit (sorry, Richard!), *Studying Popular Music* (1990) revealed to me that academic appreciation of music was, by necessity, interdisciplinary. Middleton was a musicologist but focused upon political economy, history, ethnography as well as semiotics, aesthetics and ideology. He suggested that the essential popularity of folk song demanded its analysis as a form of popular music alongside punk, disco and all the other soundtracks of the apparently inauthentic.

Secondly, Philip V. Bohlman's *The Study of Folk Music in the Modern World* (1988) was also an inspiring examination of folk as a genre. Bohlman took a cross-cultural, expansive view of folk music, espousing, as I felt that I had done in the Bothy club almost 20 years earlier, that there was a crucial folk vitality in not only music of the past, but also that of the present (and the future). Both Middleton and Bohlman appeared to me to be adopting a 'popular music studies perspective', suggesting that because folk music was an expressive act, it was intrinsically part of the modern world, not simply vested with signs and signals of the past. They further implied that our definitions of what actually constituted folk music required a radical overhaul.

It was these two scholars who finally convinced me of the relative equality of all music, and, armed with this judgement, together with an admiration for the historical writing of both Arthur Marwick and John Tosh, I joined the Institute of Popular Music at the University of Liverpool as a post-graduate student. Here I came to know and respect Sara Cohen, David Horn and Philip Tagg; these three academics further problematised binary musical oppositions for me. It was also as an MA student that I came across the excellent work of anthropologist Ruth Finnegan (1989), who, via her work in Milton Keynes, further convinced me that an in-depth external historical and theoretic survey of the second British folk revival was urgently required.

By the time that I had commenced my Ph.D. research on the British folk revival (1993), that revival had changed immeasurably from the one that I knew intimately in the 1960s and 1970s. From its apparent 'high point' during the 1970s, the revival had undergone several radical contractions (hypothesised throughout this text). There was nothing especially unusual about this. As society changes, so, too, do musical movements established in order to reflect society. But the contraction of the folk revival also appeared to occur because, as a movement, it seemed highly resistant to change. As I embarked on my study, I considered a number of differing methodological approaches in order to determine why this appeared to be the case.

I soon discovered that, while folk club attendances were in a parlous state, folk festivals were actually a growth area, and so I decided, after an initial research period, to visit as many festivals as I could, in order to familiarise myself with the zeitgeist. My conclusions are discussed in the final section of this work.

Prior to this, however, my methodologies were as follows: firstly, I had maintained a considerable amount of contacts within the folk network and inaugurated interviews to exchange ideas. My interviewees and contacts were always informed that I wished to consult them with this project in mind. I felt that this was only fair, considering the nature of the thesis, that is a re-evaluation of conventional folk 'wisdom'. I was actually refused a number of interviews because of this. I also interviewed a number of contacts that I had established in the pop and rock worlds in order to attempt a balanced dialectic between genres.

My historical research took me into a wide variety of primary and secondary sources. I was able to uncover rare and hard-to-find Workers' Music Association publications from Nottingham Libraries as part of a sheet music donation to the Institute of Popular Music, and with this primary source material, together with the assistance of Andy Linahan at the National Sound Archive and access to the Vaughan Williams library at Cecil Sharp House, I was able to piece together an illuminating political history of the advent of the second revival. Family contacts were also important. I interviewed my mother and read through the diaries of my Uncle Edgar – a supporter of the Workers' Music Association (WMA) and the English Folk Dance and Song Society (EFDSS). The only interview material that I co-opted into the study was a 1980s tape made with the late Wally Whyton.

The theoretical aspect of this book is based upon my own observations and experiences at folk clubs, venues and concerts. My performance, reception and intertextuality theories are intended to question the rather formalised ideas abounding in folk clubs about how one is inherently changed by folk music. I do not necessarily believe that this is the case, and, by using an interdisciplinary approach in my observations, I have attempted to show that folk music dissemination is far more 'up for grabs' than the folk fraternity would believe.

All of this I would describe as a 'popular music studies perspective'. I feel that popular music studies, with its interdisciplinary approach, has a great deal to offer the somewhat discrete world of folk music studies and, in making a call for greater research into all of the topics covered in this book, I would suggest that the convergence of folk and popular music studies is long overdue.

Michael Brocken

October 2002

Chapter 1

The early revivalists

Vaughan Williams was more interested in the song than the singer, in the melody than the message.

Roy Palmer, *Folk Songs Collected by Ralph Vaughan Williams*

The father of modern folksong studies was Thomas Edison.

Béla Bartók

We should never confuse history with nostalgia but, when we look at historical practice, it is very difficult to make sense of a lot of it without recourse to nostalgia. History reveals our (often confused) sense of identity, and the notion of nostalgia is a foundation for much of this historically apprised identity. We don't inherit or discover history, we create it, and, in this creation, nostalgia is often fundamental to what we feel is a 'realistic' creation of history. There are, however, no guarantees that it will always be possible to discover the truth, and nostalgia is essentially a political impulse. It insulates us from criticism; it can be implausible in its characterisation of the real; it can be nationalistic, racist and imperialist about what is seldom more than an imagined past. Nostalgia is used to help us piece together the fragments of the past and inevitably is governed by our prejudices, our ignorance and our selectivity.

For better or worse, nostalgia informs us of the enormous problems lurking behind descriptions of the past. It informs us that there are certainly no absolute ethics of reference. The writing of history is actually a corporate, politicised activity and what appear to be absolute standards usually have roots in compartmentalised ideologies, preferences and metaphors. Like the proverbial 'Chinese whisper', these metaphors of the past expand so much that we have to concern ourselves with how certain imperatives have coloured the writing of histories. The writing of history depends on the skills, weaknesses, insights and chauvinism of its writers, so 'who was saying what about which past' becomes as significant as the apparent past being narrated. That which appears to be objective may be part of an immense discontinuous network of strands, which have themselves been determined by myriad influences.

In his article 'The Philosophy of History', R.F. Atkinson portrays a number of historians as 'pathological' because they impose upon the past 'categories that are very closely and uncritically derivative from historians' personal, political or religious interests in the present'.[1] This is equally true of the ways in which wider society then appropriates and uses nostalgia-bound histories. The reconstructions of the past are, in fact, intrinsic to the cultural climate and politics of any given era (e.g. Beamish museum) and could never be considered objective truth (whatever that is).

Cultural climate is crucial. It is a metaphor for the common beliefs and shared values that flourish and have an impact on life at appropriate times. But as times change, so do value systems. R. Goldstein (1996) even suggests that the cultural revolution of one era usually turns out to be the saviour of capitalism in another. Shared ideologies and belief systems are multifarious, in any case, and folk music revivalism was but one activity among many.

But, as far as the history of the British folk revival is concerned, an upgrading of its significance has dominated historical narratives concerning its existence. In fact, so complex have been the cultural webs of meaning attached to expressions such as 'folk music' and 'folk revival' during the latter half of the twentieth century, that these very terms (and the search for sense via their presence) have, in their own right, created a kind of symbolic substance with not only aesthetic but also iconic and political significance.

There has been a series of interrelated assumptions built into the basis language that we use for understanding the British folk revival: that a 'tradition' must be preserved at all costs; that specialists are 'qualified' in this respect; that performers are middle men carrying the tradition; that folk music is a universal language; that listeners can be divided into active folkies or passive popular music consumers. These assumptions are so built into our understanding of folk music that they appear natural. We cannot see that they are, in effect, transparent. They are human constructions and, like the very history of the folk revival itself, products of social agency.

This discussion of the British folk revival will attempt to locate itself within broader social and cultural changes in British society. A relatively short work such as this must be selective and privilege certain themes at the expense of others. But its purpose is to question change at the expense of continuity, reminding readers that, although apparently new ideas were introduced surrounding folk song dissemination, older ones were not abandoned. Furthermore, it will suggest that folk ideology needs to be viewed not as a cognitive system but as something in perpetual change and subject to revisions. It will endeavour to show that the somewhat half-baked historical 'truths' by which we judge a great deal of folk music presentation are not rediscoveries of the products of nature, but political inventions of particular times and places in the twentieth century.

Let us begin with a brief historical contextualisation of the first stirrings of cultural-cum-musical revivalism of the twentieth century. The motivations of these early revivalists can be very revealing, for they involved reconsiderations of cultural practices in terms of a relationship between the aesthetic and the political.

The early revivalists: quixotic patriotism

There is no doubt that at the beginning of the twentieth century the forces of social hierarchy, parochialism and conformity were very strong. But there was also a great self-consciousness in all the arts, manifested in the emergence of modernity, and many bourgeois artists (such as those of the Arts and Crafts movement) were looking for ways to extend traditions. Furthermore, there were signs of a gestating liberal (indeed progressive) presence within the middle and higher echelons of British society. This presence was concomitant with the maturation and intellectualisation of the Labour movement (including the arrival of Guild socialism), the growing awareness of the social injustices that existed as a consequence of the Industrial Revolution (e.g. Toynbee's *Lectures on the Industrial Revolution*, 1884) and uncertainties concerning Britain's international profile and imperial development.

As a consequence, bourgeois thought was infiltrated by musicological tensions and struggles. These were manifested, for some, in an alternative interest in the music of the authentic 'vulgus in populo'. Relationships between the classes were explored and involved a debate concerning 'appearance and disappearance'. A kind of musical monument was erected upon which a shadow of a real and untainted symbolic phantom was projected (but in a constant state of disappearance). Through this authentic phantom a kind of political emancipation was sought, dependent – ironically – upon its reappearance. Salvation was at hand via the invocation of a presence of the real through its constantly threatened absence. It is from this historical subsoil of folk music revivalism that so much twentieth-century music thought grew. One might describe this constant referral to that which was no longer present as musicology's ethnocentric phase.

From the outset, the folk revival was a decidedly middle-class phenomenon whose largest constituency included young, urban adults (male and female), many with some degree of musical literacy. For example, Mrs Kate Lee was an early musically literate pioneer of folk music collecting in England (it was she who brought to public attention the Copper family of Rottingdean, Sussex). Lee produced a leaflet in 1898 entitled *Hints to Collectors of Folk Music* in which she attempted to codify the procedure for song collecting.[2] Despite her obvious enthusiasm Lee produced what could only be described as an ethogram.

At least via the evidence of this document, Lee appears to have had little time for diffusion or the creative embodiment of tradition. For example, although her musical erudition makes allowances for 'staff or tonic sol-fa notation [to be] used in taking down the tunes' she did not wish 'to encourage the singer to repeat [the words] without the music, as any alteration of the usual way in which the songs are delivered is apt to confuse the singer's memory'.[3]

Even at this early stage we have a paradox. Folk music appeared to offer some kind of autonomy that many nineteenth-century musicians and aestheticians such as Lee desired; but on the other hand it could only exist according to the rules of engagement as laid down by the middle-class mores from which she stepped forward. A tradition served as a representative function rather than as a process, a way of connecting into a selected past for the benefit of her own known way of life. In fact, one might suggest that tradition served as a source for distinguishing an identity between the collectors and the singers. Lee's advice on procedures (e.g. not accepting the variations of conscious articulation) was a template for the dogmatic and, as this extract from her leaflet insinuates, reflected her own social echelon – nostalgic, erudite, middle-class and suburban:

> IV. Although folk music may be preserved in different strata of society, the classes from which the most interesting specimens are most readily to be obtained are gardeners, artizans [*sic*], gamekeepers, shepherds, rustic labourers, gipsies, sailors, fishermen, workers at old fashioned trades, such as weaving, lace-making, and the like, as well as domestic servants of the old school, especially nurses.[4]

Apparently, according to Vic Gammon, Lee did occasionally cross over from her own social echelon 'but on her own confession managed to terrify some of her informants'.[5] Kate Lee became the first Secretary of the Folk Song Society in 1898 – a pioneer, no doubt, but given her social perspective, concepts such as 'folk music', 'society' and 'classes' are not especially useful, even as loose cultural terms. These abstractions mask the realities of myriad communities.

More eminent than Kate Lee was Cecil Sharp (b. London 22 November 1859; d. London 23 June 1924). After a period of time in Australia, he returned to England in 1892 and taught until 1896. He was Principal of Hampstead Conservatoire until 1905. After having tried, unsuccessfully, to get his own compositions published, he devoted his time to the maintenance of a 'pure' folk heritage. Many have cited the day in autumn 1903 when Sharp first heard John England, the gardener of the Somerset vicarage where he was staying, sing 'The Seeds of Love' as the beginning of the folk revival.[6] In truth, in addition to the early work of Kate Lee, the folk dance revival had already begun by Boxing Day 1899 when Sharp first heard William Kimber (junior) play concertina and saw the Headington dancers perform a Morris at Sandfield Cottage, Headington Quarry, Oxford.

Sharp's life's work became one of collecting and disseminating English folk dance and song, collecting not only in this country, but also in the Southern Appalachians in the USA, where, accompanied by his assistant Maud Karpeles, he spent two periods late in his life. Between 1903 and 1907, assisted by the Revd Marson, Sharp collected 1500 songs in Somerset alone, many of which he subsequently published in the five volumes of *Folk Songs from Somerset*. From the Appalachians he asserted to have found and gathered together another 1600 songs, declaring many to be of pure English origin. He was romantic, naïve and mistaken, however, for many other non-English elements had already eroded any 'pure' English tradition by the time of his arrival.

Sharp also turned his enthusiasm to the revival of folk dancing in England, apparently searching out and (certainly) reconstructing Morris dances and Sword dances, publishing them and teaching them to others. Three years before the First World War he founded the English Folk Dance Society. He died at the age of 64 in 1924. *Cecil Sharp: His Life and Work*, written by Arthur H. Fox Strangways in collaboration with Maud Karpeles, was published in 1933. Karpeles twice updated this work, in 1955 and 1968. The foundation stone for Cecil Sharp House, the London headquarters of the English Folk Dance and Song Society (hereafter EFDSS), was laid on 24 June 1929.

There is little doubt that Sharp and his devotees regarded folk song and dance as a powerful regenerative prescription for modern culture. By the adoption of an older, more authentic form of music (something they considered all but obliterated by the march of automation and the semi-literate masses) society could experience a musical, cultural and spiritual reawakening. Indeed, the use of the word 'revival' – indicating both a restoration and a tonic – stems from this period (see also the rival Association for the Revival and Practice of Folk Music, inaugurated in 1907). Yet, despite Sharp's inclination to 'give back to the people the songs and dances of their country'[7] it could be argued that this first revival was maintained rather like a form of latter-day Gnosticism. There appears to have been a 'knowledge' passed among an 'elevated' few, those who wished to preserve a peasant purity in music from the philistine vulgarisations of the workers, at least until such a time when the lower classes were educated enough to appreciate what they had almost lost via the 'gutter garbage'[8] of the 'popular'. Cecil Sharp:

> A lover of Beethoven's music must feel the same if ever he thought of the way his favourite composer's music is being rendered in Crouch End, Hornsey etc. If anything good is to be made popular, many things will happen which will shock the ears of the elect … I believe so sincerely in the innate beauty and purity of folk-music that I am sure it cannot really be contaminated.[9]

It has also been argued subsequently that one cannot lose what one has never actually had. *Musical Traditions* co-editor Fred McCormick remarked to me that 'the dances, the costumes were all constructions. There is no hard evidence to show that any of Sharp's dances were authentic survivals at all. Then they went out and taught them as if they were traditional.'[10]

Certainly Bampton, Eynsham and Headington were the only villages in which Sharp witnessed complete Morris teams perform; elsewhere, according to Fox Strangways, single individuals, 'many of them past their prime',[11] were responsible for passing on the movements of the dancers – not the most reliable of sources, considering the class divides of the day.

At this stage, the revival concentrated heavily upon arranging and orchestrating dance and song. Alongside Cecil Sharp and Maud and Helen Karpeles, such notable composers as Percy Grainger, Ralph Vaughan Williams and George

Butterworth – the last until his tragic death at the age of 31 at the Western Front in 1916 – were involved. Grainger famously arranged the Morris tunes 'Shepherd's Hey' and 'Country Gardens'; Butterworth's idyll for small orchestra 'The Banks of Green Willow' comprised a melody created from two folk songs. This select bunch also included Iolo Williams, Douglas Kennedy and others who, in forming the Folk Song Society (1899) and the English Folk Dance Society (1911), believed that a distillation of pure, authentic English culture could re-emerge. Sharp's archetypes of tradition, therefore (as laid out in the *Morris Books 1 & 2*), were 'necessarily' strict and meticulous in their retention of folk 'purity': 'My greatest desire is that at the outset these songs and dances shall be introduced to the present generation in the purest form possible – the next generation will have to take care of itself.'[12]

Sharp's last comment is pessimistic and alludes to what Fox Strangways summarises as the 'dangers of popularisation'.[13] Sharp's future projection of tradition was of one uncontaminated by capitalism, commerce, German lieder (despite his modelling of two of his own printed compositions on Schumann) and their dastardly effects upon English culture. Vaughan Williams concurred and penned this in *National Music and Other Essays*: 'what is the classical style? It is nothing more or less than the Teutonic style. It so happened that for nearly a hundred years, in the eighteenth and early nineteenth centuries, the great composers ... were all German or Austrian.'[14]

Richard Sykes[15] has correctly suggested that the word 'Teutonic' remains enticing here. Vaughan Williams propounded that far too much had been made of the associations of progress and genius with an Anglo-Saxon and, ultimately, 'Teutonic' heritage. According to Sharp, a new understanding of Englishness was necessary. To begin with, England (indeed, the United Kingdom) ought to disassociate herself from a nation (Germany) that was a competitor: an assault on the 'classical' tradition meant an assault on the Germanic. Sharp's view of Germany, however, was filtered through a strong degree of prejudice. He remained bitter after being 'fleeced' in Adelaide by his former business partner, the German Immanuel Reimann.

This nationalistic mood, however, was strong across certain sectors of British society and it appears not only in the writings of Vaughan Williams and Sharp, but also in the decrees of the state Board of Education, which in 1906 officially sanctioned the teaching of folk songs because they reflected the 'expression in the idiom of the people of their joys and sorrows, their unaffected patriotism'.[16]

Sharp, however, was forever the purist and was not overly impressed with the list of 50 songs suggested by the Board, fearing that folk songs were being confused with national and popular songs. In reply to this criticism, Sir Charles Stanford of the Board claimed that he had merely included 'songs of the people' and songs that had stood 'the test of a long life in the public ear' – in other words, popular songs 'which have long been acknowledged as the backbone of national music'.[17] Sharp was adamant (yet curiously vague) that there was a significant difference between the folk idiom and the popular and replied: 'The distinction is not academic; nor is it archaeological. It is intrinsic, for it distinguishes between two kinds of music that are fundamentally different from one another.'[18] Fox Strangways and Karpeles were to comment later (with, perhaps, some degree of equanimity):

> The whole thing reads to us, perhaps, like a tilting at windmills ... He was convinced now, that such a song as 'Barbara Allen' – in a mode, multiform, anonymous – was different in quality from 'Tom Bowling' – in a key, uniform, of definite authorship; and he believed that in the strength of this quality the former would, and the latter would not, win its way permanently to the heart of the singer.[19]

Sharp was not alone in considering something special – almost magical – in certain pieces of music. Right across Europe the boundaries of defining musical composition and the sources upon which it was possible to draw were being stretched in the late nineteenth century, and the Germanic grasp upon composition was already being loosened by composers such as Bartók, Grieg, Kodály, Janáček, Dvořák, Rimsky-Korsakov and Tchaikovsky (among others). Modality indicated an idealised national style and a move away from the European classical model.

George Butterworth's song cycle 'A Shropshire Lad' – first performed at the Leeds Festival in 1913 under Nikisch – can also be viewed as a fine example of this strain of thought. There is evidently a shifting of musical horizons in this work, a delicacy with little in common with German composition of the day. However, although Butterworth's melodies do owe their inspiration to English song such as 'The Cutty Wren' (a.k.a. 'Green Bushes') and are sensitive in dealing with Housman's melancholy poetry, one would have to question whether the music reveals the English people's 'true self' (as suggested by Antony Murphy in *The Times*, August 1996). In fact this very concept is little more than an (albeit contextual) idealistic middle-class construction.

For his part, Cecil Sharp indisputably aimed to transmit song and dance from one stratum of society to the broader community and, according to Fox Strangways, 'It was never in Sharp's mind to discard all but the best. The important thing to him was the establishment and recognition of a standard, not the uniform conformity to that standard.'[20] But for all of their good intentions neither Butterworth nor Sharp knew much about the history of lower-class music-making. Even if ethnicity might have been expressed musically, quite ordinary popular songs and tunes will have been invested with deep symbolic meaning in ways that would have been impossible for Sharp and his cohorts to spot.

We can actually draw upon similarities between Sharp's and Butterworth's conceptualisations of English idyll and those discussed by Peter Brooker and Peter Widdowson. They have drawn attention to a particular form of nationalism in England at the beginning of the century that was 'non-aggressive, sometimes non-militaristic ... invested in ideas of the national character, its traditions and a unifying love of the country'.[21] This appears accurate: a rather bucolic one-way construction based on a class-ridden concept of Englishness and the bond between citizen and nation – perhaps what Fox Strangways described as Sharp's 'spiritual sixth sense'.[22]

George Butterworth was undoubtedly a wonderful composer cut down in his prime. His most famous piece, the Idyll for small orchestra 'The Banks of Green Willow' (first heard at Queen's Hall early in 1914 under F.B. Ellis), is exceptional, but also tends to display a naïve, class-related romanticism – one that was soon to dissolve on the killing fields of Flanders. The musical theme running throughout 'The Banks of Green Willow' suggests shared experiences between all Englanders, a perpetuity that would continue throughout every epoch. But all that was being shared by 1916 was dirt and death. Vaughan Williams, however, concurred with the 'spirituality' of Sharp and Butterworth: 'The art of music … is the expression of the soul of a nation, and by a nation I mean … any community of people who are spiritually bound together by language, environment, history and common ideals, and above all, a continuity with the past.'[23]

Harker also stresses that, as part of Sharp's search for this spiritually bound community, the folk song was still only 'raw material' rather than 'a finished product' from 'our standpoint'.[24] These apparently binding national musical motifs were still regarded by collectors and composers as primitive because all things primitive were seen as impervious to change. The songs were also viewed as 'the heritage … of the Arian race' and in opposition to 'our system of education [which] is, at present, too cosmopolitan'.[25] The people from whom Sharp collected were authentic because they were 'out of touch with modern improvements' and 'untouched by modern civilisation'.[26] There is some very problematic and hidebound terminology here. Furthermore, it was a flawed thesis. Although the criterion of this authenticity was a kind of self-conscious oral transmission, it was still, by anybody's definition, a contemporary culture that ended up at both ends of the transmission model communicating the stuff! This later disturbed Douglas Kennedy:

> Cecil Sharp felt he had to resort to arranging and publishing his notations, and to teaching the songs and dances to schoolteachers who would teach them to coming generations. Looking back, I find it difficult to think what else he could have done at the time, yet the method itself was essentially not traditional.[27]

Well said; but what was traditional when shared values circulated in polysemic communication devices such as song and dance? Kennedy's comments highlight the eternal contradiction of revivalism: in order to popularise some kind of tradition one has to recontextualise it. Perhaps because of this, little effort was made by Grainger or Sharp to maintain any contact with living singers. In fact, according to Peter Kennedy, writing in 1959, 'most people at the time presumed that all the good young singers must have been killed in the war and the old ones passed-on'.[28] But it might have suited the purposes of composers for people to presume this. The music of the composer came to represent a plaintive folk myth, 'a source of quiet strength in the face of adversity',[29] while retaining an aura of mystery and inaccessibility: behind this world.

So, the idea of a folk revival at this early stage could be viewed as existing within a greater fashionable middle/upper-class group of concepts, part of a restoration of ideas concerning bohemian, organic intellectual communities, drawing upon the spirit of 'Merrye England'. As suggested at the beginning of this section, concepts such as these were flourishing in a cultural climate open to 'radical' thought. In fact they were not disconnected from ideas espoused by the likes of the eugenics movement, which proffered a theory that urban life had eroded the national constitution. Boer War recruitment had been seriously damaged by urban medical failures. The answer to this expanding problem was thought to lie in the maintenance of rural communities, untainted by the inherent problems of urbanites (Marie Stopes also wished to reduce the birth rate in urban areas). The folk revivalists' presumptions and presuppositions flowed from a similar source. Sharp saw song as having spiritually regenerative qualities. The Honorary Secretary of the Folk Song Society, Lucy Broadwood, never a supporter of Sharp's EFDS, even described the effects of urban culture as an 'enervating slow poison'.

Ironically, one of the classic contradictions for these enlightened Edwardians was that they also believed that the pre-industrial rural English were rather too uninhibited in their sexual attitudes. While Sharp and Stopes were advocating a return to 'country ways', they were also concerned about pastoral habits! It has long been suspected, therefore, that many of Sharp's songs were milk and water versions, thus filtering out a degree of bawdiness. Gammon suggests that Edwardian interpretations of rural songs were incongruous and somewhat paranoid (i.e. they saw sex everywhere):

> The physical and social environment in which a text is received can modify the meaning that is produced ... between individuals of the same social and cultural background the communication of identical or similar meaning may be difficult. Between individuals of different social and cultural backgrounds the communication of identical meanings is totally impossible ... People in England in the two and a half centuries before 1850 certainly made love, sometimes illicitly, but surely it is naive to view the songs of encounter as a celebration of an everyday sort of occurrence.[30]

Nevertheless, whatever class origins, fealties or motivations, the work of Sharp and other early collectors at least began to draw serious study of music away from the conservatory canons of European society, showing that music and the masses – past and present – required earnest consideration. Via the study of a hidden soundtrack Sharp brought 'other' music onto the agenda, even if it was only for a small sector of society. He certainly broadened the scope for discovering value in music. This was a considerable challenge to the musical givens of the day. Of course, if it ever existed in the first place, Sharp's 'pure' folk culture was subjected to considerable reconstruction in order to appeal to prim young middle-class ladies seated at the pianoforte in their front parlours. There were too many examples of a priori modal corrections[31] and, as Gammon suggests above, too few constructive conclusions were drawn about how the 'peasants' had previously developed and used this music, apparently discrete from the popular. Texts were doctored for a 'refined' public and, as Harker ascertains, mediation rather than restoration took place. At this early stage, 'tradition' merely linked individual preferences in song and dance to social status – what Ron Eyerman and Andres Jamison quoting Bourdieu might describe as 'habitus'.[32]

However, perhaps unlike Harker, I have no objections to mediation. Oppositions to mediation only further the concept of musical apartheid. All song is mediated as soon as somebody sings it, never mind collects it. Rather, the passing off of this music as 'pure' and 'authentic' (more English than other kinds of Englishness?) was the unforgivable petty-bourgeois postulation; ever since there has been a presumption that folk music could, indeed, be both 'pure' and 'authentic'. It is in this period that it could be said that twentieth-century folk music hagiography began.

Having introduced this music to 'our' ears, explanations were needed as to why it was supposed to be different. But the historical absolutism of Sharp was insubstantial while it claimed an over-arching authenticity for one type of music which could only be validated by an inoculation, that is using another – popular – as an anti-Christ. Sharp even admitted that these local singers with 'folk' repertoires could not 'distinguish between folk songs and other songs' – so he did this for them![33] Sadly, the British capacity for escapist whimsy can never be overestimated, and the only sure thing about discovering any evidence for Sharp's 'organic' communities was that they had conveniently disappeared.

Notes

1. Atkinson, 'The Philosophy of History', p. 26.
2. Lee, *Hints to Collectors of Folk Music*.
3. Ibid.
4. Ibid.
5. Gammon, 'Crossing Borders', p. 3.
6. Harker, *Fakesong*, p. 178.
7. Loveless, Review of Karpeles, p. 269.
8. Sharp Collection: letter from Sharp to Mrs Howard 22 December 1891, Vaughan Williams Memorial Library, English Folk Dance and Song Society, Cecil Sharp House.
9. Quoted in Fox Strangways, *Cecil Sharp*, p. 91.
10. Interview with folklorist, singer and co-editor of *Musical Traditions* Fred McCormick, March 1997.
11. Fox Strangways, *Cecil Sharp*, p. 95.

12. Sharp, 'Letter to Miss Neal of the Esperance Club', ibid., p. 77.
13. Ibid., p. 78.
14. Vaughan Williams, *National Music and Other Essays*, p. 234.
15. Sykes, 'The Evolution of Englishness', p. 469.
16. Uncredited Board of Education Decree (1906), *Suggestions for the Consideration of Teachers*.
17. Stanford, 'To the editors of the *Daily Chronicle*', 23 May 1906.
18. Sharp, ibid., 24 May 1906.
19. Fox Strangways, *Cecil Sharp*, p. 69.
20. Ibid., p. 92.
21. Brooker and Widdowson, 'A Literature for England', in Crolls and Dodd, *Englishness: Politics and Culture*, p. 117.
22. Fox Strangways, *Cecil Sharp*, p. 69.
23. Vaughan Williams, *National Music*, p. 68.
24. Harker, quoting C. Sharp, in *Fakesong*, p. 182.
25. Sharp, *English Folk Song*, p. 90; p. 135.
26. Sharp Collection: *Musical Herald*, 1 December 1905, Vaughan Williams Memorial Library, English Folk Dance and Song Society, Cecil Sharp House.
27. D. Kennedy, 'Tradition: A Personal Viewpoint', p. 207.
28. P. Kennedy, 'British Folk Music on Record', p. 2.
29. Sykes, 'Evolution of Englishness', p. 484.
30. Gammon, 'Song, Sex, and Society in England', pp. 233–35.
31. See Sykes, 'Evolution of Englishness', p. 479.
32. Eyerman and Jamison, *Music and Social Movements*, p. 16.
33. Fox Strangways, *Cecil Sharp*, p. 45.

Chapter 2

Towards post-war utopianism: the precursors and advent of the second folk revival

The distinction between past, present and future is only an illusion … if a stubborn one.

Albert Einstein

The second folk revival of the twentieth century, which began in earnest towards the end of the Second World War and was connected to the First via the upholders of the aforementioned 'tradition' at the (now amalgamated) EFDSS, has been recorded as a more accurate representation of 'workers' music' – a presentation, perhaps, of a harsher historical reality together with far greater critical examination and detail. It is actually from this revival that the more latterly coined expression of 'traditional music' stems. Indeed, by 1981 the International Folk Music Council (IFMC), which was inaugurated in 1947, adopted a new name to encompass this new expression, the International Council for Traditional Music (ICTM).

The ICTM failed to recommend any redefinition of its fields of study to any great extent, for, seen from the present, what actually constitutes 'traditional' music seems as imprecise as what defined 'folk' music. Why a folk song continues to be 'defined' in opposition to a popular one remains intangible. While it appears to be true that folk music is formed within and in turns forms traditions because it is sung, listened to and enjoyed, it is equally true that other genres of music have similar potential. One can speak of an Italian opera tradition, a punk tradition, a surf tradition or a rockabilly tradition with as much veracity. A tradition is obviously both real and imaginary at one and the same time. This chapter will attempt to examine the socio-cultural constructions surrounding the uses of folk music in Britain during and after the Second World War and, in doing so, will contextualise (and thus question) sectarian folk-versus-popular dichotomies.

There have been a few attempts to develop historical accounts of the British folk song revival from the post-war era onward. Within these histories, folk and popular music historians often regard the folk revival as something of a musical and social revolution, but this reading is a rather idealised construction. The principal problem with this kind of 'history' is that it understands the folk revival to have existed within a kind of cultural bubble disassociated from other musical activity. Fred McCormick still finds this irritating:

> The folk scene does exist in a cultural bubble. There is no doubt about it. There is the opinion that it is separate, distinct. That it has no need to interact with other genres, considers other genres unworthy. Many folkies still fail to acknowledge that the roots of, say country and western music are also folk roots. The history of the revival reflects this isolation quite clearly.[1]

Indeed, if one exposes the cultural isolationism discussed by Fred McCormick above, one can see that the folk revival was also less than revolutionary from a musical point of view.

For example, it must be assumed that following the spread of radio and record players in the inter-war era the great majority of listeners in the UK listened primarily to light music. The modes of composition of light music were undoubtedly intrinsic to Western tonal-code music. Melody, lyrics-in-performance and the performance itself all remained within the tonal codes of the European models. The BBC acknowledged this distinction and excluded certain jazz-style music by the likes of Spike Hughes and Harry Roy ('hot') from the airwaves, while championing Palm Court music and bands led by Felix Mendelssohn and Carroll Gibbons ('sweet').

The music hall song was but a variant on the European model (but little more than this) – so too was folk song. Dick Bradley (1992) suggests that folk music contained features that were not normally regarded as tonal-European (pentatonic-influenced melodies, 'coarse' singing, etc.).[2] The differences, however, are not pronounced. In fact, by the mid-period of the twentieth century European tonal composition had long included modality and pentatonics (not only the English composers but Bartók, Kodály, etc.).

In any case, by the turn of the century folk song had already merged with popular song in the hands of the older singers (many did not differentiate – it took Sharp to do this). By the time radio had appeared in the early 1920s, the presentation of folk music was orchestrated and arranged – undoubtedly a part of the tonal-European model.

Thus, one could argue that folk music was considered part of pre-existing musical systems – at least according to the most significant end of the communications model, that is the listener. Furthermore, if the very presentation of folk music is 'erudite' (as was the case with the BBC), then it further conforms with rather than reacts against pre-existing institutional models of presentation.

In decibel levels, alone, folk music of the mid-1950s was in a sound-sense far closer to the models that had preceded it than it was to rock 'n' roll and rhythm and blues. Both the noise levels and the singing styles of the folk revival were European tonal rather than African-American. After all (as we shall see) folk music was held up as a bastion against such Americanisation. So, one might propose that the perceptions of 'difference' surrounding folk music were formulated within the institutionalised European tone model framework of musical knowledge (Cecil Sharp, for example). Articulations of 'difference' were actually based on 'similarities'.

Folk music was 'more of the same' and the singing styles, beat and decibel level of Elvis Presley signified an actual difference (as the UK press noted at the time). This is why skiffle (of which more later) played such an intrinsic part in bridging the gap between similarity and difference. Skiffle provided (mostly) African-American tone-models at reduced decibel levels and in somewhat temperate, even bookish, presentations – a perfect link between what had come before and what was to come.

Much folk music history discusses the relevance of its chosen genre of music (folk) without acknowledging the existence of another, except as a 'proscribed' reference (popular). Yet the folk revival was wholly linked to other significant social processes and grew out of contextual interpretations of issues both preceding and contemporaneous with that revival. Important contextual questions, therefore, need to be raised such as:

- What were the social and cultural conditions in which this activity developed?
- What did this activity itself indicate about pre- and post-war Britain?
- What echelons of society were attracted to this music and under what ideological preconceptions? (and how and why did it enlarge?)

In order to answer these questions it is vitally important to take into account the broader context (and, in doing so, highlight the growth of the new pre-war popular entertainment 'traditions'). Although the historiography of the folk revival appears to separate itself from any greater musical activity, independent sound narratives have never existed. While identifying folk music as a hidden source of history, many folk revivalists have succeeded in diluting their sense of historical knowledge. By concealing broader popular music activity from their narratives, they have attempted to inscribe formalistic and orderly perimeters around their chosen musical eras and genres. This produces a very orderly but erroneous historical narrative. If, as the folklorists might agree, performance and reception both involve ongoing dialogue with and about the past, then that dialogue should also involve the immediately preceding past. Lipsitz describes this latter view of history as the 'product of an ongoing historical conversation in which no one has the first or last word'.[3]

New musical movements and dialectics are obviously constructed within the context of significant social, technological and political changes. John Tosh (1984) describes how historical events are produced in this way. This is a useful avenue towards understanding how musical movements reflect elements of preceding dialectics achieving some level of fruition. At the turn of the century in the United States, for example, the blues did not simply 'begin'. It emerged as a hybrid of preceding soundtracks, and existed as one soundtrack amongst many (often convergent) 'others'. Not only that, but like all kinds of popular music, the blues reflected the various social and commercial influences that worked upon it, while continuing to confirm some kind of traditional foundation.

If we look at the folk revival from a similar perspective it can be seen that it was a similar channelling of music performance and reception through social/ political/historical refractions. It was certainly a visible and clearly identifiable social movement to which an important minority were drawn. Thus the meaning and uses of folk music as an antithesis to pre-war industrial capitalism and post-war mass consumption are highly significant (as are perceptions about the survival of a British singing tradition in an ever widening hegemony of American culture).

But it would be wrong to concentrate on these causes alone if we are fully to understand the context within which the revival took flight. True, some sources of the revival lay in wilful opposition to mass consumption, but of equal importance to the historian is the recording of these agents of social change to which many revivalists objected. For many Britons mass consumption and media were benevolent, producing greater leisure time, wider musical choice and sustained social advancement. Ironically, both apparent polarities, that is the perception of an experiential lacuna in society and the understanding of mass consumption as a benign influence, can be seen by the historian as being axiomatic of the same context.

Mass consumption

For many people the VE Day celebrations in 1995 were a poignant reminder, not simply of the end of the war, but also of the immediate post-war era. I wasn't born until 1954, but my mother and my late father, who were married in 1949, often spoke of the post-war years as being a time of confused optimism. My father died in 1995. He had the (sometimes bitter) experience of growing up in Liverpool between the wars with all that that implied for him socially and politically. He served in the Army throughout the war, from 1939 to 1945, but signed on for at least another 12 months. He described to me how that extra 12 months or so helped him sort out his ideas about what to do next with his life. He came home, returned to his previous job as a bread and cake rounds man at Blackledge's bakery in Bootle (the job had been left open for him), joined the Labour Party, left the Knights of St Columba and eventually met and married my mother. Things were tight, but there was promise. I was the second to arrive into this classic example of a working-class baby-boomer family, in this 'new Jerusalem' of post-war Liverpool!

Eric Hobsbawm has argued that, prior to the outbreak of the Second World War in 1939, mass production was finally becoming a norm.[4] He also maintained, however, that the mass goods that appeared were not expensive consumer durables, for few people could afford them. Despite the growth of suburbia and a visible consumer-based middle class, the 1930s was still a decade of iniquitous social conditions for many Britons, many of whom could barely make ends meet. For example, Hobsbawm notes that, while by 1939 the USA had already provided 150 new fridges per year for every 10 000 of its population, and Canada 50, Britain by 1935 had produced only eight (the Brocken household purchased their fridge in 1965!). Even the middle classes had only begun to buy motor cars at the modest rate of four per 1000 customers by 1938. Vacuum cleaners and electric irons were probably the only pieces of domestic machinery to infiltrate many homes by the outbreak of the war – apart, that is, from the prevalent wireless sets, purchased or rented in vast amounts by the end of the 1930s.

Instead, the new goods that became available to many working-class Britons were, according to Hobsbawm, 'cheap articles of domestic and personal use'.[5] Woolworth and Boots stores rose in number and importance nationwide during the 1930s on the strength of inexpensive consumer goods such as make-up and fountain pens (for many years Woolworths were known as the 3d. and 6d. store).

Despite the recession during the 1930s, records were purchased in large quantities (around 20 million per year, and over half of these were dance band records),[6] but these were also primarily purchased by the middle classes, those families who also had the finances to buy or rent a piece of furniture that actually played gramophone discs. Even some of the cheapest discs could cost in the region of 1/- to 1/11d. (Rex, Piccadilly), and although Woolworth stores sold the ubiquitous Crystalate-pressed Victory, Eclipse and Crown discs for 6d., one couldn't hear the likes of Roy Fox, Jack Payne or Lew Stone on these releases. Many of the 'best' records still sold for as much as 3/- (HMV) and for those few interested in traditional music, folk songs and country dances, these recordings were usually on HMV, Columbia Graphophone, Parlophone or Beltona[7] and were mostly full priced.

While only a minority of working-class families had the facilities to play gramophone records, the physical act of dancing to live music was hugely popular. One statistic illustrates this well. According to a pre-war *Melody Maker (Dance Band and Syncopation News)* survey taken in the mid-1930s, 89 per cent of factory workers, 93 per cent of office workers and 84 per cent of shop assistants regularly went dancing.[8] Unfortunately there are no *Melody Maker* statistics for the unemployed! My own auntie Mary, sister of my father, was a young working woman interested in dance music and was able to save money to spend on records, which were played on her third- or fourth-hand mechanical player.

My mother often discussed these pre-war days with me, stating that her father, a time-served printer, simply wasn't able to afford such luxuries as record players and records. She also stated that my grandfather considered a lot of the current music to be 'rubbish' and, as master of the house (Liverpool Corporation notwithstanding), his statements were legislature. In any case, the family owned a rather smart piano – bought at great sacrifice from Crane's in Liverpool – for which new sheet music was occasionally purchased, especially the cheaper song books sold by Woolworths in Church Street or Davies' Arcade in Lord Street. None of the sheet music purchases were 'traditional' in the folk sense, although a favourite of my grandmother's was 'Black Eyes', the 'famous Russian gypsy song'. For my grandparents, tradition probably lay somewhere between Count John McCormack, the light classics and Billy Cotton. Even though some families in my grandparents' street (all Corporation housing) might have had a gramophone, this usually meant that they had better-paid jobs, or else had a few earners in the household at the same time.

The point of this information is twofold. First of all, under these prevailing circumstances, it was evidently mostly the middle classes (or those fortunate enough to have reasonably well-paid jobs – often one and the same) who were actively engaged in record buying in any given musical area prior to the outbreak of the Second World War; and, secondly, the importance of radio was absolutely paramount. Working-class people may have been heavily involved in the production of both forms of domestic entertainment, but were not necessarily in a financial position to enjoy both without that important radio set.

Radio introduced almost 'round the clock' entertainment into the home and workplace for the first time in history, although this did not always appear to be the primary aim of the middlebrow public corporation that controlled most of it, namely the BBC. Reithian policy dictated that entertainment was often unfavourably equated with 'Americana' and such breaches of the virginity of the United Kingdom's culture were not acceptable. Post-war, this attitude continued to prove fundamental at the BBC, particularly during the folk music revival. Typically, while the BBC in the 1930s were somewhat measured in realising the enormous potential of popular music broadcasting (endeavouring to keep pre-recorded American music at bay), European stations Radio Normandie and Radio Luxembourg (and, for some, Radio Berlin) filled the ample spaces in the dance market left by the Corporation before the war began.

Hobsbawm further states that the picture house quickly overtook the old music halls as the working-class alternative for luxury before, during and after the second war.[9] My own parents were great cinema-goers in the late 1940s, did a lot of their courting in the cinema and only acquired a second-hand record player in the 1950s as part of an old pre-war radiogram. It was the radio in this piece of polished furniture that was of prime importance, not the gramophone player. In fact it only latterly occurred to them that they could now buy gramophone records! In any case, they enjoyed their weekly visits to the pictures and tea afterwards at Sampson and Barlow's in London Road far more than the expensive luxury of records.

These immense and ornate Forums and Gaumonts could be spectacular buildings. Some also housed huge organs rising from the depths while surrounded by coloured lights, and this too contributed to a shift in tastes and sensibilities;

in fact cinema organ music became a new tradition in its own right as organists such as Reginald Dixon and Sidney Torch became household names. These new traditions of radio and cinema rose (especially inter-war) in many poorer districts abreast of the rate of unemployment[10] but were not linked, in the political sense, to concepts of social mobilisation (far from it, in fact) – hence, perhaps, their elimination from histories of popular music traditions in Britain. Nevertheless, they were essential facets of daily life and were not representations of false consciousness, but re-presentations of lived experiences.

As Hobsbawm further asserts, these cinemas were the most effective dream creators ever set up, but they also mapped out a terrain through which pragmatic ideas and feelings about reality were filtered. A visit to the cinema cost less and lasted longer than a 78rpm disc, a variety show or a few rounds of drinks, and stood alongside the radio as market leader for the entire decade. Both of these forms of media could also easily be combined with the cheapest and most rational of all entertainment and enjoyment – sex.

The BBC actually broadcast folk songs on several occasions during their first 20 years of existence but performed, as they were, by various Glee Clubs, the BBC Music Department's singers, choirs and orchestras, it has been recorded by some that these broadcasts were rather 'highbrow' and inappropriate. As I have argued, however, this could be a crucial misreading of musical transmission for it could certainly be suggested that, like their pre-World War I folkie forebears, it was largely the middle classes who enjoyed their Scottish country dances in the privacy of their own parlours; the rest of the nation was either at the pictures, in the pub, or on the couch listening to Henry Hall.

War: the radio as a catalyst for post-war utopianism

As a form of entertainment during the war years, dancing at the various palais around the country was an essential facet of wartime existence – another new tradition, perhaps. Tricia Jenkins has commented that:

> Not only did the Nazi bombers physically alter the shape of Liverpool as the 1940s dawned, but the war also altered many people's ideas about dancing and the uses of music. Liverpool still managed to keep on dancing during the war (e.g. the famous Blackout Waltz at the Rialto), but there was an increased sense of urgency attached to the dancing; personal contact increased, bearing a direct relationship to the amount of bombs falling on the city. One's home became the front line, cruelly exposing the fragility of life. The 'other world-ness' of the dance hall had given way to a marked sense of reality, and 'living for today'.[11]

During the war the power of radio also grew, not simply as an entertainment medium, but as a purveyor of a form of entertainment that was also considered to be an essential part of the war effort per se, a morale booster as well as a

Government information unit. Practically all of the dance bands playing at these venues and on the radio were of great significance to the esprit de corps of the country. Bandleader Henry Hall became a figure of indisputable national respect, as did the likes of Ambrose, Jack Payne, Lew Stone, Roy Fox, Ray Noble, Geraldo and Charlie Kunz, amongst many others.

Conscription, however, began to limit the number of bands and individual musicians available to the BBC and, in 1940, the Musicians' Union agreed to relax its radio needle-time restrictions until the end of the conflict. The BBC's use of recordings and generic programming, therefore, increased. One hitherto unforeseen side effect of the BBC's employment of records was a gradual exposure to American popular music. Only a trickle of British-made records were issued during the war in the UK owing to great shortages of materials, so the BBC came to rely on imported discs, mostly of American origin. American influence was further felt in the UK through the presence of US servicemen. In addition, the BBC made frequent use of pre-recorded American variety shows by the likes of Bing Crosby and Bob Hope, together with those made by the American Forces Network. The AFN began broadcasting in the United Kingdom in 1943 and proved to be very popular with not only the US troops stationed in the UK but also the civilian population of Britain. Indeed, it has been argued by Barnard that 'British popular culture as a whole did undergo an insidious "Americanisation" as the war progressed'.[12]

By the time of the D-Day landings in June 1944, plans were laid for a new radio service for the Allied invasion force: the Allied Expeditionary Forces Programme (AEFP). The Overseas Service of the BBC, the AFN and the Canadian Broadcasting Company managed the AEFP. It was at this time that the American Band of the Supreme Allied Command (in other words Glenn Miller's civilian band in uniform) began to make massive inroads into British popular music tastes. Theoretically, Miller's shows were not meant to be heard by the British non-military audience, but they were, and the subsequent popularity of US swing music was so great that, post-war, BBC Director-General Sir William Haley dropped US-originated shows from the BBC's schedules in an attempt to keep Americanisation at bay.

The war years also provided a national platform for songs of anti-fascist resistance. Before the war, left-wing groups such as the Workers' Music Association (WMA), the Clarion Ramblers and various Co-Op Society choirs and music groups had gathered together a repertoire of such songs – particularly around the time of the Spanish Civil War. Once WW II began they became specialists with a range of highly fashionable and politically pertinent material. For some, a tradition of the Left began to evolve, embodied in ritualised practices surrounding preferences and tastes in literature and music. For example, during the course of the war the WMA organised large-scale concerts and local get-togethers in order to send valuable aid to China and the Soviet Union (the largest of these events even taking place at the Royal Albert Hall).

National songs in a range of languages were the standard fare at such concerts and the BBC broadcast many. As a consequence, tradition was mobilised, making it possible to participate in an updated imagined community (with, for some, a sloganised Marxism as a significant pivot). In 1942, the BBC decided to record a few traditional singers such as Stanley Slade and Louisa Hooper (the latter an early source for Cecil Sharp) and *Country Magazine* began its long run (12 years) that same year. This was effectively a piece of talk radio but always included a folk song or two by a singer such as Harry Cox or the aforementioned BBC musicians and singers. War, nostalgia and nationalism, together with a contingency plan to counter-balance American cultural influences, all created a potent melting pot into which folk music was propelled.

Towards the end of the war the Workers' Music Association brought out the 'Keynote' series of low-priced monographs dealing with history, literature and music. The fourth number in this series, *The Singing Englishman* by A.L. Lloyd, issued in 1944, was a catalyst for the embryonic second revival. Lloyd was attempting to remove contemporary (i.e. EFDSS) 'misunderstandings' about English folk songs by relating them to the 'times and circumstances they were made up in'.[13] The appearance of this booklet at this moment in time was seminal, for it caught a wave of youthful and creative impulses. By 1945 Lloyd's little reader was regarded by some as a serious agent for change:

> Those who grew up in the thirties and forties now find it difficult to convey the dead hand of mediocrity and authoritarianism of those days. Britain was a class-ridden society with rigid barriers and social problems that nobody seemed to care about. The mainstream of art, literature, and poetry was largely conformist and snobbish. Even folk music was mainly a middle-class study. It is not surprising that new directions in art, literature, and social change tended to have a left-wing flavour, intensified by the drama of the Spanish Civil War and the fight against totalitarian fascism … we were all a bit left-wing in those days.[14]

Ideological and artistic imperatives were brought together as folk song became a vehicle for those (such as Leslie Shepard) interested in the rediscovery of working-class art.

Despite austerity, the utopianism of the immediate post-World War II years helped to develop a different attitude towards urban life. The Royal Institute of British Architects stated in the 1940s that a town should be for the townsfolk what a country mansion is for the rich, and that new planning developments ought not be docile ribbon developments, but involve life across a village green with active discussion and communication (as in the days of old). In a sort of architectural folk revival of its own, planning began to hark back, but in a modernist way (via new developments such as Stevenage), to a middle-class 'rural' lifestyle. There was an interest abroad in turning all things urban into all things quasi-rural (which might also mean sub-urban) and 'useful'. In 1946 the 'Britain Can Make It' design exhibition introduced major new design initiatives to the public in an attempt to persuade them that 'good' modern design had a key role in everyday life: projects could be both aesthetically pleasing and represent social and cultural values.

This pioneering idealism also had a soundtrack. It is arguable, in fact, whether this artistic impetus could have been sustained without the British Broadcasting Corporation. Regions of the country were enjoying folk song broadcasting of one form or another and, through embracing radio technology, folk music made several inroads in regions of the nation and national consciousness. *East Anglia Sings*, for example – broadcasting the voices of Jumbo Brightwell, Harry Cox and Charger Salmons in 1947 – was an initiative of producer Maurice Brown. That same year Brian George, Head of Central Programme Operations for the BBC, with the assistance of Seamus Ennis made several field recordings in Ireland. The likes of Elizabeth Cronin and Sheila and Kitty Gallagher were broadcast in *Songs from the Four Provinces* in 1948.

Following the 1944 Education Act, many of the newly trained teachers entering the expanding education system were greatly influenced by this imprecise variation on rural pioneering. The BBC had established the Third Programme ostensibly to cater for this new education system. They provided not only schools schedules of a more conventional nature, but also educational music programmes. *Singing Together with Herbert Wiseman* on the BBC Home Service was such an example, offering a chance for country-dance music to appear on the radio. Record companies such as HMV, Parlophone, Columbia and Beltona provided a supply of country-dance products for radio airplay. The regularity with which British folk music appeared on the radio was indicative of the sense of loyalty to British culture and tradition felt at the BBC and among an educated middle-class audience. HMV made recordings 'under the auspices of the EFDSS' and these could be obtained from Cecil Sharp House. Teachers were encouraged to join the EFDSS and use these recordings for organised dance classes.

The EFDSS began to run dance courses all over the regions of England. Many newly qualified teachers willing to learn and then teach English and Scottish country dancing at their schools peopled these courses. These teachers – as many children in the 1950s and early 1960s would vouch – were evangelical in their task, and they expanded the membership of the EFDSS to hitherto undreamed-of proportions. This was a classic starting point for the recruitment of people into a movement of tradition, whereby the reworking of cultural materials leaves a legacy of experiences, symbols and ideas in the heads of young children. Little surprise, then, that many of these kids went on to develop an interest in folk music in the 1960s and 1970s.

It must be emphasised, however, that (despite the aforementioned comments of Leslie Shepard) this impulse did not necessarily come from the heart of the working classes. Many of the newly qualified teachers were the grammar school 'success stories' of the post-war era. Furthermore, even though the BBC did appear committed to folk music broadcasting, it had little effect on the legions that chose not to listen to the Home Service or the Third Programme. Ultimately, the most valuable programme as far as folk music broadcasting was concerned was probably the one show that was regularly broadcast on the Light Programme: *As I Roved Out*. It replaced *Country Magazine* and lasted from 1953 to 1958; running to 53 programmes, *As I Roved Out* gave valuable Light Programme air time to the likes of Harry Cox, Fred Jordan, Maggie Barry and Frank McPeake; even so, it was scheduled to fill the Sunday morning 'dead air' slot!

Predictably, at no time during these early years of the second revival did the BBC acknowledge the obvious commercial potential of folk music. They continued to pioneer folk music broadcasting throughout the 1950s, but not to the masses, as such. A major opportunity came in 1950 when they employed American collector Alan Lomax. Between 1950 and his return to the USA in 1958, Lomax worked on several entertaining programmes such as *Song Hunter: Alan Lomax*, *Memories of a Ballad Hunter* (both about himself!) and *A Ballad Hunter Looks at Britain*. But very few of Lomax's programme ideas came to fruition. In several cases BBC producers such as Ian Grimble expressed reservations about his theories.

To be fair, Grimble was not alone in expressing concern about the overt politics of the leading folk protagonists. For most of the 1950s the 'Beeb' kept their distance from Bert Lloyd. He did, however, research the songs for *Johnny Miner, A Ballad Opera for Coal* in 1947, *White Spirituals* in 1949 and *The Condor and the Guitar* (about South American music) in 1952. In 1953 *Coaldust Minstrel* – a feature on the singer Tommy Armstrong – was broadcast regionally. By 1956 the Third Programme finally commissioned him for talks on folk music. This resulted in, amongst other items, *The Seeds of Love* (about sexual metaphor in folk song) in 1957.

The BBC had already employed Ewan MacColl during the late 1930s (as Jimmie Miller) and his ad hoc relationship with the Corporation continued during the post-war era once he had settled upon music (rather than drama) as an outlet for his considerable ego. After a few talks on the Third Programme in the early 1950s he was awarded six thematic shows featuring British and American music – *Ballads and Blues*. They were broadcast on the Northern Home Service, but only three were deemed entertaining enough to be broadcast on the Light Programme; according to one source at Oxford Road, Manchester, MacColl's intransigence and egomania proved somewhat problematic! In 1958, however, he worked in partnership with Charles Parker to produce his famous series of Radio Ballads: *The Ballad of John Axon* (1958), *Song of a Road* (1959) and *Singing the Fishing* (1960). Parker reined in MacColl's didactics and between them they produced highly entertaining programmes of immense cultural value – the series was a tour de force of radio broadcasting.

However, although these programmes kept folk music in the forefront of some kind of musical debate over aesthetics (and American influences), those that consumed other genres of popular music were largely unaffected and unconcerned.

By 1957 Radio Luxembourg, with disc jockeys such as Gus Goodwin, Jimmy Henney and Jimmy Savile, had already realised that US rock 'n' roll was not the passing fad that it was previously thought to be and most young people tried to find this station on their new transistor radios, not the Home Service (or, indeed, the Light Programme on a Sunday morning!).

A survey in 1961 showed that Radio Luxembourg had an average British audience of over two million, far greater than the Home Service, which, in any case, was the second most popular BBC station. In fact, when BBC TV were allowed to broadcast in the 'blank hour' between 6 p.m. and 7 p.m. ('toddler's truce' – time to get the children to bed) in 1957, even they chose to launch *Six-Five Special* to cater for the identifiable teenage market. It was a genuinely live show and, mixing a little rock with jazz, folk and skiffle, it caused quite a stir. However, before too long, producer Jack Good had defected to the new ITV, created a rival programme called *Oh Boy!* and effectively put the rather staid BBC offering out of business by giving the teenagers what they really wanted, that is 100 per cent US-style rock 'n' roll. Mick O'Toole testifies to the class-ridden ideology of the BBC:

> Well-intentioned as the 'Beeb' management was, it was a case of mainly middle-class producers making middle-class programmes and not having a clue as to what teenagers wanted ... but they knew a man who did ... enter Jack Good ... even Arthur Askey pranced and danced his tired old 'Busy Bee' routine to polite indifference. A definite bonus was the weekly film clip taken from one of the rock exploitation movies being made at the time ... the first clip Good featured was Little Richard belting out 'Lucille' from 'The Girl Can't Help It'. This caused a furore with the management and from then on, he felt it best to list merely 'film clip' on the schedule and thus give no clues as to the content in advance.[15]

I have written elsewhere that 'the folk revival took wing in an age of apparent certainty – that of the onward march of the "progressive" movement (with whatever more precise political inflection its individual adherents chose to add to it)',[16] but in many respects it was also a continuation of Kate Lee's, Cecil Sharp's and the BBC's engineering and shifting of music towards a pre-conceived and wilful format. Despite folk's emergence from within contemporary practices, the contemporary 'real' did not suit. So the real, the continuity, was substituted, arranged and engineered until an ideal disengaged past was itself 'real'. A genre of music was mobilised as a national contingency plan and as a counterforce to the onslaught of Americana – hardly revolutionary!

Throughout both eras of revivalism, musical 'ruins' were erected – their function to cater for an affect, to create a 'real illusion' which, through the aesthetic emotions it triggered, ceased to be an illusion. This was a contrivance, for somewhere within it lay both a block on reality and a claim to an alternative system of cognition – a post facto false picture of the past combined with an idealised, distorted version of reality. The deliberate channelling of folk music by the BBC into areas where it would not receive popular acclaim only served to feed this vision. The seriousness, hubris and ideologies of Bert Lloyd and Ewan MacColl were also at the centre of this fallacy. They accordingly directed folk music towards a tiny audience of dyed-in-the-wool listeners, rather than in the direction of the general public it so richly deserved.

Notes

1. Interview with Fred McCormick, March 1997.
2. Bradley, *Understanding Rock and Roll*, 41.
3. Lipsitz, *Time Passages*, p. 99.
4. Hobsbawm, *Industry and Empire*, p. 220.
5. Ibid.
6. Leslie, 'The Music Goes Round', p. 5.
7. Beltona was a Scottish country-dance label started in the 1920s. It was later purchased by Decca and was their Scottish music subsidiary for many years.
8. Leslie, 'The Music Goes Round', pp. 5–6.
9. Hobsbawm, *Industry and Empire*, p. 221.
10. Ibid.
11. Jenkins, *'Let's Go Dancing'*, p. 71.
12. Barnard, *On the Radio*, p. 28.
13. Lloyd, *The Singing Englishman*, p. 1.
14. Shepard, 'A.L. Lloyd: A Personal View', pp. 125–27.
15. M. O'Toole, 'The 6.5 Special … Oh Boy!', p. 5.
16. Brocken, 'The Tarnished Image', p. 227.

Chapter 3

Bert Lloyd and Ewan MacColl: a critique of the leading protagonists

Bert Lloyd (1908–82) brought a stimulating set of influences to the revival but they were highly subjective and contextual – indeed for anybody studying Lloyd, political outlook is crucial for he was an inveterate Marxist (who tended to see Marx as occupying a role similar to that of Jesus Christ in the religious sense):

> What we nowadays call English folksong is something that came out of social upheaval. That is no random remark, but a statement of what happened in history. It grew with a class just establishing itself in society with sticks, if necessary, and rusty swords and bows discoloured with smoke and age. While that class flourished, the folksong flourished too, through all the changing circumstances that the lowborn lived in from the Middle Ages to the Industrial Revolution. And when that class declined, the folksong withered away and died.[1]

Lloyd was born in Wandsworth, London and migrated as a teenager to Australia. He returned to London in the 1930s, where he became involved with the British Communist Party. He was a member of the CPGB over a long period of time and, significantly, his world view was formed in the late 1930s. By the time that war had broken out, he had already developed a strong interest in folk music from all over the world. He was interested in late Depression material from America and his song collecting while a stockman in Australia was coupled with fishing songs collected from his personal experiences on an Atlantic whaling fleet in 1937–38. He was also interested in traditional music from the Balkans, Romania and Albania and was later to collect in this area (much of which materialised on Topic long-playing albums during the late 1950s and 1960s).

During the period prior to the outbreak of war (say 1937–39) Lloyd spent a great deal of time in the Reading Room of the British Museum researching into his interests in folk music and economic and social history. A little of this research found its way into print, such as the article 'The People's Own Poetry', which appeared in the Marxist newspaper *The Daily Worker* in 1937. He also briefly worked for the BBC. He co-wrote a documentary, *The Shadow of the Swastika*, and a musical feature, *Saturday Night at the Eel's Foot*. Despite his Marxist leanings, it was not, apparently, the archetypal texts of Marx and Engels that were centrally important to his development, for according to Gammon (1986) these were very difficult to come by at this stage. Rather, it was the ethos and writings of Communist historians and Leftist intellectuals that, when coupled with his own personal experiences, became acutely meaningful. A.L. Morton's *A People's History of England*, first published in a Left Book Club edition in 1938, is important in this respect. Bert Lloyd notwithstanding, Morton's book had an enormous influence on the middle class and grammar school Left in Britain, providing a totalising view of English history from a Marxist perspective. Lloyd stated in *The Singing Englishman* that he was 'indebted to the historian A.L. Morton'.[2]

E.P. Thompson was another historian who was highly influential on Lloyd. Thompson left the Communist Party in 1956, disturbed and disillusioned at the actions of the Soviet Union in Hungary. However, his *The Making of the English Working Class* (1963) is quoted in crucial passages of Lloyd's *Folk Song in England* (1967). In addition to Thompson, the writings of J.L. and Barbara Hammond were also highly effective. Gammon (1986) states that Lloyd clearly read the Hammonds' *The Village Labourer* (1911) before writing *The Singing Englishman* in 1944. Certainly, Lloyd's style in this small book owes a great deal to that of the Hammonds. There is a suffusion of romantic regret for the passing of a lost age in both works and much of the criticism that the Hammonds have received in recent years for a cloying degree of historical romanticism could just as easily be levelled at Lloyd. When he gleefully asserted that there was a time before 'folksongs turned into something empty and vulgar and debased, before they parodied themselves to death'[3] Lloyd was using the Hammonds' sentimentalism as his sample.

By the late 1940s Lloyd had established himself as Britain's leading folk music expert. Between 1945 and 1950 he was gainfully employed by the *Picture Post* as a journalist, but left in an act of solidarity concerning his editor Tom Hopkinson. During 1950 he was asked by the National Coal Board to run a competition to unearth mining songs for the Festival of Britain celebrations the following year. This was a seminal moment for Lloyd and he soon teamed up with like-minded individuals Ewan MacColl and Alan Lomax to dominate the folk scene for at least the remainder of the decade (if not longer).

But we must understand that, for Lloyd, the folk revival's function was not simply to trace and identify neglected musical performances. He was primarily interested in the purveying of politically inspired historical concepts created by him about those performances. Many folklorists and revivalists inspired by Bert Lloyd have continued to view his historical rhetoric as inarguably accurate. This traditional/musical 'other' (i.e. 'other' to mainstream popular music) does not simply serve as an Other, but also as an invocation of the 'truth' in which that 'other' music thrives. Yet the perception that types of music can exist in opposition to an undifferentiated mainstream remains highly subjective.

Naturally, it is to Bert Lloyd that many folk music adherents still turn when any folk historical veracity is challenged, for his work remains both powerful and eloquent. Having undertaken to enlarge upon *The Singing Englishman* by writing *Folk Song in England* in 1967, he further attempted systematically to trace the development of the genre from what he viewed as its origins in agrarian songs, dances and plays into industrial song. However, it has to be said that, when Lloyd's writing is contextualised, his authority can be seen as highly subjective rhetoric. Even one of the earliest reviews of *Folk Song in England*, that of Jeremy Seabrook writing in *New Society* in December 1967, questioned this emotive subjectivity: 'He can be savage when he launches into invective against things he does not like, as when he describes the entertainment industry as "offering sickly bourgeois fantasies to audiences to suck on like a sugared rubber teat"'.[4] Francis Collinson was also to remark in his review of the same work for the EFDSS's *Folk Music Journal* in 1968:

> His reference to white collar folklorists and song collectors is surely cocking an undeserved snook at many worthy scholar-workers in the field who bore the heat of the day in the early folk song revival ... the phrase is meaningless and unfortunate ... a book that will leave a bitter taste in the mouth by reason of its class prejudice.[5]

To Lloyd, the growth of urbanised and industrialised communities had a tangible, erosive effect upon hundreds of years of oral traditions. He deemed the collection and preservation of those traditions, viewed by him as being close to irrevocable loss, of paramount importance. However, his concentration on class boundaries and industrial landscapes in his definitions of the uses of folk song in both *The Singing Englishman* and *Folk Song in England* also delivered up a sub-textual polemic about the retention of any song as a representation of political struggle, a longing for a better life. Perhaps because Lloyd's enthusiasm was so manifest, any in-depth, contextual investigations about folk–popular dichotomies were glossed over (no investigations into the history of the commercial culture industry were undertaken at all).

In criticising Sharp, Lloyd was to comment in *The Singing Englishman* 'so much collected but little commented on'. It was subsequently argued by Dave Harker (1985) that, via a mawkish deification of industrial folk song, Lloyd also adjourned any self-reflexive debate about procedure and signification. Perhaps, to Lloyd, traditional music was healthy because it manifested itself as a concrete example of immediate experience, a dissonance between life as it was and life as it might be; therefore he saw little need to examine his own preconceptions. His ideology, together with a predetermined opinion about the apparent perfunctory nature of popular music, policed future theoretical proposals. Harker remained unimpressed:

> Unfortunately, as with Sharp, Lloyd may have allowed his theoretical assumptions to work their way into his collecting and publishing activities ...The problem was, and is, that very little sustained and detailed research has yet been done on the culture of the majority of English people. This is hardly Lloyd's fault; but it does mean that his generalizations need careful scrutiny ... it ill-behoves a person unable to offer a scientific and non-contradictory definition of what he likes, and

calls 'folksong', to castigate and smear the music and songs taken up and used by contemporary working class people.[6]

Both Harker and Georgina Boyes (1993) have identified the folk revival's practice of foregrounding rhetorical excellence over historical accuracy. This was a consequence of the movement's conviction that rhetoric was essential for its continued existence, and of its subsequent over-reliance on the (admittedly awesome) communication skills of its leaders such as Cecil Sharp and Bert Lloyd (not to mention Ralph Vaughan Williams and Ewan MacColl). For example, first Harker and then Boyes on *Folk Song in England*: ˙

> Time and time again Lloyd wrenches us back in his description from the brink of a material history, trailing a liberalist-populist rhetoric … he lapses into banalities in order to rationalize what are, fundamentally, assertions based on subjective value judgements.[7]

and

> for all its apparent innovation and variety, the Revival was hidebound by historical theory. Determinedly reproducing a policy of authenticity, it became a more effective vehicle for Sharp's views than the English Folk Dance Society of the 1920s. Typifying all that had set the Revival on a return to the past was its most valued theoretical statement on folk culture, A.L. Lloyd's 'Folk Song in England'. Published in 1967, the new work accepted the survivals theory Lloyd had dismissed in 1946 as 'a lot of dark anthropological hoo-ha' and approvingly reproduced Sharp's 1907 definition of folksong in its entirety.[8]

The main strength of *Folk Song in England* probably lies in its authoritative use of language rather than any overt historical accuracy. Throughout, Lloyd was at pains to emphasise that folk song could not be separated from social validation; he claimed that folk music demonstrated utter relevance, both political and artistic, and was an important historical frame of reference for the perception of non-modern forms of life. This analysis, of course, is classically constitutive of mid-century politicised modernity. Jack Froggatt, who started the first folk club in Warrington, affirmed to me that *Folk Song in England* was a core institution of folk socialisation and collective memory processes during the late 1960s: '*Folk Song in England* was our Bible. We all "clubbed" together to buy it for the club. It was used as a reference for any debate over songs or attitudes. I still have the original copy … it was "heady" stuff!'[9]

As a thesaurus of biblical proportions, *Folk Song in England* was obviously symbolically crucial; but was it historically accurate? There appears little doubt that Lloyd lacked the skills to explain how one type of music ('folk') could be an authentic historical representation, while another ('popular') remained little more than commercial waste-produce. To Lloyd, mass production had rendered popular music stale and culturally unprofitable, but hard evidence for this conclusion remains, to this day, insubstantial. Lloyd also proposed a distinction between public and private musical worlds that is equally difficult to sustain. Perhaps an economic/political history which does not look beyond factors of production and confines itself to a Marxist perspective inevitably risks attributing too much to too few factors in its explanation of change. Harker even suggested that, for Lloyd, marking the difference between a folk and a popular song was little more than knowing 'an elephant when he saw one'.[10] Yet, for Jack Froggatt and the many other advocates of Lloyd, the belief in the power of discovering an authentic tradition, even a new approach to life, was dutiful, unquestionable.

Lloyd refused to consider not only the massive diversity of distinctive practices and tastes within popular music activity and use, but also the possibilities for all music to interact with and exist alongside each other. There cannot be one explanation suited to every aspect of the performance past; any suggestion of this merely indicates a desire to recreate rather than interpret that past. For example, Lloyd suggested in the sleevenotes to *The Iron Muse* that 'As yet the industrial community is only dimly aware of its own self-made cultural heritage; ... bounded by the bingo hall and the idiot's lantern'.[11] His distress appears more connected to the 'awful' prospect of the lower classes buying (say) Fabian records rather than (say) joining the Fabians. As Harker argued, 'which songs have not been subject to constraints imposed by material factors?'[12] Lloyd's 'self-made cultural heritage' was relative rather than absolute and was certainly not a formula that could be applied indiscriminately.

That Lloyd should so clearly see mechanical reproduction and commercial activity as the enemy is symptomatic of the profound threat to some of industrial capitalism during the middle period of the century. He is obviously groping for some kind of historical explanation, striving to create the illusion of direct experience through traditional music, evoking an atmosphere, even.

But there is a paradox at the core of Lloyd's tradition. It looks back towards a long lost past and, in doing so, transforms and reconstructs that past as the image is being realised. Although songs might be created within societies that exploit both people and nature for profit, can we regard them as 'untarnished' representations of that exploitation? Lloyd appeared to be in favour of detailed analytical interpretation, but his binary approach merely suggested that there is an acceptable ideological 'reality' at work in one type of song, but not in another. Little systematic theory comes into view in order to distinguish his musical 'authenticity' from 'dross' and *Folk Song in England* merely encourages the illusion that certain types of music can be comfortably studied in isolation. The reality of historical and musical conjuncture simply cannot support this hypothesis. In truth, the book as published remains rather shambolic and disjointed and such conclusions remain overtly ideologically orientated, rather than problem-orientated. Francis Collinson declared:

Such a preoccupation with class in a work on English folk song seems to the reviewer to give a distorted picture. This is perhaps most apparent in the last chapter, on the industrial songs, where even after the cumulative build-up of class bias throughout the book, it becomes obvious, as the songs are allowed to speak for themselves, that they are as much concerned with pride and joy of work, as with any discontent at conditions, a fact which, at a moment's glance Mr Lloyd's earlier and excellent book, *Come All Ye Bold Miners* will reinforce.[13]

Perhaps, to Lloyd, folk culture remained unconscious, even unself-conscious, whereas popular culture existed via the deliberate search for objects to gratify the senses – clothes, heroes, music, etc. Therefore, pop culture, despite all of its socio-cultural uses, was artificial because it was not 'unique'. But if popular music audiences get what they are given, does this limit them from receiving what they want? And what is unique about manufacturing a socio-political vehicle upon which the folk song is supposed to be carried (or conversely, carries the ideology), in any case? The identification of these contextual questions has been inadequately handled thus far by folk music devotees, who have revelled in an illusion of musical/social 'different-ness'. To have identified hidden musical cultures was certainly valid, but to have done so via a political connoisseurship, a collective musical consciousness as an antithesis to popular music, is a limited reading of popular music history.

Appraisal

Lloyd received the singer's prize from the EFDSS in the same year that *The People's Songbook* was published (1948) and then – rather amazingly considering his political perspective – joined the committee of the EFDSS. From the late 1940s onward a 'Mexican stand-off' between Lloyd and the EFDSS appears to have taken place. He sat on the committee of the society but did not overtly challenge the running of that body. Only a smattering of articles by Lloyd appeared in *English Dance and Song* (mouthpiece of the EFDSS) throughout the 1950s and his first review did not surface until 1955. The rather hazy body that partially funded Lloyd throughout his writing, the Workers' Music Association, also barely received a mention. The importance of these two historical 'silences' from Cecil Sharp House is fundamental. Chroniclers are influenced by the prejudices of their time and divergent histories have to be weighed against each other. There is little doubt that the folk revival according to the EFDSS and the one propounded by, say, the followers of the doctrine according to Bert Lloyd and the WMA deviated dramatically. In E.P. Thompson's telling phrase, divergent evidence (and lack of evidence) must be 'interrogated by minds trained in a discipline of attentive disbelief'.[14]

Since his death, Lloyd's collecting in Australia has also been a subject of 'attentive disbelief'. Serious doubt has been cast on the veracity of his texts by

Australian folkies. His legacy is undoubtedly interesting – perhaps even an avenue into understanding how music, for some, provides an alternative route to social and spiritual provision. But what is most disturbing about the heritage of Bert Lloyd is the way in which authenticity and purity have become associated with certain types of music as a consequence of his political beliefs. Lloyd was a rather beleaguered narrative historian who operated at too high a level of, on the one hand, generality and, on the other, political didactics.

Ewan MacColl (with Alan Lomax and Peggy Seeger)

As folk luminaries go, few come larger than Ewan MacColl. Born in Auchterarder, Perthshire in 1915 as Jimmie Miller, he died in October 1989. His loss was still being lamented some years later:

> were you to ask me just who it would be that future historians will deem the greatest loss, then there is no contest. It has to be Jimmie Miller. Jimmie who? Oh yes, I know that the cognoscenti are well aware of just who it is I am referring to, but for those of you still guessing, let me give you a clue. Born in Auchterarder, Perthshire during the second year of world war one. Composer, political agitator, playwright, essayist, folk-singer, actor, Stalinist and visionary ... Of course I refer to the great Ewan MacColl, to give him his professional name.[15]

Ewan MacColl is frequently cited as the epitome of the difference between communal and consumer music, the evidence of the truth behind that difference. He was greatly influenced by what he experienced first-hand during the Depression years, and by seeing what advanced capitalism had done to his own father and others around him, and so his life-long allegiance to the Communist Party (although he claimed to have left the Party during the 1950s) is somewhat understandable.[16] As in Lloyd's case, MacColl's own historical context created a vision of society and performance. Also as with Lloyd, as a theoretician he displayed a universalising gesture, a sign that, somewhat ironically, was historically rooted both in the bourgeois enlightenment to which he appeared opposed, as well as the Marxism he embraced.

MacColl was one of the few Britons who had made contacts with the American radical music scene in the 1930s. He had met Paul Robeson on the latter's British tour and he had arranged various assorted fund-raising events for the Republicans in the Spanish Civil War. In the 1940s he married the young actress Joan Littlewood and created their theatre company Theatre Workshop that began life with MacColl as the in-house dramatist. These two had first met in the late 1930s, having been recruited by the BBC to present the Olive Shapley-produced outside broadcasts. MacColl (then Jimmie Miller) narrated much of *Homeless People* (1938) with Wilfred Pickles; Littlewood conceived and wrote *The Condition of the Working Class in England* (1939), a programme that was later heavily criticised by Shapley for being explicitly one-sided.

Productions such as *Landscape with Chimneys* and *Johnny Noble* became staple fare at the Theatre Workshop, and it was for the former that the song 'Dirty Old Town' was written by MacColl – according to Denselow (1989) to cover a rather inexpert scene change. Theatre Workshop was an itinerant company, which suited MacColl; however a move to a permanent site in London following a funding crisis discouraged him and, as the new decade dawned, he and Littlewood separated. From this moment MacColl appears to have taken a more active interest in music rather than theatre. His musical engagement with folk song was further inspired in 1951 by the man who had also reputedly changed Pete Seeger's life, Alan Lomax. Ken Hunt accurately describes Lomax (1915–2002) as the folk revival's 'Third Man'.[17] Lomax had previously visited Britain on a field trip and had recorded MacColl's parents. He was (like Pete Seeger) already known to a few British revivalists. MacColl was later to state:

> When Alan Lomax came along with this music that had proved popular to generations and generations, I thought, 'This is what we should be exploring!' The folk revival had a lot of things in it at its inception, and one was to make songs of struggle in an idiom that would be immensely acceptable to a lot of young people.[18]

Lomax had worked alongside his father John for the American Library of Congress before the war and Alan had a reputation as a radical thinker. Perhaps more than any others, Alan and John Lomax are responsible for saving innumerable American songs and giving them public visibility. They cut 3000 78s in the 1930s alone and the Library of Congress has a collection of more than 26 000 recordings made by father and father and son. However, they were an odd pair, with Alan constructing specific music canons out of myriad sources, John writing himself into song-writing credits for some of Leadbelly's 'compositions' (themselves little more than hybrid versions of songs learned) and both generally dismissing all things popular as 'made to sell and sell quickly'.[19]

In 1948 Collet's bookshop in London, the home of Leftist literature, imported a songbook from the USA that was to cement ideas about the potential of traditional song to become a force for social change. Alan Lomax and Pete Seeger co-edited *The People's Song Book*, along with editor-in-chief Waldemar Hille. Issued by Boni and Gear in the USA, this book had its antecedents in the US Popular Front, the American Communist Party and the Wobblies of the 1920s and 1930s. John and Alan Lomax collected most of the songs, and it was one of the first large-scale compilations to appear in Britain notating and detailing lyrics of songs of protest – representing for the Leftist intelligentsia of the United States what Warren Susman has described as 'the need to feel one's self part of some larger body, some larger sense of purpose'.[20]

The book was set out in four distinct sections and listed songs as follows:

- Songs that helped build America (e.g. 'Joe Hill'; 'Oh Freedom'; 'Paddy Works on the Railway'; 'Go Down Moses')
- World freedom songs (e.g. 'La Marseillaise'; 'Peat Bog Soldiers'; 'Song of the French Partisan')
- Union songs (e.g. 'Solidarity'; 'Talking Union'; 'We Shall Not Be Moved')
- Topical-political songs (e.g. 'Strange Fruit'; 'Jim Crow'; 'Pity the Downtrodden Landlord')

Following its importation to Britain MacColl and others used this songbook as a basis for their repertoire. The book also acknowledged a 'debt of gratitude' to the Workers' Music Association in 'London, England' for their 'especially generous'[21] song contributions. Henceforth the musical/political example of *The People's Song Book* (itself inspired by Carl Sandburg's *The American Songbag*, 1927), together with the name of Alan Lomax, became synonymous with the direction and leadership of the second British folk revival. Lomax stated in the foreword to the songbook:

> Straight talk – simple tunes with a lifting quality – these songs have been tested in the fire of the people's struggle all around the world. They emerged quietly and anonymously in the vanguard of apparently lost causes … an emerging tradition that represented a new kind of human being, a new folk community composed of progressives and anti-fascists and union members. These folk, heritors of the democratic tradition of folklore, were creating for themselves a folk culture of high moral and political content … this is their book and ours, a folio of freedom folklore, a weapon against war and reaction, and a singing testament to the future.[22]

MacColl claimed to have been wholly inspired by Lomax's words to 'start' a folk revival in the UK. It is ironic in the extreme, therefore, that MacColl and his cohorts took it upon themselves systematically to delete all American influences from the history of the British revival – a most curious of acts when MacColl collaborated with Lomax on the *Ballads and Blues* radio programmes. But this event occurred after Lomax had returned to the United States in 1958 to conduct field recordings in the southern states of America. Lomax was later engaged for many years in attempts systematically to classify traditional songs and dance. This resulted in the somewhat inconclusive *Cantometrics – An Approach to the Anthropology of Music*, a set of seven cassettes with a book.

The policy decision

By pitching the forces of an anti-modern musical 'enlightenment' against the technocracy of modernity, Ewan MacColl, a classic example of a mid-twentieth-century modernist, actually reduced musical modernity to little more than degeneration. Furthermore, while claiming historical 'meaning' and 'difference' for his beloved folk music, his refusal to acknowledge any substantial reception theory in his analyses (i.e. that interpretation of text is as much the responsibility of the recipient) produced both an autonomy of the political and a holistic interpretation of musical communication – both historically questionable (and undesirable). In fact, MacColl's hagiography of folk song is one of the weakest forms of historiography being driven by a political impulse empty of critical content and full of romanticism; this whim habitually ignores the ideological inconsistencies of any musical communication model.

Despite showing some interest in the social functions of skiffle in 1956 (and going so far as recording a skiffle EP with the Lomax Ramblers for Decca) MacColl was far from impressed with the commercial success of the music. He was furious that the left-wing scenes that had openly promoted this new dialectic for popular music (trad jazz and folk) had been overtaken by a non-political, inauthentic and mercenary hybrid. His backlash to the successes of skiffle was a highly charged knee-jerk reaction, but one which also became written in folk tablets of stone for many years. This was the decree of the policy club and the formation of the Critics' Group. Even today, the repercussions can still be heard. MacColl stated that he

> became concerned that we had a whole generation who were becoming quasi-Americans, and I felt this was absolutely monstrous! I was convinced that we had a music that was just as vigorous as anything that America had produced, and we should be pursuing some kind of national identity, not just becoming an arm of American cultural imperialism. That's the way I saw it, as a political thinker of the time, and it's the way I still see it.[23]

His decision to form the Critics' Group and subsequently to create a policy in the Ballads and Blues Club and then the Singers Club was highly controversial even then, especially given the fact that, after the decline of skiffle in 1958, some fans of the popular Lonnie Donegan were drifting into folk clubs. Many felt that MacColl and the Group were setting themselves up as a politically elitist authority on folk music and, as Denselow (1989) suggests, it was undoubtedly a political as well as an artistic signal. Vic Gammon concurred:

> In the early days of the post-war folk revival, I, and I think a lot of other people, felt that MacColl and Seeger formed a point of reference against which all other performers should be judged. Gradually (and with some people not so gradually) this feeling changed into one of total rejection of what they did and represented ... [including] ... the sect-like atmosphere of the Singers' Club and the Critics' Group, MacColl and Seeger's gathered church of the elect.[24]

However, in an interesting insight into the potential power of 'sour grapes', Boyes has also suggested that MacColl was particularly vexed by the poor review that the journal *Sing* gave to his rendition on Topic of the Merl Travis song 'Sixteen Tons'! Whatever the motivations, by the late 1950s MacColl had 'decided on a policy: that from now on residents, guest singers and those who sang from the floor should limit themselves to songs which were in a language the singer spoke or understood. We became what began to be known as a "policy club".'[25] One wonders whether this edict included the man himself!

To begin with, the policies emanating from the Critics' Group addressed the rather thorny issue of floor singing. Floor singing was already a salient feature of folk clubs by the end of the 1950s and usually involved members of the audience (although this expression became less and less relevant as the decade went on) being invited to stand up and sing unaccompanied. Some regarded floor singing as an essential and democratic feature of the folk club; however it was seen by the likes of MacColl as somewhat musically anarchic. Fred McCormick remembers: 'He would allow only three floor singers and would cancel them all at a whim if he thought it was necessary. That's the real way he ran things … for himself.'[26]

It is hardly surprising that, following MacColl's intervention, the floor-singing spot subsequently became the moment at which the same person usually stood up to sing the same song at the same time at every meeting, thus creating a vocal and visible display of hierarchy rather than democracy. Given the potentially oppositional status of the folk revival at this stage, MacColl's interference was illogical. On the one hand, he was supposed to be championing a free flow of workers' music through a channel of democratic, non-mediated dissemination; yet, at the same time, he was arguing against music as an international language! If the singer was American, the song also had to be American 'so what you didn't have was a bloke from Walthamstow pretending to be from China or from the Mississippi'.[27]

It was, perhaps, inevitable that performance hierarchies should evolve. The policies of MacColl and his supporters, in searching for both the authentic and the repertoire, resulted in a kind of schema in which music was reordered into categories of tradition, realism, and fakeness. Styles of singing were also brought into the equation; it was debated, for example, whether a folk song actually remained a 'folk' song if it was performed in what was viewed as a 'contemporary' manner. Contemporary meant a number of things: firstly if the vocal inflection was 'American'; secondly if it was vocally 'syncopated'; thirdly if the singer added instrumentation to (say) a ballad that was considered to be extant as an unaccompanied artefact. Like the Marxist he was (and perhaps the Maoist he became) MacColl was a predator – sniffing out what he saw were weaknesses, persuading people to buy into an ideological package. A folkie from Beverley later recalled to me:

> I must admit I went along with it but I remember thinking that it was like trying to entertain the mother-in-law; you know, making sure that you didn't blaspheme or

laugh in the wrong place! It was quite ridiculous. What if, say, Buddy Holly was your idol? How can you stop yourself wanting to sound even a little bit like him? After all this time a lot of American music, whether it's rock 'n' roll or the Kingston Trio, is as legitimately traditional as 'Auld Lang Syne'![28]

But according to MacColl and Peggy Seeger there had to be a correct way of singing a traditional song and a level of consonance had to be reflected. Therefore the Critics' Group were also assembled in order to analyse each other's singing. The Critics' Group were interested in vocal nuances, inflections and timbres that could be described as 'authentically English' (the historical question begs to be asked 'how did they know?'). Not surprisingly they were reviled by some as being utterly dogmatic, but they prevailed. Boyes (1993) suggests that from this time the movement was turning on itself. Bob Buckle thought that this was an early indication by the revivalists of a 'death wish':

yes, a 'death wish' all right! I look back on it now and I physically cringe. I mean the policy in our club [West Kirby] was that we basically didn't have a policy. 'Come All Ye'! But the very expression 'Policy Club' became rife. 'You can't sing this, you can't sing that' … 'you must have a policy about floor singers' … even … 'you must take the musical initiative from the Singers' Club in London'. We MUST? We didn't take much notice, and when we had a singer in from that particular clique of folkies it tended to be a pretty dour affair; pretty much unaccompanied 'finger in the ear stuff'. Pete and I [The Leesiders] would have to get things going again. Word got around that we were rather liberal and one night in the mid-1960s, MacColl sort of warned me about it when we were in London. You know, sort of half-jokingly 'come the revolution' … that kind of stuff. We'd turned up at the Scots Hoose, I think, after playing at Cecil Sharp House. We'd had a few beers, sung a few songs, but Ewan was there and he wasn't pleased. We discovered that our rather irreligious reputation had preceded us![29]

And Sydney Carter, interviewing MacColl and Peggy Seeger in 1960, bemoaned:

there's no doubt that a lot of English people LIKE singing American folk songs. Now I know some people disapprove of this. Alan Lomax, for example, was always urging us to get back to our own stuff. But I'm not so sure; because I remember that in my own case my enthusiasm for folk songs really started in Greece with Greek folk songs. I should be sorry to think that we must only sing our own things.[30]

But Peggy Seeger remained unmoved: 'Well, let's put it this way, how would you like it if everybody in the world spoke one language … Esperanto …?'[31]

Folk club attendances suffered immediately after the introduction of the policy rule, but then recovered a little. People were probably still rather used to being 'organised' in the 1950s. After all, the very structure of a folk club closely resembled that of a Scout or Boys' Brigade meeting, in any case, with subscriptions, lists and parish notices. An audience was quickly built from those who were quite willing to follow the song policy. But long-term prospects for such fundamentalism were not promising. After all, how could this historical avant-garde possibly hope to continue its challenge to a perceived musical/social status quo while it receded into antiquarian connoisseurship? Fittingly by the early 1960s attendances had declined even further. Eric Winter:

> The audience figures plummeted. In 1957 John Brunner noted in *Caravan*, a US fanzine, that clubs were turning people away. If you wanted a seat at the Ballads & Blues club in 1957 you would join a queue 30 minutes before starting time. But by 1961, when Ballads & Blues moved to the Cora Hotel, impresario Malcolm Nixon saw that the audience had fallen to an average of 150 ... the divided were various ... a few [clubs] felt the need to declare themselves to be non-political.[32]

But MacColl and his devotees couldn't have cared less. They worked from a Frankfurt School reformed Marxist (Adornian-style) perspective: viewing all things popular as artificial. For 'his' sector of the folk revival to experience a decline in popularity merely 'proved' his point (i.e. 'we' weren't ready for this stuff). Like Adorno himself, MacColl was able to retreat to an 'ivory tower'. He most certainly didn't consider music as a communication device, and expressions such as 'public demand' were way beyond his political remit. The political struggle demanded correct cultural traditions in sound. Any form of cultural melting pot was total anathema to his secular religion of folk music: 'If we subject ourselves consciously or unconsciously to too much cultural acculturation, as the anthropologists call it, we'll finish with no folk culture at all. We'll finish with a kind of cosmopolitan, half-baked music, which doesn't satisfy the emotion of anybody.'[33] This remains interesting quasi-apocalyptic language from one who claimed that his policy was 'not nationalistic, but political'. Ethnic diversity in British society (MacColl's 'cosmopolitan'?) was already a reality by 1960 and, far from being 'half baked', music 'acculturation' and commerce was shaping new aesthetics out of the wealth of art and popular traditions in Britain's multicultural society.

When MacColl decided to travel the country collecting and performing in 1956–57 he argued that his policy had worked. Denselow (1989) states that MacColl claimed 11 000 members for the Singers Club alone, and 1500 clubs had opened up across the British Isles carrying his singer's policy. He also claimed that those involved with folk music were predominantly drawn from the working classes. How true these claims were is, indeed, open to debate and further research. Certainly the figure of 11 000 appears to be a gross exaggeration. Harry Boardman, often cited as the first folkie to open a club in Manchester in 1954 (see Boyes 1993, although this club was in point of fact a guitarists' club), actually stated to *Folk Review* in 1975:

> we didn't even know the term 'folk club'. It didn't exist. There was a classical guitar session in a Manchester pub called the Guitar Circle, so Lesley [Boardman] and I thought of starting a 'folk circle' ... I was not even aware of MacColl's Ballads and Blues club until 1957.[34]

And in their 'What's On and Who's Singing' column of September 1959, *Sing* (the folk music songbook) was only able to identify nine English folk clubs (Liverpool, Manchester, Bradford and six in London). Although this list is probably incomplete, it does not resemble the outrageous propaganda of Ewan MacColl.

MacColl's claims for youthful working-class loyalty was as much a political PR exercise as anything else, for while he was flogging his way around his beloved folk club network, Harry Belafonte, the Kingston Trio and Lonnie Donegan were vying for working-class appreciation of folk song in the British hit parade. MacColl refused to acknowledge not only the power of musical communication's multiplicity but also the positive potential of the proliferating media to work on behalf of the folk revival.

Yet, by correspondingly joining the recording roster at Topic in 1950 – at first as a solo performer and then with Isla Cameron and Peggy Seeger – he ensured that there were regular releases of products bearing his own (and Bert Lloyd's) name. MacColl furthered his recording career by releasing innumerable tracks for the label, some very 'committed', others – like 'Sixteen Tons', 'Fitba Crazy' and 'The Wee Cooper o' Fife' – rather less 'pure' than his political image might suggest. Also, because Topic released recordings on a non-exclusive contract basis, MacColl was free to record for whomsoever he pleased. Personal popularity was never very far away from this man's ambitious psyche.

There is little doubt that, despite MacColl's exploits, popular music from the late 1950s onward was able to ground itself more in the activities of the working classes, from both a financial and a social point of view, thus making it a real representation of common expression. While the Critics' Group approached music-making like boffin-like technicians in white lab-coats, 'folk' popularist Lonnie Donegan was actually meaning something to people.

MacColl's notion of a folk revival was constructed as a packhorse to carry an ideological burden. He was always preternaturally sensitive to the needs of what he saw as his social class. However, like Matthew Arnold before him, he also saw an urgent need to cultivate the 'philistine' middle classes who, prior to the advent of the 1945 Labour government, had been unable to underpin their growing political and economic power with a socially enriching ideology. What both MacColl and Bert Lloyd failed to realise was that their actions controlled and enslaved older musical forms as visions of a working-class past for the advantage of a beneficial middle-class present. They negated the potential not only for individual production, but also for reception.

Additionally, by authorising and accepting certain soundtracks (but not others) into his universalising museum of objects, MacColl was limiting any potentially provocative nature of his chosen music. The concept of objectifying folk music into a canonical resource ultimately rejects any revolutionary manifesto. No claim to protest can be maintained under souvenir-like conditions. Hence, perhaps, the institutionalised academic and 'arts and crafts' museum image that the folk scene has conveyed well into the twenty-first century. Martin Carthy later informed Brian Hinton and Geoff Wall that:

> Far too many doctorates, far too many professorships hang on the authenticity of all that stuff. Ewan had the same problem [as Lloyd]. He gets his Doctor of Letters, but the idea that he is actually there with his hands, working on these things, is not acceptable. And I think that's unacceptable.[35]

It is all the more ironic that MacColl is best remembered by the public for his wonderful song 'The First Time Ever I Saw Your Face'. He wrote it, ostensibly, as a personal tribute to Peggy Seeger in 1957 and throughout the mid to late 1960s it was performed by a number of 'middle-of-the-road' US folkies such as Harry Belafonte, the Kingston Trio, the Brothers Four and the Smothers Brothers. However, when released by African-American soul singer Roberta Flack in 1972, the song became a US number one hit single and an international pop smash. MacColl deservedly received an Ivor Novello award in 1973. Everybody from Elvis Presley to Mantovani then recorded 'The First Time Ever I Saw Your Face' and without the royalties from this highly successful popular song he would have been unable to start his record label (Blackthorn) the following year. But he was 'appalled'; daughter-in-law Justine Picardie:

> He hated them all. He had a special section in his record collection for them, entitled 'The Chamber of Horrors'. He said that the Elvis version was like Romeo at the bottom of the Post Office Tower singing up to Juliet. And the other versions, he thought, were travesties: bludgeoning, histrionic, and completely lacking in grace.[36]

One might argue that a few of Ewan MacColl's own songs were often dangerously close to being 'travesties ... lacking in grace'. To this writer, many (e.g. 'Schooldays Over', 'Manchester Rambler', 'Dirty Old Town') perpetuated class stereotypes to a cloying degree!

Summary

At about the time that *Oh Boy!* was broadcast on TV (1958–59), cultural critic Richard Hoggart was in the USA (Rochester) teaching and enjoying favourable reviews of *The Uses of Literacy*. Hoggart's work remains emotional and observant to this day, and is particularly important as a pioneer of textual analysis of popular culture; but, in taking its lead from the Leavisite school of literary criticism, *The Uses of Literacy* was something of a post-war period piece even by the time of its publication (1957). It was certainly expressing the same mixture of a pre-war working-class culture consciousness together with 'Enlightened' post-war optimism and intellectualism that one could find in the Critics' Group.

Hoggart was not a member of the WMA (and he was never a Communist) but an active teacher and organiser for Hull University Extra Mural Department and the WEA (Workers' Education Association). Nevertheless, the similarities between the hazy criticisms of Richard Hoggart and the indistinct polemic of Ewan MacColl are marked, indeed.

Throughout the book Hoggart expressed an anxiety for the way a certain level of literary and social 'tradition' had deteriorated. Like MacColl, he constantly searched for negative 'difference' rather than an, albeit challenging, positive 'similarity' between the new 'pop' and old popular cultures. MacColl similarly regarded anything 'folk' as sound and 'pop' as decidedly unsound, and while he and Peggy Seeger were speculating that we were heading for a form of musical 'Esperanto', Hoggart's writing was also subsumed in a nostalgia of demarcation for Britain's working classes (also reminiscent of MacColl's propaganda that the 11 000 members of the Singers Club were 'mostly young manual workers') and a resentment of the growing fluidity of life and art. Hoggart disapproved of working-class periodicals and blustered about the 'sex and violence' paperbacks of the period, whereas MacColl prattled about 'cosmopolitan, half-baked music'.

Both Richard Hoggart and Ewan MacColl were becoming self-imposed rectal thermometers for the cultural temperature of Britain. Neither recognised that many young people in the later fifties viewed a great deal of Leavisite-mediated British tradition, whether literary or musical, with a great deal of suspicion. In addition, in the wake of the Hungarian revolution of 1956, they also regarded the political systems associated with significant elements of the folk and trad jazz scenes with utter contempt. Ironically, what neither Hoggart nor MacColl could prevent was the arrival of a 'standardised' British pop figure who owed a not inconsiderable debt to both the folk and jazz revivalists, via the hybrid of skiffle: Lonnie Donegan.

Ewan MacColl was (on occasion) a first-class songwriter and interpreter and his artistic legacy is not insubstantial. His absence might appear to many like a 'gaping wound', as Dai Woosnam suggests. Looking back, however, it is very difficult to see how such a self-proclaimed folk intellectual was going to plug that gap between art and life in post-WW II Britain. This shift could only come from young people with spending power.

The apotheosis of British post-war urban experience and artistic expression was probably 'Mod', which also developed in the late 1950s. Mod not only grasped but also accentuated the dilemmas of late twentieth-century capitalism (instead of constantly whinging about them). Mods did so as an innate counteraction to their own new social and economic positions. The relative failure of the folk revival was that, ultimately, it merely replicated classical canons by offering itself up as a formal text to be learned.

Of course the highlighting of a suppression of older traditions was crucial to the understanding of the present; MacColl's folk revival, however, could never hope to represent the continuity between past and present while it perpetuated unsustainable political stereotypes produced in the euphoric, yet isolated atmosphere of post-war social intellectualism. Vic Gammon: 'In general MacColl and Seeger's self-imposed separation from the mainstream of the revival and their out of hand rejection of some important trends within it led to a strange sort of musical fossilization, a lack of openness to potentially enriching influences.'[37]

Despite formulating and representing the second folk revival's exciting beginnings, by the early 1960s Lloyd, Lomax, MacColl and Seeger were beginning to represent a rather degraded collective, gazing upon a present 'ghastly' world and then back towards a putative time in the past, merely reconstructing an idealised past history that was once itself a grim present! The monumental hypocrisy of these thinkers was their claim on incipient realism. This was little more than a confinement within the boundaries of images of the past.

Notes

1. Lloyd, *The Singing Englishman*, p. 4.
2. Ibid., p. 30.
3. Ibid., pp. 30–31.
4. Seabrook, 'The Sound of Despair', p. 868.
5. Collinson, 'Review of Folk Song in England'.
6. Harker, *Fakesong*, pp. 249–50.
7. Ibid., p. 251.
8. Boyes, *The Imagined Village*, p. 241.
9. Interview with folk singer and club organiser Jack Froggatt, July 1995.
10. Harker, *Fakesong*, p. 250.
11. Lloyd, 'Introduction', *The Iron Muse*.
12. Harker, *Fakesong*, p. 252.
13. Collinson, 'Review'.
14. Thompson, *The Poverty of Theory*, pp. 220–21.
15. Woosnam, 'The Tizer Test', p. 34.
16. 'MacColl's "lifelong allegiance" was to Communism not the CP, as such (he eventually left the CP to support a Maoist group)'. Interview with writer Dave Laing, 23 January 1998.
17. Hunt, 'The Roots of Modern Folk', p. 57.
18. MacColl, *Journeyman: An Autobiography*, p. 272.
19. Lomax and Lomax, *Folk Song USA*, p. viii.
20. Susman, *Culture as History*, p. 172.
21. Hille (ed.), *The People's Song Book*, half-title verso.
22. A. Lomax, 'Foreword' to Hille (ed.), *The People's Song Book*.
23. MacColl, *Journeyman*, pp. 287–88.
24. Gammon, 'Seeger and MacColl Revisited', p. 23.
25. MacColl, *Journeyman*, pp. 287–88.
26. Interview with Fred McCormick, March 1997.
27. Carter, 'Going American?' including interview with Ewan MacColl, pp. 19–20.
28. Interview with unnamed folkie, Beverley Folk Festival, summer 1995.
29. Interview with folk singer Bob Buckle, July 1995.

30. Carter, 'Going American?', p. 20.
31. Ibid., interview with Peggy Seeger, p. 20.
32. Winter,'Purists, Popularisers and Tolerators', p. 18.
33. Carter, 'Going American?', interview with Ewan MacColl, p. 20.
34. Schofield, 'A Lancashire Mon', including interview with Harry Boardman, pp. 4–9.
35. Hinton and Wall, *Ashley Hutchings*, p. 168.
36. Picardie, 'The First Time Ever I Saw Your Face', p. 125.
37. Gammon, 'Seeger and MacColl', pp. 23–24.

Chapter 4

Politics and obstinacy

What people mean, I suppose, is that left wing political songs appear in the columns of SING which I edit. I make no apology for this. We've never tried to hide the fact that SING is political in the same way that the Spectator or New Statesman is political. They devote a lot of their space to the arts, and so do we; but with us, it's only one art-song ... folk song, and new songs in the folk tradition.

Eric Winter to Sydney Carter, 1960

Despite being formed from within and interacting with innumerable kinetic social practices, tradition is often perceived as revolutionary. A tradition can be perceived to be older than the immediate past; hence the endorsement of tradition always implies a rejection of that immediate past in the interests of something uncontaminated, original. Such rejection is always experienced as revolutionary, an overturning of the values of an immediate past which has outlived its usefulness. This concept of tradition, together with a study of the political context of that movement, might help to make some sense of the advent of the second British folk revival. Adherents appeared to claim, amidst that immediate post-WW II environment, that, like a form of secular religion, tradition was the pathway to enlightenment – a rather revolutionary and specialised, yet 'natural' and 'truthful', way of making music.

The political ideology of the leading post-war folk revivalists was, for many years, bent on resisting the over-arching economic reality of Western capitalism. However, eventually, in order to maintain a position in the music industry marketplace, enterprises such as Topic Records (of which more later) were forced to accept a level of monetarist 'reality'. Adherence to the Marxist framework had the effect of conferring a limited reading on the world; this was replaced by an appreciation of a more inclusive historical process.

This chapter will attempt to narrate the ideological standpoint and journey of those involved. We will begin with the bizarrely dynastic (and far from Marxist) English Folk Dance and Song Society and move on to the Workers' Music Association and Topic Records. One might describe this as an expedition from incipient and ill-defined nationalists and Marxists to realistic, albeit reluctant, capitalists.

I have already expressed doubt about the revolutionary potential of folk music. Yet, within the atmosphere of post-war utopianism, the folk revival was seen by those involved as launching an important attack upon contemporary music aesthetics. Folk music was unadorned, uncomplicated, and (to some) even sounded rather mysterious. In this challenging stage, the revival contributed to many people's sense of cultural identity. There was a 'silent' history brought to the fore, a sense of power and integrity suggested by strong regionalism and political struggle. Preservation and conservation was also part of this emphasis, in opposition to the apparent outright commercial exploitation inherent in the popular. The revival even came to function as a 'natural' human sanctuary; it was a place – perhaps like a nature reserve – where 'natural' music could be saved from the menace of excessive human and industrial exploitation. A place, too, where it was envisaged that man could replenish himself with a form of music that was arguably 'truer' than that available through mediated processes. The revival was appealing because it was invested with these crucial values of 'authenticity' and 'truth'. But, conversely, it was also (as I have stated in Chapter 3) a representation of continuity, a cultural buffer against what some viewed as US carnivorous capitalism.

The issue of Americana

In the controversy surrounding the future role of the BBC inaugurated by the Beveridge Committee report of 1950, American systems of broadcasting and advertising were used as grounds against the introduction of a commercially based media. A wide variety of dominant and sub-cultural constructions around the uses and definitions of music came to combine against American popularism. Behind much of this lay a sense of national economic inferiority, provoked by Britain's dependence on American finance, together with a feeling that Britain's cultural 'pre-eminence' over the United States should not be compromised. Prior to this, Maud Karpeles had convened the aforementioned folk music conference (see Chapter 2) in London in September 1947, which led to the founding of the International Folk Music Council. Karpeles's aims were to register alarm at the poor standards of Morris dancing, country dancing and song, but she also suggested that the lowering in standards was due to the advance of popularism.

Evidently, a national debate was taking place. Alarm was expressed at the amount and substance of American popular culture in the British marketplace such as films, comics and musicals. There were political implications in these debates. The far Left were in a mood of disapprobation about all American cultural products, viewing them as manipulative, mass-produced ephemera that created unrealistic expectations about material improvements during a period of austerity. In this debate, tradition was offered as a source of new knowledge, providing resources for creative expression. Marxists did not, as is incorrectly suggested by Raymond Williams, view tradition as 'ordinarily diagnosed as superstructure'.[1] In fact, many British Marxists embraced the folk revival via the WMA in an attempt to bring about social change. The political Right viewed this Americana as weak fare in comparison with British art and culture. From their point of view it was seen as inferior low culture with few traditions to compare with 'The Great Tradition' expounded by F.R. Leavis and his *Scrutiny* chums. These Britons, therefore, used tradition in a more defensive manner!

The English Folk Dance and Song Society

The Kennedy–Karpeles axis was a dominant (indeed dynastic) force at the EFDSS. Douglas Kennedy's wife Helen was the sister of Maud Karpeles; Helen and Maud were supervised at Chelsea Polytechnic in folk dancing by Cecil Sharp and became demonstrators for Sharp's lectures around the United Kingdom. In 1911 Kennedy and Helen Karpeles met at the same time that the Folkdance Club mutated into the larger English Folk Dance Society. Helen became secretary of the larger society, Maud went on to be Sharp's assistant. Douglas Kennedy and Helen Karpeles were married in 1914 and Douglas took over the directorship of the Society in 1924 on the death of Cecil Sharp. When Cecil Sharp House was opened in 1930, Helen Kennedy established the Royal Albert Hall Festivals.

According to Boyes, the Kennedys were also founder members of the extreme right-wing 'Kinship in Husbandry' movement:

> Douglas Kennedy and Rolf Gardiner had certainly numbered the Revival among the 'many movements it was important to percolate'. And arguably, Kennedy's post war populism and reorganisation of the English Folk Dance and Song Society on a national basis, concentrating its management in his hands, was part of this strategy.[2]

This connection between the Kennedys and the ultra right-wing sympathies of Rolf Gardiner has attracted some attention from Georgina Boyes; however it has also been argued by Derek Schofield that Boyes exaggerates Gardiner's importance and influence on the Kennedys.[3] Nevertheless, it does appear that Gardiner, a known Fascist sympathiser, made an impact on the Society during the 1920s. He was an important critic of Sharp's conformity and had a substantial influence on the formation of solely male Morris clubs ('The Travelling Morrice' and 'English Mistery') during the 1920s – which the Kennedy dynasty broadly supported. Gardiner's influence did not appear to endure (but one Social Darwinian is much the same as another – right or left wing). Throughout the pre- and post-WW II era the EFDSS hierarchy remained distinctly 'Sharpian' – modernists, elitists, with interest in pre-modern aesthetic practices validated by newer sciences such as anthropology and folklore studies.

Cecil Sharp House suffered from bomb damage during the war and was still being renovated by the late 1940s, but it was regarded as something of a 'happening place' by those drawn to square dancing. There had been something of a square dance craze in the USA in the late 1940s. Peter Kennedy, the son of Douglas Kennedy, recognised this and, organising history to credit Cecil Sharp with the survival of the dances in America ('The first to recognise this American form and to recognise it as our own heritage was Cecil Sharp': Peter Kennedy[4]), became the Society's square dance specialist. From 1947 onwards Kennedy the younger took it upon himself to promote this once-removed English folk tradition. He organised barn dances and square dances at first in Northumberland and Durham and then in the West Country and they proved to be very successful. At such gatherings Kennedy persuaded local players, singers and dancers to contribute to what the Society called a 'ceilidhe [*sic*] spirit', openly singing songs in perhaps the first organised examples of singarounds. Kennedy actually rediscovered a number of little-known square dances on his travels and called them 'new-old' dances. His pro-active interest even led to a number of singers being recorded by the Gramophone Company.

The square dance was thus championed at the newly refurbished (5 June 1951) Cecil Sharp House and was introduced, in some cases as 'English Country Dancing', to schools via the BBC Third Programme. The BBC also broadcast a number of these 'Village Barn Dances' as entertainment programmes on the Home Service, and was responsible for a programme entitled *Everybody Swing*, a live square dance party from Bristol. This programme became a regular (and very popular) West Region broadcast between 1947 and 1952. The music for the programme was provided by Peter Kennedy's own band, The Haymakers Square Dance Band. Square dance tutor books also abounded, the most popular probably being the series of *Community Dance Manuals* and the *Fiddler's Tune Book*.

The Haymakers band recorded a series of records for Decca entitled *Everybody Swing*[5] and also a double-sided disc for HMV entitled 'Princess Margaret's Fancy'. This latter title was a square dance composed by Peter Kennedy for the Patron of the EFDSS, Princess Margaret. The princess was a great fan of square and round dancing and danced to Kennedy's composition when she visited Cecil Sharp House on Tuesday, 21 June 1949. The music contained some of the most characteristic movements appearing in English country dancing at that time, such as the 'millwheel', 'sashay', 'strip the willow', 'Spanish waltz' and 'heel and toe'. The record did not prove to be a huge seller, but continued to be listed in HMV's catalogue for some years, despite the wholesale deletion of 78s by EMI in 1955. By 12 October 1951 a picture of Princess Margaret square dancing in Canada had been published in the British press. As Ron Smedley, gold badge holder at the EFDSS, recalls: 'Suddenly everybody wanted to Square Dance and everybody wanted the EFDSS. The boom had begun ... things would never be the same again.'[6]

Certainly, during the Festival of Britain (1951) many fetes across the country featured square dancing in their celebrations. But, despite Smedley's genuine enthusiasm, it is arguable whether square dancing crossed many social boundaries. The square dance boom did not have any measurable impact on the lower and lower-middle classes across urbanised areas of the United Kingdom. The recording of 'Princess Margaret's Fancy' is a good indicator of the appeal of square dancing, which, although apparently collected from the English lower classes, was actually part of the upper class 'debs' circuit.

The square dance boom subsided by the end of 1952, but Peter Kennedy was still convinced that 'square dancing is something new. It is up to date, changing daily, creative and alive.'[7] He was already years out of touch and throughout the remaining years of the 1950s, the EFDSS was forced repeatedly to look over its shoulder at the Workers' Music Association-backed revivalists. These people had succeeded in changing the tenor of the revival (from dance to song) and, in the process, had thinly disguised themselves as the vanguard of a peace movement.

In 1960 the EFDSS went through a major upheaval, resulting in the eventual resignation of Douglas Kennedy in 1961. Although, by this time, the direct influence of the CP-backed WMA was beginning to diminish owing to their chronic lack of funds (brought about by a dwindling devoted), the activities of those linked to the journal *Sing* certainly influenced Kennedy's decision.

Sing

The London Youth Choir initiated *Sing* as a bi-monthly publication in May 1954. Financially assisted by the Workers' Music Association, the London (and National) Youth Choir was also linked to the Communist Party of Great Britain. Leon Rosselson, Shirley Collins and Hylda Sims were all, at one time, members of the NYC. The co-founder and editor of *Sing* was Communist Party member Eric Winter and his music editor was John Hasted. With the notable exception of Winter, all of the above were members of the Ramblers singing group, which had formed around 1952. Membership of the Ramblers was copious but also included Jean Butler, Neste Revald and Bert Lloyd. Hylda Sims joined the group, which renamed itself the City Ramblers and released a 78rpm disc on Topic (TRC101) 'Round and Round the Picket Line'/'Nine Hundred Miles'. This was not connected with the Ramblers with which Ewan MacColl and jazz clarinettist Sandy Brown later became musically involved.

In the autumn of 1954 a number of the above CP members opened the Good Earth Club in Soho. Eric Winter described this club to me as 'rather elitist and political – but that's the way we were'. In the same interview Winter also informed me of two later clubs opened by the *Sing* coterie in the spring of 1956 (Studio Skiffle at High Holborn and 44Club in Soho). He spoke of these clubs being 'extensions of the first club – all good Lefties! – but without the stiffness'.[8] Studio Skiffle featured Hylda Sims and Russell Quaye, whereas the 44Club was organised by and featured John Hasted alongside Redd Sullivan and Judith Goldbloom (the last of whom went on to find fame in Israel).

Sing's influence within the British folk revival cannot be overestimated. By 1956 it was presenting both British and American folk songs to its readership and was being mailed to interested parties the length and breadth of the country.

This little journal could correctly be described as the folk revival's first real mouthpiece, for, although the EFDSS's *English Dance and Song* had been in existence for a number of years, it was considered by some ideologically unsound and overly concentrating on dance at the expense of song.

Sing's principal duty was to print songs but also gave over a little space to copy. For its day, it was overtly political in tone. One glance at the first edition makes this abundantly clear, with material entitled 'Talking Rearmament', 'The Atom Bomb and the Hydrogen!' and 'Kenyatta' together with a feature on 'Geoff Skeet's Bucharest prizesong "The Bird with a Leaf in her Beak"'.[9] *Sing* also reprinted songs from its more illustrious colleague in the USA, *Sing Out!*, but this practice reduced considerably after correspondence in the summer of 1957 raised the issue of what constituted 'traditional' material (foredooming MacColl's policy decision in 1958). *Sing* continued to underpin its own value systems by reprinting many songs from the variety of WMA songbooks.

In October 1957 an 'English Folk Music Festival and Singing' competition was organised at Cecil Sharp House and following this event stylistic and ideological battle lines were drawn between *Sing* and the EFDSS. Disagreement emerged between Eric Winter and Fred (Karl) Dallas on the one hand, and Douglas and Peter Kennedy on the other, concerning the presentation and accompaniment of folk songs. Although there had been previous displays of divergence, from that moment on the two folk camps were most certainly codified.

In 1960, *Sing* editor Eric Winter 'infiltrated' the EFDSS and he and Sydney Carter, editor of the Society's journal *English Dance and Song*, worked together to produce a pirate edition for New Year of 1961. This was after Carter had been writing a number of provocative editorials in *English Dance and Song* during 1960. For example an editorial written by Carter pronounced:

ALL DANCE AND NO SONG?
This is the English Folk Dance AND Song Society; but you wouldn't think so, to look at our post-bag. Most of the articles and letters we receive are about the Dance, and not the Song. Delighted though we are to find the Dance so flourishing … we are a bit concerned about the Song. Does this apparent lack of interest really reflect our attitude as a Society?

Perhaps it does. But it certainly does not reflect what is happening outside the Society. There is a new interest in Folk Music (especially folk song) in circles which have never heard of Cecil Sharp. Cecil Sharp wanted to give Folk Music back to the people. Well, it has happened – though not always in the way we expected. Some of the things called 'folk' in 1960 may surprise us: but we ought at any rate to be aware of them.

That is why we have reviewed no less than eighteen 'folk' records in this issue. We could have reviewed another twenty but for lack of space. To make room for even eighteen we have had to move a few of the old landmarks. This magazine, like Folk Music itself, is in a state of flux. Ye Olde and the new are rather strangely mixed up at the moment (and this applies to our lay-out and typography as well). Things will get sorted out, we hope; but it takes time. Meanwhile, your comments, even rude ones, will be welcome. With this brief warning and apology we hand you on to the Director.[10]

The prose of Sydney Carter quite clearly displays conflicting ideologies at work at this significant stage in the development of the folk revival. Carter is criticising the antiquarian tendencies of the EFDSS, while suggesting that tradition can be mobilised in song for contemporary purposes. His perspective pre-dates the folk-rock fusion by some years, yet he clearly understands music as a kinetic social practice ('in a state of flux') rather than a fixed artefact. Carter's pronouncements are undoubtedly political. For him, the values expressed in song were a central component of the cognoscenti of the Left – the bringing together of song to reinforce a collective identity. This idea was, however, at odds with that espoused by the EFDSS – a kind of deferential glorification of the myth of people living on the land. Carter and Winter saw themselves as belonging to the future – a kind of avant-garde, perhaps; for them, the EFDSS myth of the people was associated with reaction, the forces which recreate an idealised past ('Ye Olde').

Despite a levelling off in their readership, and various funding crises, *Sing* struggled on until 1974 and, in doing so, created a fascinating archive of printed political and 'traditional' music. Its main contribution, however, was as the fulcrum of a body of Left-thinkers who placed, on the one hand, emphasis on song rather than dance and, on the other, political pressure on the direction of the EFDSS. Georgina Boyes (1993) states that the vague and varied politics of the hard Left did not leave an indelible imprint upon the revival. However, while music may not be the best medium for carrying politics, this does not mean that party politics cannot influence the conception and direction of a musical milieu. There may not have been an especially identifiable political agenda for everyone, but it is quite clear that the origin of the revival was, indeed, *political* for several important disciples.

The Workers' Music Association

The presence of the Workers' Music Association, alone, bears testimony to the vital input of a left-wing politic. The WMA helped to stimulate ideas about the authenticity of workers' song, citing it directly as a musical representation of struggle, survival and communality. Like the EFDSS, the WMA also provided an organisational backbone for the movement. It was a point of reference and authority and provided (at times limited yet) vital financial support. For example, the introduction to the WMA *Pocket Song Book*, first published in 1948, stated that: 'The majority of songs in this volume were chosen by plebiscite among members of the Workers' Music Association to provide for community singing in the larger labour movement in this country.'[11] Not only does this statement suggest organisation, formulation and fraternity, but it does so in pretty clear political language ('plebiscite', 'members', 'movement' etc.). Even though Marxist thought came in for a great deal of revisionism within the ranks of the folk revival (whilst also failing to move some of those individuals drawn to folk music) it was undoubtedly the prime mover of that revival.

The WMA was founded in 1936 by a number of choirs in the London Labour Choral Union and the Co-Operative Musical Associations (then embracing some 44 choirs and five orchestras) in order to coordinate the musical activities of what it viewed as working-class organisations. The WMA provided these groups with the necessary musical material and professional resources that it could muster as part of its resources. Composer Alan Bush (1900–95) was directly involved in this process from the outset and became the first president of the WMA. Bush, along with fellow composer Rutland Boughton, was a long-term member of the Communist Party of Great Britain. In the 1920s he was also Michael Tippett's closest musical and political ally (both were involved in socialist yeomanry). In 1929 Bush moved to Berlin and was in close contact with Brecht. But by 1936 he was back in London and President of the newly formed Workers' Music Association.

By the mid-point of the Second World War, the Association's aims and objectives (printed in *The Singing Englishman*) were as follows:

> To utilise fully the stimulating power of music to inspire the people.
> To provide recreation and entertainment for war workers and members of the forces.
> To stimulate the composition of music appropriate to our time.
> To foster and further the art of music on the principle that true art can move the people to work for the betterment of society.

It also stated that:

> At the present time the Association emphasises the need to promote music making of a character which encourages vigorous and decisive action against Fascism. The WMA is pledged to foster the development of music making wherever it can be encouraged – in the factories and in the Forces, in Civil Defence, in Youth Clubs and Schools. Many eminent musicians and dance bands are working with us; a number of choral and instrumental groups are affiliated with us; progressive educational bodies, including Co-operatives and Trade Unions, support our work; individual sympathisers are enrolled as members.[12]

From a roll call of its vice-presidents, the WMA appeared to be a very musically eclectic organisation. An early (1944) list of vice-presidents cited Benjamin Britten, Hanns Eisler, Alois Hába and Wladimir Vogel amongst its numbers. Another early WMA luminary was composer Granville Bantock (1869–1946), whose 'Celtic Symphony' the Conservative Party later used during the 1997 British elections.

Perhaps rather surprisingly, the WMA was incorporated as a limited company and initially held offices at 9 Great Newport Street, London WC2. There was also a Scottish WMA with headquarters at 60 Glenapp Street, Glasgow. However, in truth, the WMA was little more than a rather nebulous offshoot of the Communist Party of Great Britain and was, according to Harker, a 'supporting institution'.[13] For example, not only was professor Alan Bush a paid-up member of the CP, but so too was the chairman of the Executive, Geoffrey Corbett, as well as National Organiser Charles Ringrose. The publishing house Lawrence & Wishart was also directly linked to the intellectuals at the WMA and CP. The very presence of composers such as Bush and Bantock and actors such as Michael Redgrave, Alfie Bass and Harry H. Corbett further indicates the left-wing nature of British artistic communities in the post-war utopian era.

As established in the previous section, it was the WMA who commissioned Bert Lloyd to produce *The Singing Englishman* as part of their 'Keynote' series in 1944. They also asked Lloyd to compile *Coaldust Ballads* (1953) for male-voice choirs. These publications, together with the meeting of Lloyd, Lomax and MacColl, were undoubtedly major fomenters of the second British folk revival. The financial support of Bert Lloyd was an important entrustment for the WMA. As Lloyd's profile grew, the connection endured and they were also 'on hand' (although severely financially depleted by this time) in the mid-1960s when they finally persuaded him effectively to rewrite *The Singing Englishman*. This became the seminal *Folk Song in England* also discussed in Chapter 2. In the preface to this later work Lloyd was quick to give credit to the WMA for their financial encouragement:

> In America, late in the depression and early in the war years, traditional song and its topical imitations were coming into vogue, particularly among young radicals, as a consequence of the stresses of the time and the rumble of newly-found or newly made 'people's songs' was rolling towards us across the Atlantic. The WMA, that admirable but over-modest organisation, sensed that similar enthusiasm might spread in England, and they were eager to help in the rediscovery of our own lower class traditions. They commissioned me to write a brief social-historical introduction to folk song entitled: *The Singing Englishman*. It was put together mainly in barrack rooms, away from reference works, in between tank gunnery courses. It wasn't a good book but people were kind to it perhaps because it was the only one of its sort: like the okapi, not much to look at but cherished as unique … The WMA's presage was justified; the folk song revival swept in.[14]

The Executive at the WMA was fully aware of the growing importance that many left-thinking intellectuals in New York's coffee house circuit gave to folk song. It was also aware that, in the USA, the US Popular Front had accepted both jazz and folk. Thus trad jazz and folk music were viewed as being politically correct. The WMA was also supportive of theatre, and the Workers' Theatre Movement, based at 59 Cromer Street, London WC1, was closely linked to the

CPGB. Ewan MacColl and Joan Littlewood were both members of the WTM, as were the Unity Theatre's Alfie Bass and Bill Owen.

The WMA enjoyed a very active war on the home front, not only in promoting concerts and lectures about the verities of the Soviet Union, but also publishing pamphlets and songbooks of Soviet music. The Association also formed the Topic Record Club in 1939 (see below). They published a variety of successful songbooks during the Second World War. Titles such as *Popular Soviet Songs* (1941) and *Red Army Songs* (1942) were as popular as finance, printing and paper restrictions would allow. Certainly, with the vital assistance of Collet's Book Shop, 66 Charing Cross Road, WC2, the WMA distributed sheet music from the Soviet Union such as Novikov's 'World Democratic Youth Song' and the Soviet national anthem to a growing number of interested parties.

By the closing years of the war the WMA boasted an impressive list of song and choral publications, including works by Hanns Eisler ('Cradle Song of a Working Mother'; 'Ballad of Today'; 'Miner's Song'), Dunayevsky ('Land of Freedom'; 'Young Comrade's Song') and a number of political songs from around the world. Composer Alan Bush, president of the WMA in 1945, was responsible for arranging and transcribing much of their printed music. One of the WMA continual sellers in the mid to late 1940s was 'The Internationale'; arranged by Bush, the sheet music sold for 3d. The WMA continued to issue the aforementioned 'Keynote' series of journals during the later 1940s; it was in this series in 1948 that Bert Lloyd wrote a seminal article on the background to the song 'St. James' Infirmary' (also reprinted in *Sing* almost ten years later).

Poet John Manifold, together with his wife Kate – both later prominent in the Australian folk revival – were also active members of the WMA at this important formative stage. John became chairman of the Executive in 1947, having previously gathered together several seventeenth- and eighteenth-century works from the shelves of the British Museum on behalf of the WMA (John and Kate also took part in WMA recorder sessions in London). WMA Band leader Will Sahnow even set a Manifold poem, 'The Bullock and the Beef', to music. In fact Manifold's first book on music was a tutor for recorder published by the WMA in 1948 entitled *The Amorous Flute*. Its subtitle declared the booklet to be 'An unprofessional handbook for recorder players and all amateurs of music' (right on!).

In December 1948, the first edition of the *WMA Pocket Song Book* was issued. Obviously inspired by *The People's Song Book*, together with the success of *The Singing Englishman* over the preceding four years, the Association canvassed its members for a selection of songs, the majority of which were then featured in this first volume (selling enough for several reprints over the next few years). Once again Alan Bush sifted and arranged many of the songs, but was also assisted by Robert Gill, Will Sahnow, Bernard Stevens and Ralph Wood. There were some duplications from *The People's Song Book*: 'Joe Hill'; 'Pity the

Downtrodden Landlord'; 'The Marseillaise'; 'Hold the Fort', but more popular songs and folk songs from the British Isles were included. A cursory glance at the *Pocket Song Book* reveals a classic example of how the WMA contrived custom to carry their ideological burden. Songs as diverse as 'The Lincolnshire Poacher' and 'Killarney' were linked together via a political manifesto and, henceforth, the pervading folk ideology was attached to these songs, despite no literal connection – an invention of tradition, indeed.

The aforementioned song 'Pity the Downtrodden Landlord' (Woolf/Clayton) was written during the war and became something of a staple Leftist satirical song in the late 1940s and early 1950s. At a time of chronic housing shortages and before pre-fab and council house building had yet to reach a high point, landlords were often viewed as parasites (see the Topic Discography below for the Alfie Bass 78s TRC87 and TRC88 and the Stan Kelly EP *Songs for Swinging Landlords to*, TOP60). The biting satire of the song became something of a political rallying flag for those who wished to see the advance of public ownership in property:

> … You are able to work for your living
> And rejoice in your strength and your skill;
> So try to be kind and forgiving
> To a man whom a day's work would kill;
> You can work, and still talk to your neighbour;
> You can look the whole world in the face;
> But the landlord who ventured to labour
> Would never survive the disgrace.
>
> So pity the downtrodden landlord
> And his back that is burdened and bent;
> Respect his grey hairs, don't ask for repairs,
> And don't be behind with the rent!

It was published in sheet music form by the WMA from the war onward, with a catalogue number of 9029, price 6d.[15] The catalogue number is interesting, suggesting, as it does, the 29th release of sheet music by the Association – a striking anticipation of the politics of the folk revival to follow.

The Unity Theatre Club, based after the war in Goldington Street, St Pancras, NW1, was yet another outlet for political art and, like the WMA, produced small runs of sheet music from its stage productions. *People's Songs* was the name for Unity's music publishing outlet, run ostensibly from Collet's Bookshop. Songs such as 'Strike While the Iron is Hot' and 'Unity March' – the latter from the 'pantomime with a political point' *Babes in the Wood* – were published and sold for 3d. The Unity Theatre joined together with the WMA to produce recordings under the Topic label in 1939 and 1940 such as 'Brother, Brother, Use Your Head' TRC2 and 'A New World Will Be Born' TRC12. There were also a number of active Unity Theatres across the country by the mid-1950s (e.g. Glasgow, Liverpool). Renowned actors Alfie Bass, Harry H. Corbett and Bill

Owen were all prominent members of the Unity throughout this significant period.

The growth of social and cultural movements such as the WMA and WTM and the broader interest in folk and traditional jazz music were prospering as never before. Folk music writer Ken Hunt:

> Interest in folk music was swelling, not just as an art form but as an articulation of the voice of the people ... if all this sounds a smidgen political, then your antennae are attuned, because much of the later British folk revival buzzed with left-wing politics and Marxism. Even Britain's foremost folk record label was rooted there. And all this pre-dated the protest movement by at least a decade.[16]

For example, the relative popularity of folk song from 1948 onward inspired the WMA to reissue *The Singing Englishman* in 1951; described as 'A Festival Year Reissue' (the Festival of Britain) it sold for 2/-, and sold well. These sales reflected the growing memberships of both WMA and EFDSS as folk song became part of an ever-increasing underground and folk dancing became popular with the upper classes and the newly enlarged teaching profession. The Workers' Music Association's continued coordination of jazz and folk activities eventually meant that they were also on hand to assist the BBC's interest in the folk revival. In the midst of Festival of Britain euphoria, the 'Beeb' launched their aforementioned 'Ballads and Blues' radio programme (a bold step, for, prior to the Coronation of Elizabeth II, radio still ruled the airwaves). The chief contributor to these broadcasts from the jazz genre was WMA stalwart Humphrey Lyttelton, whose jazz band shared the bills with British and American singers such as Jean Ritchie, Alan Lomax, Isla Cameron and the ubiquitous Bert Lloyd and Ewan MacColl.

Humphrey Lyttelton actually became honorary vice-president of the WMA alongside Bert Lloyd, Aaron Copland, Inglis Gundry and Paul Robeson. Folk and jazz had a shared livelihood and the WMA supported both at political events, booking folk and jazz performers to entertain fans and protesters alike. If the left-wing folk and popular music scenes in the USA had all but disappeared under an anti-Communist paranoia by the early 1950s, the WMA had certainly helped to amplify the equivalent scene in the UK. MacColl, Lomax and Lloyd were able to see themselves as pioneers of a politically correct music scene, alongside their jazz counterparts Lyttelton, Ken Colyer, Sandy Brown and Bruce Turner. By 1955 there was even a generously shared benefit for the *Daily Worker*. The Marxist newspaper had a tendency to lurch from crisis to financial crisis and the concert starred MacColl, Ken Colyer's Jazzmen and the Scottish singer Jeannie Robertson. MacColl even joined the jazzmen on stage to sing an American chain-gang song.

By the early 1950s the WMA were also holding educational classes at the Association's premises. They claimed to have facilities for 'first class tuition in vocal, instrumental and theoretical training'. They also established correspondence courses throughout the country and developed their periodic music schools. Their Annual Summer School was first held in Edinburgh, but then moved to Albrighton Hall near Shrewsbury and eventually settled at Wortly Hall in Yorkshire during every third week of August. Also, by the mid-1950s, the WMA Concert Agency (licensed annually by the London County Council) was offering a complete range of artists and musical entertainment. They became an entrepreneurial booking agency for like-minded and politically correct Musicians' Union (MU) artists, many of whom worked in the folk, jazz and modernist/classical fields and advertised on the back pages of their songbooks 'full concert programmes and pageantry; lectures and recitals. Dance bands (M.U.) are also available'. They also proved a valuable link with the equally vigorous folk song revival in Scotland.

So, although the folk revival's own historiography continues to record many adherents being enlightened via a musical 'Road to Damascus' and the revival itself as developing in an 'organic' way throughout the 1950s, these constructions do not fully account for the ideological and structural support of the WMA. Indeed, the association's existence remains – curiously – a somewhat 'hidden' history within the folk revival. Perhaps praising the 'organic unity' of the sound of the music together with its associations of protest (itself a fabrication when one peruses the *Pocket Song Book*!) holds more appeal than giving due credit to the organisational determinism of a politicised backbone?

Topic Records ('a company of obstinate integrity'; the *Guardian*, 1969)

Topic Records are Britain's oldest independent record company. They began as an offshoot of the Workers' Music Association in 1939 and, mostly via mail order, distributed a few recordings of Soviet and political music on disc – 'gramophone records of historical and social interest'. The first recording to be issued under the WMA/Topic imprint was a 10" 78rpm disc of 'The Man that Waters the Workers' Beer' by Paddy Ryan (apparently a professional gentleman using an alias to conceal his political persuasions). A storming dance band version of Degeyter's 'The Internationale' was placed on the B-side of that first recording (TRC1). Will Sahnow, a prominent Left-thinking dance band leader in London, led the 'Topic Singers and Band' on that occasion. Alan Bush re-recorded 'The Internationale' with choir, orchestra and organ in the late 1940s, but his version failed to recreate the intensity of that first disc.

To begin with, there were no recognisable 'folk music' releases, as such (one wonders whether this expression abounded in 1939, and if so in what context). Current Topic Records managing director, Tony Engle, holds a mimeograph of a Topic Record Club newsletter (priced 1/2d.) from May 1941 which discusses the preceding release (TRC13) and the next available release (TRC14) while thanking its membership for their assistance in paying the purchase tax due on earlier releases – £40!

A final word of appreciation to all those members who have responded to our last month's appeal for a 1/6d levy to help us meet that dreadful bill of £40 we have to face for unexpected purchase tax imposed on certain back numbers. But we haven't nearly enough in yet to meet it – remember that many members have left to join the forces, or have been bombed or evacuated. Have you done your bit by the club yet?[17]

This gives us an interesting insight into not only British tax regulations concerning the recording industry at this time, but also Topic sales. Purchase tax was due on all sales over 99 for a record club (only a handful of independent record clubs pressed their own discs in thirties and forties Britain and they mostly comprised jazz releases, e.g. Tempo) but it was only a matter of a few coppers per disc. The implication is, therefore, that the WMA was rather 'caught out' by Topic's relative popularity. £40 is a large tax bill for 13 × 99 releases at about 3/- each. Evidently Topic re-pressed some releases without telling the taxman and was forced by law to pay tax not only on that re-pressed run, but also on the original 99!

British recordings were few and far between throughout the war years. Shellac was in short supply for the duration of the war, and pressing plants (in the case of the WMA/Topic releases British Homophone) were not ready to lend a hand to the short runs mentioned above – usually (although not exclusively) less than 100 discs for Topic releases. Venerated Topic producer Bill Leader even suggested to BBC Radio Merseyside's Geoff Speed in 1998 that production of discs effectively ceased during the war years. This remains unconfirmed, however, for, as suggested by the above-quoted mimeograph, some records were definitely manufactured up to and beyond May 1941. There was certainly a small market (as funds would allow) for such pro-Soviet propaganda within the largely middle-class WMA membership.

Runs of disc production in the immediate post-war era were infrequent, however, for not only were Topic recordings a somewhat acquired taste, Topic were reluctant to press while beset by the aforementioned purchase tax restrictions. This was a very inequitable situation during a period of financial austerity. Thus the Topic recording arm of the WMA remained partially inactive until the arrival of the growing legion of folk bourgeoisie in the late 1940s. The Alan Bush re-recording of 'The Internationale' from the late 1940s (TRC23) may well have been a contrivance to evade purchase tax on earlier versions.

As previously stated, although correctly regarded by many as the most important folk record company in Britain, initially Topic Records did not over-concentrate on British folk music at all, as one look at the following available material on a 1948 list testifies:

TRC3   'Here We Come' from the Unity Theatre revue *Turn Up the Lights*.
         'The Black Blackout' (A Souvenir of World War II)
TRC7   'The Cutty Wren' (English medieval revolutionary song). 'The People

Sing!' (English labour songs played on two pianos by Mary and Geraldine Peppin)

TRC8   Two Negro Songs of Protest (Martin Lawrence and male voice choir).'Lizzie Liberty' and 'Thompson's Last Stand' (by Aubrey Bowman, sung by Jonathan Croft)

TRC9   'The Refugees' (song of exile from Hitler's Germany)

TRC11   'Say Goodbye, Now' (aria from Mozart's 'Figaro') and Two Spanish Songs (cello, piano, played by Boris Rickelman and Alan Bush)

TRC12   'A New World Will Be Born' (sung by Michael Redgrave) and 'Me Without You' (topical dance number sung by Alan Kane)

TRC16   'El Paso del Ebro' (Spanish Republican Song) and 'Three 17th-Century Catches'

TRC19   'Cossack Song' and 'From Border to Border' (Bolshoi Theatre Chorus)

TRC20   'A Hawk Flew into The Sky' (Russian folk song) and 'The Mountain Ash' (Russian folk song)

TRC21   'The Tractor Song' and 'The Gay Girl Friends' (Red Army Choir)

TRC22   'Youth' (Russian popular song) and 'Trepak' (Ukrainian Bandura Orchestra)

Numbers omitted from this list had been deleted. Some of the music available on Topic was licensed (or more likely 'officially' bootlegged) from the Soviet Union, and the company had nothing in the way of recording facilities. Usually, once a project had been deemed viable (membership contributions were essential in this respect), Topic had to hire both the studio and like-minded musicians.

However, it was perhaps only natural that this ambitious arm of the CP should, like the EFDSS, recognise the gently growing market for not only folk music source books, but also recordings. By the turn of the decade (1950) the Workers' Music Association were recording and releasing a few British folk music discs by, perhaps predictably, Ewan MacColl (TRC39, 40, 46, 48, 50, 51 – the last two with Scottish actress/singer Isla Cameron) on their Topic label. Their runs continued to be limited (still less than 100, but with occasional re-pressings) and sales continued to be small, but a few records were apparently dispatched to the United States (especially to the Greenwich Village 'cognoscenti' around Pete Seeger).

In fact, somewhat ironically, most of these early folk music recordings were actually made possible by an American academic by the name of Kenneth Goldstein. He had a scheme for the WMA to act as agents for a series of folk song recordings that he had undertaken for the small US Stinson label. On behalf of the WMA, Ewan MacColl and Bert Lloyd supervised the recordings. Record producer Bill Leader:

Three sets of 10" LPs were completed under the Stinson deal: *Sailors' Songs and Shanties* sung by Ewan MacColl and A.L. Lloyd, with Harry H. Corbett (later

Harold in 'Steptoe and Son') giving a leery 'Blow The Man Down'; the Irish poet Patrick Galvin accompanied by Al Jeffery singing *Irish Songs of Resistance* and Ewan MacColl singing industrial ballads. The Stinson deal came to an end prematurely, but Kenny Goldstein negotiated a new deal with Riverside Records. This led to a steady flow of material between the WMA and the American market, but a clause in the new contract limited the WMA to releasing locally only one track from each LP. This clause (which seemed to be of little consequence to the WMA, then pursuing a modest programme of 78 rpm releases) would eventually reduce the supply of possible material to the slowly developing LP catalogue.[18]

Folk music aside, by the mid-1950s Topic were still holding on catalogue a variety of Soviet, Chinese and British discs on 10" and 12" shellac 78rpm discs. These included such curiosities as a multiple album release spread over five 12" 78rpm discs: Shostakovich's *Song of the Forest* (TRC41–45). Around 1953–54 Topic's first 12" microgroove long player was released in a limited run of 99 copies. This was a reissue compilation of the earlier material recorded on 78s by MacColl, Lloyd and Cameron, together with the wartime release (TRC7) of 'The Cutty Wren' by Arnold Goldsbrough. This release was quickly followed by two more limited edition LPs: TLP2 was a collection of spirituals and songs previously released on 78s in 1952–53 by the baritone Aubrey Pankey and TLP3 was material drawn from the Stinson recordings (the latter reappeared as T7 and T8 – see below).

Topic Records was located at Bishop's Bridge Road, W2 during the 1950s (moving to Nassington Road, NW3 in 1960). By 1956 Bill Leader was a member of the WMA staff and some recordings had taken place at Bishop's Bridge Road – mostly on do-it-yourself equipment designed by Leader and Dick Swettenham – and it was here that Bill Leader first learned his trade. The label's folk direction was galvanised by his presence.

Albums TRL3 (*The Singing Sailor*), T3 and T4 (Patrick Galvin) were released in 1956. Dave Harker (1985) cites the album TRL3 as being the stimulus for Topic's growing interest in the folk revival. It probably was, but featuring Lloyd and MacColl with Unity Player Harry H. Corbett, it had done so three years earlier: TRL3 was a reissue of TLP1! It is also worthy of note that, well before 1956, the astute Lloyd and MacColl had identified Topic as an outlet for their own work; after all, the first MacColl 78 appeared as early as TRC39 (1950).

The later evidence for Lloyd and MacColl's co-option of Topic is strong, as one glance through the resultant MacColl and Lloyd output on the label will testify. Rather than having to compromise their own specialised material in order to please a larger record company, it was far more judicious to co-opt the politically correct yet rather wayward and naïve Topic record label (with its continued financial support from the WMA) as their delegated disseminator. In an interview in 1996, folk singer Bob Buckle laughingly suggested to me that the Topic–Lloyd/MacColl link-up was the only time he had been aware of 'artists signing a label!'

Despite their diminutive size Topic did make an important (albeit, it must be stressed, minuscule) impression on the recording industry at a time when there were very few independent labels in existence in the United Kingdom and major label interest in folk music was negligible. In fact, although their catalogue more than reflected their political leanings, for a Communist-led label Topic was quite entrepreneurial. Many years later Bill Leader was able to throw some light on the WMA acceptance of the market economy: 'LPs sold for £2 and 78s sold for about six shillings (30p) … Thus the maximum income possible from the release of a 78rpm record was £29.70, whereas the income from an LP was a stunning £198.'[19]

A Topic press release from the late 1950s housed at the National Sound Archive refers to the company with some sense of pride as 'perhaps the smallest record company in the world'. They probably were, but by this time some expansion was taking place, for their catalogue actually included several interesting recordings licensed from the USA by the likes of Paul Robeson, Pete Seeger and Woody Guthrie (mostly from the Riverside label). This must be qualified by politics, however, for the US government persecuted all of these acts for their political affiliations during the McCarthy era. Topic's releases were a visible act of solidarity in addition to providing the British public with songs of struggle and freedom. It was seldom about money – to the extent that Topic's books rarely balanced.

All of these US recordings had been thus far available on 10" 78rpm shellac discs; however throughout the mid to late 1950s many Topic releases reappeared in an extraordinary variety of configurations. For example, reissues of early 78s such as TRC23 and TRC24 were made available on the (then) more expensive but unbreakable vinyl, creating (like Pye Records) the unusual 78rpm vinyl single. However, this policy also caused their discs to rise dramatically in price (from 3/7d. to 6/6d.) and their already small sales duly slumped. This slump, in addition to Topic's growing interest in microgroove long-players, prompted the label to experiment with a variety of cheaper pressing plants, ultimately creating the oddest releases of all, namely 8" and 7" LPs; the history of these releases is intriguing.

In the 1930s Woolworths sold a variety of sizes of cheap shellac discs including 7", 8" and 9" sizes. In 1956 Topic conceived the idea of using these old smaller shellac pressers, but for vinyl releases, thus cutting down on raw materials and costs. British Homophone and Crystalate produced the majority of these pre-war discs in the 1930s but by the 1950s their pressers were largely redundant. Decca owned Crystalate by this time, in any case; but Homophone were still independent and eager to do business.

This information attracted the tiny WMA label, which was intent on remaining in production despite rather disappointing sales, overall. Topic, according to a press release of the time, 'Old Tools do a New Job', decided to use these older sizes in an effort to keep production costs as low as possible, to suggest a certain novelty attraction to their products, and to maintain a level of solidarity with the pressing-plant operatives. The resulting records, according to the company, 'offered the playing time usually obtained on a 10" LP for two-thirds of the price'.[20] It was not an altogether successful experiment. Some pressings proved to be of very poor quality and record player auto-changers treated the 8" recordings as 7" – thus cutting off the first track! But it certainly made a few in the industry sit up and take notice and, by 1956, it also made Topic realise that if they did have a future as a record company, it would be via the release of assorted long-players rather than singles.

So, having begun to identify their market (in both format and genre) Topic announced in September 1956 that they were to become the first label in the country to have a consistent policy towards folk music. They announced the launching of their 'Blue Label', administered by Bill Leader:

> Topic have now overcome difficulties which previously limited their editions and promise that the new seven and eight inch 33 1/3 rpm discs will be available to the general public. The series, which will sell at approximately 16/- a disc, will be prepared under the guidance of experts in the field and will cover international as well as British songs. Bill Leader has just taken over as production manager with Topic. He has been associated with Sing since its first number and was instrumental in building our sales in Yorkshire before he moved to London.[21]

Bill Leader's own skills in ad hoc record production are, of course, legend. Not only did he produce classic recordings of folk artists under the most primitive of conditions, but he also realised, at an early stage, that recording folk music performers in the field was often preferable to having them enter a studio. This decision was prudent for two important reasons. Firstly, most 'folkies' were far more at home performing in situ – placing a pub fiddler such as Michael Gorman in an artificial studio environment and asking him to play on the red light did not always ensure artistic proficiency! Secondly, Topic simply didn't really have a 'studio', as such – for example, the recording of American singer Rambling Jack Elliott took place at Ewan MacColl's East Croydon home because MacColl, not Topic, owned a Ferrograph reel-to-reel tape recorder.

By 1957 a variety of Topic folk recordings (in a variety of differing formats) were available via Collet's, through the growing network of folk clubs and by mail order; they also attracted a little passing interest from those retail shops willing to place orders on behalf of their customers, but distribution was still problematic. Most record distribution was in the hands of the big players, and few retailers other than the dedicated few bothered to find out how to order Topic releases. Even fewer ran the risk of carrying any Topic product in stock. Nevertheless recording continued unabated. More Bert Lloyd and Ewan MacColl material was quickly re-released on microgroove recordings (8T7; 8T8) after the former's short contract with HMV had concluded. One or two 78rpm singles continued to be released (for example, Lloyd's recording of 'The Banks of the

Condamine'/'Bold Jack Donahue' with Al Jeffrey on guitar). But, following Lloyd's appointment as Artistic Director of Topic Records in 1958, they were completely phased out. Harker states that:

> Lloyd used this increasingly influential position not only to give an airing to the songs and music he had collected in Eastern Europe, but also to select what was suitable from his perspective for folk club performers in Britain. Lloyd exerted a strong influence in this way, at a period when the major record companies had yet to cash in on the 'folk' market ...[22]

In truth, there still was not much for any industry to 'cash in' on – and runs were so limited that, even upon release, some Topic recordings were considered 'collector's pieces'. Nevertheless, what remains of Topic's early discography bears out Harker's claim for, even though Bill Leader and Gerry Sharp (the WMA accountant who didn't like folk music) took over artistic and financial affairs in 1958, both Lloyd and MacColl continued to dominate the label. Releases such as *Row Bullies Row*, *The Blackball Line*, *Bold Sportsmen*, *First Person*, *Sea Shanties*, *The Great Australian Legend*; thematic works such as *The Iron Muse*, *Leviathan!*, *The Bird in the Bush*, *The Valiant Sailor*; not to mention field recordings such as *Rumanian Folk Music*, *Folk Music of Bulgaria*, *Folk Music of Albania* were all Lloyd and/or MacColl projects released on Topic. Although Lloyd's position as artistic director only officially lasted twelve months, his musical policies and interests pervaded the label for years to come (for example, following the young Anne Briggs's appearance at the *Centre 42* concert in Nottingham in 1962, personal support from Lloyd ensured that she would appear on Topic).

Although it took a short while for Lloyd and MacColl effectively to modify the generic direction of Topic Records (and, it has been argued by some, diminish the influence of Alan Bush), it can be seen that both had already established a fruitful working relationship with the WMA in matters other than recording. Lloyd's work has been discussed previously, but, as for MacColl, the Association had already published two of his songbooks, *Scotland Sings* (1953) and *The Shuttle and Cage* (March 1954). *The Shuttle and Cage* dealt with industrial folk ballads and, edited by MacColl, proved to be a great success, being continually reprinted up until the mid-1970s.

By 1957 Topic had become the significant disseminator of recorded folk music for the growing folk network. This was principally because they released records by three who were not only among the most important recording artists of the British folk revival, but who constituted what might be termed the 'Holy Trinity' of folk music: Bert Lloyd, Ewan MacColl and Peggy Seeger.

Survival

By the early 1960s, however, despite the artistic and pecuniary acumen shown by both Bill Leader and Gerry Sharp, Topic Records were struggling financially. By the end of the 1950s they were receiving very little financial support from the WMA because it, in turn, had also dramatically contracted. At least 10 000 members had left the Communist Party after the Hungary debacle in 1956 and the CPGB in itself became little more than a ginger group. The WMA as an offshoot of the CP was thus severely deprived of funds. By the end of the decade its London headquarters had already moved from Great Newport Street to Bishop's Bridge Road and thence to a modest basement address in Westbourne Terrace.

In fact as early as 1958 Topic were forced into relative autonomy and, by 1960, under the sole directorship of Sharp they began what they subsequently described as 'a period of consolidation … for a while new releases were few'.[23] In other words, in order to survive as a truly independent record label, they had to reconsider their ideology in a growing commercial marketplace for recorded folk song. By the sixties the impact of the folk revival was changing. A new generation of ex-skifflers were discovering folk song and were looking for it not only in the folk clubs but also on record. Sadly, being severely financially restricted, Topic was unable to capitalise on this growth area.

Topic continued to release a few 10" and 12" albums as the new decade began but they had severe competition from other labels promoting a mixture of British and American products. Two notable Topic albums from 1959/60 were *Still I Love Him* by Isla Cameron and Ewan MacColl (10T50) and *Streets of Song* by Ewan MacColl and Dominic Behan (12T41). Serious competition loomed, however. Top Rank released an album by Margaret Barry (25/020) and obtained a licence to release the Newport Folk Festival albums. Folkways, previously distributed by Topic, were made directly available through Collet's, while Jac Holzman's Elektra label obtained a British distribution deal with Pye. Decca records redesignated its spoken-word Argo series to include more folk music (Ewan MacColl and Peggy Seeger were quick to jump onto this bandwagon). Labels such as Selection, Vogue and the short-lived independent Collector label actually recorded some of Topic's 'names' such as Jeannie Robertson, Shirley Collins and Robin Hall.

Even Dobell's jazz shop was releasing occasional 'folk' music such as *Rat-a-Tap-Tap … English folk songs Miss Pringle never taught us* (Dobell F-LET1). This short-lived label later attracted publicity for releasing a track by Blind Boy Grunt (aka Bob Dylan) on one album. Collet's had already launched a bi-monthly review journal of folk recordings in January 1958 entitled *Recorded Folk Music*, edited (naturally) by Bert Lloyd. The market was, indeed, beginning to stir, but Topic had neither the financial 'clout' nor the business acumen to prevent incursions into a field that they had established and ploughed for over three years.

Still, albeit tenuously, connected to an ever-receding ideology (particularly after the erection of the Anti-Fascist Protection Rampart aka the Berlin Wall in August 1961) as a record company it produced very little during 1961 and was unable to press a single album in 1962, relying upon extended play discs only. At least three of these EPs were in great demand, but Topic even experienced difficulty in locating the finances to re-press them. TOP69: *Songs Spun in Liverpool* (a live session recorded by the Spinners), TOP70: *3/4 A.D.* (the seminal blues/jazz fusion from Davey Graham and Alexis Korner) and TOP76: *Ceilidh at the Crown – Live at the Jug of Punch* (by the Ian Campbell Folk Group) were difficult to obtain even on their release (all are now very rare).

Things began to change during 1962, when former 'artistic director' Bert Lloyd embarked upon a trades union-backed tour, organised by Arnold Wesker, entitled *Centre 42*. The tour was intended to decentralise art from London while also delivering a slab of good left-wing culture; however whether the trades unions sanctioned any out-and-out Communist messages remains doubtful, for the culture in question was a variety of musical genres, art and drama together with a smattering of poetry and jazz organised by Jeremy Robson. Robson later critically commented that despite his own eclecticism *Centre 42* still 'tended to draw one kind of audience'.[24]

Nevertheless, this tour was something of a turning point for Lloyd. He was able to witness and assess at first hand the possibilities for folk music to exist as a genre of popular music with a depoliticised message. When all was said and done, *Centre 42* drew upon a pool of first-class entertainers. From the folk field Ray Fisher, Louis Killen and Bob Davenport were present (as were the McPeakes of Ireland and the Stewarts of Blairgowrie). Youth was also taken into consideration for, after a visit to Nottingham, an 18-year-old Anne Briggs was added to the tour's roster (and that of Topic Records). Briggs's memories of Lloyd at this time make interesting reading:

> As a person he was a quiet and very positive sort of bloke. He had a great sense of humour and a tremendous insight into people and situations. He had a very delicate way of looking at things. He was a very clever bloke and I learned to appreciate that side of his nature. When you're 18, 19, 20 you're very impressionable but people like Bert don't come up more than once or twice in your lifetime.[25]

Perhaps Lloyd witnessed on this tour the potential for folk music to exist alongside other forms and for reinterpretation to take place. Jazz aficionado Gil Kendrick told me:

> [I] was at the Nottingham show and I remember it was a bloody good do! Jazz, poetry, folk – it was really entertaining and not at all overly serious. Some of the folkies were a bit self-absorbed but as a jazz fan I was surprised how commercial a lot of folk music could be – I remember Bob Davenport, he was great.[26]

The Iron Muse

The 'tremendous insight into people and situations' suggested by Anne Briggs eventually led in 1963 to Topic releasing the album that was seminal to the changing mood of the British folk revival and a salvation to the company. Including Briggs on two tracks ('The Recruited Collier' and 'The Doffing Mistress') *The Iron Muse* (12T86) was a selective study by Lloyd of what he described as 'industrial folk song', but it was far more commercial than much of his other work for Topic. In the wake of a great deal of abandonment of Communist party ideals within the folk scene, together with the mass recognition of the Beatles the same year, the album's critical regionalism and depleted political proselytising struck an appealing chord, firstly amongst the folk clubs and then among the general public, and duly sold in substantial amounts. Topic was essentially saved as a going concern by this release.

The Iron Muse had actually tapped into a growing sense of cultural awareness in the UK and Topic was henceforth no longer seen as being so essentialist in its political ties. In a sense, the times had overtaken both Topic and Bert Lloyd. By 1962 folk and jazz cellars, beat clubs, R&B venues, coffee bars and pubs with special music nights had cemented themselves on the British psyche and, depending upon the location of these venues, clientele could be drawn from a broader social class than that to which the revival had at first appealed. Anyone doubting this change in cultural climate need only look towards popular film and television programmes for evidence. *A Kind of Loving*, *Saturday Night and Sunday Morning*, *A Taste of Honey*, *Z Cars* and *Coronation Street* had already begun to draw the public's attention towards the regions in a much less stereotypical way. Unbeknown to many folkies, the dreaded US influences of rock 'n' roll and rhythm and blues had stimulated an after-dark music lover with a curiosity for the authentic. Without realising it, they had, in fact, become 'trendy'.

The Iron Muse became Topic's most commercial project to date, their saviour. Subsequently, label director Gerry Sharp steered Topic along their musically uncompromising road until his death in the mid-1970s but he followed a more indeterminate political pathway than had previously been the case. One of Sharp's most satisfying achievements was to issue in Britain, in 1968–69, the 10-LP compilation entitled *The Folk Songs of Britain* (12T157–61, 194–98). These recordings were drawn from the fieldwork of Peter Kennedy, Alan Lomax, Hamish Henderson and others, and until that time had only been available on the American Caedmon label. Topic, however, were able to obtain a licence to release these albums and sold them both as two volumes and individually. This series also sold well and introduced more Britons to the voices of Harry Cox, the Copper family, John Strachan, Elizabeth Cronin and many others.

As a direct result of the success of *The Iron Muse*, Topic were able to reach their 200th number and the 1970s at one and the same time and in some degree of financial security. The success of this important album even moved Elektra to issue it as their first Topic release in the USA in the spring of 1964. Following the critical moments of 1962–63, Topic were able to release about 10 or 12 records per year during the 1960s. Some early issues were deleted (chiefly the runs of EPs, which were proving expensive and irrelevant in a growing album-orientated marketplace), but by 1970 they developed a firm policy of keeping in catalogue all that remained while also becoming increasingly attentive to Irish music.

By the mid-1970s, connections between Topic, the WMA and the British Communist Party had ceased to occupy the minds of all but a hard core, and, although some of those involved in the label remained staunchly political, they did not allow politics overtly to interfere with the running of the company. Stalwart Tony Russell was later to state to this author that 'the less Bert Lloyd was involved the more Topic actually became a record label'.[27] In 1978 Topic and the WMA formally parted company. By the late 1970s, and after 20 years and 250 titles in their catalogue, Topic justifiably claimed to have the most substantial and wide-ranging collection of recorded British folk music in the world.

Yet, it must also be stated that it could be seen by many popular music aficionados of the 1970s that every neatly motivated effort to preserve folk music and to represent it authentically (including releases by Topic) merely contributed to a glaringly obvious opposite tendency. The great paradox of Topic's continued existence was that, to be experienced as 'authentic', folk music had to be mediated. Folk music simulation – especially recordings – can only ever be an initiative that deliberately caters for those in quest of an affect and image of musical history. Particularly by the post-punk era, Topic's catalogue could be seen as specifically designed to respond to such a demand. We had not so much inherited this music as created it and, via the challenge of punk and the new technologies, the romantic will to elevate folk 'authenticity' became unrelated to the context surrounding it.

Once more overtaken by the times, Topic was responsible not only for a canon of music (always a rather dangerous concept) but an entire hagiography of musical practice. Such collections as existed in Topic's back catalogue aimed to bring the finest 'authentic' folk music to the attention of the public. But, as with all canons, the musical objects within this catalogue were abstractions. In the everyday life of the post-punk (indeed, postmodern) era we merely integrated certain popular music forms – and not others – into our everyday practices. However unpalatable it might have been to folkies, brought into the midst of everyday existence, folk music came to be viewed as one soundtrack amongst many. As a consequence, Topic was once more to face an uncertain future as Britain's longest-running independent record label.

Notes

1. Williams, *Marxism and Literature*, p. 115.
2. Boyes, *The Imagined Village*, p. 211.
3. Schofield, review of Boyes, *Imagined Village*, pp. 512–13.
4. P. Kennedy, 'Editorial' in *'Everybody Swing'*.
5. The Haymakers Dance Band, 'Everybody Swing', Decca F 9852–9855.
6. Smedley, 'A New Society', p. 7.
7. P. Kennedy, *'Everybody Swing'*.
8. Interview with Eric Winter, 2000.
9. Uncredited information, *Sing*, 1/1 (May–June 1954), p. 1.
10. Carter, 'All Dance and no Song?'.
11. Unsigned editorial (1948), 'Introduction', *The Pocket Song Book* (London: Workers' Music Association), p. 1.
12. Uncredited aims and objectives in Lloyd, *The Singing Englishman*, reverse cover page.
13. Harker, *Fakesong*, p. 250.
14. Lloyd, Preface to *Folk Song in England*.
15. Woolf and Woolf, 'Pity the Downtrodden Landlord'.
16. Hunt, 'The Roots of Modern Folk', 57.
17. Unsigned/untitled editorial, 'A final word of appreciation ...', *The Topic Record*, 14 (May 1941), p. 2.
18. Leader, 'Topic: A People's Label', pp. 8–9.
19. Ibid., p. 9.
20. Unsigned editorial, 'Old Tools do a New Job', Topic press release (1956).
21. Winter, 'Discussion: Topic Folk Song Label', p. 51.
22. Harker, *Fakesong*, pp. 236–37.
23. Unsigned editorial, 'Prologue', *Topic Catalogue* (1974).
24. Robson, *Poetry and Jazz*, p. 15.
25. Briggs, 'Sleevenotes', *Classic Anne Briggs: The Complete Topic Recordings*, Fellside FECD78.
26. Interview with Gil Kendrick, May 2000.
27. Discussion with Tony Russell, IASPM [International Association for the Study of Popular Music] Conference, Glasgow, 1995.

Chapter 5

Challenging folk historiography: skiffle as a pop aesthetic

> Whatever the definition, folk is always seen as 'real' music, not imposed on or sold to people but produced by them ... where 'folk' and 'popular' meet, clearly important sociological consequences must follow.
>
> Middleton (1990), p. 129

In 1954 the International Folk Music Council decreed that the music they had decided to study was:

> the product of a musical tradition that has been evolved through the process of oral transmission. The factors that shape the tradition are:
> (i). Continuity which links present to the past.
> (ii). Variation which springs from the creative impulse of the individual or group; and
> (iii). Selection by the community which determines the form or forms in which the music survives.
> The terms can be applied to music that has been evolved from rudimentary beginnings by a community uninfluenced by popular and art music and it can likewise be applied to music which has originated with an individual composer and has subsequently been absorbed into the unwritten living tradition of a community.
> The term does not cover composed popular music that has been taken over ready-made by a community and remains unchanged, for it is the re-fashioning and re-creation of the music by the community that gives it its folk character.[1]

Yet by (at the very latest) 1967, appropriately cited by Simon Frith as 'the year it all came together',[2] these definitions were proving increasingly difficult to sustain for one selected type of music. Words such as 'continuity', 'variation' and 'selection' were factors impossible to consider without contextual applications. The IFMC had not so much made a decree concerning the 'refashioning and re-creation' of music, as placed all musical forms in a bell jar.

Fracture and mutation had already commenced some 10 years before Frith's year of significance. The principles as laid down in the Council's definition of aims and objectives were already grossly out of tune with the individual interests of musicians and appeared little more than hypothetical retrospections about a 'spontaneous-creative' art form. By the early 1960s the work of Davey Graham and Bert Jansch alone had heralded a different aesthetic within the folk revival. But even before this, Lonnie Donegan and the important legion of young skifflers following in his wake had already applied concepts of continuity and variation to their lives without any of the associated dogma.

Different styles and contexts produce chains of images, all of which work on the basis of shifts and progressions. For musicians these changes are fluid rather than planned and often move in sudden leaps and bounds. No international council decrees concerning what traditional music was supposed to be could have prevented links occurring where none previously existed or, indeed, prevent these musical images from oscillating between invention and convention.

Skiffle, in particular, was a process of unburdening – both musically and culturally it represented a tension inherent in British society based upon, on the one hand, small gestures of freedom and, on the other, social conformity. Ian Whitcomb from his schoolboy diary:

> We never get a moment to rehearse as a rule but nobody seems to mind. The Rev. said he'd probably lend a voice to a couple of spirituals or 'Green Grow The Rushes O' … I'm going to see if I can't get my guitar electrified … the Rev. gave a long speech about the place of skiffle in society … He said skiffle was healthy everyday music and that one could express oneself as the spirit moved one.[3]

Importantly, in not being umbilical to a totalising world view (political or anthropological), skiffle's benign musical and social eclecticism was, in fact, highly radical.

After the arrival of Donegan's 'Rock Island Line' in the British singles charts (January 1956) it was evident to many that the apparently disparate popular and folk sources enjoyed a very close, symbiotic relationship. By introducing thousands of young people to the delights of playing acoustic instruments (far more successfully than the efforts of Ewan MacColl and Douglas Kennedy), the ensuing skiffle boom changed the trajectory of all British popular music for ever. Skiffle was, as Ian Whitcomb confirms, 'a side product of the British Traditional jazz movement'[4] and, as such, operated through the presentation of real materials as an image of energy. It initially drew from different sources but facilitated personalised songwriting abilities and guitar techniques. It actually pronounced with a vengeance the indefinite and distinctive musical statements that were to follow. A brief exposition of the origins and uses of skiffle is therefore in order.

Black roots

The word 'skiffle' is American. For some, its origins are in 'music played by those too poor to buy musical instruments and who used washboards, jugs, etc.'[5] Certainly the roots of the word are immersed in African-American culture, yet to be precise about the term is to misunderstand its tautological and social status. Skiffle was just one of those expressions used to describe anything musically ad hoc – from sounds performed at a rent party to a Ma Rainey jug band session. For example, in 1929 a blues medley issued by the legendary Paramount Records was entitled 'Hometown Skiffle'. It was one of the first samplers and sported a variety of blues sounds ranging from Blind Lemon Jefferson to the Hokum Boys.

Ma Rainey, who also recorded for Paramount, was reported to have used the expression 'skiffle' when describing her repertoire for a more rural audience. In 1946 'Skiffle Blues' was among several tracks cut by Black American journalist and part-time pianist Dan Burley in New York. To perhaps confuse matters further, *Rolling Stone* magazine has reported that skiffle was New Orleans jazz and jug band music (but this is probably from a white American rock perspective). Ian Whitcomb confessed that 'people said "skiffle" was an American jazz word but I never found anybody in America who remembered American skiffle'.[6]

The expression 'skiffle' actually appears to have abounded in Chicago. The prosperity and symbolic status of that city attracted such vast internal migration of Black Americans that the city's Black population expanded nearly 400-fold in less than a century. From this perspective Chicago was seen as the Promised Land and the Black militant newspaper the *Chicago Defender* openly encouraged internal migration throughout the first 30 years of the twentieth century. Many migrants were previously farmers, itinerant loggers, and turpentine, mine and levee camp workers from the Deep South. Southern States such as Louisiana, Texas and Mississippi were inherently racist and, with rural economies dependent on the cheapest form of manual labour, openly degraded Black men, women and children. Chicago held the promise of a new life.

Between the wars, however, many migrants were packed into slums such as the notorious Mecca flats on 34th and State Streets (until the scandal of squalid, overcrowded conditions forced the authorities to pull them down). Skiffle parties, rent parties, parlour socials (call them what you will) were all means of raising funds to provide the unscrupulous landlords of these God-forsaken properties with rent. Moonshine liquor, live music and 25 cents admission would usually attract enough punters to accumulate that rent (particularly during the years of 'prohibition'). British skiffle star Lonnie Donegan was to inform the *New Musical Express* (hereafter *NME*) in 1957:

> These parties were held principally in the Chicago districts in the 1920s, their purpose being the obvious one of raising money to pay the rent ... there are obviously no genuine recordings of skiffle music proper from those days, as the very presence of microphones destroys the essential informality of this type of music.[7]

It was this music, and this somewhat idealised environment, that helped to fuel the fantasies of young British jazz and blues revivalists such as Humphrey Lyttelton and Ken Colyer (in fact the word 'skiffle' was further popularised by Colyer after he had visited New Orleans in the early 1950s).

During the Second World War British musicians such as Freddie Randall and George Webb were figureheads of a jazz movement that reintroduced the sounds of the past. It was a time when some jazz fans tired of swing music and cherished the early jazz of New Orleans. By the end of the war news of the work of Alan Lomax and Rudi Blesh (Blesh had made those 1946 recordings of Dan Burley) was also beginning to percolate across the Atlantic. As we have seen, many of these British jazz, folk and blues traditionalists were deeply rooted in the politics of the far Left, and romanticised images of the 'vulnerable yet noble' working classes of the USA (black and white alike) were inspirational, not only musically but also socially and politically. Before too long some of these (thus far) obscure American artists began to trickle through to Europe. For example, Alan Lomax's greatest 'discovery' was the Louisiana-born troubadour Huddie Ledbetter (aka 'Leadbelly').

Karl Dallas has described how, for him, the modern era of folk music in the USA effectively began with the meeting in New York City of Leadbelly's country blues, Woody Guthrie's dust bowl ballads and Pete Seeger's incipient urban folk style.[8] Leadbelly was a twice-reprieved murderer who was the source (though not necessarily the writer) for the first skiffle hit recording in the UK, 'Rock Island Line'. He came over to Europe (but not England) in 1949, the year he died.

Among those who followed Leadbelly and did make it to London were Chicago-based bluesman Big Bill Broonzy (1893–1958), whose sets included his versions of blues standards such as 'See See Rider' and 'Trouble in Mind', and Brownie McGhee (1915–96), who had recorded with both Dan Burley and Granville 'Stick' McGhee (Brownie's brother), enjoying a sizable US 'race' hit with the latter: 'Drinkin' Wine Spo-Dee-O-Dee'. Brownie also formed a long-term partnership with Greensboro, NC singer and blues harmonica player, Sonny Terry (1911–86). 'Sonny and Brownie' were frequent visitors to these shores. New Orleans-born jazz and blues guitarist/vocalist Lonnie Johnson (1889–1970) of 'Tomorrow Night' and 'Confused' fame actually played the London Festival Hall in 1952 – the occasion when British skiffler Lonnie Donegan 'borrowed' Johnson's first name!

British 'purists' – trad jazz

The aforementioned Ken Colyer (1928–88) deserves a further reference here. This Norfolk-born jazz trumpeter and guitarist taught himself music while at sea during the Second World War. He led various jazz band permutations – from the Crane River Jazz Band to the Christie Brothers Stompers to the Ken Colyer Jazzmen and, despite being a jazz fundamentalist – and difficult to work with, to boot – it was he who instigated the first skiffle sessions within the repertoire of a traditional revivalist jazz (or 'trad') band. Colyer, however, may have simply considered skiffle to be a convenient interlude music. While the band downed as many pints of beer as possible during intermissions (he was a renowned heavy drinker), two or three members would 'skiffle' their way through a few blues, folk or gospel songs to keep the audience happy until the 'authentic' stuff reappeared.

Colyer was not in fact the first British 'tradder' to seek inspiration from the African-American tradition of 'home style' music. Taking their name from the ex-jockey Red McKenzie's Mount City Blues Blowers of 1923, the Original London Blues Blowers were formed by Bill Bailey and Freddie Legon in 1945, featuring solos on kazoo and comb-and-paper in the original McKenzie style. But whereas Bailey and Legon dropped this 'hokum' for more 'legitimate' trad jazz with the bands of Charlie Galbraith, Mike Daniels and Humphrey Lyttelton (before jumping back on to the skiffle bandwagon a year or so after Lonnie Donegan became the first skiffle star), Ken Colyer stuck with the skiffle session throughout the various incarnations of his band.

A member of the post-1952 Colyer group was banjo player Lonnie Donegan. Anthony ('Lonnie') Donegan, born in Glasgow in 1931, was initially another fundamentalist (or 'purist') like Ken Colyer. Donegan had played drums in an army trad band (the Wolverines) and was one of a group of purists who gathered at the feet of Ken Colyer when the latter formed the Crane River Jazz Band (and its first skiffle group). Donegan was not one of these original members, but he joined when Colyer returned from his pilgrimage to New Orleans (the 'heart' of jazz) in 1952 and, exchanging his banjo for guitar, proceeded to lead these skiffle sessions with just a bass and washboard as accompaniment.

Colyer was undoubtedly Donegan's mentor but was, at best, an indifferent vocalist. Even though he claimed to be a purist, his vocal delivery bore no comparison in style to those of the original singers he copied. As a consequence of his own vocal shortcomings, Colyer put it about that vocals should be 'unadorned'. Donegan, however, sang with tremendous verve (he was also a natural 'show boater'). It is quite possible that Colyer may not even have realised (until it was too late) that these somewhat informal skiffle sessions were becoming just as important an attraction as his beloved trad jazz.

Inevitably, ideological and musical friction grew within the band. Trombonist Chris Barber had briefly formed his own band in 1950 but then joined (and effectively ousted) Colyer in 1954 in a disagreement over music policy. Barber wanted to broaden the band's scope, 'jazzing up' different styles of music, rather than stick with the 'authentic' but oft-repeated classic New Orleans repertoire. As a consequence, the pair fell out and the band – including Donegan – sided with Barber. It wasn't long before there were two trad bands, each featuring skiffle segments in their respective shows.

Skiffle on record

By 1954 Barber's band had recorded a 10" jazz album for Decca entitled *New Orleans Joys*. But Ken Colyer was actually the first to record skiffle songs earlier that year: 'Midnight Special', 'Casey Jones', 'K.C. Moan' and 'Take this Hammer' were recorded for Decca on 25 June 1954 and a single F 10631 'Take this Hammer' was belatedly released in mid-1955. The jazz fraternity bought both Barber and Colyer recordings but, for the time being, neither left any great impression on the general public. The Barber album was a representation of their live set and naturally included two skiffle tracks: 'Rock Island Line' and 'John Henry'.

Renowned BBC presenter Christopher Stone played the recording of 'Rock Island Line' on his radio record programme and the track was requested several times. Decca released the two songs as a novelty single in late 1955 (probably in an attempt to capture a little of the Christmas market). It was credited to 'the Lonnie Donegan Skiffle Group' and released on Decca's light blue Jazz imprint (F 10647). After receiving further radio exposure, the record went to number 17 in the British singles charts in January 1956 and then stayed in the charts for a further six months.

When 'Rock Island Line' entered the charts that January it came as a complete surprise. One British record paper declared: 'There's no accounting for taste' whereas the *NME*'s 'Alley Cat' stated: 'Here was further proof of how unpredictable the music industry is.' Even Donegan was to admit that he thought it wasn't 'a particularly good recording, and I even asked to have it withdrawn when I first heard it'.[9] 'Rock Island Line' was certainly non-commercial by contemporary standards, being raw and exciting. However, the recording undoubtedly captured the public's imagination and effectively bridged a musical gap between Bill Haley's first rock hits and the advent of Elvis Presley later in 1956 – a significant point given the title of the song (i.e. '*Rock* Island Line') and the similarity between the musical structure of Haley's brand of rock 'n' roll and Donegan's skiffle.

In March 1956 the recording was released in the USA and by the end of April was a hit there, too – shipping 150 000 in the first ten days and eventually selling one million copies around the world (for which Lonnie received the standard session fee of £3 10/-!). Donegan toured the United States in 1956 and subsequently left the Barber band. During 1956 he enjoyed another two hit records, 'Lost John' and 'Bring a Little Water, Sylvie' – he was on his way.

The skiffle craze

In the wake of Lonnie Donegan's popularity a skiffle craze erupted in Britain. Apart from Donegan himself, however, there were only three groups that reached more than a small audience: the Chas McDevitt Group, Johnny Duncan and the Bluegrass Boys, and the Vipers. McDevitt enjoyed a sizable hit with Elizabeth Cotton's 'Freight Train' in 1957 but then declined in popularity when vocalist Nancy Whiskey left in September of that year.

The Vipers, formed late in 1956, began by playing in London coffee bars (of which more later); their lead singer, Wally Whyton, wrote one of Donegan's hits ('Don't You Rock Me Daddy-o') and they had a hit (as did Donegan) with 'Cumberland Gap' in April 1957. Two of the Vipers, Terry (Jet) Harris and Tony Meehan, were to find fame shortly afterwards in the Shadows and then later as a duo. Wally Whyton found considerable long-term success in children's television and as a country music disc jockey.

Johnny Duncan was a genuine American (and strictly speaking a country and western singer – reportedly having played with Bill Monroe). He replaced Donegan in Chris Barber's Jazzmen in 1956 when Lonnie went solo but soon followed him out of Barber's band early in 1957. His second single release 'Last Train to San Fernando' – previously recorded by Bobby Short – was a storming piece of skiffle-cum-rockabilly that became a massive hit. Duncan's nasal vocal whine was certainly regarded by some as 'authentic'. Wally Whyton was to inform this writer some years later that: 'When Johnny sang "well I've gambled up in Washington, I've gambled down in Maine" you felt he could have! Not that he did, but he could have!'[10]

Skiffle competitions took place all over the UK and there was no shortage of entrants. The *Melody Maker*'s Bob Dawburn estimated that there were hundreds of skiffle combos in the London area alone. It was no different in cities such as Liverpool, where groups like the Texans and the Quarry Men crossed swords in local competitions. Even middle-of-the-road acts like Dickie Valentine, the Stargazers and the Ron Goodwin Orchestra released skiffle-related records. The *NME* described it all as 'the biggest musical craze Britain has ever known'.

A few enthusiasts were professional musicians, like Yorkshire artist and jazz fanatic Diz Disley (one of the elite who could get past the first three frets on the guitar!), but most were rank amateurs and many, such as the aforementioned left-wing intellectual John Hasted, had links with the burgeoning British folk revival. Hasted's column in *Sing* championed skiffle as a kind of music for the proletariat and his column was full of advice about playing guitar and designing tea-chest basses – obviously very legitimate, ideologically. Indeed, Alan Lomax also highlighted skiffle's political correctness. True, skiffle was American in source material (not good), but it was British in execution (very good). If rock 'n' roll sprang from the fusion of blues, gospel and country music, then, according to Lomax, skiffle was in some ways a fusion of Black rhythms and English folk music. This may not be as daft as it sounds. Certainly, 10 years before the Beatles, Donegan was the first British singer to sing American blues and country material in a decisively British manner (even if that had not really been his intention!).

Skiffle's mass following was further expanded when the BBC TV programme *Six-Five Special* was broadcast in 1957. Not only did this show use the skiffle tune of the same name as its signature tune (performed by Bob Cort's group), but it also regularly featured live skiffle groups and even ran (it must be said a rather unsuccessful) national skiffle competition. This low-budget (£1000 per programme) show was the brainchild of presenter Josephine (later Jo) Douglas and producer Jack Good (subsequently of *Oh Boy!* and *Shindig!* fame) and for perhaps the first time gave British teenagers the opportunity to see their own favoured brands of popular music performed on the small screen.

Welcome as it was, however, *Six-Five Special* is often viewed as being gutsier than it really was. In truth, it was a rather bourgeois hotchpotch and featured skiffle primarily to the exclusion of rock 'n' roll. This accurately reflected the class divide that much skiffle-related activity represented. Skiffle was welcome at the BBC and with the Left, in youth clubs and coffee bars because it was politically correct, safe and jolly – unlike rock 'n' roll, which was accused by some of being 'jungle' music. In fact, it was not only the public-school boys at the BBC and the quasi-Marxist bourgeoisie that found skiffle to their tastes. As Ian Whitcomb suggests, even the Church of England sanctioned it. The Reverend Brian Bird (a C. of E. vicar, no less) penned the first 'serious' book about the genre – *Skiffle* – in 1958.

Coffee bar culture

Donegan might have been skiffle's spokesperson but, as Karl Dallas points out, 'skiffle was not Donegan's creation.'[11] For many, skiffle exemplified the cult of the coffee bar. In the 1950s most youngsters were still living at home and many were desperate to get out for at least an evening or two each week. Before the mid-1950s the word 'teenager' barely existed, but by the time social scientist Margaret Mead was attempting to describe the differences between younger and older generations, terms such as 'teenager' and 'the generation gap' had gained wider currency. Throughout the 1950s the media used these expressions to define a new generation unaffected by the Second World War and unconcerned about British propriety. Average unemployment figures were below 2 per cent throughout the 1950s and many young people, although often stuck in dead-end jobs, were finding that they had disposable income. They came to define themselves via their creative consumption of music, clothing, hairstyles, etc. To help add a little excitement, coffee bars sprouted up right across Britain, giving teenagers further opportunities to redefine themselves socially.

The focal point in many coffee bars was usually the bulky coin-operated American jukebox, but live music sessions were also popular in some cities – particularly in London, where West End coffee bars such as the Breadbasket, the Gyre and Gimble, Heaven and Hell, Le Macabre, the Skiffle Cellar, the Nucleus and the 2I's (not forgetting Chas McDevitt's own Freight Train coffee bar in Berwick Street) played host to groups of 'musicians' strumming mutual support on cheap guitars (usually fretting the same basic three or four chords in the easy key of E). McDevitt later admitted (Granada TV 1997) that although his coffee bar became a focal point for music and debate, his takings usually fell below break-even levels, forcing the venue's untimely closure. Wally Whyton, who played at the 2I's as part of the Vipers, informed me:

> It was tiny, really. You could only get about ten people upstairs, but downstairs was a long narrow room about 12 by 20 feet where you could pack them in. We'd [the Vipers] play two sets each night. People would come from all over to hear us. The queues would be right around the block. It was all very exciting.[12]

Despite coffee bars being of great cultural importance, cultural commentators of the 1950s such as Richard Hoggart condemned their influence and their associations with American music. Left and Right thinkers alike saw an apparent erosion of the traditional processes of art and life. Hoggart attempted to rationalise this position by stating:

> I have in mind ... the kind of milk bar, there is one in almost every Northern town with more than, say, fifteen thousand inhabitants, which has become the regular evening rendezvous of some of the young men. Girls go to some, but most of the customers are boys between fifteen and twenty, with drape suits, picture ties and an American slouch. Most of them cannot afford a succession of milk-shakes, and make cups of tea serve for an hour or two, whilst, and this is their main reason for coming, they put copper after copper into the mechanical record-player ... Compared with even the pub around the corner this is all a peculiarly thin and pallid form of dissipation ... Many of the customers: their clothes, their hairstyles, their facial expressions all indicate, are living to a large extent in a myth world compounded of a few simple elements which they take to be those of American life ... they are ground between the millstones of technocracy and democracy: society gives them an almost limitless freedom of the sensations but makes few demands on them ... they are in one dreadful sense the new workers ... the directionless and tamed helots of a machine minding class.[13]

Hoggart appeared to 'blame' the jukebox for being an agent of social change. He certainly viewed technology as a prime mover in history and, like many cultural critics, fell into the trap of technological and cultural determinism. He saw what was merely a product as a 'creator' of a fundamental condition triggering the social patterns of (in this case) Teddy Boys. But it remains implausible to isolate a single cause for any set of social processes (and to prove that it is the primary determinant). Hoggart is bewildered, disorientated even, but one should not mistake this disorientation for constructive criticism. It is, in fact, an unduly simplified point of view.

Were one to doubt the importance of coffee bars as an integral and meaningful part of 1950s British teenage lifestyles, it would be sufficient to look at the UK pop films of that era. Many of these were centred on youth clubs and coffee bars (not folk clubs) and included a variety of musical genres (skiffle, rock, trad, folk, calypso). *Serious Charge, Some People, The Tommy Steele Story, The Golden Disc* all confirmed that a quintessential musical intertextuality was intrinsic to the 1950s British coffee bar. But, of course, these movies have also been written off by some such as Hoggart as insubstantial mass-produced 'pseudo-Americana' surplus.

Skiffle in decline

Skiffle was easy to play and Donegan (almost literally) placed guitars into the hands of hundreds of young men across the UK. It was given the intellectual stamp of approval by the BBC and folk traditionalists. It had a brand of authenticity, coming, as it did, from African Americans via trad jazz, but it had a sameness that could not be ignored. Despite its popularity, record sales remained poor (Donegan aside) throughout 1957, suggesting that, although it was enjoying mass appeal, it was probably music to be played, not listened to. Even before the summer of 1957 it was only Donegan who was still reaching the Top 20. Many unrewarding releases by the likes of Les Hobeaux, the 219 Group, the Delta Group, Dickie Bishop and Don Lang (who cut a tedious skiffle album that year) rightly failed to capture the public's imagination.

By the end of 1957 the craze was losing momentum; the media was asking 'is skiffle dying?' and by 1958 the boom had definitely ended. Astute skifflers, however, knew exactly what to do next. Many, such as Cliff Richard and Adam Faith, followed the rock 'n' roll path; some, such as Martin Carthy, went into the folk clubs; others, like that seminal musical mentor of the 1950s Alexis Korner (who replaced Donegan in the Colyer skiffle group), began to electrify the blues. Skiffle's life was short but it was, without doubt, the foundation upon which the next two decades of British popular music was built.

Donegan's mainstream success continued, but it was not without criticism. For many, he was a figure of national adoration and respect, but others, such as the 'purists' he had long left behind, pilloried him for being too successful. Lonnie Donegan had committed the cardinal sin of popularising skiffle, of turning it from the obsession of a small coterie of aficionados into music of mass popularity. He was also, perversely, reproached for pillaging the works of 'composers' such as Leadbelly and Woody Guthrie. But it remains arguable that, without recordings like his version of Woody's 'Grand Coulee Dam', later performers (perhaps even Dylan himself) might not have beaten their way to Guthrie's door. Skiffle authority Mick O'Toole recalled that, for him, skiffle was:

> a window into America. Excitement! The folk scene inherited so much from skiffle, but only grudgingly acknowledged it because of that American connection.

For example, Donegan has always been discredited as being inauthentic ... but why? He introduced so much new stuff to us? All because he didn't stick his finger in his ear and liked to play the London Palladium? If MacColl had been offered the same chance, he'd have jumped at it![14]

One could state that without Donegan's recording of 'Rock Island Line' British and American popular music would not be as we know it today. This may appear a rather exaggerated statement, but consider the facts. He was undoubtedly the most significant (and successful) British recording artist of the pre-Beatles era and his influence on the Beatles was also seminal. Lonnie was also the man said to have inspired Phil Spector to take up the guitar. One could also cite the fact that Cliff Richard, Hank Marvin, Jet Harris and Tony Meehan were originally skifflers; that a young Jimmy Page's first appearance on TV was as a schoolboy skiffler; that other virtuoso rock guitarists such as Ritchie Blackmore, Robin Trower and David Gilmour began as skifflers (the list is almost endless). But it's not simply about Donegan and skiffle inspiring a host of future rock stars. The point that needs emphasising is that the (e.g.) Quarry Men-into-Beatles development (say 1957–62) was a typical result of the skiffle and post-skiffle eras. Skiffle's (and Donegan's) legacy is a sincere reflection of our social mores, our folkways.

The legacy is also one of access; historically, the skiffle experience has taught us that opening the door to 'non-musicians', inviting them to play E, A and B7, involving them in musical practices without the slightest knowledge of (say) a 'flattened thirteenth' has left us with some of the most enduring musical moments of the twentieth century. It is a salutary lesson that periodically needs revisiting. Skiffle was to inform the closed-shop, 'bell jar' world often inhabited by folkies and ethnomusicologists alike of precisely what they did not wish to hear, that is that via a couple of chords and a battered guitar literally anybody could play music. As one ex-skiffler informed this writer: 'three chords – you formed a group; four chords – you went on the road!'[15]

Pseudo-Americans?

When skifflers were added to the folk revival, new hypotheses were posed about influences, performance strategies and musical-historical processes. The traditionalists were challenged. While the folk club might appear from this historical distance a natural habitat for some ex-skifflers, the matrix of their artistic incursion was marked by an intertexture of influences and a growing subjectivity – neither of these features were hitherto salient characteristics of the folk revival. Popular acclaim, for example, did not necessarily demonstrate inauthenticity. Singer/songwriter Harvey Andrews:

The very interesting thing is that Lennon and McCartney came through [Buddy] Holly; and all of the great songwriters that I love – [such as] Paxton, Paul Simon –

came from Holly. There is something about Holly that got them; he was the first singer-songwriter. We didn't know that at the time but his lyrics are incredible. If you turn over to the b side of 'That'll be the day' – which every one bought – you've got a lyric on 'Looking For Someone To Love' which goes [sings] 'drunk man, street car, foot slipped, there you are' … now that's a book a novel a play and a film. Nine words – and lyric writing of the very highest level! Holly is the one that everybody relates to.[16]

Despite the almost congenital antipathy displayed by folk's deep-seated political philosophies, via skiffle a pop aesthetic permeated the folk revival. Intertextuality had dawned. Like those of Harvey Andrews, Bob Buckle's musical influences do not fit the official 'credo':

I'd played around with Buddy Holly songs a little, but not seriously … I still admire him, of course. Folk music, to me, when I was about 16, was rather twee, to be honest. I came to love a lot of it, but at that time I wasn't very impressed. Then my brother brought home a Burl Ives record from America; he used to go to sea. I'd actually asked him to bring back a rock & roll record, but he was hopeless as far as music was concerned, and because the album had Burl Ives playing a guitar on the front he presumed it was rock! I remember throwing it to one side. But one rainy day when I hadn't anything to do, I played it. It was a completely different experience … simple, but effective, traditional, but commercial. Burl Ives was seminal. We [the Leesiders] came into the folk scene because of Ives, not Lloyd, and I know that was the case for many people. Between them, Lloyd and Kennedy were strangling it at birth. I wanted to be a professional folk singer from that moment onward. But being professional didn't always please everybody![17]

There was, however, a backlash. Both Bob Buckle and Jack Froggatt testified to me that several leading folk club traditionalists condemned this US textual incursion. According to Froggatt, Co-Op and WMA education officer Bill Reddish was one of the first of a large minority in the folk clubs to coin the phrase 'pseudo Americans' for the undesirables inspired by the USA. This phrase stuck and came to be used to invalidate American influences.

This anti-American stance was created not only via the fear of standardisation associated with commodity production, but also through the 'traditional' conservative and nationalist mirror of British society held up by schooled Leavisites within the EFDSS and the WMA. The impact of Elvis Presley on British society was anathema to both the reactionaries of the far right and the eastward looking thinkers of the left. For some, the folk revival was much more than simply a musical re-evaluation: it reflected nothing less than a whole reading of national music history. Sydney Carter detected this xenophobic intransigence in 1960:

It looks as if the dream of Cecil Sharp has now come true: people sing and actually play folk music, not because it's educational, but because they actually like it! Up at Cecil Sharp House [near the Zoo] you'd think they'd be putting flags out. But are they? …The Dance, they feel, is going on quite merrily [safely within the wall of the Society] but the song is getting out of hand. The wrong sort of people are singing it. Folk song is going commercial, going American, going [worst of all!] Political. Well, is it?[18]

Undoubtedly American and commercial influences were pivotal. As we have seen, Douglas Kennedy resigned as director of the EFDSS in December 1961. He was not only wary of the Left's politicising (as explained in the previous chapter), but also unable to compromise his middlebrow anti-Americanism. Ironically, Kennedy's departing message was printed on the same page of *English Dance and Song* (25/1, December 1961) as the final sentences of Sydney Carter's typically cryptic editorial:

> The Kipsigis tribe in Kenya are entranced by the guitar of Jimmie Rodgers ... Cross-fertilization of traditions is occurring at a speed we never dreamed of. All this applies to song more than dance. But even dancers were affected by the Square Dance craze which rocked our society a dozen years ago. Some deplored it, because it was not purely English. But the only 'pure' folk music of the future may be (to use an Irishism) the folk music of the past. All new shoots on the old trunk of tradition will be hybrids; and this goes for the English as well as the Kipsigis.[19]

Jacquie MacDonald of both the Spinners and the renowned folk duo Jacquie and Bridie also testified to this mixture of influences described by Carter as 'new shoots on an old trunk':

> I was teacher training up in Yorkshire when Burl Ives came to play in Leeds. I was getting interested in music and liked skiffle a bit and because I was at teacher training college, we all tried to do something ... I was transfixed ... I'd never seen or heard anything like it – this little man singing with just a guitar. He was SO professional, I suppose. I became interested in folk music and eventually became a member of the Spinners, then I met Bridie and we began to sing together ... the rest, as they say, is history. For me, the folk clubs came later, really![20]

Yet by 1960, American Peggy Seeger had adopted her own utterly untenable jingoistic position. She openly criticised British singers for being culturally disloyal by singing American songs:

> to me, as an American, the fact that the Americans have built up a culture, which is American, which is absolutely unique, is valuable to me. And that's why I sing American songs. Because they represent to me the particular struggle of a particular people at a particular point in time. But when I hear a British person singing a folk song from America I feel that there's an anachronism, a spiritual anachronism, if you want to put it that way, there's something which is not quite right.[21]

There was, indeed, an anachronism. Seeger's unique antiquarian holding-place – her 'museum' – did not actually exist. By 1960 a conceptual framework had evolved from within the folk revival: certain music was able to take its place in the cultural heritage of the United Kingdom. But there was a cost. Out of Seeger's revival had evolved a canon, a repertory. Certain music was eligible for inclusion in this canon but others were not. Perhaps without realising, Peggy Seeger had adopted the currency of the classical, applying an impenetrable benchmark by which other forms were judged.

In 1960 in fact most British youth still had little or no knowledge of the existence of the folk revival. It was the development of non-literary forms like commercial television that really started to ask questions about devolving societal structures. Once the independent TV networks began, the exposition and then erosion of cultural stereotypes started to become evident. It is no coincidence that the biggest inroads that not only rock 'n' roll but kitchen sink realism made in 1950s Britain were directly linked to the output of ITV, rather than the (albeit pioneering) product of the BBC.

Technology

By the 1960s, with technological developments leaping ahead almost month by month, rapid changes in the very sound of music were affecting all musicians. In 1966, Brian Wilson of the Beach Boys made a monumental step forward in pop soundscape painting with *Pet Sounds* and by the following year a wide variety of foot-pedals such as 'wah-wah', phase shifters, 'fuzz' distortions had appeared in the electric guitar marketplace (and Marshall amplifiers were also in production). Walter Carlos's experimentations with electronic music were even staple album chart fare by 1969 (*Switched on Bach* CBS (s) 63501). With Carlos's assistance, Robert Moog's synthesiser was also in its final stages of development. Moog's comments on his expansions in electronic music now make fascinating and relevant reading:

> The question 'is electronic music less natural than music played on acoustic instruments?' No music is natural! Music is produced only after people invest strenuous and extended effort to gain intimate control over vibrating systems such as vocal cords, a violin, or a synthesiser. Furthermore, all musical instruments, except for the human voice, are highly contrived technological artifices. They are differentiated not by their degree of 'naturalness', but by the technological periods in which they were developed. The string instruments were perfected when woodworking was a flowering technology. Piano designers utilised the processes of a fully industrialised society. And the electronic music medium is being developed now, a time when electronic technology is dominant and the golden age of manufacturing appears to be yielding to what people are calling the 'post-industrial era'.[22]

Evidently, the pleasure and value derived by musicians from being involved in making such technologically facilitated music should never be underestimated or ignored.

One could even argue that Moog's statement totally fulfils the IFMC criteria set out at the beginning of this chapter. By the 1960s popular music technology was helping to reinvent and rearticulate musical practices. 'Continuity' with past music was retained while creative variation blossomed (e.g. Cream). Even at the other end of the musical continuum, consumer-based refashioning and recreation (e.g. Mod, Skinhead) meant that meaningful social practices emerged. Many young people were exposed to the growing counterculture of the neo-Marxist 'New Left' (including the folk revival), the existentialists and the 'beats', but variations of rock 'n' roll (including folk-rock) remained the primary sources of cultural expression for the next 25 years. It is hardly surprising that rock 'n' roll has now achieved 'folk' status!

The products of the culture industry may have played an important part in strengthening the domination of patriarchal capitalism but they also performed fascinating reciprocal functions. British youth used commerce as art and involved themselves in creative consumption. Furthermore, mass communications were vitally important in transmitting teenage preoccupations to a wider society. Technology was essential in making possible a significant indigenous cultural activity out of what was originally viewed as dissipated 'Americana'.

For example, the Beatles movie *A Hard Day's Night* demonstrated in 1964 that pop was not false consciousness. The film displayed a real sensitivity to British working-class 'folklore' in its own right. It presented little Irish granddads, pompous ex-army officers and decaying television theatres in a fascinating pop jigsaw puzzle that posed questions rather than providing answers.

Mass media folk music

In any case, interest in folk music was fuelled by mass media broadcasting. Julie Felix, Jake Thackray, and Robin Hall and Jimmy McGregor were all regulars on television (so too, the ubiquitous and highly influential group the Seekers). There was a wide-ranging assortment of British folk artists such as Donovan, David McWilliams, Friday Brown, the Leesiders and the Settlers making regular appearances on TV and radio. Bruce Woodley of the Seekers co-wrote songs with Paul Simon, who also sang on the religious *Five to Ten* slot on BBC Radio in March 1965, introduced by Judith Piepe. In doing so, Simon opened the door for other contemporary singer/songwriters.

In fact, one might argue that in the years before the advent of Radio 1 in 1967, the populist appreciation of contemporary folk song emanating from the broadcasting 'establishment' of the BBC, the kind of 'middle of the road' form of folk singers such as the aforementioned Friday Brown (who appeared regularly with Max Jaffa on the Light Programme) and the Settlers, effected a greater appreciation of folk music than any revivalist connected to the MacColl/Lloyd axis. The radio listener was able to hear the likes of Jake Thackray establish himself as a troubadour in the wake of what Piepe was to describe as the 'folk poets'. This acquaintance involved daily household procedures such as hoovering rather than attending a folk club!

The Paul Simon song 'Carlos Dominguez', recorded by Val Doonican, even filtered in a Latin agit-prop feel, as did the later (September 1966) Latin American song originally purveyed by the Weavers, 'Guantanamera'. The BBC even broadcast Latin 'folk' music at peak listening times. Amongst the repertoire of Dorita y Pepe and David and Marianne Dalmour were protest songs from South and Central America. Dorita y Pepe sang songs by Argentinian troubadours Ramon Ayala, Cholo Aguirre and Atahualpa Yupanqui on mainstream daytime radio, enabling a wider listening demographic to hear folk music of one sort or another without entering any internecine debate over thematic specialisation, authenticity or social relevance. Dorita y Pepe were Londoners with no family connections with Latin America; they were ex-jazz musicians who simply became interested in Latin American folk music. Critic Herbert Krezmer penned the following sleevenotes to David and Marianne Dalmour's first album, released in 1965 (Columbia 33SX 1715):

> One of the most endearing things about the entertainment offered by the attractive and musicianly Dalmours is that they do not burn, in public, at any rate, with the sort of overblown social conscience that nowadays seems obligatory among professional singers.
>
> Nowhere in this enchanting catalogue of a dozen songs are we pursued by the voices of social protest. Nowhere are we warned about the ominous mushroom cloud settling like a pall of doom on our civilisation; nor about what Strontium 90 is doing to our milk. Nowhere are there jeering references to the faceless conformists who live in little ticky tacky boxes on the hillsides of California, and nowhere is the listener scorned for the racial and colour prejudices he is assumed to possess and of which stains all guitar-toting cellar singers are assumed to be free.
>
> David and Marianne Dalmour ... cover a wider range of songs than is normally essayed by this breed of entertainer. They have, in short, conducted a merger between the simplicities of folk singing and even such tin-pan-alley improbabilities like 'A-tisket-A-Tasket'.
>
> The effect, strangely, has been not to narrow the 'folk' field, but to enlarge it. The results are undemanding, unpretentious and eminently listenable. (Let me say, lest certain citizens get too hot under the hoot'nanny, that my respect for certain social protest singers is immense, but that I suspect all those who protest too much, too stridently, and too profitably).[23]

Both the Dalmours and Dorita y Pepe sold thousands of record albums across the country. They did not trouble the weekly album listings of the day, but neither did Topic releases! Sales of folk-related albums were distributed over a much longer period of time than weekly lists could reflect. Dorita y Pepe's album *Latin American Folk* (Pye NSLP 18215, 1968) was a formidable seller at the famous Musical Box in Liverpool. Proprietor Diane Caine told me:

We sold lots of copies of that album. It's funny when you look back now, but it's not really, say, the Dylan or Pentangle records that seem to have sold the most, but the more 'middle-of-the-road' folk artists. There was a call for the 'Latin American Folk' album. I can remember re-ordering that one many times. It was full-priced to begin with, too, not a budget item ... although it probably later became that. Pye used to place everything on Golden Guinea and Marble Arch eventually ... even Dominic Behan![24]

Caine further informed me that 'traditional or folk music sales were actually far smaller than they have been given credit for' and also remembers Topic lurching from crisis to crisis. She recalls them wholesaling records from 'the back of an old van. When we did get enquiries for stuff like *The Iron Muse*, it was invariably out of stock at Topic, and we'd keep people waiting for weeks, months sometimes! It was a little embarrassing, actually.'[25]

From personal experience I can also vouch for the cumulative effect of the American folk-rock singers on the British singles and album charts of the day (the Byrds, Dylan, Simon and Garfunkel, Bob Lind).[26] In fact, by January 1964 Irwin Silber, the editor of the influential American folk song magazine *Sing Out!*, was already acknowledging that:

> The Beatles, at least, gave us 'Hard Day's Night', and if any reader has missed this film, our advice is to rush out and see it next time around. It's one of the great film comments of our age. Compare it to 'Hootenanny Hoot', for instance, and a lot of things fall into place. The basic fact, of course, is that folk music and rock and roll are not the two separate worlds that many think. Much genuine folk expression of our time has come through the medium of rock and roll, and we venture the thought that Chuck Berry, B.B. King, and Tommy Tucker have created an identification with this generation that few folk singers can duplicate. Perhaps if more folk singers did not choose to hold themselves aloof, some of the great realistic elements of the folk tradition would merge with the basically healthy moral outlook and musical sound we now call rock and roll.[27]

Many subsequent letters to *Sing Out!* declared support for Silber's populist eclecticism. Take this, for example, from the September 1965 edition (after *Billboard* had run the headline 'Folk + Rock + Protest = Dollars'): 'I think that the Beatles should be on the cover of *SING OUT!* Also the Rolling Stones. I'm sick of arguing about Dennon, Lylan [misspelling intended here], Seeger, commerciality, ethnicity and all these exhausted targets.'[28]

Together with the earlier skifflers and the BBC-validated populist folk singers mentioned above, these Americans widened musical horizons. Two comments from fans rather than practitioners illustrate this well. First, Anne Thomas:

> I came to love folk music around about 1965 or 6, but I was 14 ... too young for a folk club! I'd never heard of them in any case. No, I was at Blackburne House School in Liverpool at the time and some of us girls thought that it was very cool to try to read Sartre and/or Camus and 'dig' Bob Lind and Paul Simon. We never had a suitable record player or the money to buy records at home so it was down to

catching them on the telly or listening to a few different radio shows. Believe it or not Val Doonican was regarded as something of an interpreter of folk songs for a while! Also singers like the Seekers, David and Marianne Dalmour, Marianne Faithfull and Friday Brown. I thought Lind, especially, was quite sexy! I liked Donovan, too, but thought he was a bit of a wimp. I'd never heard of Renbourn or Jansch. I remember seeing the Ian Campbell folk group on the telly around that time and thinking, well if that's British folk music, you can stick it![29]

Anne Thomas's rather bitter comments about the Ian Campbell Group undoubtedly suggest a weariness of the myth of folk music coherence. They also suggest that direct communion with the folk revival was impossible for a generation of young people. The totalising histories of the folk revival, represented by a stringent arrogance, are inaccurate in suggesting an encompassing cognitive praxis. According to Bill Pook, fragments gathered from popular culture were just as significant:

I think it's incredible; it appears to me that most histories about the British folk scene have been written by those with vested interests in one stage of history. So, you don't get, maybe with the exception of Laing or Humphries, the real influences coming through. TV was bloody important; Robin Hall and Jimmy McGregor, Diz Disley, even Alexis Korner on *Five O'Clock Club*. Many weren't fucking old enough to get into a pub during the early part of the sixties, never mind join or run a folk club! Seeing Donovan on *Ready Steady Go* was really important![30]

Two camps: a generation gap

Even if one was old enough to be a member of a folk club, this diverse behaviour would have been clearly evident. The revival was divided into two distinct camps. On the one hand a few clubs became exclusively tied to the diatribes of the Critics' Group and were populated by mainly finger-in-the-ear singers performing mostly unaccompanied or with approved traditional instrumentation (such as fiddle or concertina). Robin Denselow:

clubs started to take on specific characteristics. Some became exclusively traditional, approving only of hand-on-the-ear unaccompanied singers … Gradually, the easy-going acceptance of different forms of music broke down. The traditionalists created a ghetto, and a host of excellent musicians were trapped inside.[31]

On the other hand, the contemporary clubs featured exponents of acoustic blues and ragtime (among their heroes were the Revd Gary Davies, Blind Blake, Sonny Terry and Brownie McGhee, etc.) and experimentalists in fusion. Two of the most celebrated contemporary folk clubs were to be found in London – Les Cousins in Soho and, to a lesser extent, the Scots Hoose in Cambridge Circus. These clubs, in their ascendancy in the mid-1960s, played host to such performers as Paul Simon, Al Stewart, Davey Graham, Donovan, Ralph McTell, Roy Harper,

Bert Jansch and even, on occasion, Bob Dylan. But open hostility on the part of the 'purists' remained. Eric Winter:

> Broadly the battle of ideas raged between the 'purists', the 'popularisers' and the 'tolerators' (the terms are my own). The purists were of various shades, ranging from those who believed that all folk songs should be passed on orally and those who thought that they should be sung only by those who 'had them from tradition', to those who sing only traditional material. The popularisers were largely anti-purist – they were known to the purists as 'ethnics', a term arising from the concern of some purists with the racial origins and significance of the songs ... The tolerators had taken their watchword from the American singer Pete Seeger, who coined the phrase 'cultural coexistence'.[32]

A point well made, but Winter's language also reveals much. Words such as 'tolerate' still suggest orderly parameters. A cardinal mistake of the folk revival of the 1960s was to impose strict musical and social codes on reception while culture and meaning were becoming ever more diverse.

The traditionalists of the revival severed themselves from the modern world, objectifying song along the way. They implied that an articulate and authentic soundtrack would help ordinary working people to take more control over their lives, but they ignored the fact that people also needed to grasp an understanding of the forces which moulded their world – not reject them out of hand. The pop-influenced singer/songwriters accepted this challenge (in doing so, Dylan apparently described the folk legacy as 'nothing but mystery'), whereas the traditionalists merely reinforced their own superficial distortion of history.

It is historically naïve to suggest that people listened to folk music to the exclusion of everything else, especially during the eras of (say) Elvis, Donegan, the Beatles, the Stones, Motown, Stax, Nat King Cole and Andy Williams. The questions beg to be asked: how? where? when? Even if the syncretism that I depict is neither sought nor desired by the folk listener, it still has an effect. It is not only illogical to ignore BBC radio and TV shows such as *Five to Ten*, *The Sam Costa Show*, *Two Way Family Favourites* or *The White Heather Club*, but outrageous to dismiss them as examples of force-feeding the public a diet of music 'pap'. If communication fluctuates in meaning as it passes between us, these programmes effectively 'produced' not only folk music within folk clubs (whether desired or not), but also a variety of receptive strategies about folk music, outside them.

By the late 1960s there was a clearly defined generation gap within the folk revival. Tim Hart, one of the forces behind the folk-rock aggregation Steeleye Span, informed the writers of *Electric Muse* that the folk movement:

> built its own limitations within itself. It came out of skiffle, a popular movement, and popularised traditional music for a while, but then went backwards ... No one said 'let's glamourize it a bit, let's do a bit of publicity, let's really try to sell folk records, let's try to sell a folk act to a larger market'... My personal philosophy is

that most English traditional song is unaccompanied song, and the only argument is ... should you or should you not accompany it at all? After that I'm not interested in any argument as to what degree you can go to.[33]

By 1969 Hart was one of a vanguard of folk musicians, nurtured on rock and skiffle, who questioned the assumptions of the revival. It became obvious to a younger generation of folk performers like Hart that recordings, radio, television and the increased mobility of artists had contributed to, not detracted from, folk music writing, dissemination and production. *Electric Muse* reported that Tim Hart and his singing partner Maddy Prior set off in a Ford Anglia to 'conquer the British folk scene'. This they accomplished quite easily in a very short space of time (turning full professionals in 1967). Hart realised that 'the crock of gold at the end of the rainbow on the folk scene wasn't that difficult to achieve ... once you get £25 at clubs and headline at occasional festivals, that's it. You either become a folk intellectual or you become an alcoholic.'[34]

Hart and Prior, like others, were very conscious of not becoming part of a folk meritocracy. Like a typical member of the teenage subcultures spoken of earlier, Hart desired to fulfil a musical potential. This led him into experiments with technology and musical amalgamation, stretching the limits of his own discourse – actually the real tradition of any musician.

Like the Seekers and Donovan, Tim Hart did not dilute folk music. Whatever his proximity to a perceived, 'pure' cultural carbon, he encouraged a new generation to appreciate differing forms of popular music, some of whom evidently owed as much allegiance to Buddy Holly as they did to Maggie Barry.

Notes

1.   *International Folk Music Council 1954* (pamphlet).
2.   Frith, 'The Year it all Came Together'.
3.   Whitcomb, *After the Ball*, p. 243.
4.   Ibid., p. 244.
5.   Clarke (ed.), *The Penguin Encyclopedia of Popular Music*, p. 1078.
6.   Whitcomb, *After the Ball*, p. 242.
7.   'Donegan, L. to New Musical Express (1957)', in McAleer, *Hit Parade Heroes*, p. 64.
8.   Dallas, 'Lonnie Donegan and Skiffle', p. 125.
9.   McAleer, *Hit Parade Heroes*, p. 66.
10. Interview with Wally Whyton, 1987.
11. Dallas, 'Lonnie Donegan and Skiffle', p. 125.
12. Wally Whyton, 1987.
13. Hoggart, *The Uses of Literacy*, pp. 248–50.
14. Interview with Mick O'Toole, May 2001.
15. Ibid.
16. Harvey Andrews to Spencer Leigh, 'On the Beat', BBC Radio Merseyside, 14 November 1987.

17. Interview with Bob Buckle, July 1995.
18. Carter, 'Editorial: Pop Goes the Folk'.
19. Carter, 'Editorial', *English Dance and Song*, 25/1.
20. Interview with Jacqueline MacDonald, November 1995.
21. Peggy Seeger to Sydney Carter in Carter, 'Going American?', p. 20.
22. Robert A. Moog to V. Vale, in Vale, *Incredibly Strange Music II*, p. 135.
23. Krezmer, 'Sleevenotes'.
24. Interview with Diane Caine, proprietor of the Musical Box, Rocky Lane, Liverpool.
25. Ibid.
26. The Byrds' singles successes at this time were: 'Mr Tambourine Man' CBS 201765, no. 1, June 1965; 'All I Really Want to Do' CBS 201796, no. 4, August 1965; 'Turn! Turn! Turn!' CBS 202008, no. 26, November 1965.

   Bob Dylan's single successes from 1965 were: 'The Times They Are A-Changin'' CBS 201751, no. 9, March 1965; 'Subterranean Homesick Blues' CBS 201753, no. 9, April 1965; 'Maggie's Farm' CBS 201781, no. 22, June 1965; 'Like a Rolling Stone' CBS 201811, no. 4, August 1965; 'Positively Fourth Street' CBS 201824, no. 8, October 1965.

   Joan Baez had (technically) four hit singles in 1965, but the media only really recognised the top 20 at that time, which rules out three of them. The Phil Ochs song 'There but for Fortune' Fontana TF 587 attained the number 8 position in July 1965.

   Simon and Garfunkel's small run of hit singles did not begin until March 1966 when 'Homeward Bound' CBS 202045 reached number 9.

   This was the same month that Bob Lind scored a big hit on the British singles charts with 'Elusive Butterfly' Fontana TF 670 reaching number 5. Val Doonican also held this position with the same song during the same month, Decca F 12358. The aggregate sales of the two records would undoubtedly have resulted in a number 1 record. 'Elusive Butterfly' was Bob Lind's only 'real' hit in this country, but it was Doonican's fourth hit of a strong run that lasted until 1973.

   These statistics suggest three things:

   Firstly: that American folk/rock was an important influence on a younger generation of would-be folkies (I include myself here).

   Secondly: that artists like Val Doonican (and the Seekers – see *Guinness British Hit Singles*, 11th edn, p. 313) were also important and successful disseminators of folk approximations during the mid-1960s.

   Thirdly: that the song 'Elusive Butterfly' was as important as the work of Dylan at that time in raising the profile of acoustic singer/songwriters. Lind was a 'clean-cut Dylan' with a 'pleasant voice' (Buckle) and was 'less challenging' (Pook). Many people I have spoken to outside the British folk scene cite this song as a memorable piece of American folk, whereas few remembered what 'Positively Fourth Street' was all about. It should be noted that, by 1966, none of the above artists, with the possible exceptions of Val Doonican and the Seekers, would have regarded themselves as singles-orientated artists.

   All of Dylan's albums attained top 10 status on the British LP sales lists up until 1970, with the exception of his first, which didn't chart until 1965 (reaching a retrospective number 13); six albums reached the number 1 position. *The Freewheelin' Bob Dylan* CBS BPG 62193 spent 49 weeks on the chart; *Greatest Hits* [1967] CBS SBPG 62847, 82 weeks.

   Bob Lind released three albums in the UK in 1966: *Don't Be Concerned*, *The Elusive Bob Lind*, *Photographs of Feeling*. None charted.

   Simon and Garfunkel's album successes began in April 1966 with their second album (discounting *The Paul Simon Song Book*) *Sounds of Silence* CBS 62690.

That great Irish 'traditional' group the Bachelors (!) gave Paul Simon a 'leg-up' in March 1966 with a successful cover of 'The Sound of Silence' Decca F 12351: number 3 on the singles charts. Another Paul Simon song that was especially popular on the radio during the mid-1960s was 'Carlos Dominguez'. Simon had released the song as a single under the name of Paul Kane, Oriole CB 1930 without any success. It became a staple part of Val Doonican's live and radio act for many years. His albums were enormously successful between 1964 and 1969. For example: *Lucky Thirteen Shades of* Decca LK 4648, no. 2, 1964; *Gentle Shades of* Decca LK 4831, no. 5, 1966 (52 weeks on charts) and *Val Doonican Rocks but Gently* Pye NSPL 18204, no. 1, December 1967.

The Seekers spent a total of 268 weeks on the British album charts! Of the six albums that charted between 1965 and 1969 (when they disbanded for the first time), four spent lengthy periods in the top 10, with *The Best of the Seekers* Columbia SCX 6268 reaching number 1 and spending 125 weeks on the listings. They also contributed to the rise of Paul Simon by successfully recording his composition 'Someday One Day' Columbia DB 7867 (no. 11, March 1966).

Joan Baez's album successes go back to July 1964: *In Concert Vol. 2* (Fontana TFL 6033). She enjoyed three British hit albums during 1965.

The Byrds were altogether rather less successful, saleswise, in the UK. Only one album: *Mr Tambourine Man*, August 1965 CBS BPG 62571, reached the top 10, and although practically all of their subsequent albums charted, they spent only a few weeks on the charts.

There are, indeed, lies, damn lies and statistics but all of the above details help to show that American and so-called 'middle of the road', 'non-committed' artists appearing on Independent Television and the 'Variety' wing and Light Programme of the BBC were as responsible for the growing interest in folk music in Britain as the 'purists'. The Bachelors, for example, may not have been everybody's idea of 'carriers of a tradition', but they were successful singles and album artists at a crucial synchronic moment in time (in 1964–66 they also had four hit LPs on Decca). Doubt their motivations if you must, but rewrite the history, please.

27. Silber, 'News and Notes', p. 3.
28. Magriel, 'Letter to the Editors of *Sing Out!*', p. 118.
29. Interview with Anne Thomas, June 1993.
30. Interview with Bill Pook, May 1995.
31. Denselow, 'Folk Rock in Britain', p. 143.
32. Winter, 'Purists, Popularisers and Tolerators', pp. 18–19.
33. Tim Hart to R. Denselow, in Denselow, 'Folk Rock in Britain', pp. 164, 140.
34. Ibid., p. 140.

Chapter 6

Folk-rock

The purpose [of genre is] to organise the reproduction of an ideology.
Robert Walser, quoted in Hamm (1995), p. 373

I'm glad Fairport existed. I'm glad they re-exist and I think in a sense they are a certain yardstick by which modern electrified traditional music is measured.
Richard Thompson to Sarah Coxon, *Folk Roots* (Dec. 1988), p. 15

When I started to learn my instrument all those years ago it was Johnny and the Hurricanes and Bill Black's Combo I wanted to emulate, not the Spinners or the Kingston Trio; in the early days of Fairport there was very little folk music.
Ashley Hutchings, founder of Fairport Convention, October 1995

Authenticity

Authenticity is an often-used expression within the British folk revival. It appears to reveal or clarify a particular musical history ('authentically English'; 'authentically original'; 'the authentic sound of the bagpipes'). Authenticity is used as an index or an indicator of a musical past, as a historical meter in the re-establishment of a living dialogue with a tradition. It can suggest an active involvement with history. But this involvement can also imply an affirmation of dogma, unity and coherence. To those historians who maintain that research ought involve an immersion in the widest possible range of primary sources, notions concerning musical authenticity require great caution. For it becomes quite clear that any search for musical authenticity can involve the creative appropriation and mythologising of the past. Political evidence rather than musical evidence is often used as an indicator of authenticity (e.g. 'an authentically Black soundtrack'; 'the authentic sound of Scotland') and when this occurs, a historical amnesia can be created by a search for a musical history from a limited amount of possibilities. This is a recipe for musical parochialism rather than a critical regionalism and, for the folk revival, remains a paradox.

This is because the unity of an emancipatory project such as the folk revival actually calls for an acknowledgement of plurality and dispersion rather than a historically authenticated soundtrack. The search for authenticity in traditional music can actually deny the possibility for music to exist as a vast argumentative texture through which people construct their own reality. Conventional wisdom appears to dictate that authentic representation begins with the basic axiom that the sign and the real are equivalent. Simulation, argues Baudrillard, appears to start from the converse point of view, that the sign is a reversion and 'death sentence of every reference'.[1] One might look at successive phases of musical/ cultural/artistic representations along Baudrillard's model to discover where perceptions about the authentic and the simulated diverge for lovers of folk music. This would then give us an insight as to why certain musical soundtracks and accompanying representations are regarded as 'fake' and others as 'genuine'. For example, common assumptions concerning images surrounding the mediation and simulation of folk music might be divided into four distinct types.

First, that the musical representation is a reflection of basic reality. This is a good, wholesome image, a natural appearance or sound that represents a truth. The work of, say, Aly Bain might cover this area: 'authentic' Hebridean fiddle-playing of a virtuoso standard without any 'frills'. The artist is playing natural music within his natural environment.

Another depiction that masks and perverts a basic reality is, according to Baudrillard, a base appearance. In this case, the music is being transformed and fails to deal with the natural truth. The electrification of folk music might be an appropriate illustration here, where the 'natural' sound of (say) a Fylde guitar, being made from one piece of wood, is preferable to the distorted sounds from a Fender/Marshall amplification set-up. The filtering processes of tradition have been loosened (by technology), leaving many dubious musical items to survive with 'quality' clearly in doubt: 'Modern recording is now so accessible that many items pass directly from the writer's pen to the CD. Is it now too easy to record new work? and whose job is it to pass judgement on the value of the writing?'[2]

There is a more extreme interpretation of simulation when the musical representation masks the entire absence of basic reality. This means that the music plays at being the natural in a system that is actually designated for other uses – music is artifice disguising itself as original. The use of (say) 'Wild Mountain Thyme' in a Scottish Tourist Board advert might be an appropriate example. However, the song (Scottish) actually promotes Scotland, therefore it could be considered an acceptable process. Advertising Danish lager on an English beach, together with cricket wickets being embedded in the sand to the sound of Runrig (Carlsberg advert), is probably not! Here, nationalist paradigms of authenticity are important features of a musical 'masking of reality'.

Perhaps the ultimate insult to the aesthetics of the authenticist might be that the musical image bears no relation to any concept of historical 'reality' whatsoever and is pure simulation. There is a suggestion that the musical image does not even warrant inclusion as a reference point even within its own simulated appearance; that it is almost non-existent as a piece of traditional music because it is so reliant on the immanence of its own appearance. The image has subsumed any influences into a nightmarish scenario and that image bears no relationship to (and fabricates, insults and destroys) the sources of the original. A line is drawn in the sand beyond which this type of image leaves no concept of (in this case) folk music. Perhaps a good example of this might be the work of the folk-influenced group Mouth Music.[3] A leading member of the Frodsham folk club described it to me as 'insulting sad-bastard unlistenable crap'. The overriding impression is that when the real is no longer viewed as being what it used to be, it is a corrupted simulation. In this instance, nostalgia assumes the major significance and 'tradition' appears more valuable and rewarding than any other musical text.

The drawback with these claims is that they are clearly unreliable: many musical discourses have great value, but not all of them have value thrust upon them in the same 'authentic' manner. By limiting certain works to ideas about value we ignore the fact that that value criticism is part of the institutions that constitute value in the first place. There are indefinite ways of discussing music, and not all of them fall within the canonical nature of 'authenticity' and 'value'.

Furthermore, performance is never intrinsically 'natural'. However determined a singer is to express a message, one can never guarantee that the listener will appreciate that message – the reception of a song or tune cannot be fully controlled. In fact, attempts at control can restrict the message by limiting, stylistically, the emotional power of the music. The paradox is that folk performances often attempt to be precise in order to deliver a message. That message, however, can never be totally explicit (and can actually be at its most effective when there is a loss of stylistic control). What is more, in addition to the irregularity of a song's message, there is the inconsistency of a listener's strategy.

Listening strategies

Suppose, for example, we have been listening to a Martin Carthy performance. What have we been doing? Firstly, not simply listening, for I do not believe that this isolated activity exists; this implies the possibility of pure (that is, disinterested) perception. Rather, we are using at least two predetermined interpretive decisions: one, that the music is 'folk', two, that it is being sung by Martin Carthy. Moreover the ideas of 'folk' and 'Carthy' are also an interpretation – they do not stand for a set of indisputable facts.

Once those predetermined interpretations are in place, we then perform certain listening acts according to our predisposition towards concepts surrounding the expression 'folk music', together with the proximity of Carthy's performance to our predispositions and preconceptions: to find, for example, similarities between our concepts of Carthy and folk – indeed, our concepts of Carthy and Carthy as a live performer. We might also look for 'themes' in his songs, or look for histories of people in the songs and listen to Carthy relate his preambles and retune his guitar in order to 'understand' the songs better. We might compare this Carthy with previous 'Carthys', this repertoire with previous repertoires, in order to confer a degree of significance on the performance; or we might wish to mark folk concepts in the musical structures (ballad, broadside, jig, reel, hornpipe, contemporary, Scottish, Irish). Our inclination to perform these acts (and others; this list is not exhaustive) constitutes a set of interpretive strategies which, when put into execution, become part of the listening process attached to our interpretation of folk music.

We are, therefore, adopting a listening 'type' just as much as Martin Carthy is adopting a performance 'type'. But our 'type' may not have anything to do with another person's 'type', as such. Others listening might dispute my interpretations; they might complain to me that I could not possibly be listening to the same song, and they would be right because each of us would be interpreting the song that each of us had made out of that particular performance of Martin Carthy. Our interpretations give the songs shape, not the other way around, and we formulate the songs in interpretation. We place our own strategies on them, and even if both listeners are roughly conforming in some respects to the patterns laid down above, this does not exclude the possibilities for one song to become two (at least), and for those two songs to become relatively discrete. They don't have to, but they can.

Perhaps the notions of 'same' and 'different' musical texts can be fantasies. Perhaps truth in a song is forever mediated, not only by the rhetorical nature of song but by predetermined listening strategies. If I listen to (say) 'Lord Franklin' and 'My Way' differently, I form the songs from my own interpretive strategies based on my social and cultural construction of genre. This is not because 'Lord Franklin' is 'great' folk or 'My Way' is 'great' pop. Neither of them is great 'anything' without the constructions that I have built for them. In fact, inasmuch as this is a personal interpretation, 'My Way' and 'Lord Franklin' can actually be similar for me; I am not simply formed by them. Undeniably, the songs have an impact and reality but I like them (or hate them) not only because they remind me of a certain place, time or era, but also because they remind me of me. I also listen to these two songs differently as I get older. The impact of hearing 'Lord Franklin' the first time is lost, filed or subsumed in the intervening time, mingled with the formulations I have made in that time.

If this is valid so far, one then needs to question one of the most fundamental assumptions of the folk revival concerning musical perception: that by listening to 'traditional' song, our musical interpretations can be almost spiritually altered. Although music has vital transformative qualities, ought we not also take into account our predispositions towards interpreting folk music via our social and cultural constructions and experiences? Perhaps people differ about musical 'quality' not because quality is different but because people are different in terms of experience.

So, where does this leave the aforementioned ideas about authenticity? How can music actually authenticate any history without significant contextual and intertextual interpretation? Finding new meanings in rediscovering and revaluing what is on offer as being cheap and readily available is possible. Even more satisfying must be the ability to create new aesthetics both from what society has thrown out and from what has previously been regarded as 'tradition'.

Folk-rock

In this way, the hybrid genre of folk-rock is of vital importance to record. It remains something of a peculiarity as far as its inclusion in the larger British folk scene is concerned, for it is often tolerated rather than exalted: it fails to be grounded in any algorithmic certainty. It does, however, require investigation, for if one mixes certain aspects of an increasingly multi-layered society into a musical genre initially based on 'authenticity' then the results are of primary significance. The crossbreed of folk-rock can be viewed as both an attempt to overcome revivalist concepts of authentic re-performance ('do it this way, and this way alone') and an acknowledgement of the intrinsic value of musical traditions. It is a great example of dialectic processes at play and, like skiffle before it, an expansion on any concept of a 'folk revival'. For example, Dave Swarbrick, formerly of Fairport Convention, stated:

> It was starting to become a real minority thing. It was a musical closed shop. Now, in the wake of all of the things that were happening then ... how could I sit and watch all of that ... especially Richard's [Thompson] playing? You need to find out whether it'll work for you, too.[4]

However, for many, Swarbrick's enthusiasm for embracing and experimenting with an amalgam of 'commercial' rock music and 'authentic' folk music remains anathema. Folk music signifies the participant within the collective, whereas rock music is still viewed by many as the individual and exploitative. The following contrasting quotes indicate a real level of disagreement which still exists within the folk movement about the hybrid of folk-rock; firstly from *The Living Tradition*, July–August 1994:

> An article on folk rock – that bete noire for the purists of the folk world – surely out of place in a magazine like this! Well maybe, but to my ears at least the grafting of our traditional lyrics and tunes onto harder-edged rock roots has produced a hybrid that deserves to be listened to. The genre has always had its critics ... and I find it rather sad that today 'folkies' (their label not mine) base their criticisms, in the main, on the noise level rather than the merits or otherwise of the lyrics and tune.[5]

But from *Taplas*, April–May 1995:

> Then, of course came folk/rock, a peculiarly mismatched hybridisation for 95% of the time. And it still is. That's not to say enjoyable things haven't come out of it,

but I'll be amazed if much of it lasts for fifty years. It won't get a listen once the nostalgia's worn off.[6]

The development of folk-rock was much more than simply a new wave of musicians investigating the potential of electrifying traditional music; it was a cultural transformation of the representative values of that very music. The work of Fairport Convention, Steeleye Span, Mr Fox and the like was not musically determined. One musical 'activity' could not have occurred without the presence of an 'other'.

However difficult it may be for hardened folkies to accept, folk and rock music had become mutually dependent by the late 1960s. The transformation of folk music was dependent on the popular culture within which it truly existed and the popular forms that resulted were totally dependent on the tradition that formed its models of representation. Interestingly, many interpreters of the 1960s have noted the role played by folk music in the development of rock, but few have reversed this equation. Yet reverse it we must, for the majority of musical innovation during the 1960s dialectic of liberation was indeed from the rock, not the folk, field. Furthermore, the cultural resonance of rock music was (and remains) far greater because of its indisputable commercial strength.

Impact

The Britain of the post-World War II era was subject to a great deal of musical cross-fertilisation of one sort or another. By the latter half of the 1960s, this inherent hybridisation had actually become the norm. After all, the Black US rhythm and blues that had inspired countless British groups to play music had been exported back across to the United States by white British youth, so anything appeared possible.

All kinds of popular music hybrids began to emerge between 1967 and the end of the decade. Not only had musicians who had originally entered the pop scene covering American rhythm and blues progressed to emulate their heroes by developing a British hybrid of their own (e.g. the Action, the Creation), but many were dropping their 'soul' moniker and taking themselves very seriously (e.g. Black Sabbath, Spooky Tooth, Procol Harum).

The sonic heights reached by the Beatles on the *Revolver* album (1966) and the 'Penny Lane'/'Strawberry Fields' single (1967) re-influenced an entire generation of musicians. The Beatles released their masterpiece *Sergeant Pepper's Lonely Hearts Club Band* in 1967 and in the wake of such ground-breaking material came a whole host of new groups, all intent on using a wide variety of popular music traditions and stretching recording and compositional boundaries. The emphasis was on 'serious' music and the 45 single was (perhaps somewhat sadly) no longer seen as an adequate medium to express artistic ideas. Many albums became quasi conceptual in nature and were snapped up by an eager 'underground' audience. This activity also attracted the attention of disaffected folk musicians.

In fact, cross-fertilisation in all of the arts was at a peak, in what Arthur Marwick has described as 'the high sixties, 1964–1969'. He further states:

> Many of the great intellectuals of the time were fascinated by popular culture and the mass media. Classical musicians have long borrowed from folk music and, from at least the 1920s, from jazz: but, in fact, in the sixties the effort was much more concentrated and much more concerted; furthermore the movement was two-way.[7]

This interest in cross-fertilisation also took a quantum leap forward with the profile raising of marijuana and LSD during 1965 and 1966. Both drugs influenced countless (mostly musically illiterate) beat and R&B musicians who began taking chord structures apart, experimenting with time signatures, sound effects and studio techniques. Just as skiffle had revolutionised music 10 years earlier, the psychedelic era revolutionised the modus operandi of many rock and pop musicians.

Psychedelia in Britain also affected those of a bourgeois but traditionally liberalist sensibility (particularly when mixed with a little nascent Marxism). As with all drug cultures and their distillation through cultural echelons, psychedelia was both revolutionary and orthodox. However revolutionary it might have been in its initial influence, practitioners could not really 'escape' from their own cultural circumstances. Psychedelia became an important touchstone for an entire generation (even if many never actually experienced an LSD 'acid trip'). When mixed with heavy doses of grammar school aesthetics and middle-class sensibilities it mutated into an aesthetic of embryonic pastoralism, not unlike that created and experienced by early revivalists such as Sharp and Grainger. While the burgeoning counterculture found it could tap into a cult of innocence and fairytale gardens, rock musicians also discovered that this fad of incorruptibility was a platform for musical conceptualisations of a rural idyll.

For example, the work of Donovan, the Incredible String Band and Tyrannosaurus Rex all reflected an acoustic Tolkienesque blend of mystery, English folklore and children's fairytales. When mingled with American musical influences from the likes of Joni Mitchell, Buffalo Springfield, Love and the Byrds, innocence was elevated as an important marker (hence the renaissance in popularity of William Blake). Innocence marked the point before one grew up and became serious – very much part of the hippie aesthetic – whereas 'tradition' appeared to some rather po-faced and academic.

The attraction of a folk music sound divorced from the social mores of the folk scene was, for a pop and/or rock musician, very appealing. One could develop a music that explored the complex changing milieu of British society without being locked into a framework of musical intolerance. For bands such as

Jethro Tull, Barclay James Harvest, Gentle Giant and Genesis, this was an intoxicating prospect. Released from the somewhat dry explanations emanating from within the revival, folk music served a different purpose, symbolising something of the enchanted, heroic and organic. A musical spectrum appeared signifying (perhaps as Vaughan Williams had demonstrated previously) a crossover between popular and 'serious' music. However, unlike 'Uncle Ralph's' model, the agent of change was not the orchestra but the rock group. By 1970, disparate factors had developed into a coherent musical culture.

These experiments of the late 1960s provided substantial evidence to suggest that, despite complaints from predisposed authenticists, music will always be able to digest augmentation. Rock music had been misinterpreted by even the most sensitive of critics (actually right up until the mid-1970s). On the one hand, it was dismissed by high art elitists, on the other it was 'Mellers-ised' (Wilfred Mellers wrote the musicological *Twilight of the Gods* about the Beatles in 1973) and analysed like classical composition. Rock was therefore crucial in deconstructing any institutionalisation of traditions. In the process, the rock incursion into the folk revival persuaded many within that scene to look beyond the discursive boundaries of the folk movement. Two apparently incompatible genres were forced together – a coupling of the didactic tendencies of folk with the hedonism and (hitherto) 'low art' of rock. Of course, it soon became apparent to all those willing to experiment that distinct similarities existed between the increasingly explicit nature of late-1960s rock romanticism and the ruralist idylls extolled by the purist folk revival.

Disaffection

For example, as I have previously suggested, by the mid-1960s many younger folk musicians working in Britain had also been influenced by the American amalgam of folk and rock music. This hybrid, however, having been created by US folkies, was subject to much indigenous prejudice from those musical anti-commercialists who found a refuge in folk music. US folk-rock continued to remain castigated and isolated by elements of the British folk club movement for its lack of 'authenticity' (American origins still equated with promoters and hucksters) and the use of electronics. Indeed, the folk revivalists found themselves bitterly divided over Bob Dylan's 1965 adoption of electric instruments and amplification – tantamount to a heresy for some ('Judas' was the call from the Manchester auditorium that year).

Sweeney's Men, from Ireland, were amongst the first folkies to experiment with electric folk music in 1966 (sadly not on record) but their path was tortuous because of continued intransigence within the folk hierarchies. This legendary group (Andy Irvine, Johnny Moynihan, Terry Woods and – latterly – Henry McCullough) were not only among the prime movers in the resurgence of interest in Irish music in the late 1960s, but they fostered it utilising a vast range of instruments on their albums (for which they were greeted with considerable acclaim by the British and Irish music press at that time).

By the time they had recorded *The Tracks of Sweeney* for Transatlantic (TRA 200, 1969), Andy Irvine had left the band. His replacement was the electric guitarist Henry McCullough (ex-Eire Apparent) who played with the group at the Cambridge Folk Festival of 1968. His hippie-cum-rock background was enormously influential on the band and, although the line-up was rather short-lived and McCullough did not actually play on *The Tracks of Sweeney* album, the musical mould had been broken at Cambridge. Unfortunately, amid artistic frustration created by this encroaching eclecticism, Sweeney's Men split in 1969.

Any great strides to ally folk to rock in Britain had to come from without. Rock musicians 'dabbling' with folk were uncontrollable and could experiment with folk music well away from (e.g.) the restrictive confines of a folk club. Rock's pastoralism was, of course, an idealised musical assembly from the outset. As I have previously suggested, folk music was used rather like Cecil Sharp's 'raw material' and Paul Stump suggests that 'the fascination with the rustic often reflects a view of the countryside inherited through the refracting lenses of a century of popular, mass-cultural idealisations of rural life'.[8] But Stump's somewhat sour rationalisation does not account for folk-rock as a viable cultural currency. Of course it was a refracted view, but what else could it have been? Many mid to late sixties band members were raised in suburbia with grammar school educations. They were liberalist, idealist and democratic units from the outset – organic assemblages of school friends and siblings – a bunch of squabbling families who looked after each other. Moreover, almost without exception, the generation of young people that colonised these bands were collectors of music just as much as purveyors. US blues and country music had real esteem as living issues in history and any interest in all aspects of American culture involved serious research. Furthermore, blues, folk and hillbilly recordings were not the easiest to find in the Woolworths of 1960s Britain!

It is, therefore, not hard to understand why some, such as bass guitarist Ashley Hutchings (by 1967 leader of Fairport Convention), went on to research and then refract British pastoralism with great fervour. His bourgeois upbringing in Muswell Hill probably contributed to his willingness to experiment, his unflappability and his relatively easy-going nature. This was as contextually relevant to Hutchings's development as Vaughan Williams's backdrop of intellectual aristocracy and Alan Bush's CP-based international modernism.

Fairport Convention's guitarist Richard Thompson displayed this typically communal, erudite yet still rather self-abnegatingly humble folk-rock attitude by stating to *Beat Instrumental* in August 1968: 'the group as a whole are drawing from English roots. The fact that we're electric doesn't make any difference.'[9] But, of course, it most certainly did. The late 1960s produced different sets of musical and social reference points but high on the list was the electric guitar and amplifier. The time had arrived for Thompson's social mores to intertwine with the music of mass communication. It was an appropriate moment for the liberalist hippies from good homes to find an idiom to reflect their cultivated tastes. Balance, genre, variation, contrast, quietude and irony were all important features of this socially informed musical exposition.

While Sweeney's Men's personal and musical problems hampered their progress, other moves were afoot to harvest this aesthetic. Pentangle (Bert Jansch, John Renbourn, Jacqui McShee, Danny Thompson, Terry Cox) organically united in 1967 to draw folk, jazz and blues aesthetics together (while remaining, to begin with, defiantly acoustic). Eclection (George Hultgren, Gerry Conway, Kerilee Male, Mike Rosen) took their name from the contrasting backgrounds of their line-up and recruited Australian folkie Trevor Lucas (who had made recordings with A.L. Lloyd for Topic) and, later, Black American vocalist Dorris Henderson (a one-time musical partner of John Renbourn) in the process. The Strawbs (Dave Cousins, Tony Hooper, Arthur Philips, Ron Chesterman) also came together that year. They were previously a bluegrass outfit (the Strawberry Hill Boys) but began to experiment with a kind of 'progressive Byrds' sound, briefly attracting by 1967 a musically discontented Sandy Denny – probably the foremost female folk singer in the south of England – along the way.

However, it is the formation of the aforementioned Fairport Convention, which also came together in 1967, that is of the greatest interest here. At this early stage the group consisted of Ashley Hutchings, Judy Dyble, Martin Lamble, Ian Matthews, Simon Nicol and Richard Thompson. Typically, blues, jug band and US West Coast music heavily influenced Fairport Convention. Even the line-up of West Coast band Jefferson Airplane (female vocalist, male band) was highly influential. Via demos supplied by their young American manager Joe Boyd, Fairport were familiar with the songwriting talents of the then little-known US folkies and folk-rockers Joni Mitchell, Emmitt Rhodes and Richard Farina. It could be said, in fact, that the group was born out of an unswerving attempt to emulate heroes.

By the spring of 1967 Fairport Convention were a regular attraction at the most significant underground rock venues in London – the UFO and Middle Earth clubs. After an interesting debut album for Polydor, singer Judy Dyble departed and it was then that Fairport scored a major coup by recruiting to their ranks the darling of the London folk scene, Sandy Denny. Denny, by this time, was attempting to sing and write her way out of what she saw as an unadventurous folk scene and had already recorded a demo of her celebrated song 'Who Knows Where the Time Goes' with the Strawbs in 1968.

Naturally, Denny brought a more folk-oriented approach with her, and the subsequent album *What We Did on Our Holidays* (Island Records ILPS 9092, 1969) was hailed by the British music press as a major step forward in the band's musical development. A month before the release of their second album for

Island Records (*Unhalbricking* ISLP 9102) in 1969 the group and entourage (minus Denny) was involved in a serious motorway crash, resulting in the death of drummer Martin Lamble and the American girlfriend of guitarist Richard Thompson, Jeannie Franklin.

To survive this tragedy as a musical group was, alone, a major achievement, but they did so in such a way as to re-evaluate themselves as individuals and artists. This course of action initially included Fairport recruiting two new members from equally diverse backgrounds. Firstly, Dave Mattacks was brought in as a replacement drummer. Mattacks was essentially a session player with little or no knowledge of folk music. Secondly, the group caused yet another shock to the folk scene by recruiting Dave Swarbrick, erstwhile fiddler in the Ian Campbell Group and performing partner of Martin Carthy. Swarbrick (actually a devoted jazz fan) was a renowned interpreter of traditional material and he played with Fairport Convention initially as a session player but then, impressed by the direction of the group and the guitar playing of Richard Thompson, he agreed to become a permanent member.

Liege and Lief

It is worth a historical reminder that, by the time of the release of *Liege and Lief*, the group had recorded four LPs in a period of a little over 12 months. Not only was this a truly remarkable achievement for any young rock band, but also in the light of the motorway crash that almost ruined the group, together with the fact that we have the genesis of a new genre of rock music, these events are of considerable historical and artistic magnitude. Fairport Convention's fourth album, *Liege and Lief* (Island Records ILPS 9115, 1969), was therefore a key historical moment. It represented a point at which apparent disparities in musical practices and sensibilities began to flow together.

Liege and Lief was a mobile and shifting investigation into the possibilities opened up by preceding folk and rock models. The album was pieced together at the old Queen Anne rectory at Farley Chamberlayne, near Winchester, for three months in the summer of 1969. But it was a project certainly outside the logic of planning to any great extent. The important point is that this aesthetic in creation opened up a passage to hitherto uncharted musical territory.

The Fairport Convention of that summer was a group of musical risk-takers in the real artistic sense of the word. The album is a classic example of a micro-event that starts from the inside and develops, almost organically, into a historical landmark. Like many great works of art, its invention, therefore, was not explicit or obvious to many at the time of its release. The originality of *Liege and Lief* consisted in bringing forth the disparate emotional, cultural and conceptual latencies that were condensed during the band meetings in Farley Chamberlayne and creating, in the process, a musical and social climate within which it became acceptable to perform folk music in a rock context and even (for some) rock music in a folk context – no mean achievement!

The phrase 'getting it all together in the country' has been part of most music journalists' stock-in-trade of cynical remarks since the 1970s, but this idea has actually led to a number of popular music successes (*Led Zeppelin 4* and the first two Barclay James Harvest albums are two such examples), and the physical displacement of artists can bring about the pleasure, pain, joy and anxiety, respect and melancholy such as existed at Farley Chamberlayne. In this particular chain of events, elements of the sublime came to be at work. As a consequence, we can acknowledge *Liege and Lief* as great art – but it remains a project that the British folk revival cannot directly lay claims to.

Liege and Lief now sits as an image of the solidification of numerous currents, as an agent of innumerable factors that guide the creative impulse and, in doing so, stands as a true piece of folk music. The album also became the template for future work – some fascinating, some less interesting. The artists became vehicles for a certain sensibility, leading to future mutation. This, in its ultimate persistence, is how great popular music works. It might be part of the standardisation process of modern society but never submits itself to that standardisation. Popular music, and in this case folk-rock, responds to the requirements of unrepeatable chance, because, despite the end-result being a 'product', the relationship between the artists and the musical means of expression is actually unrepeatable (and takes place in non-repeatable historical circumstances).

The music on *Liege and Lief* remains very questioning, especially in the juxtaposition of 'traditional' and 'contemporary' material. How could a young music lover actually tell the difference between the traditional 'Matty Groves' and the contemporary 'Come All Ye'? or between the contemporary 'Crazy Man Michael' and the traditional 'Tam Lin'? The answer, quite clearly, was that he or she couldn't; and more to the point, it didn't really matter. And so *Liege and Lief*, and the listeners to the same, gloried in that very muddle. The ultimate questions raised by this amazing recording – as important, in its own way, as *Sgt. Pepper* – are evident: why should it be true that what comes later is less valuable than what comes before? What entitles a sort of centrality in music to be more important than the peripheral?

Fairport Convention questioned the presupposition that a copy is secondary to the original and is somehow less valuable. This seminal record does not leave one with the impression that differences ought to be subsumed in a folk category of undifferentiation where a thematic sameness survives. This is often an unfair criticism that rings from within the folk revival. The album affirms that difference and contradictions can be allowed space to stand freely within a loose framework, which acknowledges both the centre and the divergencies and has the potential to reverse both. All music signifies other music, commenting on other performances and other styles along the way. The key to the appreciation of folk-rock lies in the acknowledgement of how it can draw our attention to other forms through its very resonance. That is the very principle on which *Liege and Lief* stands.

Consequences

Fairport Convention were (are) not only a testimony to an era of musical ideas and idealism but an embodiment of critique: they captured our attention through extending and elaborating on previously created themes while, at the same time, illustrating deep significances in the work of both the folk revival and rock music. Attention was drawn to the responsibilities on the shoulders of the revival: had it succeeded up to that point? had it actually captured our imagination as a nation or posited musicology in a museum? Indeed, *Liege and Lief* implied that folk music could never be simply an object, but was a cultural negotiation, overlaid with the values of a specific historical context and in need of continual arbitration to understand and/or modify the values on offer.

The cultural stratification of the folk movement in the 1960s was thus challenged by an effort to rethink historical 'authenticity'. Folk purists might have 'screamed with anguish';[10] but folk-rock was a soundtrack that moved beyond the somewhat mechanistic cause-and-effect theories of the folk hierarchy. In a 1969 interview in *Disc & Music Echo*, Fairport Convention's Simon Nicol attempted to explain what they were trying to achieve on *Liege and Lief*:

> When it comes down to folk, it's still a form of music that's very alive, but has always been restricted. The songs exist in libraries and in folk clubs, but the people who play in folk clubs, and the people who go to listen, never advance. It's always been the same people singing the same songs to the same audience. A kind of innate snobbery … I'm sure the kids are completely unaware of their heritage. I count myself among the kids, because I was reared on music that was always a distillation of American influences. We feel the time is right to bring the music out – getting away from the blues scale and introducing something completely new. All the folk songs have reached a very pure form by now – a kind of sorting the wheat from the chaff. And there are some fantastic songs about. I mean there's nothing like a good murder ballad to get them going![11]

Fittingly, perhaps (even before *Liege and Lief* was in the shops), the group began to fracture and two members ('leader' Ashley Hutchings and 'leading lady' Sandy Denny) left in November 1969, as if to confirm that the group representation in itself was also open to fracture. Denny went on to form Fotheringay and then record a succession of albums which also place the later work of Mary Black (ex-DeDannan) into a similar important historical context: that of a graduated musical move away from conventional wisdom about tradition. Sadly, Sandy's career was marred by inveterate alcohol abuse, although she rejoined the group for 12 months before finally leaving in 1974; she tragically died from an accidental fall in 1978.

However, even the fractured Fairport Convention paved the way for add-ons to their cultural dimension, haunting and contradicting the folk purists along the way. Ashley Hutchings initially formed Steeleye Span. This second aggregation included Andy Irvine, Johnny Moynihan and Terry Woods from Sweeney's Men along with Terry's wife Gay. Moynihan and Irvine were early casualties and were replaced by another highly respected folk duo, Tim Hart and Maddy Prior. This line-up recorded *Hark, the Village Wait* (RCA SF8113) in 1970 in an attempt to take electric folk music off in a different direction from Fairport Convention. The shared vocals of Gay Woods and Maddy Prior alone are astounding on this album, never mind the fascinating selection of material. Later that year the equally celebrated folkie Martin Carthy was persuaded to plug in with this crossbreed.

Hutchings's musical wanderlust in the 'garden of England' led to his own departure in 1972 but not before Steeleye Span had become the highest profile purveyors of folk-rock by extensive touring on the rock circuit. While exploring an increasingly distinctive sound, the group was still able to create a fascinating and highly original version of Buddy Holly's rock 'n' roll classic, 'Rave On' (B&C CB164, 1971), thus keeping alive the mosaic of forms. Their tour de force was undoubtedly *Please to See the King* (B&C CAS 1029, 1971). This album attempted to take popular music into further unexplored areas by amalgamating various musical traditions with an electric melange of sound without a kit drum. All the tracks were 'traditional' in the accepted sense of the word, but the group effectively rewrote each song in that search for the removal of the hermetically sealed, bounded domain of the folk revival.

As a result, their sound – augmented by Tim Hart's electric dulcimer – was utterly unique. The almost heavy metal sound on the traditional 'Lovely on the Water' remains, to this day, a model for critical engagement with musical pigeonholes. In an interview with Hinton and Wall, Ashley Hutchings stated: 'If we don't muck around with these things and sing them, and bring them into the vernacular, they will die. Or they'll freeze, which is equally as bad.' Martin Carthy concurred with Hutchings: 'I don't mind it dying if you're the only person who knows the song, and you die, that's tough! If you freeze the fucker – I could kill you!'[12]

Fairport's *Liege and Lief* was a musical time bomb and turned the folk scene inside out. It also had an undoubted effect on the rock scene of that period, but with only the remains of a band to promote it, the album quickly became an Island back catalogue number recommended for investigation. *Please to See the King*, however, had an arguably greater residual effect on rock. Steeleye Span toured extensively on the back of the album (not always happily, it must be said) – particularly with Jethro Tull – and the two bands cut quite a dash together in concert. As an experienced rock band, 'Tull' were influential in tightening up Steeleye Span's rather loose, 'folkie' stage sound and presence; the work of 'Steeleye', on the other hand, was highly important to the songwriting of Tull's

Ian Anderson (and, according to certain sources, that of David Bowie). Jethro Tull, in fact, became something of an occasional folk-rock band themselves in later years.

Upon his departure from Steeleye Span in 1972 Hutchings founded (rather than formed) the Albion (Country) Band project for his future experiments to amalgamate English folk and rock music. Rather like Fairport Convention, the 'Albion' bands have involved too many changes to constitute one permanent identity. Early members included Shirley Collins, Royston Woods, Dave Mattacks and Simon Nicol, and re-formations have included Richard and Linda Thompson, Martin Carthy, John Kirkpatrick and Sue Harris. But perhaps the greatest influence on the Albion projects has been from John Tams, formerly of the Midlands folk group Muckram Wakes. Tams, Rick Sanders (ex-Soft Machine) and Graeme Taylor (ex-Gryphon) were members of the Albion Band that recorded *Rise up like the Sun* (Harvest SHSP 4092) in 1978 – this album, like *Liege and Lief* and *Please to See the King* before it, established the possibility for others to follow in the pursuit of an English folk-rock aesthetic.

Rise up like the Sun was another fine example of how the monolithic ideas of the folk revival could be presented but also *re*-presented; concentrated but also *de*-concentrated. But, importantly, the album also appeared at an interesting moment in the history of popular music. Punk rock had challenged all of the progressive concepts abounding in the 'post-Pepper' period of 1967–74, but was itself also levelling out (1978). Punk soon discovered that as it, too, was grounded as a critical practice. Existing within rock, its soundtrack of resistance was also subject to an encircled discourse. The biographer of Ralph McTell, Chris Hockenhull, discussed this period with me:

> To be honest, I felt that the punk thing was rather disingenuous. It takes a long time for an artist to develop, hone his/her craft. Songwriting and the kind of fusions that Fairport were attempting to achieve were organic processes ... not something that could be written off with the waggle of two fingers in the air. It was inevitable to me that punk lasted only a brief time whereas the Albion Band and Fairport soldiered on and kept folk-rock firmly in the driving seat. *Rise up like the Sun* was like a beacon in the dark in that respect.[13]

What was at stake in this late 1970s debate was the issue of popular music gravitating towards commodity; that, in a period of vast urban decay and (conversely) Lear jets for rock stars, the conventional rock scene was merely feeding the media society with gratuitous images rather than proffering, as rock had claimed, a creative canvas. It was certainly true that the rock scene from which Fairport and the like had arisen could no longer be simplistically identified as liberating, in part because of the domination of mass culture by the media industry and in part because the trajectory of modernisation had brought us to the threshold of self-destruction, as represented by the 'winter of discontent'. John Savage:

Warner Brothers' 1970 success with the cross-media marketing of the chaotic Woodstock festival set the pattern which would emerge during the 1970s: 'It was the beginning of the end', says Country Joe McDonald, a Woodstock star, 'the music industry learned to market million upon million of records by safe hippie groups.' The true beneficiaries of this process were not the first blazing hippies – like Country Joe and the Fish – but survivors like the Rolling Stones, Paul McCartney and Wings, the Californian school of cocaine country-rockers like the Eagles and Linda Ronstadt, or soft-poppers like Peter Frampton. The whole process was brought to its height by Fleetwood Mac, whose Rumours stayed at number one for thirty-one weeks in 1977 with sales of 7 million.[14]

Folk music, too, was seen by many young people of the late seventies as an artistic cul-de-sac, its initial utopian promise having been overrun by dogma. In fact, punk signalled (perhaps for the first time since the advent of the post-WW II revival) a period when the revival failed to recruit – en masse – a generation of young people. Geoff Davies of the pioneering independent Probe Records told me:

> We saw it coming at Probe. We sold plenty of folk music between 1970 and 1975 – it was part of the underground, in a way; but after that sales died. We had our regulars but the kids weren't into it at all. One minute it was the height of underground, the next they thought it was a load of irrelevant pretentious crap.[15]

Curiously, however, by adopting a kind of arrière-garde position that distanced itself from both rock and folk myths of progress(ive rock) and from punk's reactionary unrealistic impulse to return to the primordial popular music past, the Albion Band's *Rise up like the Sun* was an entirely appropriate record for its era. This seminal album was yet another stepping stone for folk-rock in that it refused to regress into nostalgic historicism – which the folk scene had done during the 1970s (with particular emphasis on the myth of the 'Celt') and which certain elements of punk were about to follow with their own 'Mod' revival. The traditional song 'Poor Old Horse', for example, was a reflection on some kind of tradition but was also a critique of 1970s Britain. As a cultural stratagem, Ashley Hutchings and John Tams were able further to deconstruct music genres as bounded domains – as one listen to 'Afro Blue'/'Danse Royale' and 'Ampleforth'/'Lay Me Low' from the album clearly shows. It is no coincidence that the finest Albion Band performance witnessed by this writer was in 1978 at Eric's Club in Mathew Street, Liverpool, ostensibly the 'home' of punk!

Carrying the baton

Many bands have followed the Fairport/Steeleye/Albion axis but only a few have achieved national success. The Pogues were formed out of the Nips (short for Nipple Erectors) around 1982. They occasionally supported the Clash and, in

1984, signed to Stiff Records. At various times the Pogues included figures from both the folk-rock scene of the early 1970s (Terry Woods) and the punk movement of the late 1970s (the early band was a punk outfit and leader Shane McGowan was later briefly replaced by Joe Strummer of the Clash in 1991–92) and for a while displayed a great deal of promise.

However, while the Pogues delighted the young with their rebellious approach – almost single-handedly recontextualising the sound and status of the ceilidh (these days more wedding parties book ceilidh bands than discos) they also let slip a great opportunity to continue the folk-rock dialectic. Despite the occasional presence of venerated producer Steve Lillywhite (*If I should Fall from Grace with God* WEA WX243, 1988), they made rather ramshackle recordings (in one small paragraph the *Music Hound Folk Album Guide* (1998) uses the words 'clumsy' and 'rag tag'[16]) and allowed their off-stage antics to upstage their music. Their descent into 1990s chaos remains an unsatisfactory chronicle.

The Oyster Band, on the other hand, developed out of possibly one of Britain's worst-ever folk groups. Fiddler's Dram were a group of Steeleye Span soundalikes, 'one-hit wonders' with little to commend them. Their freak hit single 'Day Trip to Bangor' (no. 3, December 1979) shot them to brief but rather uneventful fame and their first album represented a well-worn repertoire (songs such as 'Peel the Tatties', 'Two Brothers' and 'False Knight on the Road' graced *To See the Play* [Dingle's DIN 304 1979]).

Vocalist Cathy LeSurf left for the Albion Band in 1980 and the remaining musicians – Ian Telfer, John Jones, Alan Prosser and Ian Keary – adopted the name the Oyster Ceilidh Band. This was later shortened to the Oyster Band (occasionally the Oysterband) as the group moved in a folk-rock direction. Despite all of the folk-rock activity over the previous 10 years or so, this was still an unusual move for dyed-in-the-wool folkies to make (that other folk miscreant June Tabor has also been an occasional vocalist).

The Oyster Band's musical development during the late 1980s and early 1990s is worthy of note. For example, their sound became decidedly harder once they signed to the folk-rock/indie label Cooking Vinyl in 1986. The 1987 album *Wild Blue Yonder* was certainly more disjointed than previous releases and, by 1990, the album *Little Rock to Leipzig* even contained a very furious country rock version of the Bobby Fuller Four sixties garage 'classic' (and also latterly recorded by the Clash) 'I Fought the Law' while also accommodating a very moving unaccompanied lament for the British miners, 'Coal not Dole'.

By 1995 they were moving even further into what some commentators described as 'indie rock' with their album *Holy Bandits*, something that would have been considered anathema even to the most hardened folk-rocker in the late 1970s and early 1980s – at least until the arrival of the aforementioned former friend of the Sex Pistols, Shane McGowan, and the Pogues. And yet they continued to play traditional material and draw attention towards their inspirational sources. Their reputation as a folk festival band par excellence has now grown to such a level that they are considered to be amongst the elite of the folk-influenced acts currently performing in the British Isles. An approving 1993 review of the album *Deserters* described the group as 'The Levellers after a good bath' and now no reviews contain any references to their earlier folk incarnation as Fiddler's Dram. A real reverse legacy of Fairport Convention, one might say. In an interview with *Rock 'n' Reel* in 1994 John James of the band stated 'I've always thought this music, "roots", "folk", call it what you like, should stand alongside the hardest rock music.'

Assimilation

But we need to understand that the Oyster Band has also enjoyed osmosis of its sound by folkies. The musical identity of the group and the responses from the folk revival to that identity have modified over the passage of time. Abandonment of the myth of authenticity leads to a proliferation of discursive musical interventions and arguments. One night even argue that their kind of rock has now been assimilated into an aural mainstream, enough for a large section of folk fans to understand and buy it. The dissolution of the myth of authenticity releases not only emancipatory possibilities but also the possibility of cultural assimilation. Niall MacKinnon concludes his work by suggesting as much:

> One of the reasons for the extraordinary success of rock music is that its ideological attachment to 'newness' means that it could readily utilise new sound potentialities and use this to restructure musical communication, in essence rock music evolving through and via the development of sound technology. However, just as this 'newness' can be equated with 'that which is modern and fresh', so this contains within it an essential periodicity. The symbolic function of electronic sound as an emblem of modernity has already waned and as it loses this connotation, when the musical meaning of electronic sound does not mean the negation of other forms of musical communication, then I suspect we will see the integration of the potentialities of electronic music-making within other genres. I believe this is true of the folk scene today and, in consequence, we may even see a 'reverse newness'.[17]

By the late 1990s the folk and rock worlds had long established their own institutions. Thus, the previously unstable relationships between folk and rock music had acquired canonic tendencies: whereas in previous eras folk-rock was part of a striving to become part of a recognised musical discourse, by the turn of the millennium it was providing a context. MacKinnon's 'integration' is actually an important feature of all popular music history.

MacKinnon's final sentence of *The British Folk Scene* is also revealing. He circumscribes the folk world's social status by acknowledging that 'perhaps the folkies have found their niche as the reluctant bourgeois of contemporary popular culture'.[18] If this is the case, perhaps the historical underlying impulse of folk-rock music – to undermine the status quo – is spent!

Certainly, that particularly postmodern form contemporary dance music (which distinguishes itself for some as existing outside of rock's canon) operates for some folk music artists as an aural and social discourse in much the same way as Fairport and Steeleye Span once did. Indeed, some of the most interesting folk music of the past few years – the Afro-Celt Sound System, Paul Mounsey, Eliza Carthy, Talitha McKenzie, Shooglenifty, etc. – has come from this sector, integrating (as MacKinnon suggests) 'the potentialities of electronic music-making' with folk music.

So, maybe any musical output, once metered by a historical idealised performance model, can result in being rather stylised – having to conform to certain culturally incorporated traditional prerequisites. Folk's classifications dictate that both the performance and the music have to conform to a certain relationship with the invented historical folk (and now folk-rock) community – a process of cultural assimilation. What once were musical vices eventually become habits – or traditions, if you like. Thus perhaps folk-rock of the Oyster Band variety (a 30-year-old folk-rock hybrid, after all) is a convenient pseudo-oppositional soundtrack to hide behind. Rock guitarist Steve Hillage:

> It's been going for 30 years without any really major change, and it can't change its sound. It is how it is. Like it or not, the house or techno end of things is now where all the radical, progressive and revolutionary ideas are. It's just the way it is. It's unfortunate, but rock music is not the same sort of experimental force it used to be and, as a guitar player, I've found a new forum for that sort of invention.[19]

What next? Who knows!

Fairport have always celebrated their ability to transcend conventional wisdom and expectations. The 1980 reunion from which the Cropredy Festival sprang was such a success that it was decided to keep it on a regular basis. The band's fan base was not at that stage sufficient to keep the group surviving for 12 months of the year. The Cropredy celebrations duly exceeded all expectations as an event and led to the Fairports not only holding their own very public party, but also having their own marketing, recording and reissue conduit nearby at Woodworm Studios. This enterprise had developed by the twenty-first century into a sizable venture somewhat removed from its beginnings as a small, cosy, folk-related enclave. The historical example of Fairport Convention displays to us that all music exists in a polymorphous state and an essential ingredient of popular music is its ability to change.

Musical roots indicate where popular styles have been and are most vital when one recontextualises them, rather than holding them up as an untouchable icon. Fairport and the Oyster Band are no longer on the cutting edge (whatever that is) of popular music, but they do represent a break with the formalised perceptions of a performing past – even if their model has now been culturally assimilated into the British folk revival. This leaves the groups as not only spokespersons for attacks on musical traditions, but also as ironical advocates of 'becoming' rather than simply pausing at 'being', the fun that comes from the invention of new rules.

Perhaps, we can even draw a comparison between these bands' treatment of folk music and the iconoclastic reactions of late-seventies Punk: placing the unpresentable in live performance, denying the 'enlightened' versions of folk via the usual prevailing themes of 'good taste', ignoring shared romantic nostalgia. Fairport Convention did not simply 'borrow' 'Matty Groves'. They transformed it, used it rhetorically and figuratively. They were able to show great respect for concepts about 'tradition', but also goad and poke fun at those concepts. They showed both reverence and irreverence towards previously agreed musical conclusions and values.

So, despite their relative acceptance as folk icons (in fact in ironic facsimile of it) these folk-rock bands discussed above (and others, too) still proceed to 'invent' tradition even if, perhaps, the rock music that they use may no longer be at the forefront of popular music development. The straightforwardness of their approach to folk-rock has helped to simplify and release apparently fixed relationships between 'authentic' tradition and popular music. They demonstrate that music created out of the folk 'legacy' involves conscious artifice – which can also be described as future tradition! And, as young folk-rock performer Vera Dalcis reminded *Folk Roots* in 1995: 'Folk-rock is an accessible form that attracts young audiences … which is what folk music needs to survive. Martin Carthy says he would like to hear young people playing folk music … we are … you're not listening.'[20]

Perhaps the amalgam of folk-rock reveals that the aura of authenticity can be exorcised. What on earth *is* authentic, in any case? Fintan O'Toole:

> Tourism, anyway, makes it very hard to remember what is authentic in the first place. Some years ago I went for a drink in the 'Irish' pub in the basement of the Europa Centre in Berlin. The place was expensively decorated with authentic Irish road signs, shop fronts and post boxes. On a low stage was a trio of musicians playing Irish folk tunes. Two of them were execrable, playing out of tune, and occasionally dancing on the table with gyrations that owed more to Zorba the Greek than the Man of Aran. The third, the banjo player, was terrific … quiet, serious, with an unmistakable feel for the authentic pulse of the music.
>
> I analysed the situation instantly: two German chancers had teamed up with one genuine Irish traditional musician. When they finished playing, I went up to the banjo player to sympathise and let him know that although the burghers of Berlin couldn't tell the difference between his authenticity and the awful antics of his companions, I could. He looked at me with hurt in his eyes. As it turned out, he was Austrian, and the two chancers were from County Roscommon. He loved Irish music very deeply and considered it a great privilege to be allowed to play with two native and authentic masters of the form.
>
> I resolved there and then that if I ever wrote a best seller and made enough money to buy a pub in the West of Ireland, I would hire only Austrians to play Irish traditional music for my American tourists.[21]

And so say all of us. Musical conservatism, however, remains strong in the folk revival because it is both a methodology and an ideology that wishes to turn us towards an idealised past. But the implication that music is 'authentic' effectively isolates the text. All music is fluid. It exists by anticipating the potential of the next phase, not by reflecting in its entirety on the 'once was' – which, historically, is usually the 'never been'!

Notes

1. Baudrillard, *The Evil Demons of Images*, pp. 28–31; p. 33.
2. Heywood, 'Editorial', *The Living Tradition* (1994), p. 3.
3. Martin Swan, a Sheffield-born Scot, and Talitha McKenzie, an American, formed Mouth Music. They debuted in 1990 with a fusion of Gaelic vocals, African percussion and synthesisers. An EP *Blue Door, Green Sea* followed in 1992. *Mo-Di* (1993) followed and unveiled moves towards dance music. Talitha McKenzie departed and is now a solo artist (e.g. *Solas*, Riverboat Records TUGCD 1007, 1993). Jackie Joyce replaced McKenzie.
4. Interview with Dave Swarbrick, Chester, 1995. Patrick Humphries (1982) relates a similar tale in *Meet on the Ledge*, London: Eel Pie.
5. Ridgeway, 'Folk Rock', pp. 16–17.
6. Freeman, 'Freeman in the Fray' (1995), p. 9.
7. Marwick, *The Sixties*, p. 316.
8. Stump, *The Music's all that Matters*, p. 149.
9. R. Thompson (1968) to *Beat Instrumental*, August, in Hinton and Wall, *Ashley Hutchings*, p. 71.
10. Phillips, *Music Master Folk Music of the British Isles Catalogue Edition 1*, p. F1.
11. S. Nicol (1969), to *Disc & Music Echo*, in Humphries, *Meet on the Ledge*, p. 49.
12. Hinton and Wall, *Ashley Hutchings*, p. 168.
13. Interview with Chris Hockenhull, November 2001.
14. Savage, *England's Dreaming*, p. 434.
15. Interview with Geoff Davies of Probe Plus, November 2001.
16. Walters and Mansfield (eds), *Music Hound Folk*, p. 640.
17. MacKinnon, *The British Folk Scene*, p. 133.
18. Ibid., p. 137.
19. S. Hillage to Tim Barr, in Barr, 'Guitars and Dance', p. 25.
20. Dalcis, 'Homeless Folk Rock', pp. 113–14.
21. F. O'Toole, 'The Authentic Irish Tradition of Impersonating Elvis'.

Chapter 7
Rituals of retreat: folk clubs, connoisseurs, hierarchies

I remember taking Font Watling [the Suffolk step dancer] to a folk club, we sat there in rows of chairs, and he turned round to me and said, 'This is like a Chapel'. And it is ... sitting there for three hours in total silence, accepting what's on. The 1970s template for a folk club ... is maybe not the way forward.

Ian A. Anderson, in *Folk Roots*, 136 (Oct. 1994), p. 29

The 1950s and 1960s ushered in new eras in the history of British popular music. Many young people were desperately seeking answers to sociological questions. Much of the roots of the conflict ideology of the folk revival during these years can be traced to Karl Marx. The conflict perspective adopted by many folk music lovers included a view of society as being composed of diverse groups who had conflicting values and interests. It was believed that nothing unites a group more strongly than a common enemy. Capitalism, and within capitalism the popular music industry, was seen as living proof of the unequal distribution of power.

By the 1970s, these conflict philosophies were gradually replaced by a growing attention to micro-level social processes, personal meaningful symbols and an examination of definitions and redefinitions of interactions with each other. In the folk scene of the 1970s the rallying calls from the likes of the Workers' Music Association appeared dated (Topic Records severed all connections with the WMA by 1978) and a great deal of the music was of a 'looking glass self' style with far greater emphasis on a kind of dramaturgical analysis.

Performers such as Dick Gaughan, Keith Christmas and Vinny Garbutt all expressed deeply held personal beliefs. The music press (especially the *Melody Maker*) described their like as 'singer/songwriters' rather than 'folk singers' (by now a rather archaic term). Singer/songwriters such as Cat Stevens, John Martyn, Al Stewart, Clifford T. Ward and Nick Drake became (and remain to this day) admired for levels of introspection hitherto unseen since the early days of the Blues.

The remains of the 1960s counterculture popularised the idea that young people were now victims unable to cope with the strains of everyday existence. An image of vulnerability was thus explored by singer/songwriters. Folk's collective identities were stitched into much of this, but there was also a discernable degree of disengagement. The celebration of alienation and 'bed-sitter images' (actually the title of an Al Stewart song) contributed to a social and cultural retreat from the here and now. It could be argued that the 1970s brought about the seeds of New Age-ism in both rock and folk music.

The folk style certainly became associated less with overt politicising, and more with agency for cultural change on a personal level. For example, by 1972 this proclamation graced the dust jacket of *Songs of the Midlands*, edited by EFDSS member Roy Palmer:

> Can the generation gap be bridged? Is society now nearer to being classless than ever it was? Is there a setting in which race colour and creed can become less immiscible than behind the cherty partitions that our newspapers tend daily to buttress than demolish? If the answer to these questions is yes, then a not too gracile portion of the credit belongs to an element that is attaining the proportions of a sociological phenomenon: the folk music revival.[1]

However, Palmer's 'New Agey' optimism was but one end of a social continuum that also shaped a level of relativism and pessimism. Introspection bred alienation and alienation produced sobering observations. Dissenting voices began to question assumptions concerning folk music as a cultural power for change. Renowned performer (and latterly EFDSS committee member) Dave Arthur in his review of the aforementioned work remarked:

> So begins the publishers blurb on the back of Roy Palmer's collection, propounding the myth that we live on the brink of a classless, religiously tolerant and non-racialist society ... If as suggested folk music has affected, or is capable of affecting, the social, political, economic and religious climate of this country, it is being very secretive about its progress. I can't remember the last time I saw a black face in a folk club.[2]

And by 1976 Bob Pegg – performer, writer, and erstwhile leader of the pioneering folk-rock group Mr Fox – had also confirmed that, for him, folk music was:

> an illusion created unconsciously by the people who talk about it, go out looking for it, make collections of it, write books about it, and announce to an audience that they are going to sing it or play it. It is rather like a mirage which changes according to the social and cultural standpoint of whoever is looking at it.[3]

In fact, by 1984 singer/songwriter Dick Gaughan had informed Mark Moss and Judy Weglarski of *Sing Out!* (the US folk song journal) of his growing dissatisfaction with the revival's conventional wisdom:

> I don't agree with the predominant definition of what folk music is because I think it's too narrow. There's a growth of antiquarianism in folk music, where folk music is the music of the past, and it therefore has to be performed exactly the way it was in the past ... I have a great respect and love for the whole process of tradition, but I do not think that it is sacred. I do think that we have to constantly develop the music and play it as we feel, with all the influences that we have ... to

say that we must preserve it for all time the way it was played hundreds of years ago is like collecting stamps.[4]

Arthur ('secretive'), Pegg ('mirage'), and Gaughan ('collecting stamps') were referring to a significant characteristic of the 1970s folk revival – that of the esoteric introverted connoisseur. It is to this connoisseur, his/her social echelon and habitat to which we must now turn. The word connoisseur is not common parlance within the folk revival; however, those with a depth of knowledge about canons certainly created hierarchies that still remain to this day. The folk revival of the 1960s partly achieved its goals via the accumulation of detail, but by the 1970s it was also responsible for unyielding echelons – particularly within the ubiquitous folk club.

The connoisseur

A connoisseur can display great knowledge and can be regarded as an expert judge in matters of taste but this is often manifested as a preference for a limited domain, dealing with systematic exclusion as well as inclusion. All knowledge can be hierarchically useful in one way or another by creating and reinforcing echelons. Yet, any mapping of musical performance via history inevitably faces disassociated histories and disassociated views from without. Music has its own ways of creating new values and can be absorbed and reused through time and geographical space; it is not buried in local lifestyles for ever, even if it may have originated there. To the connoisseur, however, such a broad church is not always agreeable, for thematic specialisation is intrinsic to the discipline.

The connoisseur seldom embraces historical complications. He/she stands in judgement and guarantees folk music a distinct and identifiable place in a museum via stylistic analyses. To authenticate folk music in this way requires all of the machinery of the antiquarian, which includes both rhetoric and the subjectivisation of history. Antiquarians convert chance moments of performance into 'historically based' connoisseurship.

According to the above comments of Arthur, Pegg and Gaughan the political/ antiquarian interpretations of (e.g.) Bert Lloyd and Ewan MacColl were coming under pressure from a variety of differing sources. In fact, Dave Arthur further stated in 1973 (perhaps with some degree of exasperation):

> The folk music revival in this country seems to have been built and fostered on misconceptions. For a start it was not started, or perpetuated, by the working classes, who to this day are blissfully unaware of its existence. It would appear to be the product of left wing intellectuals who somehow lost control of things when it was taken up by the young middle class intelligentsia, grammar school boys, university graduates, teachers and the like. The movement rather than breaking

down barriers has set up a whole load of its own, with the conventions upheld by romantic idealists, and pedants, of which the revival has more than its fair share.[5]

Strong words, indeed, from one of the revival's most active performers and writers of the early 1970s. So, what had happened to the folk scene in the short period between the end of the optimistic 1960s and the derelict mid-1970s? Why was the folk scene of the 1970s so introverted?

By 1970 it could be stated with some justification that the revival had triumphed. Folk music performance styles were accurately regarded as significant: an intrinsic part of our culture. But British society and culture was also experiencing further radical change. By focusing upon the private, the idea emerged that one could, like a child, also find a refuge in the confidential (and privileged). This resulted in abdication – which was also unproblematic when one had relocated to the suburbs. Despite the undeniable effects of the counterculture, during 1970 there was a substantial shift in the living patterns of many of this country's young bourgeois. Countless numbers withdrew from urban living into their private spheres within Britain's new suburban landscapes. Undeniably, many folk adherents were drawn from this 'graduate' sector of society (the lecturer and teacher, the social worker, the local government official) and they proceeded to reinvent the folk revival as a playful abstraction, a representation of cultural autonomy for childlike suburban retreatists. Jeff Nuttall noted that: 'Naivety was equated with honesty, ineptitude was equated with sincerity, and merit was gauged in terms of proximity to the animal and the vegetable.'[6]

Peter York also bore witness to this dearth of ideas, recalling a period he ironically branded 'babytime': 'a magic time when thousands of adult, sane, bourgeois men and women aspired to Babyhood. The man with the child in his eyes, Kickers on his feet and dungarees round the rest, walked the land.'[7] Thus the folk club became both a nether world and a power-base for those who had profited from their own social and economic circumstances over the previous decade. The British folk revival turned away from the last vestiges of collective association and towards a 'childlike' antiquarian connoisseurship – like collecting stamps or football programmes (a few even embraced religion via assemblages such as Fisher Folk).

This diminution was typical of the early 1970s trade-off between the alienated sensibility and collective action. Most folk club-goers chose the former while pontificating about the latter and, in doing so, unwittingly enforced one of the great socio-musical U-turns of the post-World War II era. The meaning of folk music within the British folk club came to 'belong' to a cultural hierarchy of those who sought refuge in the self and an intellectualised echelon of antiquarian connoisseurs – a folk ruling class. The musical value-word that became most associated with this phase of the folk revival was 'tradition'. This word became an encapsulating get-out clause for any debate about the future social role of the revival, and the whiff of snobbery on the part of initiates towards the uninitiated knew few bounds (certainly the only feature of the folk *club* scene that was not restricted by the word 'tradition' was conceit). By 1976, this had the effect of turning an almost entire generation of young people away from the folk scene.

Folk clubs – 'beating the retreat'?

By 1993, Niall MacKinnon was stating that, for him, the expression 'folk scene' was intrinsically connected with that of 'folk club'.[8] This has a certain historical logic, for during the 1970s the folk club came to view itself as the backbone of the British folk revival. During the mid-1960s it was estimated by the EFDSS that there were upwards of 300 folk clubs in Britain; by the mid-1970s that figure had quadrupled – a massive power base.

But Georgina Boyes, also writing in 1993, questioned this command structure:

> Through the later 1960s and into the 1970s [folk clubs] became a way of life – a major source of a Revival subculture … in pursuit of more authentic traditional material club members researched and photographed and taped … The movement had never been as widespread and active. But for all its apparent innovation and variety, the Revival was hidebound by historical theory. Determinedly reproducing a policy of authenticity … The Folk Revival had succeeded … but unless its fundamental concepts of the Folk and folk culture were rejected, the movement had no possibility for development.[9]

Boyes was suggesting that, while these folk club systems appeared to establish continuity, they also endowed the folk scene with a bulwark against reality. The world of the 1970s folk club had, indeed, become increasingly intense. Skiffler and folk-clubber Mick O'Toole informed me that, for him, from the 1970s onward folk clubs became 'populated by virtuoso Luddites'. He continued:

> As I saw it, willingness to embrace change became a reluctance to witness change. An interest in the music of the past became an immersion in the images of that past. An interest in alternative music practices turned into a dogged reluctance to acknowledge stylistic and technological change – they wouldn't grow up. It was ok to immerse yourself because there was nobody around from your imagined past to argue the toss. Also, disenchantment with contemporary society had created a propensity to abdicate decision-making (in favour of e.g. a club committee)![10]

By 1989, social anthropologist Ruth Finnegan, in discussing folk music activity in Milton Keynes, was suggesting that 'understanding the folk music world can best start from some description of the folk clubs'.[11] But while Finnegan theorised that 'folksiness' was confirmed by its setting and concepts, and discussed folk activity via location, organisational membership and participation (describing the identity of a folk club as 'sometimes the most meaningful experience of their lives'), she also noted that the folk ideology she came across in Milton Keynes was a historically established amalgam put together via 'the intellectual perceptions of certain scholars and collectors'. She recorded that in the clubs she surveyed professional and higher education classes predominated: 'If any of the local music worlds could be regarded as "middle class" it would be that of folk music … those operating mainly on the folk club and folk festival circuit [were] often well educated, professional and middle-aged with few if any teenage adherents.'[12] Finnegan did not even deem the folk clubs she surveyed as constituting a 'scene' per se (preferring the ambiguous expression 'worlds', suggesting encapsulation, exclusivity and isolation). She further stated that musicians wishing to experiment were 'regarded as fringe by the more purist enthusiasts. Bands in this mode – Merlin's Isle, for example – could not always find a ready niche for their performances: not "folk" enough for the folk clubs.'[13]

Undoubtedly within every aspect of popular music one can discover distinctive lifestyles across various groups of people whose worlds are closely bound together by music. These associations are reliant on adhesives of persuasion and the attachment of labels. But it is intriguing that the suburban sleight of hand of the 1970s surrounding truisms such as 'tradition' and 'heritage' created a value framework of recidivism.

As Britain became more and more embattled as a nation throughout the 1970s, the folk club cultivated a concomitant resistant, identity-giving culture. However, this kind of approach was able to serve only a limited amount of functions because it existed, effectively, 'within itself'; one might say in a state of cultural pessimism. During the 1970s there was a great deal to be pessimistic about, of course, but ultimately folk club regulars of that era began to project into folk performances particular kinds of social and musical fantasies that gratified their 'folk' senses.

One example in my own neck of the woods was the fascination with Lancashire and Liverpool dialect singing. Artists such as Gary and Vera Aspey, Bernard Wrigley, Brian Jacques, the Oldham Tinkers, Billy Maher, Bob Williamson and the Houghton Weavers purveyed songs and poetry in 'cod' dialects that insulated the listener from the present while also supplying a cloying romantic regret for the passing of a bygone era – a classic fabrication of 'tradition'. Listeners were patronised and invited to compensate for their own lack of experience by vicarious identification with the endorsements of these artists.

By the time I was a regular at various clubs in Liverpool in the period between 1970 and 1974, I had discovered that such projections were regarded as genuine authorisations. The past was, without a doubt, *very* vivid. The problem was that it was more vivid than the present! These Liverpool folk clubs had become domesticated and semi-detached; made safe, even. Chris McKenna also remembers:

It was the same all over Liverpool. I'd been interested in folk music and went at
first to the Clubship Landfall where the Crofters were residents. It wasn't bad but
was rather 'twee'. I then went to the 2 plus 1 Club at the Centre Hotel behind
Lime Street and that was terrible. Long tables ... sitting next to people you didn't
know. You were expected to know the songs. I'd gone to see Tim Hardin, who was
great, but I went again and I could see it was a closed shop – it was like shaking
hands at the end of a Mass. If you went along expecting to hear stuff like the
Pentangle, you were disappointed![14]

Perhaps as a direct result of this state of 'social grace' folkies of the late 1980s
were, as Ruth Finnegan observed, 'only a small and select minority'. This was
not as a result of the unpopularity of the music (far from it, in fact), but because
the folk club had become part of a striving to elude broader social interaction.
Sounds, artefacts, instruments and even alcoholic liquids were edited to conform
to intellectual predispositions. Rather than reflecting the social cohesion with
which it was endowed in the 1950s and 1960s, the folk club of the 1970s to the
1990s reflected the language of musical déjà vu, even of simulacrum (the
pastiche of the stereotypical past): displaying a failure to fashion meaning out of
contemporary, heterogeneous experiences. That which appeared to be the
sustaining lifeblood of the folk scene was actually draining it of any power for
survival.

The folk club coterie of the 1970s transformed the folk revival by acting out a
fantasy of authenticity that their own time denied them. They remoulded the past
into a 'world', because the present could not be moulded to serve such desires
(after all, we have to share the present with others!). The past was malleable
because its inhabitants were no longer around to contest the manipulations; thus
their 'world' projected a historical totality. These folk categories of musical
totality would need rethinking if turned to contemporary times, but they were
able to survive intact in the folk club because they were dealing with an
internalised narrative.

As part of this process of benign recidivism, expectancy came to be especially
important in the folk club scene. One of the primary concepts behind folk listening
practices has been knowledge of historical performance givens concerning levels
of socio-musical democracy and de-staging: the song is 'carried', the performance
is de-staged. Performance was, therefore, expected to unfold within this spiritual
mode, just as it was entangled in it 'in the beginning'. The radical 1950s concept
was of unfixing performer–audience relationships. By the 1970s a model
performance was an inscription of cultural coherence and, together with a concept
of the performer as a 'specialist', incorporated abstractions surrounding the
importance of listening space (the club) and a vigilant listener/receivership (the
'folkie'). The organisation of performance space had to include the serious listeners,
for they were regarded as equal to the performer in every way.

In order to incorporate and then validate this performance/reception model,
folk clubs became self-absorbed in a passion, a certainty, that the musical

authentic could be relocated. Within folk clubs, what began as an in-built provisionality came to be regarded as an ineluctable sign. Many folkies came to appreciate 'their' music by basing their tastes on what they and their listening colleagues discerned to know already rather than what they were willing to learn – a musical cul-de-sac.

1980s, 1990s – aural hierarchies

If connoisseur listeners become torpid while remaining the most significant feature of the process, if their methodologies remain unchallenged by performers simply wishing to support the principles of the listening process, an aural hierarchy is created. A real democracy in performance may persist only if that democracy is constantly brought under pressure. If the democracy slips too far into the hands of the receiver, the power of the performance dialectic is diminished, thus producing a musical stalemate. Consequently the music, as a kinetic practice, ceases to reflect external challenges and pressures, adopting internal rhetoric and modes of associative and acceptable behaviour. The maintenance of stylistic listening processes becomes rigorous and strict; relationships are refixed. This is especially true in the case of musical movements that have expressed their culture through forms of resistance, such as the folk revival. As Judith Young was to ask in the EFDSS journal *English Dance and Song* in 1983: 'why this continual bias towards middle-aged, old or deceased performers ... why not include more articles and pictures concerning the up and coming generation of young "folk" ...?'[15] Roger Marriott attempted to explain on the very next page:

> The Society [i.e. EFDSS] is, and has been for many years, an amalgam of various interests. There are plain hedonists, who just like to dance and sing; there are mystics, who see in ritual dance some expression of the life force and the folk consciousness; there are scholars; there are keep fit enthusiasts; there are musicians; there are political activists, who see folk song and dance as the voice of the people; there are ... you name them, we have them.[16]

It is undeniable that Marriott appreciated that our perception of and response to music is influenced by the position it appears to occupy in our value framework. But his failure to include the young in his potted assemblage of folkies remains revealing. We not only respond to sound materials and identify with the expressive character of certain types of music, but also take into account the structural resonance of that music – in this case, a perception of an internalisation and institutionalisation of performance and reception.

By the mid-1990s both Niall MacKinnon and Hazel Fairbairn (1994) had identified performance in club and session as encompassing a necessary and unique element of social identity. MacKinnon's approach was especially positive and his use of expressions such as 'destaging', 'destruction of performance', 'listening as engagement' and 'informal participation' was benevolent. However, if the social location and thus identity of the folk club audience had undergone important changes since the early days of the revival, these performance and related reception strategies could have been described far less magnanimously (i.e. strictly regulated and musically demarcated).

MacKinnon failed to take due account of the social hierarchies that were created via reception in a club, together with the shifting social status of his folkie in society during the more recent history of the revival. Fairbairn, in discussing the ubiquitous session as an example of de-staged performance democracy, also failed fully to consider the social echelons involved in folk performance (related hierarchies, social mores, spontaneity and expectancy). She somewhat blithely assumed that every folkie wished to play, when, quite clearly, many people found equal enjoyment in unaffiliated listening. Chris McKenna: 'I never wanted to play. I never wanted to sing. I can't imagine anything worse, personally. So why was I made to feel almost guilty when I declined the "do you want to sing" look? Can't I just listen?'[17] Fairbairn, in fact, placed 'passive' listening beneath 'spontaneous' performance in a hierarchy of strategies – a curious approach if one takes into account the process by which many people approach genres of popular music. Both MacKinnon and Fairbairn are typical examples of internalised perspectives inherent in the folk revival as reformulated since the 1970s – one had to 'do', as it were.

The folk club powers actually managed their 'hidden authority' via performance well. This hierarchy existed in compensation for the absence of any over-arching technical and administrative apparatus; the clubs existed via a 'system' of clienteles, allegiances and legitimacies, none of which was obviously hierarchical. While folk clubs sought to make themselves independent of the structures and financial fluctuations of mainstream music appreciation, they were able to do so only through justification, control and organisation of performance space: one set of rules replacing another.

As a result, the power in the folk club developed via subtle and close-knit procedures for the control of all performance models and networks, thus giving an outward impression of less authority, even laissez-faire, but actually having great power and control. Hobsbawm and Ranger (1983) used this concept to account for a specific type of canon-formation: one for which the past is largely fabricated, via the decisions of a few individuals. They described this as an invented tradition. An invented folk music tradition centres on a canon and the ascription of value to certain aspects of performance history in canonical fashion.

Expressions of community via the invention of tradition

The insularity of the folk scene over the past 30 years now dictates policy. Those few individuals drawn to folk music and its associated activities do so because of a network of musical activity perceived as representing an identifiable corpus. Musical affectation appears to exist around a centre of musical truth and a feeling of enfranchisement that comes with it. A variety of folk dancing, mummers, passion plays, workshops, real ale festivals and canal festivals have all been cited to me as having an essential 'folksiness'. Even ideas abounded concerning arts and crafts, such as this comment from Nantwich: 'I even find a connection between the canal boat painting and selling canal crafts, and the music. There just seems to be a sense of reality about all of it. This is what people did; this is what people sang, you know. There are connections.'[18] To invent a folk tradition certainly involves decision-making processes around a sense of community, but there are substantial historical-cum-ideological tools at work amongst the folk fraternity involving ideas about community as arbiter of musical performance and taste.

This internalised aural arbitration has created a 'catch 22' situation for some clubs. Faced with dwindling finances brought about by performance constrictions, some clubs have rejected performers outright. An emphasis has swung towards perpetuating the membership, at the expense of performers. Some singers' clubs ideologically attempt to bestow on folk music a singular dignity that relates only to itself. Helen McCall, former organiser of the now defunct 'Mags' in New Brighton, told me: 'We didn't have guests. It was an expensive luxury, but in any case, we believed that the song was the important feature of the club. The singer was carrying a tradition.'[19]

This is an interesting abstraction, but it suggests that folk's so-called democracy has weighted itself far too heavily on the side of the connoisseur listener. Folk club performance as an expression of community remains restricted to that community being elevated enough to appreciate the second revival's constructions of folk song. While the reaction of the folk revival to so-called intellectual complexity was, indeed, a valid one, this intellectual complexity appears to have resurfaced in the folk revival via an aural connoisseurship.

This is linked in no small measure to the pre-eminence of ideas about the very transmission of the music. To some in the folk scene, the folk performance should actually eschew all aspects of 'performance' in contemporary terms. This means that the singer 'carries a tradition' and suppresses the performance in order to transmit the song. For example, describing the singing of Fred Jordan, fellow unaccompanied singer Roly Brown stated that Jordan was 'a true carrier and offers multiple satisfactions, never predictability; intelligence, passion, and awareness'.[20] Brown recognised that Jordan had acquired and formulated identifiable skills and musical focus. But one might also describe the work of (say) Tony Bennett in the same way.

The difference between Jordan and Bennett is perceived to lie in the idealistic concept that what the folk musician is seen to absorb in musical terms he or she is expected to disseminate with a minimum of extra cultural 'baggage'. This also means that for some folkies, the folk singer or instrumentalist has to be rather dispassionate, maintaining a certain non-emotional style, perhaps even a 'distance' from the music being performed. This distance is then expected to maintain a certain level of purity and probity. But if a folk singer is supposed to express his communality, is not cultural baggage part of that expression?

Ultimately, an aural hierarchy sits in judgement on generic appropriateness. The knowing receiver judges the performer so that the structures surrounding folk identification avoid uncomfortable pressures. The values associated with appropriate de-staged folk club spontaneity are social constructions to support continuity with an imagined, yet strangely immutable, past. Yet, if one examines folk performance away from this isolationist social construction, intertextuality immediately questions folk music repertoire. Unrestrained performance of traditional music can draw one towards 'folk music' in ways unimagined by such illusory criteria. Bob Buckle, for example, remembers a school performance in Everton in 1994:

> I was showing the youngsters the array of instruments that I play and I found that they were fascinated by the 5-string banjo. In my ignorance I thought that I had made a real breakthrough, but when I asked whether they had any questions, quite a few asked me whether I played like the Grid. I didn't know what they were talking about but they told me there was a dance track by a duo called the Grid. They'd sampled a 5-string banjo. So I played them a similar breakdown and they went mad! Now don't tell me that the pop charts are worthless when that sort of thing happens because I have the evidence to show you that it's the reverse. The Grid unknowingly drew attention towards what I do. My instrumentation didn't seem half as archaic.[21]

Buckle witnessed that historical conditions precluded any organic evolution of folk music reception. For the children cited above, the 'real' aural/oral root into any musical tradition was little more than a pot-pourri of soundtracks: whether they were 'appropriate' or not depended on matters such as age, gender, class and ethnicity. For them, tradition could be discovered in the computer circuitry of a modern dance tune just as much as in a jig played on the fiddle. If some members of the folk movement regard the sound of the Grid as an inappropriate melding of two sounds, perhaps they would also like to explain which sound is more appropriate? Has tradition never interacted?

Although tunes and styles can be shared, and the activity of performance can further expand this shared basis, canonical delineation ultimately dictates what can be shared and what cannot. What the collective club 'authority' deems good or bad 'taste', appropriate or inauthentic music, remains the rule of thumb. This seems little removed from the policies adopted in many popular music venues, where, say, an R&B or dance club dictates musical policies as an act of course. However, it cuts against the grain of the initial impact of the revival that attempted to remove (and succeeded, to a degree) the social glue from musical relationships, freeing people to explore and to realise the potential of extending musical relationships. The balance between appropriate performance and collective reception has certainly swung away from the musician. Philip Bohlman has recognised how this imbalance has affected the approach of folk music scholars over the past 30 years or so:

> The long-standing failure of folk music scholarship to take account of individual creativity is perhaps the most visible testimony to the undercurrent of conservatism that has saturated many of our most entrenched concepts of folk music. Considerations of cultural and musical change, for example, muddy this undercurrent and thus are too often channelled into the 'nondescript' pools of popular music.[22]

We can see from this, therefore, that musical performance in folk clubs is not as relaxed as one might at first imagine. It is, in fact, tenaciously preserved via folk club reception modes that are tightly structured and organised formally. Although the clubs have a friendly atmosphere and a spontaneous and 'natural' environment, their reception and socialisation expressions are neither natural nor stable representations (after all, the folk club is a relatively new concept and context for folk music performance). Tension exists through a judgemental appropriateness of genre or style in proportion to the construction of a canon of 'tradition'.

These ideas of informality and de-staging, as desirable as they appear to be in the removal of expectations of performance behaviour, are inaccurate. They can frighten off those new to the folk scene and make hypotheses about the performance-self no other genre in music would dare to make. Both style and content in performance are based around the socialisation processes that established the clubs in the first place, rather than on any proximity to an authentic model. As society changes, so do musical sounds. The folk club fraternity, however, have evaded social kinesis. If one retreats from the present day, one should not bemoan a fall-off in recruitment.

Conclusion

These arrangements at work in performance and participation stemmed from specific contextual responses to a given era in British social history. They continue to reveal significant structuring ideologies in folk music that are carefully contrived to convey a sense of informality. This is attractive to some, less so to others, but all are utilised at both a communal and an individual level in ways which come to be at odds with the ethos that they were erected to sustain. Informality, spontaneity, continuity and the idea of participation are all dominant features of the folk movement, but they are organised concepts that have been used as ideological tools. These canonical constructions are articulated through models of performance and reception and effectively control the balance of power, status and recognition within the movement.

In effect, the folk establishment has based its performance models on unstable and idealised representations. Consequently the performance preconditions adopted in many folk clubs can, at best, be described as debatable antiquarian re-enactments. The performance/reception model that the folk world contrives to sustain is both socially more complex and historically less locatable than it at first appears.

Despite many claims that the popular, the professional and the experimental remove the performer from the sanctions of tradition, quite the reverse is often the case. Even an extreme form of experimentation within traditional music forms requires that the performer understands both the social and musical tolerance levels of that tradition. Ultimately, static folk performance without dialectic fails to refer to any musical tradition whatsoever, for the real performance tradition at work within the British Isles is one of expansion of musical and cultural boundaries. Most folk musicians are innovative and creative on one level or another; they might accept or reject change; they might observe tradition or violate it. Now that folkies have experienced a time of self-protection, they are in a position to consider how much a juxtaposition between change and stability, between popular and folk, determines a future for folk music.

The balance in performance dialectic, which has swung away from the musician and towards the antiquarian listener, needs to be restored so that creativity, rather than re-enactment, is paramount. I draw this section to a close by quoting, once again, from Dave Arthur's 1973 review of *Songs of the Midlands*: 'It would be a far more profitable way of expending time and energy if we were to start studying folksong as a communications medium, which is what it is, instead of as a quaint museum piece.'[23] By doing as Arthur suggests, the folk musician's tradition of innovation and kinesis will come to underpin the future of the folk revival, rather than the social mores and clandestine hierarchies that have continued to surround the singing traditions of this country. Like-minded people can actually share the same degree of ignorance.

Notes

1. Palmer (ed.), *Songs of the Midlands*.
2. Arthur, review of *Songs of the Midlands*, pp. 327–29.
3. Pegg, *Folk: A Portrait of English Traditional Music, Musicians and Customs*, quoted in Yates, review, in *Folk Music Journal*, 3/3, p. 285.
4. Moss with Weglarski, 'Meeting the Needs of the Time'.
5. Arthur, review of *Songs of the Midlands*, p. 328.
6. Nuttall, *Bomb Culture*, pp. 37–38.
7. York, *Modern Times*, p. 64.
8. MacKinnon, *The British Folk Scene*; see chs. 4, 5, 6.
9. Boyes, *The Imagined Village*, pp. 240–41.
10. Interview with Mick O'Toole, December 2001.
11. Finnegan, *The Hidden Musicians*, p. 58.

12. Ibid., p. 68.
13. Ibid., p. 69.
14. Interview with Chris McKenna, May 2002.
15. Young, 'Letter to the Editor', p. 26.
16. Marriott, 'Letter to the Editor', p. 27.
17. Chris McKenna, May 2002.
18. Interview with unnamed Nantwich folkie, 1997.
19. Interview with Helen McCall, July 1995.
20. Brown, 'Fred Jordan', p. 412.
21. Interview with Bob Buckle, September 1996.
22. Bohlman, *The Study of Folk Music in the Modern World*, p. 69.
23. Arthur, review of *Songs of the Midlands*, p. 328.

Chapter 8

What of the folk scene now?

Some of the informal amateur structures within the folk scene are at times one of its
greatest strengths but at other times one of its weaknesses.
                        Peter Heywood, 'Editorial', *The Living Tradition* (Jan.–Feb. 1996)

I have proposed that the main problem with the British folk revival has also
been the source of its initial strength: namely the hypothetical homogenisation
of a form of performance history one should associate with a wide variety of
socially, politically and culturally heterogeneous processes. Therefore the
meaning of folk music that has emerged has been used as a distinctive (but
illusory) form or quality of social experience. This folk discourse has become
caught up in a consolidation and a permanence that has relations only to, or
with, the images created at its own inception. There are few possibilities of
transcending a priori meaning, of unfolding dialectic of its own history. The
folk club, for example, is there because without it, it would not be there. The
musical and visual images in a folk club remain just that and attract few new,
young outsiders. They are put off by an inward-looking self-replication, as
Andrew Weskett observes: 'Traditional music is fine, but we need to be open-
minded when considering the spectrum which is available to possible audiences,
or else clubs will continue to be closed shops, full of introverted cliques,
blinded by their own shallowness when considering folk music.'[1] In what was
originally a space for absence of rules, a rejection of musical rules, the folk
club has now become caught up in the revival's own rituals. The images
portrayed by a folk club are now more real than real and are sustained like a
lifeblood, rather than the recreated images that they are. The folk club has now
become the tradition, only resembling itself.

   I have also implied that a curious perfection process has developed within the
folk revival whereby performers have consummated their performance models.
Guitarists play like other guitarists; singers sing like other singers – those who
scrupulously wish to resemble somebody else of note beset the folk club. Playing
has become a striving towards a disturbing perfection, a perfect replication. All
potential miasmas have been removed and a perfect prescription of folk remains.
All of the ingredients are present, but in precise doses and perfect quantities.
There are too few mistakes rather than too many and an entire generation of
adolescents has been frightened off by this performance rectitude.

   In Chapter 1 it was stated that during the first revival Vaughan Williams
collected and arranged folk song as a contemplation of alternative pre-modern
society, something that could meliorate the advancement of the contemporary

nation. This unerring musical confidence has been sustained by the second folk revival; there has been precious little doubting of the universal grounding of folk's values and status. While presenting this selective history, I have also attempted to argue that while the present folk movement continues to be supremely confident, involving a firm hierarchy of values and supported by an overwhelming consensus, it has marginalised history, music use, performance and reception.

The folk club, especially, is fascinated with itself as a lost object, but some, such as John Moulden, are evidently frustrated by this 'universal wisdom': 'If clubs become restrictive and exclusive they are of no possible use to the tradition and should be dispensed with. But it's always hard to abandon old markets and look for new.'[2] This work calls for such 'abandon[ment of] old markets'. The result would certainly begin to attract younger participants. What constitutes 'tradition', then, becomes responsive to the diverse arguments taking place in society. A lack of certainty about one's historical past, a refusal of the foundations set out by the two folk revivals of the twentieth century, does not negate the meaning of these actions; it only confirms their limits and their historicity. Some revivalists are now considering this lack of historical assurance, and the physical and cultural site of the folk festival appears to be an interesting home for discursive possibilities.

The festival

The folk music festival has become an extremely important feature of folk music activity in this country. It has matured into possibly the best medium for presenting the eclectic and idiosyncratic in folk music, whilst at the same time drawing attention to the folk scene as an important feeder network. The festival is seen as part of a pyramid organisation the culmination of which is the explosion of performances at places as diverse as Sidmouth, Cambridge, Fylde, Edinburgh, Cleethorpes, Fort William and Pontardawe. Whereas the folk club and the EFDSS can still be heavily criticised as elitist, the festival can be seen as an influential folk activity which has not only germinated via the historical and political contexts and motivations of the revival, but also exists as a dialectic about its own historical and social position within that revival.

Whereas the folk club is a construct of the revival itself, festive occasions have always been part of social and community life in the British Isles, and people in every generation and of every immigrant background have sought to keep this form of entertainment alive. The beginnings of folk music festivals in this country certainly took their lead from those in the United States such as at Newport in the late 1950s, but there have always been celebrations concerning the turning of the seasons, sporting and popular pastimes, theatrical entertainments and the like. A festival, in principle at least, does appear to have a claim on a historical past.

There has been very little written about the growth of folk festivals in the British Isles since the advent of the second revival. In retrospect, one can perhaps partially understand the reluctance of folklorists to consider the growing folk festival phenomenon. Festivals such as Cambridge and Keele began in 1965 and immediately celebrated that murky no-man's-land between the 'authentic' and in-context culture of the real folk and the non-folkloric popular culture of American folk music. The Clancy Brothers and Tommy Makem, Paul Simon and Hedy West all appeared on the first Cambridge bill alongside Cyril Tawney, Pete Sayers and Dorris Henderson: 'the token black lady on the bill'.[3]

So, although folklorists were involved to varying degrees as informal advisers to some of the festivals, they were also quite aware that the festival did not primarily have the 'purity' of (say) an EFDSS enterprise. Most folklorists apparently perceived it as happening (and perhaps better left) outside the locus of their concern. The late Ken Woollard, organiser of the Cambridge Folk Festival between 1965 and 1993, confirmed this rather 'snooty' attitude from what he described as 'traditionalists':

> It was the traditionalists who objected to the Clancy Brothers being booked for the first festival. One of the criticisms of Cambridge in the early days was that we didn't put on enough traditional music and that this was what the working class was all about. When traditionalists said that to me I would reply that I'd never known an electrician who sang a sea-shanty while he pulled a string through a hole. They'd be more likely to be singing a Beatles song![4]

It is essential that folk festivals come under the academic microscope for they continue to present some of the most important musical events within the British music calendar. They are not restricted by the social mores of folk clubs, but, rather, exist as an embodiment of resourceful musical programming. They continue to attract thousands of visitors and artists from all over the world and are, in a real sense, the future of folk music. Festivals remind us that folk music is, after all, a shifting signifier, something that is continually subject to modification. Even though the constructions surrounding a festival might have been formed from within a folk social consensus, the festival cannot succeed unless it attracts 'passive' or even non-folkies. It is hardly surprising therefore, that Niall MacKinnon (1993) struggles with this performance polyglot, for the musical performances and social identities that he claims to be so intrinsically linked within the folk scene are far more up for grabs on the festival site.

For example, important performance and cultural dialectics are able to manifest themselves at differing folk festivals, one being between passive or value- and agenda-free presentations on the one hand and musical/cultural advocacy on the other. By variable programming some festivals allow people to listen to a great diversity of sounds, whereas others present something of a musical 'fait accompli', tending to impose their own concept of what is traditional on people. Also many festivals in Britain such as WOMAD openly celebrate the concepts of pluralistic and multi-layered societies, despite overwhelming evidence to the contrary and despite Black audience numbers remaining minuscule. These visual and aural challenges within the festival scenario derive at least partly from the uneasy coexistence within many festival producers of a conservative personal music aesthetic and left-wing politics, together with a growing appreciation of the indeterminacy of musical traditions. Festivals, therefore, are unquestionably and openly challenging.

For instance, there is considerable evidence to suggest that folk festivals serve primarily as entertainments and annual meeting places for an audience of mellow, suburban, middle-class people who have literally grown up with festivals. Over two distinct periods (the summers of 1995 and 2001) I attended over 20 festivals in England and Wales and found myself asking whether they served to encourage or enhance public understanding of different soundtracks or whether these events simply provided the same, mobile audience with a rather sanitised and unchallenging folk artefact. A number of important questions arose from my festival tours. For example, should a folk festival be an arena of cultural affirmation or the scene of cultural and political debate? It could be argued that festivals should only reflect the related functions of celebrating, socialising, sharing and participating, but one could also suggest that the festival is an appropriate vehicle to address tensions and disagreements.

Additionally, are festivals successful only because the producers, participants and audiences are of a similar socio-economic class? (Or do they have an important community-based role to play?) I discovered enough evidence to suggest that the folk festival-goer acknowledges the potential of festivals (at least while in progress) to alter the social and cultural dynamics of adopted areas and that festivals were viewed as challenges to conventional concepts about performed music and the status of performers. Folk festivals were also seen as vehicles for cultural forms usually overlooked by general public. For example, it was suggested to me by Chris Wade, organiser of the Beverley Festival ('Open Forum 1995': discussion group at the Beverley Festival), that festivals served a useful purpose by allowing alternative social, cultural and even political divergence to be addressed alongside music. For Wade, the very presence of a folk festival in a conservative town such as Beverley was a visible reminder that communal activity could exist in a variety of forms, and that alternative and yet traditional forms of music were alive and kicking.

However, organisers from both Warwick and Fylde Folk Festivals suggested to me that festivals also had a rather negative function. For these interviewees, there was evidence that the organisational structures and pricing policies had contrived to place a mask over cultural differences and structural inequities in the social system. My informants were particularly concerned that festival ticketing policies systematically excluded large sections of the population because tickets were prohibitively expensive and that, once the festivals were over, there was little cultural consequence.

As I travelled from festival to festival in 1995 and 2001 I found no real consensus. Perspectives and analyses were very wide-ranging. The festival is, therefore, an ideal monitor for the future role of musical traditions in modern society and an in-depth study of British folk festivals is obviously long overdue. Future works might ask, for example: what conditions the perceptions of traditions represented at a festival? Upon what ethical warrants (if any) does the festival enterprise rest? How is a major British folk music festival to be understood sociologically – in its class and race representations, for example? What are its political implications? How should festivals be comprehended within the realm of public spending policy?

Few of these questions have yet to be addressed in anything but the most cursory and fragmentary fashion. This is a pity, for they are all meaningful and urgent areas of discussion. The last of these points, for example, demands attention and research. In circumstances where the range of any music that reaches the public ear is determined at least partly by the nature of the establishment that produces and disseminates it, any such sanction inevitably influences the course of a 'scene's' mercantile development.

For example, one of the few advances in profile amplification that the folk commerce sector appears to have made in recent times is in receiving more grant aid from regional and government arts development directorates. Alan Bell, organiser of the aforementioned Fylde Folk Festival, became chairman in spring 2000 of a new organisation named Folkus (the Folk Arts Network of the North West) because he was 'frustrated by the lack of recognition for the folk arts on his home patch'.[5] Bell is regarded highly in the North West of England for his tireless campaigning for folk music and dance, and it was expected that he would succeed in attracting sponsorship from a variety of funding bodies. Similarly, the relative success of the Folkworks organisation in the North East remains a credit to the hard work of fund and image expansion on behalf of folk music.

However, activity of this kind hardly signals economic growth. In fact, one could view this tendency to seek external sponsorship as a desperate measure to underwrite the accumulated debt incurred by various folk-related projects – including festivals. Folkworks rely upon funding from Northern Arts, Durham City Arts, Durham County Council and the Arts Council of England. It is also a registered charity. These networking bodies have not elicited any notable creative successes in the folk music sector, nor have they expanded investment or production. In fact, they appear to exist for the purpose of rescuing festival societies from non-profit situations while maintaining, on the musical front, a 'them versus us' stance. One has to ask whether they unwittingly encourage a commercial backwardness.

The 2000 Edinburgh Folk Festival was forced to fold prior to its customary Easter event because the previous November 1999 'Shoots and Roots' fell short of its budgeted income targets. The basic problem was that not enough people were attracted by the presentation of the programme, even though, according to its artistic director Dave Francis, the festival sported 'a balanced commercial and artistic blend and [was] supported by a good publicity campaign on a limited budget'.[6] Perhaps folk music is now failing so spectacularly to sell itself that it has to resort to funding applications to prop up unstable financial proposals. The Scottish Arts Council and Edinburgh City Council both decided not to fund after considering the size of the EFF Society's overdraft. The same commentator who recorded the words of Dave Francis quoted above relayed the following 'off the cuff' comments of an unidentified festival organiser:

> We really set ourselves up as suckers, don't we, when we believe something is worth doing because of its intrinsic worth. Better to be thoroughly crassly commercial – the folks with the purse strings seem to understand that so well; they know the price of everything and the value of nowt! Thatcher's legacy.[7]

Thatcher's legacy, perhaps, but the decline in the revival's ability to market itself has recently been reflected widely in similar falling figures and failing projects. The closure of the Edinburgh Folk Festival followed closely on the heels of the failure of the 'Continental Ceilidh' in Lanark, which left a trail of debts to artists. In June 2000, the HTD Records Summer Folk Day was cancelled on account of 'very bad advance ticket sales'.[8] The label then experienced considerable financial difficulties and folded – reinventing itself as Talking Elephant in 2002.

My own experiences of co-promoting the folk duo Show of Hands at Liverpool's Neptune theatre in May 2000 bears similar witness not only to apathy or declining public interest but also to misdirected, irrelevant and consequently unsuccessful marketing. Despite the relative success of the venture, the nature of the promotional material foredoomed it to unprofitability. Indeed, the 'traditional' associations suggested by the advertising material probably bewildered many. The number of people willing, under these terms, to invest culturally or financially in folk music reception in Liverpool is undoubtedly decreasing. So far as one can see, this process looks like continuing while promotion remains tied to a prescription.

Perhaps, as Peter Heywood, editor of *The Living Tradition*, admitted in March 1996, some organisers are their own worst enemies:

> My editorials seem to be a constant battle with underlying concerns with the structure of the folk scene. I have lost count of the number of times I have heard the words 'don't quote me but ...' to then hear what is really going on and how people really feel. Organisers are under a lot of strain and I know that some will eventually take the closure option or quietly run down their work.[9]

Heywood was remarking upon the failure of the Girvan Festival that very year.

So, while it has been estimated by the EFDSS that three million people now attend folk festivals each summer, one could also argue that some folk festival organisations continue to teeter on the brink of a financial abyss. During the summer of 2000 a spokesperson for the Chester Folk Festival expressed to me concern that festival presentations were failing in their duty by not marketing folk music as a form of popular music. She also stated that this led to the music being 'exhibited inside a neutral event culture where the music merely accompanied the happening'.

All depictions have their problems, of course. While reflecting a respect for heritage and tradition such folk performance and reception processes no longer represent the informal rules and expectations that guide our everyday behaviour (our 'folkways', so to speak). In fact, they can (and do) reek of the aforementioned musical virtuosity and elitism. Sessions and singarounds do not belong to the common musical parlance of young people of the twenty-first century and do not relate to their social mores or everyday social interactions. In an interesting struggle, the social/musical language of the folk festival is experiencing considerable popularity but is also constrained by its most visible expositions (coming across as antiquated and esoteric). A debate has been established on the festival fields that appears hopeful (dialectic processes are kinetic, after all). But how would any folk music commercial sector cope with such expansion?

Marketing

Any hope of a revival *of* the revival could founder, for at least some in the folk commercial sector remain subject to over-sensitivity and socio-political (and thus generic) pressures and judgements. They allow themselves to be deflected from the pursuit of expansion by continuing to perceive an opposition between heritage (the natural) and enterprise (the mass-produced); for some this dichotomy remains central to a continual struggle for meaning.

As a consequence, the music of the folk 'movement' (if it may still be described as such) still remains largely hidden from, and consequently unheard by, the vast majority of the general public. Moreover, despite the efforts of such singers as Billy Bragg, and certain progressive elements within the folk music industry (the internet-based magazine *Musical Traditions*, for example) to raise the profile of the genre in the United Kingdom, it seems to me that what little is revealed of folk music participation remains tarnished by the revival's own countenance.

In fact, the relationship between what can be conceived as folk music and its presentation remains a significant and persistent problem for the commercial sector of the folk revival. This relationship dictates that the methods and forms of presentation are accompanied by an ever-present sanction of the unacceptable. This is a serious problem when the inherited categories of high culture, folk culture and popular culture, together with the host of associated aesthetic gatekeepers (who include critics, reviewers and opinion makers), are being subverted by the heterogeneous mass-mediated cultures of our own age. A voice crying in the wilderness is not necessarily a marketable commodity.

For any popular music genre to survive in the twenty-first century its commercial arm needs to understand how to market that music. Perhaps the one basic axiom valid for all popular music presentation is that the music is obliged to speak on at least two levels at once: first, to other musicians and to the concerned minority that cares about specific meanings; second, to the public at large that cares about other issues pertaining to its own chosen way of life. However, the revivalists tend to demarcate themselves strictly in the marketplace: either as increasingly dated but charming 'ancients' (note the William Jackson album *Celtic Tranquility*), or else as partisans endorsing the solemn 'historical' burden of the coal mine and the pawn shop. It is this second association, perhaps more than anything else, that alienates the youth of the twenty-first century and the aspirations arising from them.

To be involved in folk music commerce is to align oneself with one or the other version of an apparently fixed musical-cum-social policy at a time when the predominant drive in British society and trade is to move away from integrated packages of this kind. In an explosive age of social pluralism and new forms of stratification that is witnessing a rebirth of social snobbery via hedonism and liberal elitism as well as multi-cultural tolerance (and its obverse, racial hatred) the activities and language of the folk revival look increasingly anachronistic. Conversely, the modern world of commerce appears to many folk revivalists as increasingly degenerate in relation to a putative past.

The fear of affluence

A significant proportion of active folkies react negatively towards anything resembling popular music 'business'. At times, they seem to prefer an inefficient marketing network that remains true to its traditions to an efficient one modelled on commerce. Moving forward via individual initiative, a basic tenet of the popular music industry, often appears less acceptable than advancing via group activity. As a result, there is a very deep-rooted hostility to any attempts at increasing sales via outright commercialism; ambitious projects such as the English Folk Dance and Song Society's *Root and Branch* (of which more later) have first to justify themselves by being 'thoroughly stimulating ... extremely important and worthwhile'.[10]

Yet, despite an ideological reluctance to admit that the capitalist system and present-day reality can have anything to commend them (coupled with a general feeling that once the folk revival ceases to appeal to idealists and starts to attract careerists it will lose the moral force which is its greatest traditional asset), the folk music industry in Britain stubbornly endures through a network of relatively small, independent businesses (many of them part-time) and the devotion of enthusiastic amateurs. This network includes record companies, distributors, instrument makers and repairers, retailers, festival organisers, promoters, artist agencies, folk clubs and a periodical-dominated media system. All of these business and media strands compete with each other for musicians, articles and, indeed, consumers; but they also attempt to coordinate their activities informally through the folk music-related social networks that have survived into the twenty-first century. These networks are bound together in a kind of ideological commonwealth. From a pragmatic business perspective, however, this network often turns out to be something of a chaotic labyrinth. Jeremy Horrall, proprietor of the Telford's Warehouse venue, has complained:

> it can be a bit of a nightmare, to be honest. We've had to cancel many times after having a folkie on our [advertising] board for ages. Alexander's [another venue in Chester] have had the same trouble – even with Martin Carthy – he was due there last autumn but failed to show … didn't know anything about it, apparently. It's no good, really. I'm not suggesting that Martin is unprofessional – far from it – but the (I think) Farndon folk club who 'booked' him into Alexander's certainly are![11]

Horrall is suggesting here that folk networks are habitually rather dispersed communities. Some parts of these communities do attempt to make a living out of the genre (the Adastra agency, for example), but many others, among whom one might cite Rita O'Hare of the Nantwich festival, Alan Surtees, organiser of the Bridgnorth Folk Festival, and promoters and writers such as Bill Pook and Chris Hockenhull, do not. All of them appear to desire a wider recognition for the music – but not under 'any' terms. For example, advertisements in volume 37 of the folk magazine *The Living Tradition* entice prospective purchasers with such descriptions as 'folksinger, storyteller and community musician' (Pete Castle, p. 24), 'a cerebral musician' (Cormac Breatnach, p. 26), 'spirited sets and honest songs … and love of the tradition' (Firebrand, p. 48). In this way, the folk music trading sector and media see as their joint task to confirm not only the existence of a musical style, but also a valuable historical-cultural existence. There is a general consensus for non-concession – a fear, even, that the music or the artist as a visible embodiment of an authentic aesthetic could in some way be compromised.

While such anxieties are perhaps understandable, given the apparent historical nature of the music, they shade into another fear that is far more pernicious (and financially damaging): that once a folk music artist acquires the trappings of popular music he or she will begin to adopt popular music attitudes and habits of mind, becoming totally commercial and corrupt or, at best, losing touch and sympathy with the folk revival. Although there is a history of folk artists leaving the revival for the sake of commercial success (the names include Isla St Clair, Billy Connolly, Mike Harding, Richard Digance, Gerry Rafferty and Barbara Dickson), it is easy to show how inconsistent this negative attitude is, since all of the above-named artists, among many others, have proudly drawn attention to their folk origins. It also appears ill considered to take as axiomatic that authenticity and commercial success are antithetical, since both can logically be components of the same accomplishment. The problem with the categorisation by rank of musical parameters is that there is, quite literally, no area in music (not excluding Gregorian chant!) that has not at some time or other been visited and uplifted by musicians of a commercial persuasion.

We have already seen that the folk revival took wing in an age of apparent certainty; it was further rearticulated in the light of social and economic circumstances abounding in the 1970s – but it was in time overtaken by a different era symbolised by the world of late twentieth-century capitalism, to which it reacted by becoming further embattled, uncertain and protectionist. Thrown back for support on a hard core of older adherents in the 1980s and 1990s, it found its appeal increasingly narrowed to the horizons of this declining group, trapped among the slogans and banners of the past (as witness, the 'Raise Your Banners' event in Sheffield). For this reason, its ability to attract the young steadily declined. Today, much of the folk media finds itself continuing to express the ideas and ideals of a conservative (with a small C) minority group resistant to change.[12]

The folk music 'industry' continues championing, and attempting to merchandise, a way of life that is in several respects whole decades out of date. If one is to talk sensibly of a growth within folk music's commercial sector to reflect that of the festival, the primary objective must be to deflate its pretensions and empty it of outdated ideological baggage. This may appear an over-harsh indictment since, after all, there are many enlightened musicians active in the revival. But the folk 'industry' and media taken as a whole remain overly cautious and preservationist, and these actions reflect not only their origins in the aftermath of World War II, but also the deceleration that took place in the early 1980s.

Record labels – plausible inefficiency?

As we have seen, by the late 1970s popular music reception had visibly fragmented and the folk scene failed – perhaps for the first time since the war – to recruit en masse a new generation of followers. In addition, by the early 1980s the major industrial players in the popular music marketplace, having temporarily lost ground to a host of independent labels, were forced to reinvent themselves with leaner, younger, more dynamic appendages that were also bent on using technology rather than tradition to its fullest capacity. Furthermore, many major record companies began also to employ teams of young accountants who saw little future in non-commercial acoustic music and systematically removed from their rosters many leading British folk artists, among whom were Ashley Hutchings, John Martyn and Al Stewart.

In consequence of the growth–contraction economic cycle that had begun to overtake many small businesses and entrepreneurs by the mid-1970s, such independent record companies as Transatlantic, Island, Topic, Leader, Trailer, Ash, Kicking Mule, Village Thing, Peg and Mooncrest (B&C), and Criminal – all previously very sympathetic to folk and folk-rock – began either to mutate, sell out to a major company with little interest in their back catalogues or disappear altogether. This caused a huge depression in the folk 'industry' (which places music before economics, as we have observed). The highest-profile casualty was Nat Joseph's Transatlantic label, but Topic (by that time Britain's longest-running independent record label) also found the going very tough.

Topic survived thanks to the managerial acumen of Tony Engle, who set up a wholesale distribution network similar to the once defunct but now re-emergent independent Rough Trade cartel. Direct Distribution (as it was named) came to handle at least 50 per cent of all United Kingdom folk distribution and was also a clearing house for independent American labels, among them Bearcat, Black top, Philo and Rounder. With the assistance of their wholesale markets, in alliance with Engle's proactive reissue campaigns, Topic reached its golden anniversary in 1999, despite almost ruining itself with the 20-CD *Voices of the People* series.

Yet, like most record labels centred on folk music, this albeit stubborn company has a vacillating approach to business and periodically lurches into crisis. During 2000 Proper Distribution lured several Direct Distribution staff away from Topic and the latter was plunged into financial jeopardy once again. Thankfully, the label recovered and a subsequent arrangement with Proper has eased matters (although as I write – October 2002 – Proper are also displaying signs of business fatigue) but at least two perspectives on this unhappy event spring to mind. One could argue with some force that poaching of this kind reflects the unacceptable face of the record industry – the sort of activity that Topic disavows by its very existence. Conversely, however, one can hardly blame staff for wishing (as this writer was anonymously but reliably informed) 'to escape the incessant amplification of compliant inefficiency'.

In fact, a disturbingly large proportion of folk music record labels are, like Topic, in deficit even at their present rate of expenditure, which in most cases is well below the requirements of even moderate efficiency. Yet this weak business sense in the folk music industry ironically confers plausibility on it among its leaders and consumers (often the same individuals) by appearing to validate the mystifications of the 'them versus us' ideology embedded in the revival. So it is no surprise to learn that many folk music labels continue to exist uncomplainingly as hand-to-mouth organisations that scorn forward planning. While there is almost a dread of competition, sales and marketing remain sluggish and inefficient.

However, a handful of folk music labels have shown an ability to become 'materialist' organisations, attracting both idealists and the vilified careerists mentioned earlier in their bid to establish viable businesses. Survivors such as

Cooking Vinyl and Fellside have found themselves having to engage with those very market forces that were redefining traditional ideas about music-making and recording. Cooking Vinyl, for instance, is a fiercely independent label from London launched in 1986. Of all the independents, they have come closest to attaining a 'folk' hit single with Ancient Beatbox (1989) and Billy Bragg (various releases). Arguably the 'biggest' folk-rock band of the 1990s, the Oyster Band, remains signed to Cooking Vinyl. The same label also markets a few rock groups having little or no connection with the folk scene, but at least in possession of an indie or punk kudos (Poison Girls, Pere Ubu, the Wedding Present, etc.). This suggests that Cooking Vinyl is fully aware of the capacity of differing genres to follow their individual paths and refuses to accept the conventional quiescent concept of an archetypically 'traditional' (i.e. 'folk') music.

For many years Fellside was a typically folk part-time operation, but in order to present folk music professionally to a wider public its proprietor, Paul Adams, went full-time. The company now has an active jazz subsidiary (Lake), a URL (www.fellside.com) and a catalogue of releases by luminaries such as Sandra Kerr and the experimentalists Trykster. It has also reissued former Topic releases, including Frankie Armstrong's 'Lovely on the Water' (FECD 151). In the autumn of 1999 Fellside intelligently issued a CD of the original music for the 1970s children's TV series 'Bagpuss' (mainly the work of Sandra Kerr and John Faulkner with Oliver Postgate). Perhaps not surprisingly, this release became its best-seller to date.

The survival and modest growth of Cooking Vinyl and Fellside suggest that at least some folk-based labels have responded to the need to broaden the genre (and thus its appeal), taking their products successfully to purchasers outside the 40–55 age range, where folk's most loyal public is now concentrated. This is an important step since it is still young people, of whatever social group and disposition, who set trends. Any record company has eventually to come to the realisation that it cannot avoid engaging with the youth market, irrespective of the musical genre purveyed. Not only is British society obsessed with the idea, the image, of youth: it is also a fact that consumers between the ages of 10 and 24 are the most avid purchasers of discs.

There is some evidence, then, that a handful of folk music independents are at last recognising a need to 'follow the money' and to market themselves in a more dynamic, less staid, way in order to reach out to the legions of youth. These companies have remained steadfastly independent. Yet they have managed to upgrade their media relations via press releases, kits and advertising material aimed at stimulating first-time interest in folk music. Other small-time operators such as instrument makers have made similar attempts to combine economic development with a salutary relativism. Perhaps the reservoir of pure idealism is indeed starting to run dry.

Small-time operators

The folk 'industry' harbours a number of specialist instrument manufacturers. Guitars, melodeons, bodhrans, mandolins, pipes, citterns, bouzoukis, flutes, harps, whistles and fiddles are often handcrafted, their makers relishing the chance to produce an instrument for a connoisseur. There are many craftsmen-manufacturers who produce high-quality instruments in small production runs. These include Andy Perkins (banjos), Dave Shaw and Julian Goodacre (pipes), P.G. Bleazey (flutes, recorders and drums), Tim Phillips and Andy Holliman (violins), Kevin O'Connell (bodhrans), Colin Keefe and John Marlow (various plucked stringed instruments such as mandolas, citterns and guitars) and Hugh Forbes (harps). Pen pictures of two of these dedicated makers can shed light on developments in a different area of the folk revival.

Hugh Forbes has built harps, many of which are modelled on medieval or Pictish designs, for 14 years. He is a Canadian who began by building guitars but was captivated by the romance of Celtic Britain and now sells harps to continental Europe, Japan, North America and South Africa. He freely admits, however, that whether many of the instruments actually get played is another matter! Forbes has identified an interest in the mythologised history of Scotland and Ireland and exploited it. Nonetheless, he also sees himself as belonging to a local community:

> Yes, I do all sorts of things … I run 'build a harp in a day' courses for youngsters, and two-week courses, too. I dearly want more harps in schools. Cost has been against it previously, but now I'm offering a basic kit instrument at around £150, easily affordable … I'm establishing a trust, also; the Historic Harp and Clarsach Trust for educational and research work. I'm handing over designs for my cheaper instruments so they can control the royalties.[13]

On the other hand, Colin Keefe of Luthier Instruments (who in 2002 finished building a new finger-picking guitar for me) constructed his first guitar – an electric – on a Black & Decker 'workmate' bench in his bedroom and between 1985 and 1991 went to college to study instrument making. After a short time with Patrick Eggle Guitars he took a certificate in adult education teaching and initiated the manufacture of his own instruments. For Colin, education, craftsmanship and a heavy dose of musical broad-mindedness have been part of his rite of passage:

> I'm now teaching just the one evening class at a local community college. Business is busy enough for me. I currently have 14 instruments on order … from a 34-string Celtic harp to an 8-string electric! Along with this, I have a large workload of restoration and repair jobs.[14]

The future direction for these small manufacturers is difficult to predict, but noteworthy changes in attitudes and values are occurring. Many ingrained music stereotypes are being challenged by their existence, and both men mentioned above seem to be generating kinds of business that were not open to them only a few years ago. The experiences of these entrepreneurial-minded craftsmen suggest that, in reality, outright ideologies are only ideal types that are rarely, if ever, encountered. Consideration of any economic situation must include context and contingency: rhetoric about purity, class struggle and sell-outs is unproductive. Forbes and Keefe, for example, belong to a new breed of craftsman that manages to combine central elements of both capitalism and altruism, refusing to elevate one musical genre over another or trade in rhetorical platitudes about the specialisation of musical traditions. What, however, of the media?

Broadcasting

Throughout the 1950s the exposure of folk music on the radio gradually increased to a point where, by the 1960s, folk artists could be heard at various times on the BBC. Following the advent of Radio 1 in 1967, however, folk music was perceived as being too specialised for pop listeners. Radio 2 producers likewise viewed folk as a specialised genre and effectively ceased to broadcast it during the day. This specialisation (and thus marginalisation) was highly contextual since, by the late 1960s, all popular music was undergoing pigeonholing of one form or another on the part of so-called experts.

Thematic specialisation and the social codes and conventions that went with it overtook folk music, so producing a specialised context within which it was subsequently to be confined. Indeed, Frances Line, a great supporter of folk music, described her station's main objective during her period as head of BBC Radio 2 in the 1980s as 'ratings by day, reputation by night'. Retrospectively, it can be seen that a process of cultural prioritisation and categorisation developed and then compacted; as a consequence of massive digital communication/ recreation competition during the 1980s, night radio specialisation only succeeded in further marginalisation.

But there are other, more strictly pecuniary reasons for the dearth of folk music on the radio. During the late 1990s BBC local radio stations became increasingly more orientated towards sport-and-talk. Although this worked to the financial advantage of local radio, it tended to erode its long-standing support for folk music. Inherited needle-time and performance fees are a perennial source of conflict between PPL (the licensing body Phonographic Performance Ltd) and the BBC local stations, for which PPL and Performing Rights Society fees can amount to as much as 10 per cent of the annual turnover. In these circumstances it pays to minimise the broadcasting of music of any kind.

Special deals are struck, however, for the repeated use of certain tracks. In 1999 a new contract to that effect was signed between BBC local radio stations and PPL. As a result, the BBC produced a new batch of 'continual play' in-house

CDs. With the possible exception of a few numbers by such artists as John Denver, Cat Stevens and the Seekers, songs that could accurately be described as 'folk' scarcely figured in this new batch of 'core radio-play' CDs. This problem for folk music has worsened with the introduction of 'Radioman' – a hard drive wavfile version of the above, which even precludes the need for CDs (and by doing so perhaps actively discourages a presenter to be 'imaginative').

Folk music programmes invariably occupy evening slots on BBC local or regional radio. This means that they have also suffered from the growth of interest in Premier League football. Practically all folk and jazz programmes are required to be pre-recorded for local radio. This enables them to be rescheduled (or 'dumped', as I was informed by a BBC Radio Merseyside personality) should a football occasion prove too enticing.

It would be fair to claim that folk music has been condemned to a degree of radio exile. After much media speculation, Andy Kershaw was finally removed from the DJ roster at Radio 1 in May 2000. Mike Harding's Pebble Mill-based hour of folk music each Wednesday on Radio 2 is now the sole nationally broadcast folk programme in the United Kingdom. Very few commercial radio stations display anything more than a fleeting interest in folk music, and their DJs seldom have any knowledge whatever of the genre. Most of the regional folk programmes that have been broadcast have been entrusted to enthusiastic amateurs.

My own experience of broadcasting at BBC Radio Merseyside confirms that local radio has come to rely entirely on enthusiasts such as Geoff Speed and Stan Ambrose, without whom there would probably be no folk music programmes left on air at all. But the neglect has arisen not simply because the institutions have treated folk music unfairly. It is quite clear that the traditional authority of folk music, grounded in custom and habit, no longer reflects the roots of many visible aspects of British society.

For instance, while the BBC continues to promote the Radio 2 Young Tradition Awards, one wonders whether the award has an unintentionally adverse effect on the stimulation of interest in folk music amongst younger listeners. The most obvious points remain that, although Radio 2 is currently the most popular BBC national radio station, the vast majority of its listeners are white and aged over 40. The editor of *Folk Roots* (now known as *F-Roots*), Ian A. Anderson, commented in 1996:

> As far as I know the entry rules have never specified what tradition the competitors should come from, but the finalists are always white anglo/celts. There has never been any sign of young musicians from the multiplicity of other cultural traditions in the UK today, and no clue apparently given that they would qualify, be welcome or be fairly judged. Of course I don't know what efforts the BBC makes to remedy this, but they aren't working.[15]

Over half a decade later, little appears to have changed. In this case, 'tradition' is defined by the myth of its origins – those that appear to predate the contaminating expansion of the culture industry of multinational capitalism. This view, both essentialist and metaphysical, of what constitutes folk identity continues to be mythologised and turned into folklore in a number of disturbing ways: indigenist, nationalist and 'thirdworldist'.

Publishing: a hidebound medium?

There are a number of folk publications available in the twenty-first century. It would be misleading, however, to declare that they are all accessible on the 'open' market. They range from fanzine-like publications, processed on computers and/or photocopiers (e.g. *North West Buzz*, *Folk Orbit*), to the long-established EFDSS publications (*English Dance and Song* and *Folk Music Journal*), not forgetting such top-of-the-range products as *F-Roots* itself, which is very glossy and highly professional, even giving away a couple of free CDs every year. *F-Roots* can occasionally be purchased at W.H. Smith, but many of the others are harder to find.

In between *North West Buzz* and *F-Roots* there exists a pyramidal structure of magazines with regional perspectives. Examples are *Taplas*, *The Living Tradition*, *North West Folk*, etc. Magazines remain important points of contact for local musicians and mouthpieces for the local folk organisations such as the North West Folk Federation. Despite the proliferation in the UK of media conglomerates (e.g. Emap), none of the British folk journals has fallen under their sway.

For instance, the EFDSS has always published writings for its members. The *Journal of the Folk Song Society* was founded in 1899 for the purpose of publishing collected songs. Since 1936 the society has also published a quarterly entitled *English Dance and Song* that enjoys runs of about 4500–5000. Both publications have an academic slant and for many years represented the rather cloistered opinions of the EFDSS hierarchy. More recently (2000), however, the Society attempted to address the changing nature of folk music definitions with projects such as the CD-magazine *Root and Branch*. This was perhaps the most radical venture in policy and marketing that has ever come from this organisation, a bulwark of folk music preservation: the creation of a linked CD and magazine that aimed to explore the diversity of music traditions.

Root and Branch contained a full-length CD, articles and essays, facsimiles and photographs. Its content embraced song, music, collectors, performers and historiography. A theme linked the text, graphics and music; for example, the second issue ('Everybody Swing') dealt with the post-World War II era in which the folk revival gathered momentum, delivering an interesting historical account of those years. The selection of tracks on the CD, however, was even more absorbing, for it included music from such diverse sources as Big Bill Broonzy, Lord Kitchener, Ken Colyer and George Webb's Dixielanders. In June 2000 Phil Wilson stated on behalf of the Society:

Times have changed and we need to look to the future. We need to think about the role of the EFDSS in a world that is progressively becoming globalised. Cultural differences are breaking down ... so what is our role? As a first question who do we represent? ... We need to ask more questions. How many people in Britain are involved in folk culture? ... Are there as many people involved as some people say? three million go to festivals but how many of these are the same people? Are we really reaching new audiences?[16]

Wilson's point about 'new audiences' is a genuine concern. Sadly, *Root and Branch* ran for only two issues. Production costs incurred by the rather extravagant Unknown Public production company, together with typically weak promotion, killed this fine project at an early stage.

The magazine with the highest profile and the biggest sales in the folk world remains *F-Roots*. The name of the journal was changed from *Southern Rag* in the 1980s in order to encompass the growing market in this country for world music. In 1998 the word 'folk' itself became abbreviated to 'F' in its title – perhaps a symbolic shift in the magazine's ethos: an attempt to capture the attention of a younger readership.

Sadly, despite this transformation, *F-Roots* continues to present folk music as an anodyne substance soaked in the values and mores of its largely middle-class clientele. Folk music soundtracks are mediated in terms of what the journal perceives its audience demographics to be. This approach takes account of age, class, ethnic and gender locations and (not least) financial stability; but it fails to subject to debate its own global perception taken from that demographic standpoint or its own sense of good taste. Describing this form of literature as 'cultural capital', Roy Shuker cites an apt aphorism of Bourdieu to the effect that 'nothing more clearly affirms one's class, nothing more infallibly classifies, than tastes in music'.[17] Certainly, if *F-Roots* is anything to go by, it would appear that nothing more clearly affirms class than the media's interpretation of one's taste in music!

F-Roots presupposes (true to EFDSS tradition) a core of natural, unspoilt musical truth: a distinction between 'real' music and the 'artificial' products of the manipulator. Interestingly, the use of the word 'roots' in the context of a British folk magazine clearly conveys the idea that 'folk' is of the First World, whereas 'roots' are apposite to the Second and Third Worlds. British musical isolationism may have been successfully challenged by *F-Roots*'s warm embrace of 'roots' music, but the implication remains that foreign forms are to be sampled as exotic novelties. 'Roots' music is written about as if it were the creation of 'unspoilt' (for which read: backward) natives, who, as much for our benefit as for their own, continue to interpret reality in a way forgotten by time. The term carries strong hints of an imperialistic past and a neo-imperialistic present.

Even in the most recent copies of *F-Roots* (2002), the demand that attention be paid to, say, African or Latin art is still framed within a dichotomy that ascribes essences to categories (see no. 227: 'Mariza – fado's new face'). This opposition is articulated in various ways: as that between the local (pure) and the international (corrupted); between the past (rooted-ness) and the present (dissolution); between popular culture (participation) and mass culture (alienation). In this Manichaean scheme of things, modern life is found guilty of having destroyed the characteristics of true identity through a conglomeration of external influences that are invariably deemed baneful and threatening and which lead to falsifications or travesties of original, authentic culture. *F-Roots* is, perhaps, a good example of a cultural product that finds itself obliged to authenticate its own judgemental relevance. Even though it is itself a product, it cultivates the self-image of an arbiter of aesthetic pleasure and a cheerleader of collective nostalgia without ever acknowledging the limits of its own discourse.

Analysis

The presentation of folk music assumes something more than just a musical style. It is a point of identification, an expression of something 'authentic', and a source of affective alliances between fans, business partners and professional musicians (indeed, many professionals could earn far more money in non-musical careers). However, the needless polarisation that opposes the authentic to the commercial has stultified growth in all but the most progressive areas of the folk commercial sector. The folk media still largely feel that folk music portrayal cannot encompass both polarities. In volume 157 of *Folk Roots* a reader, Ian Croft, asked for the destabilisation of the reasons for being involved in the first place. Peter Heywood of *The Living Tradition* continues to question whether a traditional music agency (such as exists in the United States) would seek to serve the folk scene or to control it. It appears that, for these writers at least, folk music has become rationalised as 'artistic' and specifically traditional music that needs vigilance and networking on the part of its adherents to prevent it from 'selling out'.

This sell-out, however, remains problematic as long as the folk media deliver up a Pygmalion-style judgement on tradition in such an idealised, obsessive manner. Folk music rationale continues to be encased within a self-fulfilling prophecy of dissociation and isolation from pop traditions. This is clearly illogical. Economic and political circumstances have changed so much that many folk music perspectives created and nurtured within the era of post-World War II utopianism have been obsolete for some time.[17] Yet the folk media's theoretical development since the glory days of quasi-Marxism has been modest, and a simplistic hate–love attitude towards popular music and urban society still saturates most folk writing, leaving the reader with a composite image of twisted dialectics and inextricable contradictions.

Folk music is still seen as having heroically evaded commercial structures, whereas mass art has been captured by them and watered down as a consequence. I quote the words of folk writer Chris Sugden on this point:

I have a vision. I think that we could work towards a folk equivalent of real ale. Real ale aims to be an honest, natural product, not altered to suit some idea of modern tastes ... promoted for its own intrinsic qualities ... The Campaign for Real Folk – I'll drink to that.[18]

Folkies who share Sugden's outlook always assume that technology and trade have historically been external influences upon music: that music has somehow struggled against these authorities. Yet to divide music communication from technology, production and finance, even in a pre-industrial society, is as fraudulent as separating 'real' from 'manufactured' ale. As Keith Negus writes:

Musical composition and performance have always depended on the instrument technologies available; whether European classical music, orally transmitted folk music, music of different regions of the African continent or contemporary popular music with its complex industrial networks of production and distribution. The character, conventions and reception of a particular music have been shaped by the machines of sound creation.[19]

No genre of music can ever achieve full independence from the economic pressures of a market economy. Sugden's view leads to an impasse: the folk industry and media attempt to function as relatively non-commercial businesses, marketing and discussing a potentially commercial music, while at the same time protecting that same music from the influence of a commercial structure that would bring its message to an infinitely larger number of people. As long as this relationship with an 'outside world' of popular music continues to be a problem, folk music will forever be hard to find on the radio, on stage and in the record shops. Only the already converted, willing to expend effort on searching out products, will be served with any degree of satisfaction. Folk music lovers themselves are not only the ones responsible for folk's failing visage: in a very real sense, they are also its main victims.

For some years, there has been a folk magazine on the internet that goes by the name of *Musical Traditions*. Its co-editors, Rod Stradling and Fred McCormick, understand music as a cultural text subject to change and mutation. They allow the site/magazine to be a home base for important arguments over where contextuality stops and textuality begins. Another internet magazine called *freefolk.com*, the editor of which is guitarist par excellence Mike Raven, has recently joined the fray. The aforementioned Unknown Public produces a CD journal that (it claims) is mailed to 50 different countries. So perhaps e-mail and the World Wide Web can reconfigure and recontextualise avowedly 'authentic' folk art in the most modern of all contexts. The folk revival, which traditionally has looked towards the past, must now widen its focus to include the future if it is to be commercially viable.

Of course, any reconfiguration must also include a reformation of the structure of the folk business world, purging itself of its stagnant, conservative elements and harnessing the winds of change instead of resisting them. The folk industry has to make itself more purposeful, more cohesive, more effective and (that dread word!) more popular. The present splendid isolation of folk, which finds itself disassociated even from other popular music genres, is largely antediluvian, reflecting the issues and events of yesterday, not of today. The revival has to find a new dynamic to replace the old, fading appeal to working-class solidarity and opposition to capitalism in any form. The commercial sector has to break down the rigid generic barriers and remove the paralysing sense of 'superiority' (and, conversely, of insecurity) that underlies the presentation of the music.

But in order to do this the folk media have somehow to question the attitudes of those whose aspirations they exist to express. These several encounters must go hand in hand if the folk revival, its 'industry' and its networking, are to get anywhere. For let us be clear about the alternatives. The choice certainly lies between growth and stagnation, but it will rarely be posed directly. There will always be extraneous issues that intrude – special complications or mitigating factors. If the folk music related 'industry' and media will not jump the hurdle, the consequences will not be immediately catastrophic. It may well be some time before these consequences become noticeable at all. All that will happen is that the slow slide towards impotence and failure will accelerate until it is finally too late to do anything about it.

A few concluding remarks

I have attempted to show, via this contextual and intertextual study, that the second folk revival was vital: a valid identification of hidden soundtracks; but I have also endeavoured to question the assumption that a historical consensus existed between the folk apotheosis and those being historically represented. This consensus was only 'valid' as a politicised socio/economic history at the revival's instigation: it could never be a universal 'truth'. I have also attempted to dispute the assumption that consensus existed among its contemporary representatives and, via a popular music studies perspective, have suggested that if we continue to look to the 'handcrafted' history of the folk revival for firm answers about how musical traditions work, we will be disappointed.

I have further suggested that we can no longer allow the folk revival to legislate comfortably between opposing or competing musical genres, between superior and inferior representations (à la Lloyd), for popular music history cannot subscribe to such totalising binary forms. Instead, by addressing certain historical instances in an attempt to clarify something perhaps less tangible but in the long run more valuable, I have submitted that the meaning of folk music has been continually contextually subjugated to political 'reason'.

By providing variable historical readings of the revival and showing the relative equality of all popular music, including the genre of folk, I have argued that nothing can be gained from providing a musical history constructed from apparently luminous absolutes. This reading of music history does entail frustration (for any work is frustrating if it avoids a hierarchy of meaning) but it also reveals that an eclectic musical language speaks to a wider, more divergent audience – something of a necessity for any folk movement. External histories such as this also show that the reaction of folklorists to the homogeneity of mass-produced music was not simply a reaction to music, but to the cultural and industrial systems that appeared to bring that music about. Thus, as times and music changed, the political antithesis of 'tradition' could not continue being successfully validated in the music, but only in the past systems which brought that validation about; it became illogical not only to fence off folk music from other genres, but also to confine folk's role in society as a narrative of political events.

Just as twentieth-century mass-produced music presented complex conceptual problems for folklorists in the 1950s, so the predicaments posed by the twenty-first century of how to contemporise and yet illuminate sources also call out. They cannot be circumvented by folklorists condemning the thrust of global imperialism while retreating back into their manuscripts. Further research into the uses and definitions of folk music will have to include perceptions of folk as one soundtrack amongst many. Folk music retains the capacity to arouse the impulses, but when it is applied as a historical veil over the surface of reality it merely replicates Benjamin's vision of the 'Angelus Novus': 'The storm irresistibly propels him into the future to which his back is turned, while the pile of debris before him grows skyward. The storm is what we call progress.'[20] Such actions deny the co-creative potential of our musical universe and reek of cultural pessimism.

Notes

1. Weskett, 'Come Write Me Down', p. 82.
2. Moulden, 'Is our Tradition Living?', pp. 20–23.
3. Dallas, '1965–74', p. 25.
4. Ibid., p. 11 (Ken Woollard to Dave Laing).
5. Heywood, 'Flowers of Edinburgh Wilt!', p. 12.
6. Ibid., p. 14.
7. Ibid., p. 15.
8. Unsigned editorial, *Hit the Dust,* 27 (HTD Records newsletter) (June–Sept. 2000), p. 1.
9. Heywood, Editorial: 'Tighten Your Belts!', p. 4.
10. Upton, 'What's Afoot?'
11. Interview with Jeremy Horrall, proprietor of Telford's Warehouse, Chester, June 2000.
12. For example, see letters page, *The Living Tradition*, 36 and subsequent replies.
13. McGrail, 'The Harpmakers', quoting Hugh Forbes, p. 47.
14. Interview with Colin Keefe, Luthier Guitars, June 2000.
15. Anderson, 'The Editor's Box' (Oct. 1996), p. 17.

16. Wilson, 'Who Are We?', p. 9.
17. Shuker, *Understanding Popular Music*, p. 16.
18. Sugden, 'There are Three Ways of Being "Folk"', p. 37.
19. Negus, *Producing Pop*, p. 28.
20. Benjamin, *Illuminations*, pp. 259–60.

Topic Records Discography

This discography is by no means complete (and let us all hope that it remains but a fraction of Topic's output in future years). It would not have been possible in its present state without assistance from the following: The Vaughan Williams Library (VWL) at Cecil Sharp House, The National Sound Archive (NSA), Tony Engle, Rod Stradling at *Musical Traditions* and, last but by no means least, Alistair Banfield (AB/Banfield) – thanks to all.

SHELLAC

1939–1940/1

TRC1   *The Man that Waters the Workers' Beer* (Paddy Ryan; arr. Alfred Roberts): Paddy Ryan (of the Unity Theatre) with guitar accomp. CP 889. 1CS0020192. *The Internationale* (Degeyter; arr. A. Bush): The Topic Singers and Band cond. by Will Sahnow. CP 892. later reissue of TRC1: The Internationale with different B-side.

TRC2   *Fags Are Up* (Arthur Pooley and Alfred Roberts). Recorded as a quickstep with vocal verse and chorus. From the Unity Theatre revue 'Turn Up the Lights': The Topic Variety Chorus and Band. CP 888. *Brother, Brother, Use Your Head!* (Geoffrey Parsons and Berkeley Fase). From the Unity Theatre revue 'Turn Up the Lights': Martin Lawrence (bass) with The Topic Band. CP 891. 1CS0020193.

TRC3   *Here We Come* (Roger Woddis and John Berry). Recorded as a quickstep with vocal verse and chorus. From the Unity Theatre revue 'Turn Up the Lights': The Topic Variety Chorus and Band. CP 890. 1CS0020194. *The Black Blackout* (Steve Weaver; arr. by Aubrey Bowman), a souvenir of WW II: sung by Jonathan Croft (at the piano, Ethel Green). CP 906.

TRC4   *Song Poem in E major for Vio* (Aram Khachaturian): Edward Silverman (violin) and Alan Bush (piano). CP 914. 1CS0020195. *Van Diemen's Land* (ballad of transportation), *Harvest Song* (from Purcell's 'King Arthur'): John Hargreaves (baritone) with male voice choir. CP 914-1.

TRC5   Balalaika Selection Number one. *The Soviet Airman's Song*; *Soviet Land*: The Medvedev Balalaika Sextet. *Poor Man's Heaven*: Paul Wesley.

TRC6   Balalaika Selection Number two. *Bravely Forward Comrades* (trad. Russian); *Salute to Life* (Shostakovich): Arr. and played by the Medvedev Balalaika Sextet. CP 954. 1CS0020197. *Left! Left!* (the international marching song of the people, including: *The Carmagnole, Bandita* [sic] *Rossa, United Front, Whirlwinds of Danger* and *Solidarity Forever*). Arr. for two pianos by Alan Rawsthorne, recorded by Geraldine and Mary Peppin. CP 959.

TRC7   *The People Sing!* A selection of English period songs arr. Alan Bush for two pianos recorded by Mary and Geraldine Peppin. CP 962. *The Cutty Wren* English medieval revolutionary song ('14th. century folk song'): Una Brandon-Jones, Hertzel Goldbloom and Martin Lawrence with The Topic Singers and pipe and tabor; accomp. cond. Arnold Goldsbrough. CP 963.

TRC8   Two Negro Songs of Protest: *How Long Brethren*; *Ah's De Man*: Martin Lawrence and The Topic Male Singers. *Lizzie Liberty* and *Thompson's Last Stand* (by Aubrey Bowman): Jonathan Croft.

TRC9   *The Refugees* (fugitives from Nazi oppression). Words by John Heartfield; music by Peter Baker. Sung by Mara Menshikova (Czech) and The Topic Singers cond. Arnold Goldsbrough. CP 972. (Also noted as 'song of exile from Hitler's Germany' in early catalogue). *The Peatbog Soldiers* (composed by prisoners in Nazi concentration camps). Tune noted by Hanns Eisler; arr. Alan Bush. Sung by The Topic Male Singers, cond. Arnold Goldsbrough. CP 973. 1CS0020203.

TRC10   *Truth on the March* (from the play 'Freedom on the Air' by Randall Swingler). Music by Alan Bush; sung by Michael Percival (baritone) with The Topic Singers and Unity String Orchestra cond. by the composer. CP 982. *Salute to Life* (English text by Nancy Head; music by Shostakovich). Topic Singers and Unity String Orch. Arr. and cond. Will Sahnow. CP 983. 1CS0020205 (NB. white label at NSA, different logo – reissue?).

TRC11   *Say Goodbye, Now* (Figaro's aria from Mozart's 'The Marriage of Figaro' – English text by Prof. E.J. Dent): Martin Marshall (baritone) with the Unity Orchestra cond. by Alan Bush. CP 985. 1CS0020207. Two Spanish Songs (cello and piano): *Tonada*; *Granadina*: Boris Rickelman (cello) and Alan Bush (piano). CP 986.

TRC12   *A New World Will Be Born* (from the Unity Theatre pantomime 'Jack the Giant Killer' by Geoffrey Parsons and Berkeley Fase): Michael Redgrave with Rhythm Band. CP 990. *Me Without You* (from the Unity Theatre pantomime 'Jack the Giant Killer'): Alan Kane with Rhythm Band. CP 991.

1941
TRC13   *Soviet Fatherlands Song (Land of Freedom):* The Soviet State Choir and Orchestra. *The Winkle Woman*: Della Facer with Alan Bush.

TRC14   *Trio* (1932) by Aram Khachaturian. 1st Movement: *Andante Dant* [*sic*] *Con Doloro*. Phil Cardew (clarinet), Edward Silverman (violin), Ben Franke (piano). CP 1028. *Monologue from Soviet Opera 'Yemelian Pugachev'* by M. Koval. Text by V. Kamenski, English text by Will Sahnow: Martin Lawrence (bass) with Topic Orchestra cond. Will Sahnow. CP 1029.

1942?
TRC15   *Young Comrade's Song* c/w Two Soviet Folksongs: *The Cruel Sweetheart*; *Song of the Collectives*: The Topic Singers. 1CS 0020212, 1CS 0020213? CP 1030/1?

TRC16   Three 17th-Century Catches: 'Catch as Catch Can': *Come Hither, Tom* (anon.); *Cursed Be the Wretch* (H. Carey); *Say What You Will* (H. Turner): Jonathan Croft with David and Michael Percival. No matrix no. *El Paso del Ebro* (The Crossing of the Ebro)

Spanish Republican song from the Civil War: Topic Choir and Orchestra. Arr. and cond. Rodolfo Halffter. No matrix no. Different pressing.

TRC17   *Soviet Airman's Song*: Soviet Choir and Military Band (sung in Russian). C 17. *Chapayev*; English text by Ben Blake, music by V. Sedoy: John Hargreaves (baritone) accomp. by Arnold Goldsbrough. H. 072.

1942–45
nil?

post-war 1945–48 (matrix numbers change – different pressings)
TRC18   *Tachanka*; words by M. Ruderman, music by K. Listov XYZ RA6 c/w *Kalinka*: USSR Red Banner Ensemble of the Red Army Songs and Dances, cond. A.V. Alexandrov 'People's Artist of the USSR'. XYZ RA7 new matrix, therefore next 5/6 releases issued in series?

TRC19   *From Border to Border* sung by Krasovsky with choir and orchestra of the Bolshoi Theatre, Moscow, cond. S.A. Samosud. From Dzerzhinskey's opera 'Quiet Flows the Don'. XYZ RR5790. *Cossack Song* sung by P.T. Kirpichek and P.S. Sellinik with the Bolshoi Theatre Chorus as above, from Dzerzhinskey's opera 'Virgin Soil Upturned' XYZ RR 5864.

TRC20   *The Mountain Ash* (Russian folk song): V.P. Vinogradov (tenor) with choir and orchestra. *A Hawk Flew into the Sky* (Russian folk song): Bolshoi Theatre artist P.T. Kirpichek (baritone) with choir and orchestra (see IPM archive).

TRC21   *The Tractor Song* from the film 'The Rich Bride' c/w *The Gay Girl Friends*: USSR Red Banner Ensemble of the Red Army Songs and Dances, music by Dunayevsky. XYZ RN 5860.

new matrix
TRC22   *Trepak* (Russian dance): Bandurist Orchestra of the USSR, directed by M.M. Michailoff. GRK 4. SOV. 623. *Youth* (Russian popular song); words by Danziger and Doleff; music by Blanter: The Glinka Orchestra and Chorus directed by V.W. Knushevitzky. GRK 749. SOV 4245B-1.

All of the above are before December 1948 (Topic Song Book; see inside back page). Available records are up to but not including TRC23.

VINYL AND POST-VINYL SHELLAC
It has been recorded (Topic catalogue 1970s) that TRC vinyl begins with 23. The NSA copy of 23 is shellac. Their copy of 24, however, is vinyl. Shellac/vinyl is probably an option. The NSA have only one Topic vinyl 78rpm. Surely the copy at NSA is a reissue; Pye (and Mercury) vinyl 78s only begin circa 1956.

late 1949
TRC23   *The Internationale* (Degeyter, arr. Alan Bush): The Centenary Choir with organ and orchestra cond. Alan Bush. 1CS0020227. *The Red Flag*, arr. Alan Bush: The

Centenary Choir cond. Alan Bush. 11880. NB. NSA copy is white (demo or reissue) with 'Topic Record Company' in bold black.

TRC24   *England Arise!* (Edward Carpenter): The WMA Singers conducted by Lawrence Leonard 11881. *The Partisan Song* (Aturov, arr. Alexandrov): The Centenary Choir with orchestra and organ cond. Alan Bush 11879. The copy of this record at the NSA is vinyl – post 1955?

1950

TRC25   12" double-sided (two records with TRC26): *Paul Robeson's Message of Peace.*

TRC26   The same. If this is the speech that Robeson delivered in Paris, 1949 ('loved Russia more than USA') – then we could date this as (probably) 1950–51.

TRC27   *Soviet Fatherland Song*: The WMA Singers c/w *Freedom's Song (Song of Democratic Youth)*: The WMA Singers.

TRC28   *Our Song Will Go on (The Peekskill Story)*. Paul Robeson, Howard Fast, Pete Seeger, The Weavers (sides a, b). Written and directed by Mario Casetta. No separate matrix nos. except IIIV. Weavers misspelt on label: 'Weevers'. The rally at Peekskill in upstate New York was 1949 – conflict with right-wing racists. The Weavers existed from 1949 to 1952, 1955–63 (–58 with Seeger).

TRC29   *Ami Go Home*: Ernst Busch with choir c/w *Sing a Song of the Blue Flag*: Youth Choir of the Mitteldeutscher-Rundfunk.

TRC30   *The Swallow* c/w *Along the River (Echo di Lasso):* State Choir of the USSR.

TRC31   May Day Greeting: The Choir of Women Teachers' Faculty of Cinkota, Hungary c/w *Song of the Tractor Drivers of Deszk*: Central Song and Music Ensemble of the Ironworkers' Union, Hungary.

TRC32   *Song about Schorsa* (Blantet and Golodni): Kromchenko and Kirichek. O 2131. *The Death of Chapaiev*: Korolev and the Moscow Philharmonic Orchestra, cond. Schteinberg. O 2132.

TRC33   *The North Wind Blows* ('from the new opera "The White-haired Girl" by Zhang Lu, Ma Ko, Xo Gingzh'): The Orchestra and Chorus of the Central College of Drama. O 2134. *Arise and Sing for Joy* (folk song of North Shensi): Li Bo with Arts Section of the China Democratic Youth.

TRC34   *Flax* (folk song): The Piatnitsky State Choir, chorus masters Zakharov and Kazmin. O 2135. *My Red Rose Bush*: The Piatnitzky State Choir with the State Orchestra of the USSR, cond. Chvatov. O 2136.

TRC35   *Suite* from music for the film 'Fall of Berlin' by Shostakovich, words by Dolmatovski: Choir and symphony orchestra cond. A.B. Gauk. Sides a, b. O 2430/O 2431.

TRC36   *The Capitol of Sovietland* (music by Kruchinin, words German). The Piatnitzky State Choir, solo: Khvatova. O 2432. *Kolkhoz Song about Moscow* (music by Maslov and Gusiev): The Piatnitzky State Choir. O 2433.

TRC37   *Green Grass, Green Carpet* (folk song): The Piatnitzky State Choir, solo: Guliaeva. O 2434. *I Am a Young Maiden Going to Fetch Water* (Russian dance song): The Piatnitzky State Choir, accordion: Filin. O 2435.

TRC38   *The Stripe* (Russian folk song): The Piatnitzky State Choir, solo: Lapina. O. 2436. *Kolkhoz Song-Chastushki:* Women soloists of the Piatnitzky State Choir: Guliaeva, Podlatova, accordion: Filin. O 2437.

TRC39   *The Asphalter's Song, I'm Champion at Keeping 'em Rolling* c/w *Four Pence a Day*; *Barnyards of Delgatie*: Ewan MacColl.

TRC40   *The Four Loom Weaver* c/w *McKaffery*: Ewan MacColl.

TRC41–TRC45   *Song of the Forest* (Shostakovich/Dolmatovsky): The State Choir of Russian Song, Boys' Choir of the State Choral School, State Symphony Orchestra of the USSR, cond. Mravinsky, I.I. Petrov, V.I. Kilchevsky. Also on one side of TRC41: *Song of Peace* from the film 'Meeting on the Elbe' (Shostakovich/ Dolmatovsky): The A.V. Alexandrov Song and Dance Ensemble of the Soviet Army, cond. B.A. Alexandrov.

TRC46   *As I Went Out One May Morning* c/w *Keach in the Creel*: Ewan MacColl.

TRC47   *The Song of Momus to Mars* (Boyce) c/w *O What a Charming Thing's a Battle* (Dibdin): Martin Lawrence and the WMA Orchestra.

TRC48   *Collier Laddie* (Scottish folk song) c/w *Johnny Lad* (Scottish folk song): Ewan MacColl with Al Jeffrey.

TRC49   *The Brewer Laddie* (Scottish folk song) c/w *Johnny Lad* (Scottish folk song): Ewan MacColl.

TRC50   *Poor Paddy Works on the Railway*: Ewan MacColl c/w *Cannily, Cannily* (Tyneside folk song): Isla Cameron with Al Jeffrey – banjo.

TRC51   *Moses of the Mail* (English work song): Ewan MacColl with Al Jeffrey c/w *The Fireman's not for Me*: Isla Cameron with Al Jeffrey.

TRC52   *The Song for Stalin* folk song from Timisoara region of Rumania: Maria Lataretu with Folk Orchestra accomp. O 3235. *The Peace Hora* folk song from the Ploesti region of Rumania: Ioana Rad accomp. by the Rumanian Radio Committee Folk Orchestra. O 3236.

TRC53   *The East in Red Glow*: solo voice with choir and piano accomp. from the People's Republic of China. *The People of the Whole World Are of One Heart:* choral song with piano accomp. from the People's Republic of China. O 3237/8.

TRC54   *The Ballad of Stalin*: Ewan MacColl and Al Jeffrey c/w *Sovietland*: The Soviet Choir and Orchestra.

TRC55   *The Coalowner and the Pitman's Wife* c/w *Jamie Foyers* (Scottish traditional ballad with words by Ewan MacColl): Ewan MacColl (side a with Al Jeffrey – banjo; side b unaccompanied). O 3617/8.

1952

TRC56   *Dirty Old Town*: written and sung by Ewan MacColl c/w *Sheffield Apprentice* (a 'come all ye'): Ewan MacColl (side a unaccompanied; side b with Al Jeffrey – guitar).

TRC57   *Browned Off* c/w *The Union of the Fire Brigade Song:* Ewan MacColl with Al Jeffrey.

TRC58   *He Met His Death in a Far Away Land* (Moussorgsky) c/w *Lyubimy Gorod* (Dear Home Town); words: E. Dolmatovsky; music: N. Bogoslovsky: Paul Robeson. O 4046/7.

TRC59   *Ch'i Lai* (Ching-hua jen min kung ko ku Nieh?) (Ny Erh); Chinese national anthem sung by Paul Robeson in English and Chinese. O 4048. *Fengyang* – old Chinese folk tune dating back some 400 years, Ming Dynasty. Words from time of Japanese invasion: Paul Robeson. O 4049.

TRC60   *The Chinese Soldiers' Song* (modern words to an old tune), *Riding the Dragon* (old children's song of China). O 4050 c/w *Joe Hill* American union song by Earl Robinson: Paul Robeson. O 4051.

TRC61   *Ballad for Americans*: text by John Latouche, music by Earl Robinson. Sung by the London Youth Choir with Martin Lawrence (bass). Cond. John Hasted, arr. Arnold Clayton. Parts one and two. O 4106/7.

TRC62   As above, parts three and four: The London Youth Choir. O 4108/9.

TRC63   *Kawaliry*. Polish folk song from Radzonow arranged by T. Sygietynski for the Mazowsze Song and Dance Ensemble, English text by Stewart Farrar. Sung by Elvira Childe and The WMA Singers, cond. Alan Bush c/w *A Bridge to the Right*. Lyrics: H. Kolczkowska, English text: Honor Arundel, music A. Gradstein: The WMA Singers with Martin Lawrence.

TRC64   Two Ghetto Songs *Wilno Ghetto Song* c/w *Warsaw Ghetto Song*: The WMA Singers with Martin Lawrence.

TRC65   *Shule Agra* (Irish folk song arr. Mátyás Seiber): sung by Anna Pollack with The WMA Singers cond. Alan Bush c/w *Mrs McGrath* (Irish ballad) arr. Christian Darnton: Anna Pollack and Cragg Sinkinson with The WMA Singers.

TRC66   *Festival Seasons*, *A Village Song* c/w *Love Song of the Grasslands*: Yu i-Husuan (China).

1953

TRC67   *Bonny Boy* c/w *She Moved Through the Fair*: Patrick Galvin with Al Jeffrey.

TRC68   *Brown Girl* c/w *My Love Came to Dublin*: Patrick Galvin with Al Jeffrey.

TRC69   *Wild Colonial Boy* c/w *Football Crazy*: Patrick Galvin with Al Jeffrey.

TRC70   *Wackfoldediddle* c/w *Johnson's Motor Car* (Irish Rebel Songs): Patrick Galvin with Al Jeffrey.

TRC71   *Ballad of New Poland* c/w *Trafford Road Ballad*: Ewan MacColl with Brian Daly.

TRC72   *Strange Fruit* written by Lewis Allen arr. and sung by Aubrey Pankey (baritone) accomp. by Frederick Bontoft. *John Henry* ('words and music by Aubrey Pankey' – not!). Sung by Aubrey Pankey (baritone) accomp. by Frederick Bontoft.

TRC73   *Jim Crow* c/w *Tarrier's Song* (arr. Irving Heller), *Great Gittin Up Mornin'* (arr. Lawrence Brown): Aubrey Pankey with Frederick Bontoft.

TRC74   *Deep River* c/w *Out in the Rain* (arr. Irving Heller), *Didn't My Lord Deliver Daniel* (arr. Lawrence Brown): Aubrey Pankey with Frederick Bontoft.

TRC75   *Girl at Stzalinvaroz* c/w *It's Only Propaganda*: Ewan MacColl with Brian Daly – guitar.

TRC76   *Es Brent* (The Flames); song from the Warsaw Ghetto; English text by Stewart Farrar, music by Hersch Glick; sung in Yiddish and English by Martin Lawrence (bass) with The WMA Singers, cond. Alan Bush. *Zog Nisht Kainmol* (Tell Me Not) song from the Wilno Ghetto; English text by Stewart Farrar, music by Gebertik; sung in Yiddish and English by Martin Lawrence and The WMA Singers cond. Alan Bush.

1954

TRC77   *Johnny Breadisley* c/w *Henry Martin*: Ewan MacColl with Brian Daly.

TRC78   *Johnny Todd* (Traditional English Ballad) c/w *Cosher Bailey's Engine* (Welsh Industrial Song): Ewan MacColl with Brian Daly – guitar.

TRC79   *Wull Cayrd* (words by Alex Russell; trad. Scots tune): Ewan MacColl with Bryan [*sic*] Daly – guitar c/w *The Swan-Necked Valve*: Ewan MacColl and Brian Daly – guitar. Matrix: WMA 5776/7.

TRC80   *A Hawthorn Blossoms* (as sung by the Beryozka Dance Co.) English text by Paul Fineberg, music by M. Isakovsky: The Middlesex Youth Choir, cond. Gladys Ritchie c/w *The Birch Tree* (trad. Russian folk song), *The Road is Bright* (music by I. Dunayevsky): The Middlesex Youth Choir, cond. Gladys Ritchie.

TRC81   *The White Haired Girl* (1 and 2): The Chinese Operatic and Orchestral Ensemble.

TRC82   *Who Dares to Speak?* c/w *Johnny, I Hardly Knew You*: Patrick Galvin.

TRC83   *The Women are Worse Than the Men* c/w *Whiskey in the Jar*: Patrick Galvin.

TRC84   Two Australian Bush Ballads: *Bold Jack Donahue* c/w *The Banks of the Condamine:* A.L. Lloyd with Alf Edwards – concertina.

1955

NB. Weavers re-form.

TRC85   *Talking UnAmerican Blues*: Betty Sanders c/w *Banks of Marble*: The Weavers.

TRC86   Test pressing?

TRC87   *Pity the Downtrodden Landlord* (Woolf/Clayton): Alfie Bass and the Four Bailiffs (Unity Theatre) c/w *Housing Repairs and Rents Act* (Fred Dallas): Alfie Bass and the Four Bailiffs with instrumental accompaniment.

TRC88   *Pity the Downtrodden Landlord* (Woolf/Clayton): Alfie Bass and the Four Bailiffs c/w *The Oakey Evictions* (a Northumbrian ballad *c*.1870): George Burn with Al Jeffrey (banjo).

TRC89   Test pressing?

TRC90   Test pressing?

TRC91   *Young Dimiter* c/w *Saucy Dilmano* (folk songs arr. Kutev): Bulgarian Song and Dance Ensemble. 2486.

1956
TRC92   *Dark as a Dungeon* (written by Merl Travis) c/w *Talking Union Blues:* Pete Seeger. 'Recorded at a Hootenanny'. Released Jan. 1956.

TRC93   *The Iron Horse* (Scottish railway ballad), *Four Pence a Day*: Ewan MacColl and Brian Daly – guitar c/w *The Wark o' the Weavers*: Ewan MacColl. Partial reissue of TRC39?

TRC94   *Oh No John* (English folk song) c/w *No More Auction Block* (spiritual): Paul Robeson.

TRC95   *Joe Hill* c/w *John Brown's Body*: Paul Robeson, piano accomp. Alan Booth.

TRC96   *Kevin Barry* (Irish ballad) c/w *The Four Insurgent Generals* (song of the Spanish Civil War): Paul Robeson, piano accomp. Alan Booth.

TRC97   *Sixteen Tons* ('American work song'; NB. actually written by Merl Travis) c/w *The Swan-Necked Valve* (British Foundry Workers' song): Ewan MacColl with Brian Daly (guitar).

TRC98   *Talking Miner Blues* c/w *Pretty Boy Floyd*: Jack Elliott.

TRC99   *The Blarney Stone* c/w *If You Ever Went to Ireland*: Margaret Barry with banjo. WMA 99-1/2.

TRC100   *The Bridge Below the Town:* Written, sung and played by John Hasted (banjo). *Keep Talking*: Al Jeffrey (vocal, guitar) with Ted Andrews (banjo). WMA 100-1/2.

TRC101   *Round and Round the Picket Line* c/w *Nine Hundred Miles*: (Hylda Sims and) The City Ramblers. WMA 101-1/2. The Ramblers were: Russell Quaye, Shirley Bland, Eric Bunyan, Vic Pitt, Bobby Taylor, Jimmie McGregor (see *English Dance and Song*, 46/3). Released May 1956.

TRC102   *The Banks of Sweet Dundee*: Ewan MacColl with Alf Edwards. WMA 102-1 c/w *Fitba' Crazy*, *The Wee Cooper o' Fife*: Ewan MacColl with Brian Daly. WMA 102-2.

1957
TRC103   *Old Blue* c/w *Rambling Blues*: Jack Elliott. WMA 103-1/2.

TRC104   *Streets of Laredo* c/w *Boll Weevil*: Jack Elliott. WMA 104-1/2.

TRC105   *Villikins and his Dinah* (Cockney ballad): Wendy Corum and chorus with

Elsie Bracher, piano. *The Coachman* (Cockney ballad): Wendy Corum with John Hasted (accordion). WMA 105-1/2.

TRC106   *The Collier's Rant* c/w *The Row Between the Cages*: Alex Eaton with John Hasted. WMA 106-1/2.

1958
TRC107   *Freight Train* c/w *Cumberland Gap*: Peggy Seeger. WMA 107-1/2.

TRC108   *Pretty Little Baby* c/w *Child of God*: Peggy Seeger (side a guitar; side b banjo). WMA 108-1, WMA 108-2. Label change: different logo, light green background. 1CS0020280.

National Sound Archive: 'this appears to be the end of the 78s'.

LPs, EPs AND SINGLES: 7", 8", 10" and 12"

English Dance and Song, autumn 1969, stated: 'The name TOPIC first appeared on 78 rpm records produced by the Workers' Music Association, and in fact the first LP to bear the name (a 12" record in a white sleeve, consisting of dubbings from 78 recordings) also appeared under these auspices.'

1953–54 three sets of 10" LPs were completed under a deal with US label STINSON – see TLP3.

TLP1   *Sailors' Songs and Shanties*: Ewan MacColl, A.L. Lloyd, Harry H. Corbett. Also included: reissue of TRC7.

TLP2   A collection of spirituals and songs by Aubrey Pankey (baritone) dubbed from 78s.

TLP3   Material from the STINSON set of sailor's songs … part of which were later released as T7 and T8 in the 8" format.

TRL3   A reissue of TLP1 (RL could stand for re-release?)   *The Singing Sailor*: Ewan MacColl, A.L. Lloyd and Harry H. Corbett (1956). The Ship in Distress/Johnny Todd/ Haul on the Bowline/The Cruel Ship's Captain/The Dreadnaught/Santy Anna/The Coast of Peru/Row, Bullies Row/Blood Red Roses/Off to Sea Once More/Blow the Man Down/ The Flying Cloud/Lord Franklin/Paddy Doyle/Van Diemen's Land/The Greenland Whale Fishery.

T1   *Warsaw Festival Souvenir 1955*.

T2   *Festival of Folk Music* (extracts from above, 1955).

T3   *Irish Songs of Resistance 1* (Nov. 1956): Patrick Galvin with Al Jeffrey – banjo.

T4   *Irish Songs of Resistance 2*: Patrick Galvin with Al Jeffrey – banjo.

8T5   *Woody Guthrie's Blues*: Jack Elliott. Talking Columbia Blues/Talking Dustbowl Blues/1913 Massacre/Hard Travelling/Ludlow Massacre/Talking Sailor Blues.

10T6   *Street Songs and Fiddle Tunes of Ireland*: Margaret Barrie [*sic*] and Michael Gorman (with Tommy Maguire, Paddy Breen and Patsy Goulden). Songs: The Wild Colonial Boy/Our Ship is Ready/The Factory Girl/The Cycling Championship/Her Mantle so Green. Reels: The Bunch of Keys/The Heather Breeze/Dr. Gilbert/Hornpipe: The Boys of Blue Hill. Polkas: Maguire's Favourite/Trallee Jane/Maggy in the Wood.

8T7   *Row, Bullies, Row*: A.L. Lloyd and Ewan MacColl (1957). Row, Bullies Row/The Dreadnaught/Johnny Todd/Paddy Doyle, etc. All with chorus and concertina.

8T8   *The Black Ball Line: Sea Songs and Shanties*: A.L. Lloyd and Ewan MacColl (1957). The Black Ball Line/Do Me Ama/Reuben Ranzo/The Handsome Cabin Boy/A Hundred Years Ago/Stormalong/The Coast of Peru/The Gauger/Sally Racket.

10T9   *Eleven American Ballads and Songs*: Peggy Seeger (1957). Devilish Mary/ Cumberland Gap/I Never Will Marry/The Lady of Carlisle/The Fair Maid by the Shore/ The Deer Song/Come All Ye Fair and Tender Ladies/The Wife of Usher's Well/Soldier's Joy/Shady Grove/Georgia Buck.

7T10   *Nancy Whiskey Sings*: Nancy Whiskey 1SE0049879 (1957). Recorded prior to her hit with the Chas. McDevitt Skiffle Group. This recording originally included the Irish rebel song 'The Bold Fenian' but the track was withdrawn before release. The recording may include The Calton Weaver – the source of Nancy's stage name.

10T11   *John Gibbon's Disc*: John Gibbon (1957). John Henry/Stakolee/Another Man Done Gone/True Religion/You're Going to Leave me Baby/Can't You Line 'em/Kansas City Blues/Corina.

10T12   *Rumanian Folk Music*: field recordings edited by A.L. Lloyd (1958). Geamparalele/Ca Din Cimpoli/Miorita/Ca La Breaza/Bogatul Si Saracul/Briu/I-Auzi Mindro Pitigoiu/Arcanul/Bugeacul/Miu Haiducul/Riule Pariule/Pe Picior/Pendem Devla Draboro/Tumbe Tumbe/Calusarii Si Ciocirlia.

10T13   *Shuttle and Cage*: Ewan MacColl with Peggy Seeger (banjo and guitar) (1958). Twelve industrial songs: Tha Wark of the Weavers/The Blantyre Explosion/Moses of the Mail/Fourpence a Day/Champion at Keeping 'em Rolling/The Four Loom Weaver/The Plodder Seam/Cosher Bailey's Engine/The Gresford Disaster/Cannily, Cannily/The Coalowner and the Pitman's Wife/Poor Paddy Works on the Railway.

10T14   *The Rambling Boys*: Jack Elliott and Derroll Adams (1958). Rich and Rambling Boys/Buffalo Skinners/Wish I Was a Rock/State of Arkansas/Mother's Not Dead/East Virginia Blues/The Old Bachelor/Danville Girl/The Death of Mr. Garfield/Roll On Buddy. Query on track 9; on reissue but not on this?

10T15   *Jack Takes the Floor*: Jack Elliott (1958). San Francisco Bay Blues/Ol' Riley/ Boll Weevil/Bed Bug Blues/New York Town/Grey Goose/Mule Skinner's Blues/Cocaine/ Dink's Song/Black Baby/Salty Dog.

12T16   *Chorus from the Gallows*: Ewan MacColl and Peggy Seeger (1960?). Derek Bentley/The Black Velvet Band/Jamie Raeburn's Farewell/Minorie/Hughie the Graeme/ Johnny O'Breadiesley/Treadmill Song/Turpin Hero/Crafty Farmer/McKaffery/Jimmie Wilson/Lag's Song/Van Diemen's Land/Go Down Ye Murderers.

10T17   *Paul Robeson's Transatlantic Concert*: Paul Robeson with piano accomp. Winifred Harrison. Water Boy/Scandalise My Name/Lullaby/All Through the Night/Ol' Man River/ Curly Headed Baby/Star Vicino/Song of Freedom (Smetana)/Schlaf Mein Kind/Kevin Barry/No More.

7T18   *Come Along, John!* 8 American folk songs for children sung by Peggy Seeger with Barbara and Penny Seeger. Come Along John/All Round the Kitchen/Billy Barlow/ Old Aunt Kate/Little Bird/Lula Gal/Rissolty Rissolty/The Derby Ram.

7T19   *Round and Round with the Jeffersons*: The Jeffersons (Al Jeffrey, Barbara Young, Ted Ford, Ted Andrews). The Rakes of Mallow/I Gave My Love a Cherry/Poor and Rambling Boy/Coortin' in the Kitchen/The Drover's Dream/Keep Your Feet Still Geordie Hinny.

12T20   *Pete Seeger's Guitar Guide for Folk Singers* (1958). An instructional record with booklet demonstrating folk-style guitar technique. A Folkways (USA) recording.

10T21   *Israeli Songs*: Zimra Ornatt with Leon Rosselson – guitar (1958/9). Ashira Ladonai (I Will Sing to the Lord)/Ki Tinam (Because it is Pleasant)/Pizmon Lyakinton (The Hyacinth)/Rachel, Rachel/Roeh Vroah (Shepherd and Shepherdess)/Yesusum Midbar Vtsia (The Wilderness Shall be Glad)/Orcha Bamidbar (Desert Caravan)/Hafle Vafele (Miracle of Miracles)/Taam Haman (The Taste of Manna)/Agada (The Legend of Kineret)/ Dodi Tsach Vadom (My Beloved)/Haderech Leilat (On the Way to Eilat).

12T21   *Bound for Glory*: Woody Guthrie, told by Will Geer (1958). Stagolee/Little Sack of Sugar/Ship in the Sky/Swim, Swim, Swimmy/Vigilante Man/Do Re Me/Pastures of Plenty/Grand Coulee Dam/This Land is My Land/Talking Fish Blues/The Sinking of the Reuben James/Jesus Christ/There's a Better World A-Coming. A Folkways (USA) recording. Only Topic issue with duplicated number. 12" issue, rather than 10". VWL has this as 12T21. See 12T31.

10/12T22   Test pressing?

10T23   *Play the 5 String Banjo*: Pete Seeger's 5-String Banjo Tutor with booklet. A Folkways (USA) recording.

10T24   *Mountain Songs and Banjo Tunes*: Guy Carawan (banjo and guitar). The Crawdad Song/Charlie/Sourwood Mountain/Ida Red/The Young Man Who Wouldn't Hoe his Corn/ Who's Going to Shoe your Pretty Little Foot?/Railroad Bill/Poor Little Turtle Dove/ Cindy, Cindy/The Three Little Pigs/The Kentucky Moonshiner/Chilly Winds/The Kicking Mule/Whoa Buck.

10T25   *Second Shift*: Ewan MacColl with Peggy Seeger. The Song of the Iron Road/ Droylsden Wakes/The Calton Weaver/Twenty One Years/The Best Little Door Boy/Oh, Dear Me/Will Caird/The Iron Horse/The Durham Strike/The Collier Laddie/The Colour Bar Strike/The Swan-Necked Valve.

10T26   *Barrack Room Ballads*: Ewan MacColl with Peggy Seeger (banjo and guitar), Jimmy MacGregor (guitar) and John Cole (harmonica). Join the British Army/The Ghost Army of Korea/The Ballad of Wadi Maktilla/The Young Trooper Cut Down in his Prime/ Bless 'em All/Any Complaints/The Second Front Song/Seven Years in the Sand/Farewell to Sicily/Browned off/When this Ruddy War Is Over.

TOP27 *Liverpool Packet*: Stan Kelly (with Leon Rosselson and Geoff Rose) sings songs from Liverpool (1958). Maggie May/Away, Haul Away/Lowlands Away.

10T28 *Irish Songs Recalled*: Dominic Behan accompanied by John Hasted. Zoological Gardens/Love is Teasing/The Poor Lone Boy/The Maid of the Sweet Brown Knowe/ Coolin/Maureen/The Blind Man/Lagan Love/The Old Triangle/She Moved Through the Fair/Poem.

12T29 *Brownie McGhee and Sonny Terry Guitars, Harmonica* (acc. Gene Moore drums). Better Day/Confusion/Dark Road/John Henry/Let Me Make You a Little Money/Old Jabo/If You Lose Your Money/Guitar Highway/Heart in Sorrow/Preachin' the Blues/ Can't Help Myself/Best of Friends/I Love You, Baby. A Folkways (USA) recording.

10T30 *Harmonica Blues*: Sonny Terry. Alcoholic Blues/Women's Blues (Corina)/ Locomotive Blues/Bad Luck Blues/Lost John/Shortnin' Bread/Fine and False Blues/ Harmonica Stomp/Beautiful City. A Folkways (USA) recording.

12T31 *Bound for Glory*: Woodie Guthrie with Will Geer. Reissue of 12T21 with different album sleeve.

TOP32 *Robeson's Here!*: Paul Robeson, piano accomp. Alan Booth. Going Home/ Curly Headed Baby/Eriskay Love Lilt/Now Sleeps the Crimson Petal.

TOP33 *Pete and Five Strings*: Pete Seeger. Penny's Farm/John Riley/Rissolty Rissolty/ Jam on Gerry's Rocks/Come All Ye Fair and Tender Ladies/Git Along Little Dogies. A Folkways (USA) recording.

TOP34 Test pressing?

12T35 *Down by the Liffeyside – Irish Street Ballads*: Dominic Behan with Peggy Seeger, Leon Rosselson and Ralph Rinzler. Get Me Down Me Filling Knife/The Saint/ Down by the Liffeyside/Ross' Farewell to Dublin/Waxy Dargell/Red Roses for Me/ Thank You Mam, Said Dan/John Mitchell/The Finding of Moses/Master McGrath/Dicey Riley/Finnegan's Wake/The Women are Worse than the Men/Easy and Slow/The Spanish Lady/The Twang Man/Bold Robert Emmett/Biddy Mulligan.

10T36 *Bold Sportsmen All*: Ewan MacColl and A.L. Lloyd with Steve Benbow, Peggy Seeger (guitars), John Cole (harmonica). Govan Pool Room Song/Old Bob Ridley/The Sporting Races of Galway/The Old Bitch Fox/Football Crazy/Creeping Jane/Card Playing Song/The Cock Fight/Bold Thady Quill/The Turpin-Sugar Ray Fight.

TOP37 *Hootenanny New York City*: Pete Seeger with Sonny Terry, Bob de Cormier and Jerry Silverman (1959). Mule Skinner Blues/Talking Union Blues/Dark as a Dungeon/ California Blues/Wimoweh. A Hootenanny (USA) recording.

TOP38 *Shine Like a Star*: Peggy Seeger and Her Sisters (1959). Amen/Child of God/ Pretty Little Baby/Great Big Stars/Shine Like a Star/The Angel Band/Watch the Stars.

12T39 *Spirituals by the Fisk Jubilee Singers*. I Couldn't Hear Nobody Pray/O The Rocks and the Mountains/Rockin' Jerusalem/When I Was Sinkin' Down/You May Bury Me in the East/He Arose/The Angels Done Bowed Me/There's a Great Camp Meeting/ Were You There?/Done Made My Vow to the Lord/I'm A-Rolling Through an Unfriendly World/Lord I'm Out There on Your Word. A Folkways (USA) recording.

12T40

12T41   *Streets of Song* – Childhood Memories of City Streets from Glasgow, Salford and Dublin: Ewan MaColl and Dominic Behan (1959). See Robert Shelton Collection, The University of Liverpool for complete transcription as supplied with recording. See also The Singing Streets Folkways FW 8501; USA copy.

12T42

12T43

12T44   *Easter Weekend and After – Songs of the IRA*: Dominic Behan acc. John Hasted. Erin-go-Brath/It's a Grand Old Country/The Recruiting Sergeant/Slean Libh/Sgt. William Bailey/Barry's Column/Roscarberry/The Boys of County Cork/Johnston's Motor Car/ Sean Tracy/Take it Down from the Mast/The Castle of Brumboe/The Merry Ploughboy/ The Old Alarm Clock/The Patriot Game.

12001   *Songs Against the Bomb* (1960). 12" LP. Some live tracks at the Ballads and Blues (Ewan MaCColl and Peggy Seeger) and the Partisan Coffee House (London Youth Choir with Fred and Betty Dallas). Brother Won't You Join in the Line? – Ewan MaCColl, Peggy Seeger and Jack Elliott 1958; The Crooked Cross – Ewan MaCColl and Peggy Seeger 1960; Strontium 90 (Dallas) – Fred and Betty Dallas with Ron Fielder (banjo) 1959; Hey Little Man (Sinner Man) – Fred and Betty Dallas; Doomsday Blues (St. James Infirmary Blues) – Fred Dallas (sung in the film *Aldermaston*) 1958; The Ballad of the Five Fingers (MaCColl) – Ewan MaCColl and Peggy Seeger 1957 (from the play *So Long at the Fair*); There are Better Things to Do – Peggy Seeger (banjo) with Jack Elliott (guitar) 1958; The H-Bomb's Thunder (words by John Brunner, tune the American Union song Miner's Lifeguard; arr. John Hasted) – The London Youth Choir, soloists Wendy Edwards and Ron Fielder (banjo) with Leon Rosselson (guitar) 1958; Song of Hiroshima (Koji Kinoshita; English text Ewan MaCColl; arr. Alan Bush) – The London Youth Choir, soloist Wendy Edwards 1955; Hoist the Window (a Negro Spiritual arr. John Hasted) – The London Youth Choir, soloist Marlene Tallman with Leon Rosselson (guitar) and Ron Fielder (banjo) 1952; That Bomb Has Got to Go (words MaCColl, Seeger; tune traditional shanty A Hundred Years ago) – Ron Fielder, Ray Edwards and members of the Robin Hood Singers 1959; The Dove (MaCColl). Freely based on the old English folk song The Cuckoo is a Pretty Bird; arr. Leon Rosselson – Margaret McKeown with Leon Rosselson (guitar) 1954; The Family of Man (Fred Dallas) arr. Wendy Edwards – The London Youth Choir, soloist Ron Fielder (banjo), Margaret McKeown, Marlene Tallman and Ray Edwards, with Leon Rosselson (guitar) 1957. 1LP0129508.

TOP45   *Songs and Dances of the French Cameroons*: Mouan(tan)gue and his Drummers. Sondi Di Bwea/Bele Mama/Congo/Tondo Mba/A Ndolo.

TOP46   *Songs and Dances of Argentina*: Leda and Maria: Zambita Arribena/Una Lagrime/Manchay Pulto/Their di Querer/Probrecito/Mi Caballo/Huachi-Tori/La Mota/El Humahuaqueno.

TOP47   *Songs and Dances* contd.?

TOP48   *Songs and Dances* contd.?

10T49   *Songs of the Aegean*: Pieris Zarmas. NSA … 2LP0076751

10T50   *Still I Love Him* – 'Great Traditional Singers' series: Ewan MacColl and Isla Cameron (1960). The American Stranger/Geordie/Are Ye Sleeping, Maggie?/The Bleacher Lass of Kelvinhaugh, etc.

12T51   *Outback Ballads – Songs from the Australian Bush and Outback*: A.L. Lloyd accompanied by Peggy Seeger, John Cole, Ralph Rinzler. Flash Jack from Gungadai/ Lachlan Tigers/The Cockies of Bungaree/South Australia/The Banks of the Condamine (Nile)/Bluey Brink/The Overlander/A Thousand Miles Away/The Flash Stockman/ Wild Colonial Boy/Brisbane Ladies/Bold Jack Donahue/The Shearer's Dream/The Derby Ram.

10T52   *Jeannie Robertson* – 'Great Traditional Singers' series. The Bonnie Wee Lassie Who Never Said No/What a Voice/My Plaidie's Awa'/The Gypsy Laddies/When I Was New but Sweet Sixteen/MacCrimmon's Lament/Roy's Wife of Aldivalloch/Lord Lovat. World of Jazz series.

12T53   *The Music of New Orleans Vol. 1*: The Music of the Streets and the Music of Mardi Gras. A Folkways (USA) recording.

12T54   *The Music of New Orleans Vol. 2*: The Eureka Brass Band. A Folkways (USA) recording.

12T55   *The Music of New Orleans Vol. 3*: The Music of the Dance Halls. A Folkways (USA) recording.

'World of Jazz series ends'. (NSA)

TOP56   *Vive La Canadienne*: Perry Friedman. Vive La Canadienne/The Shining Birch Tree/Mary Ann/The Grand Hotel/The Red River Valley/Great Big Sea Home.

TOP57   *Hush Little Baby*: Sandy and Caroline Paton. Hush Little Baby/Lord Bateman/ Tittery Nan/Perry Merry Dixi Domini/Katy Cruel.

TOP58

10T59   *Working on the Railroad*: Jesse Fuller. Railroad Work Song/Lining Up the Tracks/John Henry/Railroad Blues/San Francisco Bay Blues/Hangin' 'Round/The Skin Game.

TOP60   *Songs for Swinging Landlords to*: Stan Kelly. Greedy Landlord/Oakey Evictions/ The Man that Waters the Workers' Beer/Pity the Downtrodden Landlord.

TOP61

TOP62   *Paul Robeson Sings Freedom Songs*.

TOP63   *Songs of Liberty*: Paul Robeson.

TOP64   *Yugoslav Dances*: The Tine Rozanc Ensemble. Zabaljka – Serbia; Tandrcak – Serbia; So mamca mi rekil – Slovenia; Kortensko na pojas – Macedonia; Bohinjski Polka – Slovenia.

TOP65   *Dancing Sardanas – Catalonian Dancers*: Orquestra Cobla Soleris.

TOP66 *All for Me Grog – English Drinking Songs*: A.L. Lloyd. All for Me Grog/Foggy

Dew/The Butcher and the Chamber Maid/John Barleycorn/Jug of Punch/The Drunken Maids.

TOP67   *Far Over the Forth*: Ray and Archie Fisher. The Night Visiting Song/Far Over the Forth/The Twa Corbies/Kilbogie.

TOP68   *By Mormond Braes*: Dolina Maclennan and Robin Gray (1962). Gin I wa' fer the Gandie Rins/Fil-u-o Ro Hu-o/The Gypsy Laddies/Bratach Bana/Port a Beul/Hug O Ran O Ro/Mormond Braes.

TOP69   *Songs Spun in Liverpool* (live): The Spinners (1962). The Whip Jamboree/The Liverpool Barrow Boy/Hayarden/The Champion of the Seas/Judy Drownded/John Peel.

TOP70   *3/4 AD*: Davey Graham and Alexis Korner (1962). Anji/Davey's Train Blues/3/4 AD.

TOP71   *Gamblers and Sporting Blades*: A.L. Lloyd and Ewan MacColl acc. Steve Benbow – guitar. Skewball; Heenan and Sayers; The Bold Gambler Boy – A.L. Lloyd. Reynard the Fox; Morrisey and the Russian Sailor – Ewan MacColl.

TOP72   *Troubled Love*: Peggy Seeger. A Rich Old Man/The Rambling Gambler/The Cruel War is Waging/The Trooper and the Maid.

TOP73   *Early in the Spring*: Peggy Seeger. Madam I Have Come to Court You/When I Was in My Prime/So Early in the Spring/The Chickens They Are Crowing.

TOP74   *The Collier's Rant*: Louis Killen, Johnny Handle, acc. Colin Ross (1962). Blackleg Miners – Louis Killen; Collier's Rant – Johnny Handle; Aw Wish Pay Friday Would Come – Louis Killen/The Putter – Johnny Handle; The Trimdon Grange Explosion – Louis Killen; The Waggoner – Johnny Handle. See Topic 189.

TOP75   *Northumbrian Garland*: Louis Killen, Johnny Handle, acc. Colin Ross (1962). Anti Gallician Privateer/Sair Fyeld Hinnu/Keep Your Feet Still/Up the Raw/Dol-Li A/ Derwentwater's Farewell. See Topic 189.

TOP76   *Ceilidh at the Crown – Live at the Jug of Punch*. An evening at the Jug of Punch folk club at the Crown, Station Street, Birmingham: The Ian Campbell Folk Group (1962). Paddy on the Railroad/The Twa Corbies/Our Ship is Ready/By Broom Besoms/The Nutting Girl/Jolly Beggar/Boatman/A Hundred Years Ago.

TOP77   *Songs for City Squares*: Leon Rosselson – with spoken comments (1962).

TOP78   *Stottin' Doon the Waall – Mining Songs from Northumberland and Durham*: Johnny Handle (1962): The Collier Lad/Big Meeting Day/The Stoneman's Lament/ Strutting Alang the Wall/Farewell to the Monty/The Day We Went to the Coast. See Topic 189.

12T79   *Jacobite Songs – The Two Rebellions 1715 and 1745*: Ewan MacColl with Peggy Seeger – guitar and banjo (published 1962, released 1963). Ye Jacobites by Name/ Such a Parcel of Rogues in a Nation/Will You Go to Sherrifmuir/Wae's me for Prince Charlie/Charlie is my Darling/Haugh's o' Cromdale/Bonnie Moorhen/Johnnie Cope/ Cam Ye o'er frae France/There's Three Brave Loyal Fellows/This is No my Ain House/ Piper o' Dundee/Donald MacGillavry/MacLean's Welcome/Will Ye No Come Back Again.

TOP80   Test pressing?

TOP81   *The Butcher's Boy*: Enoch Kent. Donal Don/The Beggar Man/Bonnie Lass Come Ower the Burn/The Butcher Boy/Erin Go Bragh.

TOP82   *Songs of Protest*: The Ian Campbell Folk Group (1962). Viva La Quince Brigade/ We Will Overcome/The Boys of Wexford/Peat Bog Soldiers/Domovina/Cutty Wren.

TOP83   *Wor Geordie*: Bob Davenport (1962). Hot Asphalt/Bog Down in the Valley/ Tramps and Hawkers/Wor Geordie's Wife.

12T84   *The Roving Journeyman*: The Willet Family (1963). Lord Bateman/The Blacksmith Courted Me/The Little Ball of Yarn/Died For Love/The Rambling Sailor/ Riding Down to Portsmouth/As I Was Going to Salisbury/The Roving Journeyman 1 and 2/While Gamekeepers Lie Sleeping/The Old Miser/Game of Cards.

TOP85   *Peelers and Prisoners*: Dominic Behan (1963). The Old Triangle/The Smashing of the Van/The Peelers and the Goat/The Mountjoy Hotel.

12T86   *The Iron Muse – A Panorama of Industrial Folk Song Arranged by A.L. Lloyd* (1963): Miner's Dance Tunes – The Celebrated Working Man's Band/The Collier's Rant – Bob Davenport/The Recruited Collier – Anne Briggs/Pit Boots – A.L. Lloyd/The Banks of the Dee – Louis Killen/The Donibristle Moss Moran Disaster – Matt McGinn/ The Durham Lockout – Bob Davenport/The Blackleg Miners – Louis Killen/The Celebrated Working Man – A.L. Lloyd/The Row Between the Cages – Bob Davenport/ The Collier's Daughter/The Weaver's March – The Celebrated Working Man's Band/The Weaver and the Factory Maid – A.L. Lloyd/The Spinner's Wedding – Ray Fisher/The Poor Cotton Wayver – A.L. Lloyd/The Doffing Mistress – Anne Briggs/The Swan Necked Valve – Matt McGinn/The Dundee Lassie – Ray Fisher/The Foreman O'Rourke – Matt McGinn/Farewell to the Monty – Louis Killen/Miner's Dance Tunes – The Celebrated Working Man's Band.

12T87   *Irish Traditional Songs: The McPeake Family* (1963). McLeod's Reel/Bucket of the Mountain Dew/Eileen Aroon/An Durd Fainne/My Singing Bird/Lament of Aughrim/ Carraigdoon/Derry Hornpipe/Old Piper/Slievegallion Braes/Ireland Boys Hurrah/Cock Robin/Coolin/Verdant Braes of Skreen.

12T88

12T89   *Irish Pipe and Fiddle Tunes*: William Clancy and Michael Gorman. Hardiman the Fiddler/Coleman's Favourite/Chief O'Neill's/The Maid I Ne'er Forgot/The Tempest/ Colonel Rodney/The Chanter's Song/The Mountain Road.

12T90

12T91   *Irish Traditional Songs in Gaelic and English*: Joe Heaney. Rocks of Bawn/One Morning in June/Casadh an Tsugain/Wife of the Bold Tenant Farmer/Trees they Grow Tall/Peigin is Peadar/Cunnia/Caoineadh na Dtri Mhuire/An Tighearna Randal/Bean an Leanna/John Mitchel.

TOP92   *Wild Mountain Thyme*: The McPeake Family. Will Ye Go, Lassie Go/I Know My Love/ Juanita/Jug of Punch.

12T93   *Talking Woodie Guthrie*: Jack Elliott. Talking Columbia Blues/Pretty Boy Floyd/ Ludlow Massacre/Talking Miner Blues/Hard Travelling/So Long its Been Good to Know You/Talking Dustbowl Blues/1913 Massacre/Rambling Boys/Talking Sailor Blues.

TOP94   *The Hazards of Love*: Anne Briggs (1963). Lowlands Away/My Bonny Boy/ Polly Vaughan/Rosemary Lane.

TOP95   *Heroes in Love*: Shirley Collins (1963). The False Bride/Locks and Bolts/ Rambleaway/A Blacksmith Courted Me.

12T96   *The Great Scots Traditional Ballad Singer*: Jeannie Robertson (1963 reissue of 10T52, 1959). The Bonnie Wee Lassie Who Never Said No/What a Voice/My Plaidie's Awa'/The Gypsy Laddies/When I was New But Sweet Sixteen/MacCrimmon's Lament/ Roy's Wife of Aldivalloch/Lord Lovat.

TOP97   *The Summertime is Over*: Judith Silver. Ya Se Fuel Verano/The Crow on the Cradle/The Two Brothers/Shura Eiloi.

TOP98   *Blow the Man Down*: A.L. Lloyd and Ewan MacColl with Harry H. Corbett (originally recorded 1956). The Black Ball Line/Reuben Ranzo/Do Me Ama/Blow the Man Down.

TOP99   *A Hundred Years Ago*: A.L. Lloyd and Ewan MacColl (originally recorded 1956). Blood Red Rose/The Handsome Cabin Boy/A Hundred Years Ago, etc. 1SE0049912.

TOP100   *The Coast of Peru*: A.L. Lloyd and Ewan MacColl (originally recorded 1956). The Dreadnought/The Coast of Peru, etc.

TOP101   *Dominic Takes the Floor*: Dominic Behan. The Blind Man He Could See/ Love is Pleasing/Zoological Gardens/A Sailor Courted a Farmer's Daughter.

STOP101   *Black and White* c/w *Bahnuah* (45): The Galliards (Robin Hall; Jimmy McGregor; Leon Rosselson; Shirley Bland).

STOP102   *The Sun is Burning* c/w *The Crow on the Cradle* (45): The Ian Campbell Group 1SE0049915.

STOP7001   *Dance for Your Daddy* c/w (45): The High Level Ranters 1SE0049919.

STOP7002   *Bonny Lass of Anglesey* c/w (45): Martin Carthy.

12T103   *English and Scottish Folk Ballads*: A.L. Lloyd and Ewan MacColl (1964). Henry Martin (L)/The Baron of Brackley (MacC)/Cruel Mother (L)/Lord Randall (MacC)/ The Bitter Withy (L)/The Sweet Kumadie (MacC)/Demon Lover (L)/Hughie the Graeme (MacC)/The Prickly Bush (L)/The Beggar Man (MacC).

12T104   *Steam Whistle Ballads*: Ewan MacColl (1964). Wark of the Weavers/Droylsden Wakes/Four Loom Weaver/Calton Weaver/Oh Dear Me/Coal Owner and the Pitman's Wife/Four Pence a Day/Gresford Disaster/Will Caird/Iron Horse/Poor Paddy Works on the Railway/Cannily Cannily/Song of the Iron Road/Blantyre Explosion/Collier Laddie/ Moses of the Mail.

12T105   *Roll On Buddy*: Jack Elliott and Derroll Adams (1964). Reissue of 10T14 plus? Rich and Rambling Boy/Buffalo Skinners/I Wish I Was a Rock/It's Hard, Ain't it

Hard/All Around the Water Tank/Mother's Not Dead/East Virginia Blues/The Old Bachelor/Danville Girl/The State Of Arkansas/The Death of Mr. Garfield/Roll On Buddy.

12T106 *Muleskinner*: Jack Elliott. San Francisco Bay Blues/Ol' Riley/Boll Weevil/Bed Bug Blues/New York Town/Old Blue/Grey Goose/Muleskinner Blues/East Texas Talkin' Blues/Cocaine/Dink's Song/Black Baby/Salty Dog. Retitled reissue of 10T15.

12T107 *Folk Music of Bulgaria*. Collected and ed. by A.L. Lloyd (1964). Side One. W. Bulgaria: Sofia District/Pirin Region. Side Two. S., E. and N. Bulgaria: Rhodope Region/Thrace/Dobrudzha and N. Bulgaria.

STOP108 Unreleased single by The Ian Campbell Group.

TOP109 *True Loves and False Lovers*: Alice Brenan.

12T110 *Sea Songs and Shanties – Farewell Nancy*: Various Artists (1964). Wild Goose/Lovely Nancy – Ian Campbell with chorus and Dave Swarbrick, fiddle/The Nightingale/Heave Away My Johnny/Row Bullies Row/The Fireship – Cyril Tawney/Tom's Gone to Hilo/Ship in Distress – Louis Killen/Lowlands Low/One Morning in Spring – Cyril Tawney/Hilo Johnny Brown/Poor Old Horse/Bold Princess Royal – Louis Killen/Billy Boy – Bob Davenport/Bold Benjamin – Cyril Tawney/Hog Eye Man/Goodbye, Fare Thee Well – Louis Killen with chorus and Dave Swarbrick, fiddle.

STOP111 *Hanging From a Tree* c/w *Where Have All the Flowers Gone* (45): Vanessa Redgrave (1964). 1SE0049916.

TOP112 *Macedonian and Albanian Dances*: Tine Rozanc Ensemble. Dances from Povarderje/Soto/Frulaska Oro/Cacak/Makedonsko Oko.

12T113 *Who's Going to Shoe Your Pretty Little Foot?*: Peggy Segger and Tom Paley with Claudia Paley (1964). Who's that Knocking at my Window?/Lone Henry/The Lass of Roch Royal/Who's Going to Shoe Your Pretty Little Foot?/Pretty Polly/Englewood Mine/Buck Dancer's Choice/Just as the Tide Was Flowing/The Kicking Mule/The Heartless Lady/The Fiddling Soldier/Tittery Nan/Loving Reilly/The Cuckoo/If He'd Be a Buckaroo/The Girl on the Greenbriar Shore.

TPS114 *Folk Songs – An Anthology. Topic Sampler 1*: Various Artists (1964). Heave Away My Johnny – Louis Killen 110/Skewball – A.L. Lloyd 71/Cutty Wren – Ian Campbell Group 82/Let No Man Steal Your Thyme – Isla Cameron 50/Dr. Gilbert – Maggie Barry 6/Blow the Man Down – Harry H. Corbett 98/Jug of Punch – McPeake Family 92/Up the Raw – Louis Killen 75/Donal Don – Enoch Kent 81/My Bonny Bonny Lass – Anne Briggs 94/Miner's Dances – Celebrated Working Men's Band 86/Johnnie Cope – Ewan MacColl and Peggy Seeger 79.

STOP115 *The Patriot Game* c/w *Erin Go Brath* (45): Dominic Behan (1964).

STOP116 *Ol' Man River* c/w *Kevin Barry* (45): Paul Robeson. 'First Published 1957'; this release 1964.

12T117 *Old Times and Hard Times*: Hedy West. The Wife Wrapt in Wether Skin/Fair Rosamund/Barbara Allen/Old Joe Clark/The Coalminer's Child/Gambling Man/Brother Ephus/Polly/Davidson-Wilder Blues/Rich Irish Lady/Shut Up in the Mines at Coal Creek/The Wife of Usner's Well. Reissued 1981.

12T118   *First Person*: A.L. Lloyd (1966). Four Drunken Maidens/St. James' Hospital/ Kelly Gang/I Wish My Love/Jack Orion/Lover's Ghost/Rocking the Cradle/Drover's Dream/Short Jacket and White Trousers/Sovay, the Female Highwayman/Reynardine/ Farewell Nancy/Fanny Blair/Shickered as He Could Be.

12T119

12T120   *The Singing Campbells – Traditions from an Aberdeen Family*: The Campbell Family. Fur does Bonny Lorna Lie/Sleep Till Yer Mammy/Nicky Tams/Road and the Miles to Dundee/Drumdelgie/I Ken Fur I'm Gaun/My Wee Man's a Miner/Fa Fa Fa wid be a Bobby/Foul Friday/Me an' me Mither/We Three Kings of Orient Are/Bogie's Bonnie Belle/Cruel Mother/Lang a-growing/Lady Eliza/Will Ye Gang Love/I Wish I Wish/ McGinty's Meal and Ale.

12T121   *R & B From S & B*: Sonny Terry and Brownie McGhee. Old Jabo/Heart in Sorrow/Preachin' the Blues/Can't Help Myself.

12T122   *Tommy Armstrong of Tyneside*: Louis Killen, Tom Gilfellon, Johnny Handle, acc. Colin Ross and Maureen Craik (1965). Durham Gaol – Tom Gilfellon/Row Between the Cages – Louis Killen/The Birth of the Lad – Tom Gilfellon with Handle, Ross/Marla Hill Ducks – Louis Killen/Oakey's Keeker – Tom Gilfellon/Durham Lockout – Maureen Craik; Colin Ross/Wor Nannie's a Maizor – Gilfellon; Handle; Ross/Oakey Strike Eviction – Gilfellon, Handle; Ross; Killen/Sheel Raw Flood – Louis Killen/Hedgehog Pie – Handle; Gilfellon; Ross/The Ghost that Haunted Bunty – Louis Killen/Skeul Board Man – Handle; Gilfellon; Ross/Trimdon Grange Explosion – Maureen Craik/South Medomsley Strike – Handle; Gilfellon; Killen; Ross.

12T123   *Her Mantle So Green*: Margaret Barry and Michael Gorman. The Cycling Champion of Ulster/Flower of Sweet Strabane/Turfman from Ardee/Galway Shawl/Wild Colonial Boy/My Lagan Love/The Factory Girl/Her Mantle So Green/3 Polkas/2 Reels.

TOP124   *More R & B From S & B*: Sonny Terry and Brownie McGhee. Confusion/Dark Road/John Henry/Blues on the Highway. Taken from 12T29.

12T125   *New Voices – An Album of First Recordings*: The Watersons, Harry Boardman, Maureen Craik (1965). Boston Harbour – The Watersons/To the Begging – Harry Boardman/The White Cockade – Maureen Craik/Owdham – Harry Boardman/The Greenland Whale Fishery – The Watersons/Hard Times – Harry Boardman/The Sandgate Girl's Lament – Maureen Craik/Three Score and Ten – The Watersons/The Broom of Cowdenknowes – The Watersons/Bonny at Morn – Maureen Craik/The Hand Loom versus the Power Loom – Harry Boardman/A U Hinny Burd – Maureen Craik/The Shurat Weaver – Harry Boardman/King Arthur's Servants – The Watersons/The Weaver of Wellbrook – Harry Boardman.

12T126   *Ballads and Broadsides*: Louis Killen (1965). Young Edwin in the Lowlands/ As We Were a-Sailing/The Flying Cloud/All Things Are Quite Silent/One May Morning/ The Cock/The Bramble Briar/Thorneymoor Woods/The Banks of Sweet Primroses.

12T127   Test pressing and/or not used. VWL/NSA.

12T128   *Bonny Lass Come O'er the Burn*: Various Artists. Twa Corbies – Ray Fisher; Fil Uo Ro Hu-o – Dolina MacLennan; Gypsie Laddie – Robin Gray; Beggarman –

Enoch Kent; Hug O Ran O Ru – Dolina MacLennan; Donal Don – Enoch Kent; Kilbogie – Ray and Archie Fisher; Night Visiting Song – Ray and Archie Fisher; Bonnie Lass Come O'er the Burn – Enoch Kent; Far Over the Forth – Ray Fisher; Butcher Boy – Enoch Kent; Puirt a Beul – Dolina MacLennan; Erin Go Bragh – Enoch Kent; Bratach Bana – Dolina MacLennan.

12T129   Test pressing and/or not used. VWL/NSA.

12T130   *Bundook Ballads*: Ewan MacColl. Any Complaints/Fortress Songs/Farewell to Sicily/Ballad of Wadi Maktilla/Dying Soldier/Ghost Army of Korea/Browned Off/When this Ruddy War is Over/Join the British Army/On the Move Tonight/Second Front Song/ Seven Years in the Sand/Hand Me Down Me Petticoat/Young Trooper Cut Down in his Prime/Bless 'em All.

12T131   Test pressing. VWL/NSA.

12T132   Test pressing. VWL/NSA.

12T133   *New Voices from Scotland*: Gordeanna McCulloch, Norman Kennedy, The Exiles (1965). The Exiles – Soldier's Joy/Tae the Beggin'/The Toon o' Kelso/The Bonnie Lass o' Bon Accord/The Haughs o' Cromdale/Campbell's Farewell to Redcastle/Moulin Dubh. Gordeanna McCulloch – The Kirk o' Birnie Bouzle/The Dowie Dens o' Yarrow/ The Lichtbob's Lassie/Will Ye Gang, Love. Norman Kennedy – Sleepytoon/Puirt a Beul/ The Haughs o' Cromdale/My Son David.

12T134   *Move on Down the Line*: Jesse Fuller (1965). Move on Down the Line/Stealing/ Ninety-nine Years and One Dark Day/Animal Fair/Sleeping in the Midnight Cold/ Stackolee/Railroad Worksong/Lining up the Track/Hangin' Round a Skin Game/Railroad Blues/San Francisco Bay Blues.

12T135   *The Bird in the Bush – Traditional Erotic Songs* (1966): A.L. Lloyd, Anne Briggs, Frankie Armstrong, with Alf Edwards (concertina) and Dave Swarbrick (fiddle). Two Magicians/Old Man from Over the Sea/Wanton Seed/Gathering Rushes in the Month of May/Bonnie Black Hare/Whirly Whori/Pretty Polly/Old Bachelor/Stonecutter Boy/Mower/Bird in the Bush/Pegging Awl/Martinmas Time/Widow of the Westmorland's Daughter.

12T136   *Frost and Fire*: The Watersons (1965).

TSCD136   CD reissue: Here We Come A-Wassailing/The Derby Ram/Jolly Old Hawk/ Pace-Egging Song/Seven Virgins (the Leaves of Life)/The Holly Bear a Berry/Hal-An-Tow/Earlsdon Sword Dance/John Barleycorn/Harvest Song – We Gets Up in the Morn/ Souling Song/Christmas is Now Drawing Near at Hand/Herod and the Cock/Wassail Song/God Bless the Master/The Bitter Withy/Emmanuel/Idumen/Sound, Sound your Instruments of Joy/Come All Ye Faithfull Christians/Green Fields.

12T137   *The Fisher Family* (1966). Come All Ye Fisher Lassies/Schooldays Over/Rigs O'Rye/Donalogue/For Our Lang Biding Here/Joy of My Heart/Hey Ca'through/What's Poor Mary Weeping For?/Bonnie Lass O'Ballochmyle/I am a Miller Tae ma Trade/Birkin Tree/I am a Freeborn Man/Aince Upon a Time.

12T138   *The Stewarts of Blair*: The Stewart Family. Huntingtower/Caroline of Edinburgh

Town/In London's Fair City/Queen Amang the Heather/Dowie Dens o' Yarrow/The Lakes o' Shillin/Ower Yon Hill There Lives a Lassie/The Convict's Song/Young Jamie Foyers/ The Corncrake amang the Whinny Knowes/Busk, Busk, Bonnie Lassie/Fagail Liosmor/ 74th Farewell to Edinburgh/Shepherd's Crook/Miss Proud.

12T139   *A Wild Bee's Nest*: Paddy Tunney (1965). The Rollicking Boys Around Tandaragee/The Colleen Rue/The Flower of Sweet Strabane/The Waterford Boys/Easter Snow/I Once Had a True Love/Sheela Nee Eyre/When a Man's in Love/The Banks of Dunmore/Bonny Tavern Green/Castlehyde.

12T140   *A Canadian Garland – Folksongs from the Province of Ontario*: LaRena Clark. Kettle on the Stovepipe/Lord Gregory/Thyme, 'tis a Pretty Flower/Rifle Boys/ House Carpenter/Gallant Hussar/Banks of the Nile/I Once Loved a Lass/Dapple Grey/ Old County Fair/There was a Lord in Edinburgh/Faggot Cutter.

12T141   Test pressing and or not used. VWL.

12T142   *The Watersons* (1966). Dido, Bendigo/The North Country Maid/Brave Wolfe/ The Jolly Waggoners/I Am a Rover/Fathom the Bowl/The Thirty Foot Trailer/The Holmfirth Anthem/Twanky-Dillo/The White Hare of Howden/The Plains of Mexico/All for Me Grog.

12T143   *Freedom, Come All Ye*: The Exiles. Ballad of Accounting/Moving On Song/ We're Only Here for Exploration/Thank Christ for Christmas/Pigeon/Pound a Week Rise/Freedom, Come All Ye/For a That and a That/Arthur McBride/Willie Brennan/ Wae's Me for Prince Charlie/La Pique/Van Diemen's Land/Twa Recruiting Sergeants.

12T144   Test pressing and/or not used. VWL.

TPS145   *Folk Song – An Anthology. Topic Sampler 2*: Various artists (1966). Whip Jamboree – The Spinners/Hedgehog Pie – Johnny Handle/The Sailor Cut Down in his Prime – Stan Kelly/Fair Rosamund – Hedy West/Four Pence a Day – Ewan MacColl/ Master Magrath – Dominic Behan/Buy Broom Besoms – Ian Campbell Folk Group/The Overlander – A.L. Lloyd/The Broom of Cowdenknowles – The Watersons/Rambleaway – Shirley Collins/Buck Dancer's Choice – Tom Paley/Night Visiting Song – Ray and Archie Fisher.

12T146   *Pretty Saro*: Hedy West (1966). The House Carpenter/Pretty Saro/Old Smokey/ Blow Ye Gentle Winds/My Love's Full of Glory/Promised Land/Over There/Little Matty Groves (Ch 81)/Rake and Rambling Boy/Joe Bowers/Whistle Daughter, Whistle/I'm an Old Bachelor/Johnny Sands/My Good Old Man/Frankie Silvers/Lee Tharin's Bar Room (Cowboy's Lament).

12T147   *The Manchester Angel*: Ewan MacColl (1966). We Poor Labouring Men/ Georgie/Barbara Allen/Sheepcrook and Black Dog/Bramble Briar (Strawberry Town)/ One Night as I Lay on my Bed/Grey Cock/At the Begging I will Go/Sheep Stealer/ Manchester Angel/Bold Richard/Press Gang/Round Cape Horn/Through Moorfields/ Homeward Bound.

12T 148   Test pressing. VWL/AB.

12T 149   Test pressing. VWL/AB.

12T150 *Songs of a Shropshire Farmworker*: Fred Jordan (1966). We Shepherds are the Best of Men/The Ship that Never Returned/Down the Road and Away Went Polly/All Jolly Fellows that Follow the Plough/The Watery Grave/The Dark Eyed Sailor/Three Old Crows/John Barleycorn/The Banks of Sweet Primroses/The Bonny Boy/Polly's Father Lived in Lincolnshire/The Royal Albert/Down the Green Groves/The Farmer's Boy.

12T151 *Vagrant Songs of Scotland*: Isabel Sutherland (1966). King Farewell/The Brewer's Daughter/Griogal Cridhe (Gaelic Lament)/Soda Scones/Waulking Song/Father, Father (Sweet William)/The Two Brothers (Child ballad number (Ch)49)/Iomavaibh Eutrom (Row Lightly)/False Hae Ye Been/Lord Bateman (Ch53)/Dance With Me, Morag/ Sandy's Mill/The Beggin' Man (Ch279)/The Four Maries (Ch173).

12T152 Not used. NSA.

12T153 *Ireland Her Own*: Paddy Tunney, Arthur Kearney, Frank Kelly, Joe Tunney (1966). Paddy Tunney – Sean O'Dwyer a Gleanna/The Ribbon Blade/The Bold Fenian Men/John Mitchel/The Valley of Knockanure/The Grand Oul' Dame Britannia/Kevin Barry. Arthur Kearney – Follow Me Up to Carlow/Jackets Green/General Munro/The Felons of our Land/The Song of the Dawn. Frank Kelly (violin) and Joe Tunney (melodeon) – The Battle of Aughrim/The Memory of the Dead/The Dawning of the Day.

12T154 *The Folk Music of Albania*. Recorded in the field by A.L. Lloyd (1966). North Albania: Kenge Maje Krahe (mountain signal): Zef Deda/Valle Lezhes (dance): Mark Pashku (cifteli)/Kenge Djepi (lullaby): Mri Jaku/Ti Ne Koder Un Ne Koder (dance song): Tom Nikola (acc. cifteli)/Vajtim (funeral lament): Dila Gjoni/Dhent Ne Mrize (shepherd's melody): Martin Vata (fyell)/Kenga E Cun Mules (ballad): Tom Marashi and Zef Deda/Zenel Kadrija (ballad): Mark Pashku (acc. cifteli)/ South Albania: Valle E Gadjes (dance): Sadik Diko (gadje) and Reshit Shehu (daire)/O Bilbil Sakat, Sakat (lyrical song): Vangjel; Nikollaq; Kili and Kristo Dano/Vatjim (shepherd tune): played by Sadik Diko (cyledy jare)/Llazore (ritual song): Kili Dano/Avazali Dy Motrave (instrumental improvisation): Qerim Baki (llaute) acc. by Riza Muhaxhiri (llaute)/Do Dalim Nga Myzeqeja (political song): Vangiel, Nikollaq, Kili and Kristo Dano/Kaba Vence (instrumental improvisation):Refki Taho (clarinet), Hysen Zizolli (accordion) and Ahmet Metolli (drum)/Fuat Bahani (historical song): Ali Kondi, Nevruz Kondi and group/Valle Kolonjarce (dance): Feim Feizo (gadje) and Riza Muhaxhiri (daire)/Kaba Me Gernete (instrumental improvisation): Rakip Muhaxhiri (clarinet), Festim Permeti (violin), Qerim Baki (llaute) and Qerim Hajre (accordion). See TSCD904 reissue.

12T155 Test pressing.

12T156 Test pressing.

12T157 *The Folk Songs of Britain, Vol 1. The Songs of Courtship* (1968). Original issue Caedmon TC 1141 (USA) 1961. Green Grow the Laurels – Jeannie Robertson/The False Bride – Bob Copper/Our Wedding Day – Francis McPeake/When a Man's In Love – Paddy Tunney/Aileen Duinn – Flora McNeill/Bonnie Kate – Agnes Whyte/Old Grey Beard Newly Shaven – Jeannie Robertson/The Sweet Primeroses – Bob and Ron Copper/ The Coolin – Paddy Taylor/Shule Aroon – Elizabeth Cronin/The Brown Thorn – Seamus Ennis/As I Roved Out – Seamus Ennis/The Magpie's Nest – Jane Kelly/Dame Durden – Bob and Ron Copper/Casadh an tSugain – Maire O'Sullivan/The Girl was Smart for the

Fiddler – Michael Doherty/My Darling Ploughman Boy – Jimmy McBeath/The False Young Man – Frank and Francis McPeake/I'm a Young Bonnie Lassie – Blanche Wood/ No John, No – Bob and Ron Copper/Bogie's Bonnie Belle – Davy Stewart.

12T158 *The Folk Songs of Britain, Vol 2. The Songs of Seduction.* The Nutting Girl – Cyril Poacher/The Bonnie Wee Lassie Who Never Said No – Jeannie Robertson/Bundle and Go – John Doherty/ Blow the Candle Out – Jimmy Gilhaney/The Foggy Dew – Phil Hammond/Toorna Ma Goon – Jimmy McBeath/Rolling in the Ryegrass – Paddy Taylor/ The Jolly Tinker – Thomas Moran/Long Peggin' Aw – Harry Cox/The Thrashing Machine – Anne O'Neill/The Rigs of London Town – Charlie Wills/The Wind Blew the Bonnie Lassie's Plaid Awa' – Jimmy McBeath, Duncan Burker, Jeannie Robertson/The Cunning Cobbler – George Spicer/Dublin City – Seamus Ennis/The Light Dragoon – Harry List/ The Orkney Style of Courtship – John Findlater/The Cuckoo's Nest – Jeannie Robertson, John Maguire, John Strachan/The Soldier and the Lady – Raymond and Frederick Cantwell/Behind the Bush in the Garden – Seamus Ennis/Never Wed an Old Man – Jeannie Robertson/The Maid of Australia – Harry Cox/The Merchant's Son and the Beggar's Daughter – Davy Stewart/The Bold English Navvy – Lal Smith/Cruising Round Yarmouth – Harry Cox.

12T159 *The Folk Songs of Britain, Vol. 3. Jack of All Trades.* Jovial Tradesman – Bob and Ron Copper/Roving Journeyman – Paddy Doran/Candlelight Fisherman – Phil Hammond/Canny Shepherd Laddies – Jimmy White/Dairy Maid – John Maguire/Green Brooms – Sean McDonagh/Gruel – Jimmy McBeath/Jug of Punch – Edward Quinn/ Gresford Disaster – Mrs. A. Cosgrove/Jolly Miller – John Strachan/Irish Washerwoman – John Docherty/Farewell to Whiskey – Jessie Murray/The Roving Ploughboy – John McDonald/The Buchan Miller – John McDonald/Fagin the Cobbler – Whickets Richardson/Ould Piper – Frank McPeake/Sweep, Chimney Sweep – Bob and Ron Copper/ Mason's Apron – Agnes and Bridie White/Rhynie – John Strachan/The Tailor by Trade – Joe Tunney/Wee Weaver – John Doherty/Jim the Carter Lad – Jack Goodfellow/ Drumgeldie – Davie Stewart/Merry Haymakers – Bob and Ron Copper/I'll Mend Your Pots and Kettles – Seamus Ennis.

12T160 *The Folk Songs of Britain, Vol. 4. The Child Ballads 1 [2–95].* Original issue Caedmon (USA) 1961. Side One. The Elfin Knight (An Acre of Land; Strawberry Lane): Bob and Ron Copper, Rottingdean, Sussex, Thomas Moran, Mohill, Co. Leitram/ The False Knight on the Road: Frank Quinn, Coalisland, Co. Tyrone/Lady Isabel and the Elf Knight (The Outlandish Knight): Fred Jordan, Aston Munslow, Salop/The Twa Sisters (Binnorie): John Strachan, Fyvie, Aberdeenshire/Lord Randal (Lord Donald, My Son): Jeannie Robertson, Aberdeen; Elizabeth Cronin, Macroom, Co. Cork; Thomas Moran, Mohill, Co. Leitrim; Colm McDonagh, Carna, Galway; Eirlys and Eddis Thomas, Glamorgan, South Wales/Edward (My Son David): Jeannie Robertson, Aberdeen; Paddy Tunney, Beleek, Co. Fermanagh; Angela Brasil, Kent/King Orfeo: John Stickle, Lerwick, Shetland/The Cruel Mother: Thomas Moran, Mohill, Co. Leitrim/The Broomfield Wager: Cyril Poacher, Blaxhall, Suffolk. Side Two. Captain Wedderburn's Courtship: Seamus Ennis, Dublin/The Twa Brothers: Lucy Stewart, Fetterangus, Aberdeenshire/Lord Bateman (Young Beichan): Thomas Moran, Mohill, Co. Leitrim; Jeannie Robertson, Aberdeen/ Lord Thomas and Fair Ellen: Jessie Murray, Buckie, Banffshire/Lord Lovel: Mrs Ethel Findlater, Dounby, Orkney/Lord Gregory (The Lass of Roch Roy): Elizabeth Cronin,

Macroom, Co. Cork/Barbara Allen: Jessie Murray, Buckie, Banffshire; Fred Jordan, Aston Munslow, Salop; Charlie Wills, near Bridport, Dorset; May Bennell, Amersham, Bucks; Thomas Moran, Mohill, Co. Leitrim; Phil Tanner, Gower, South Wales/ George Collins: Enos White, Axford, Hants/The Prickelly Bush (The Maid Freed from the Gallows): Julia Scaddon, Chideock, Dorset.

12T161   *The Folk Songs of Britain, Vol. 5. The Child Ballads 2 [110–299].* Original issue Caedmon (USA) 1961. Side One. The Royal Forester (The Knight and the Shepherd's Daughter) – John Strachan, Fyvie, Aberdeenshire/The Baffled Knight – Emily Bishop, Bromsberrow Heath, Herefordshire/Johnie Cock – John Strachan, Fyvie, Aberdeenshire/ The Jew's Garden – Cecelia Costello, Birmingham/The Battle of Harlaw – Lucy Stewart, Fetterangus, Aberdeenshire/The Four Maries (Mary Hamilton) – Jeannie Robertson, Aberdeen/The Gypsie Laddie – Harry Cox, Catfield, Norfolk; Jeannie Robertson, Aberdeen; Paddy Doran, Belfast/Georgie – Harry Cox, Catfield, Norfolk/The Dowie Dens of Yarrow – Davy Stewart, Dundee, Angus. Side Two. Glenlogie – John Strachan, Fyvie, Aberdeenshire/The Grey Cock (Willie's Ghost) – Cecilia Costello/Henry Martin – Phil Tanner, Gower, South Wales/Lang Johnny More – John Strachan, Fyvie, Aberdeenshire/Willie's Fate – Jeannie Robertson, Aberdeen/Our Goodman – Harry Cox, Catfield, Norfolk; Mary Connors, Belfast; Colm Keane, Glinsk, Co. Galway/The Farmer's Curst Wife – Thomas Moran, Mohill, Co. Leitrim/The Jolly Beggar – Jeannie Robertson, Aberdeen/The Auld Beggarman – Maggie and Sarah Chambers, Tempo, Co. Fermanagh/ The Keach in the Creel – Michael Gallagher, Beleek, Co. Fermanagh/The Golden Vanity – Bill Cameron, St Mary's, Isles of Scilly/The Trooper Lad – Jimmy McBeath, Elgin, Moray.

12T162   *North Carolina Songs and Ballads*: Frank Proffitt (1966). Trifling Woman/ Cluck Old Hen/Morning Fair/Bonnie James Campbell/Lord Randall/Handsome Molly/ Reuben Train/Tom Dooly (Dula)/I'm Going Back to North Carolina/Moonshine/Rye Whiskey/I'll Never Get Drunk No More/Wild Bill Jones/Gyps of David/Song of a Lost Hunter or Lone Henry/Sourwood Mountain/Going Across the Mountain. First issued on Folk Legacy FSA1, 1962.

12T163   *Ballads*: Hedy West.

12T164   *The Hale and the Hanged*: The Exiles. Jolly Beggar/Fair Flower of Northumber-land/Corner House/Sally Gardens/Laird o' the Windy Wa/Dainty Davie/Le Reel Du Pendu/Queen Eleanor's Confession/Plume an' Laddie/Shoals of Herring/Coolin/I Walked Up to Her/Rocky Road to Dublin/Wee Weaver/Battle of Harlaw/I Will Lay Ye Doon, Love/Planxty Davis.

12T165   *The Irish Edge*: Paddy Tunney. Craigie Hill/Lark in the Morning/Johnny, Lonely Johnny/The Cow that Drunk the Poteen/Blackwaterside/Out of the Window/The Month of January/Rambling Boys of Pleasure/Lowlands of Holland/Wearing of the Britches/ Old Man Rocking the Cradle/She's a Gay Old Hag/St Peter's Day was a-Dawning.

TPS166   *Men at Work. Topic Sampler 3*: Various Artists (1966). Hilo Johnny Brown – Louis Killen and chorus/Three Score and Ten – The Watersons/The Shining Birch Tree – Perry Friedman/Drumdelgie – Dave Campbell/The Row Between the Cages – Bob Davenport and the Celebrated Working Men's Band/The Davison-Wilder Blues – Hedy West/Santy Anna – A.L. Lloyd and chorus/The 1913 Massacre – Jack Elliott/Poor Paddy

Works on the Railway – Ewan MacColl with Peggy Seeger/The Factory Girl – Margaret Barry/Slieve Gallon Brae – Kathleen and Francis McPeake/The South Medomsley Strike – Johnny Handle with Louis Killen, Tom Gilfellon and Colin Ross.

12T167   *A Yorkshire Garland*: The Watersons (1966). Poacher's Fate/Morning Looks Charming/Pretty Drummer Boy/Tour of the Dales/Willy Went to Westerdale/L'anson's Racehorse/Ploughboy/White Cockade/Sorry for the Day I was Married/Ye Noble Spectators/Stow Brow/Wanton Wife of Castlegate/Yorkshire Tup/Whitby Lad.

TPS168   *From Erin's Green Shore. Topic Sampler 4*: Various Artists. Zoological Gardens – Dominic Behan and John Hasted/Cunnia – Joe Heaney/Our Ship is Ready – Margaret Barry/Boys of Blue Hill – Michael Gorman and Margaret Barry/Rollicking Boys Around Tandaragee – Paddy Tunney/Will Ye Go, Lassie Go; An Durd Fainne – McPeake Family/Castle of Drumboe – Dominic Behan and John Hasted/Chanter's Song (march) – Willie Clancy/Song of the Dawn – Arthur Kearney/My Lagan Love – Margaret Barry/Maguire's Favourite; Tralee Gaol; Maggie in the Wood – Michael Gorman; Margaret Barry; Tommy Maguire; Paddy Breen; Patsy Golden.

TPS169   *A Prospect of Scotland. Topic Sampler 5*: Various Artists. King Farewell – Isabel Sutherland/Bratach Bana – Dolina MacLennan/The Boatman – Lorna Campbell and the Ian Campbell Folk Group/The Bonnie Wee Lassie who Never Said No – Jeannie Robertson/Sleepytoon – Norman Kennedy/Pipe Tunes: Fagail Liosmor; 74th's Farewell to Edinburgh; the Shepherd's Crook; Miss Proud – Alex Stewart/Joy of My Heart – Ray and Archie Fisher/Bogie's Bonny Belle – Winnie Campbell/Minorie – Ewan MacColl/Dowie Dens of Yarrow – Belle Stewart/The Spinner's Wedding – Ray Fisher/For A' That and A' That – The Exiles.

12T170   *Sweet Primroses*: Shirley Collins (1967). All Things Are Quite Silent/Cambridgeshire May Carol/Spencer the Rover/Rigs of Time/Cruel Mother/Bird in the Bush/Streets of Derry/Brigg Fair/Higher Germanie/St. George Collins/Babes in the Wood/Down in Yon Forest/Magpie's Nest/False True Love/Sweet Primroses.

12T171   *A Girl of Constant Sorrow. Songs of the Kentucky Coalfields*: Sarah Ogan Gunning (1967). I Am a Girl of Constant Sorrow/Loving Nancy/Old Jack Frost/May I Go With You, Johnny?/The Hand of God on the Wall/Down the Picket Line/I Hate the Company Bosses/I'm Going to Organise/Christ was a Wayworn Traveller/Why Do You Stand There in the Rain?/Dreadful Memories/Old Southern Town/I Have Letters from My Father/Captain Devin/Gee Whiz What They Done to Me/Davy Crockett/Battle of Mill Spring/Just the Same Today/Sally/Oh Death. First issued on Folk Legacy. FSA26, 1965.

12T172   *Dublin Street Songs*: Frank Harte. Traveller all over the World/Shamrock Shore/Rag Man's Ball/Henry My Son/Bold Belfast Shoemaker/Night That Larry was Stretched, etc.

12T173   *Wild Rover No More*: Jimmy MacBeath. Bold English Navvy/Come a' Ye Tramps an' Hawkers/Johnny McIndoe/Wind Blew the Bonnie Lassie's Plaidie Awa'/Merchant and the Beggar Maid/Nicky Tams/Barnyards of Delgaty/I'm a Stranger in this Country/Moss O' Burreldale/Highlandman's Ball/McPherson's Rant/Groat for Gruel/Drundelgie/Wild Rover No More.

12T174 *Leviathan! Ballads and Songs of the Whaling Trade*: A.L. Lloyd with Alf Edwards – concertina, Dave Swarbrick, Martin Carthy, Trevor Lucas, Martyn Wyndham-Reade (1967). The Balaena/The Coast of Peru/Greenland Bond/The Weary Whaling Grounds/Cruel Ship's Captain/Off to Sea Once More/The 23rd. of March/The Whaleman's Lament/The Bonny Ship the Diamond/Talcahuano Girls/Farewell to Tarwathie/Rolling Down to Old Maui/Greenland Whale Fishing/Paddy and the Whale/The Eclipse.

12T175 *The Minstrel From Clare*: William Clancy (1967). Langstern Pony/The Templehouse, Over the Moor to Maggie/Bruachna Carraige Baine (The Brinks of White Rock)/Erin's Lovely Lea/The Killavel Fancy, The Dogs among the Bushes/ The Family Ointment/The Dear Irish Boy/Caoineadh an Spailpin (The Spalpeen's Lament), The Cuckoo's Nest/The Pipe on the Hob/The Legacy Jig/The Flogging Reel/The Song of the Riddles/Spailpin a Ruin (Spalpeen, my Love).

12T176 *Paddy in the Smoke – Irish Dance Music from a London Pub*: Various Artists (1968). Side One. 1a. Reels: Hall's Favourite and Lafferty's Reel; 1b. Jig: Paddy Fahey's Jig (Martin Byrnes – fiddle). 2. Reels: Eileen Curran and the Bunch of Keys (Martin Byrnes – fiddle). 3. Reel: Paddy Ryan's Dream (Danny Meehan – fiddle). 4. Reels: Lucy Campbell and Toss the Feathers (Tony McMahon – accordion, Martin Byrnes – fiddles). 5a. Reel: The Ragged Hank of Yarn; 5b. Reels: The Bank of Ireland, The Woman of the House and Morning Dew (Bobby Casey – fiddle, John McLaughlin – spoons). 6. Hornpipe: Denis Murphy's Hornpipe (Sean O'Shea – fiddle, Bobby Casey – fiddle). 7. Reels: The Yellow Tinker and The Humours of Scarriff (Sean O'Shea – fiddle, Bobby Casey – fiddle). Side Two. 1. Reel: The Chorus Reel (Con Curtin – fiddle, Denis McMahon – fiddle, Julia Clifford – fiddle). 2. Reel: Callaghan's Reel (Con Curtin – fiddle, Denis McMahon – fiddle). 3. Jigs: Kitty's Rambles and Dan the Cobbler (Jimmy Power – fiddle) 4. Reels: Jenny Picking Cockles and Kitty in the Lane (Jimmy Power – fiddle). 5. Reels: The Graf Spee and Ballinasloe Fair (Lucy Farr – fiddle, Bobby Casey – fiddle). 6. Reel: The Moher Reel (Lucy Farr – fiddle, Bobby Casey – fiddle). 7. Reels: Farewell to Erin and Duffy the Dancer (Jimmy Power – fiddle, Lucy Farr – fiddle). 8. Jigs: Doctor O'Neill and the Battering Ram (Jimmy Power – fiddle, Lucy Farr – fiddle, Andy O'Boyle – fiddle).

12T177 *Grand Airs of Connemara – Various Traditional Irish Songs*. Mainstir na Buille – Sean MacDonnachadha/An Caisdeach Ban – Padraic O Cahain/Piopa Andy Mhoir – Tomas O Neachtain/Una Bhan – Feichin O Connluain/Bean on Fhir Rua – Padraic O Cathain/Stor Mo Chroi; Noirin Mo Mhian – Sean MacDonnachadha/Caillin Schoth na Luachra – Padraic O Cathain/Peigi Mistreal – Tomas O Neachtain/An Goirtin Eornan – Feichin O Connluain/Cuaichin Ghleann Neifin – Padraic O Cathain/An Spailpin Fanach – Sean MacDonnachadha.

12T178 *Scots Songs and Ballads*: Norman Kennedy. Merchant's Song/Corachree/ Forester/Jolly Beggar/Kismuil's Galley/Guise o' Tough/Drumdelgie/Night Visiting Song/ Wi Me Rovin' Eye/I Wish I Wish/Auld Beggar Man/Puirt a Beul/Bonnie Highland Soldier/Johnny My Man. A Folk Legacy recording.

12T179 *The Travelling Stewarts* [incl. Lizzie Higgins] (1968). Johnnie My Man/ Willie's Fatal Visit/Battle is O'er/Scotland the Brave/51st Division in Egypt/Bogie's Bonnie Belle/McGinty's Meal and Ale/My Bonnie Tammy/McPherson's Lament/

Drunken Piper/Brig o' Perth/Reel of Tulloch/Loch Dhui/Dawning of the Day/Donald's Return to Glencoe.

12T180   *Back o' Benachie – Songs and Ballads from the Lowland East of Scotland*: Various Artists. Forfar Soldier – Rob Watt/Bogieside – Lizzie Higgins/Tarves Rant – Davy Stewart/Back o' Benachie – Maggie MacPhee/Guise O'Tough – Rob Watt/Bonnie Hoose o' Airlie – Bella Stewart/Billy Taylor – Rob Watt/I Canna Wash – Jane Turriff/ Willie Graham – Cameron Turriff/Orange and Blue – Cattice Stewart/Lothian Hairst – Rob Watt/Mill o' Tiffy's Annie – Sheila Stewart.

12T181   *Festival at Blairgowrie*: Various Artists recorded at Blairgowrie (1967). Festival o' Blair – Belle Stewart/I Am a Miller tae ma Trade – Davie Stewart/Irthing Water Hounds/An Old Man Come Courting Me/My Johnny/Bellingham Boats/Smash the Windows/My Old Man/Puppet on a String/Nam Shuidh So Gad Chuimhneachadh/Bas An Eich/Nucan Bhalallan/MacCrimmon's Lament/Berryfields o' Blair.

12T182   *Ulster Ballad Singer*: Mrs. Sarah Makem. Farewell My Love/Remember Me/ Banks of Red Roses/It was in the Month of January/Robert Burns and his Highland Mary/Factory Girl/Jolly Thresher/Caroline and her Young Sailor Bold/Wind that Shakes the Barley/I Courted a Wee Girl/Servant Maid in her Father's Garden/Barbara Allen.

12T183   *The Shepherd's Song*: Willie Scott. Shepherd's Song/Piper MacNeil/Kielder Hunt/Jamie Reaburn/Bonnie Wee Trampin' Lass/Bloody Waterloo/Jock Geddes/Dowie Dens of Yarrow/Herd Laddie o' the Glen/Lads that Were Reared Among the Heather.

12T184   *The Breeze from Erin* – Irish folk music on wind instruments.

12T185   *Princess of the Thistle*: Lizzie Higgins. Wha's at the Windy/Lovely Molly/Fair of Ballnafannin/Young Emsley/Bonnie Udby/Far Over the Forth/Laird of the Dainty Downby/Seasons/Davy Faa/Red Roses/Young But Growing/Lass o' Glenshea.

12T186   *Northumberland Forever – Dance and Song From the North-East*: The High Level Ranters (1968). Shew's the Way to Wallington/Peacock Followed the Hen/Sandgate Girl's Lament/Elsie Marley/Bellingham Boat/Lamb Skinnet/Adam Buckham/Maggy's Foot/Lads of North Tyne/Redesdale Hornpipe/Hexhamshire Lass/Breakdown/Blanchland Races/Lads of Alnwick/Lamshaw's Fancy/Byker Hill/Whinham's Reel/Nancy/Because he was a Bonny Lad/Salmon Tails up the Water/Sweet Hesleyside/Dance to Your Daddy/ Billy Boy/Nae Guid Luck About the House/Mi Laddie Sits Ower Late Up/Keel Row/ Kafoozalum/Washing Day.

12T187   *The Old Timey Rap – American Songs and Instrumentals*: Hobart Smith. Soldier's Joy (instr.)/Peg and Awl/The Great Titanic/ Banjo Group: a) Cindy; b) The Girl I Left Behind Me; c) John Hardy/ Short Life of Frankie/The Devil and the Farmer's Wife/Soldier's Joy (fiddle)/Sitting on Top of the World/Stormy Rose the Ocean/Bonaparte's Retreat (fiddle)/Cuckoo Bird/Columbus Stockade Blues/ Banjo Group: a) Black Annie; b) Sally Ann; c) Chinquapin Pie; d) Last Chance; e) John Greer's Tune/ Meet Me in Rose Time, Rosie/Uncloudy Day.

12T188   *Deep Lancashire – Songs and Ballads of the Industrial North-West*: Various Artists (1968). The Hand-Loom Weaver's Lament: Harry Boardman/Hop Hop Hop: The Oldham Tinkers/Beg Your Leave: Pete Smith/Ale is Physic for Me: Mike Harding/Gettin'

Wed: Harry Boardman/Clogs: recited by Harvey Kershaw/The Merry Little Doffer: Harry Boardman/Rawtenstall Annual Fair: Lee Nicholson/Coalhole Medley: The Oldham Tinkers/Cob-a-Coalin': Harry Boardman/Seaur Pies: John Howarth and the Oldham Tinkers/The Bury New Loom: Harry Boardman/Ten Per Cent: Pete Smith and Mike Harding/A Mon Like Thee: John Howarth and the Oldham Tinkers/The Lancashire Liar: Harry Boardman. KTSC188 – cassette.

12T189 *Along the Coaly Tyne – Old and New Northumbrian Songs*: Louis Killen and Johnny Handle with Colin Ross (originally issued by Topic in 1962). Anti Gallican Privateer/Collier's Rant/Up the Raw/Farewell to the Motly/Blackleg Miner/Collier Lad/ Dollia/Waggoner/Derwentwater's Farewell/Stottin' Doon the Waal/Keep your Feet Still/ Stoneman's Song/Aw Wish Pay Friday was Come/Durham Big Meetin' Day/Trimdon Grange Explosion/Putter/Sair Fyeld.

12T190 *The Lark in the Morning*: Dave and Toni Arthur with Barry Dransfield, fiddle (1969). All Frolicking I'll Give Over/Death of Queen Jane/Creeping Jane/Merchant's Daughter of Bristol/Bold Dragoon/Cold Blows the Winter's Wind/Lark in the Morning/ Poor Old Horse/Hey John Barleycorn/Bedlam/Admiral Benbow/Father, Father Build Me a Boat/Press Gang/Six Jolly Miners.

12T191 *North Indian Folk and Classical Music*: The Batish Family (1970). Side One: Folk Music. Tappa (NW Frontier dance)/Albelua (Kashmiri Hill Song)/Dhola (Punjabi love song)/Darya Dama De (Punjabi wedding song)/Dara Avalare Di Peer (Punjabi lyrical song)/Raste Bazzron Mein (Urban folk song from Delhi)/Kanakam Lammi Yan (Punjabi woman's song)/Snake Charmer Theme. Side Two: Classical Music. Raga Pat Multani/ Raga Todi/Raga Shudh Sarang/Raga Khamaj.

12T192 *All Bells in Paradise*: The Valley Folk (Jean and Elaine Carruthers, John Dickinson and Stephen Heap). Christmas: The Babe of Bethlehem/On Christmas Day it Happened So/Come All You True Good Christians/Welladay, Christmas Too Soon Goes Away. General: Sons of Levi/All You that Are to Mirth Inclined/Come All You Worthy Christian Men/All Bells in Paradise/The Joys of Mary. Easter: Tomorrow Shall Be My Dancing Day/O Mary Mother, Come and See. Harvest or Midwinter: The Two Brothers. General: Oh, Mary with her Young Son/The Bitter Withy/The Cherry Tree. New Year: The Moon Shines Bright.

12T193 *Once I Had a True Love*: Phoebe Smith (recorded in Suffolk, 1969, issued 1970). Once I Had a True Love/A Blacksmith Courted Me/Young Ellender/Higher Germany/Molly Vaughan/The Tanyard Side/The Yellow Handkerchief/The Wexport Girl/ The Dear Little Maiden.

12T194 *The Folk Songs of Britain, Vol. 6. Sailor Men and Serving Maids*: Various Artists. Paddy West – Timothy Walsh/Liverpool Packet – Billy Barber/Green Banks of Yarrow – Mrs. Maguire/Our Gallant Ship – William Howell/Alehouse – Elizabeth Cronin/Rosemary Lane – Bruce Laurenson/Ratcliffe Highway – Jim Baldrey/Lowlands of Holland – Paddy Tunney/Quaker – Dorchester Mummers/Beninn a' Cheathaich – Flora McNeil/Whale Fishery – Philip Hamon and Hilary Carre/Grey Silkie – John Sinclair/Warlike Seaman – Bob and Ron Copper/Boat that Brought Me – Thomas Moran/Handsome Cabin Boy – John Stickle/Smacksman – Sam Larner/Sweet Willie – Lal Smith/Campanero – Bill Cameron/Andrew Ross – Ned Adams/Boatie Row –

Jessie Murray/Our Ship is Ready – Robert Cinnamond/Nancy of Yarmouth – Fred Ling.

12T195 *The Folk Songs of Britain, Vol. 7. Fair Game and Foul*: Various Artists. Northamptonshire Poacher – Jim Baldrey/Jimmy Raeburn – Jessie Murray/Drumhullogan's Bottom – Thomas Moran/Sweet Fanny Adams – Vashti Vincent/Sylvia – Timothy Walsh/Young Willie – Paddy McCuskey/Lakes of Shillin – Mary Reynolds/Brennan on the Moor – Robert Cinnamond/Butcher Boy – Jeannie Robertson/Three Jolly Sportsmen – Bob Scarce/Jack Hall – Jack Endacott/Standing Stones – John and Ethel Findlater/ Polly Vaughan – Harry Cox/Lion's Den – Mrs Maguire/Van Diemen's Land – Jimmy MacBeath/Blind Man He Can See – Mary Connors and Paddy Doran/Oxford City – Mary Doran/Erin Go Brach – John Strachan/Derry Gaol – Sarah Makem/Newlyn Town – Bob Scarce.

12T196 *The Folk Songs of Britain, Vol. 8. A Soldier's Life for Me* (1971): Various Artists (originally Caedmon TC1164, 1961, USA). List, Bonny Laddie – John Strachan/ Swansea Barracks – Phil Tanner/The Dying Soldier – Mary Doran/Willie O'Reilly – Robert Cinnamond/The Banks of the Nile – Jean Matthew/The Recruiting Song – William Rew/William Taylor – Harold Covill/Johnny Harte – Mrs. Maguire/The Soldier and the Sailor – Arthur Lenox/Bold General Wolfe – Bob Scarce/Muddley Barracks – Jumbo Brightwell/Handsome Polly-O – Thomas Moran/The Deadly Wars – Jeannie Robertson/McCaffery – Peter Reilly/Drink Old England Dry – Carol Singers/Prince Charlie Stuart – Brigid Tunney/My Son Tim – Timothy Walsh/Napoleon Bonaparte – Robert Cinnamond/The Bonny Bunch of Roses O – Louise Holmes/Napoleon's Dream – Sam Larner/The Forfar Soldier – Jimmy McBeath.

12T197 *The Folk Songs of Britain, Vol. 9. Songs of Ceremony*: Various Artists. Cornish Wassail Song/New'r Even's Song/Mari Lwyd Ceremony/Joys of Mary/Holly and the Ivy/ Twelve Days of Christmas/Bitter Withy/As I Sat on a Sunny Bank/Singing of the Travels/ Dives and Lazarus/Gower Wassail/Taladh an Leinibh Losa/St Clements Song/Shrove Tuesday Song/Cherry Tree Carol/Somerset Wassail Song/Hunting the Wren/Cheshire Souling Song/Six Jolly Miners/John Barleycorn/Hal-an-tow/Huntingdonshire May Carol/ Cornish May Carol.

12T198 *The Folk Songs of Britain, Vol. 10. Songs of Animals and Other Marvels* (1971): Various Artists.

12T199 *(The King of the) Highland Pipers*: John Burgess. See TSCD466. The Baldozer/ Centre's Bonnet/Cork Hill/John MacDonald's Jig/Loch Monar/Inveran/The Ewe wi' the Crookit Horn/The Rejected Suitor/Donald MacLean/Paddy's Leather Breeches/The Desperate Battle of the Birds/The Old Wife's Dance/The Kitchen Maid/The Irish Washerwoman/The Wandering Piper/Parker's Welcome to Perthshire/Achany Glen/The Duchess of Edinburgh/Thick Lies the Mist on Yonder Hill/Rose Among the Heather/The High Road to Linton/The Pretty Apron/The Highland Lassie Going to the Fair/The Ladies from Hell/Delvin Side/Hearken My Love/John MacCall's March to Kilbowie Cottage/Athole Cummers/Thompson's Dirk.

12T200 *The Fox Jumps Over the Parson's Gate*: Peter Bellamy. Spotted Cow/Two Pretty Boys (The Two Brothers)/Female Drummer/Here's Adieu Sweet Lovely Nancy/ Ghost's Song/The Cruel Ships Carpenter/Carnal and Crane/Little Black Horse/The Penny

Wager/Barley and the Rye/Turkish Lady/Warlike Seaman/Blackberry Fold/St. Stephen/ Rigs of London Town/Fox Jumps over the Parson's Gate.

TPS201 *Ballads and Broadsides Topic Sampler 6*: Various Artists. Brave Wolfe/Bonnie Ship the Diamond – A.L. Lloyd. Pace Egging Song/Droylsden Wakes/Johnny Todd/The Gresford Disaster – Ewan MacColl. John Barleycorn/Blackleg Miner/Jolly Waggoners/ Trimdon Grange Explosion/Sweet Primroses/White Cockade.

12T202 *More Grand Airs From Connemara*: Various Artists.

12T203 *The Great Australian Legend – A Panorama of Bush Balladry and Song*: A.L. Lloyd, Martyn Wyndham-Read(e) and Trevor Lucas (1971). Waltzing Matilda – A.L. Lloyd and chorus/Jim Jones at Botany Bay – A.L. Lloyd/The Wild Colonial Boy – A.L. Lloyd/The Streets of Forbes – Trevor Lucas/The Hold-up at Eugowra Rocks – A.L. Lloyd and chorus/The Fash Stockman – Martyn Wyndham Reade/Five Miles from Gungadai – Trevor Lucas/The Lime Juice Tub – A.L. Lloyd, Martyn Wyndham Reade and chorus/Euabalong Ball – A.L. Lloyd/Banks of the Condamine – Trevor Lucas/Click Go the Shears – Martyn Wyndham-Reade/Flash Jack from Gungadai – A.L. Lloyd/The Road to Gungadai – Martyn Wyndham Reade/Hard Tack – Martyn Wyndham-Reade/On the Road with Liddy – A.L. Lloyd.

12T204 *'Owdam' Edge – Song and Verse from Lancashire*: Various Artists.

TPS205 *Sea Songs and Shanties Topic Sampler 7*: Various Artists. Blood Red Roses – A.L. Lloyd and chorus/The Black Ball Line – Ewan MacColl and chorus/Maggie May – Stan Kelly/The Plains of Mexico – The Watersons/The Dreadnought – Ewan MacColl and Alf Edwards/Reuben Ranzo – A.L. Lloyd and chorus/Lowlands Low – Ian Campbell with Chorus and Dave Swarbrick, fiddle/Do Me Ama – A.L. Lloyd and Alf Edwards/ Boston Harbour – The Watersons/Blow the Man Down – Harry H. Corbett and chorus/ The Handsome Cabin Boy – Ewan MacColl and Alf Edwards/Away, Haul Away – Stan Kelly/The Coast of Peru – A.L. Lloyd/All For Me Grog – The Watersons/The Greenland Whale Fishery – The Watersons/A Hundred Years Ago – A.L. Lloyd and chorus/Goodbye, Fare Thee Well – Louis Killen with chorus and Dave Swarbrick, fiddle.

12TS206 *Oldham's Burning Sands – Ballads, Songs and Daft Ditties*: The Oldham Tinkers. Success to the Weavers/The Lancashire Miller/Charlie Chaplin/Eawr Market Neet/The Owdam Chap's Visit to th' Queen/In Our Town/Oldham's Burning Sands/A Fine Old English Gentleman/Peterloo/We're Off in a Motor Car/The Oldham Pensioner/ The Stockport Strike/Th' Childer's Holiday/The Owl of Oldham.

12T207 *Anne Briggs*. Blackwaterside/Snow it Melts the Soonest/Willie O' Winsbury/ Go Your Way/Thorneymoor Woods/Cuckoo/Reynardine/Young Tambling/Living By the Water/Ma Bonnie Lad.

12T208 *Matching Ballads of the British Isles and America*: Hedy West and Ian Manuel.

12TS209 *Songs, Ballads and Instrumental Tunes from Ulster*: The Irish Country Four. Reels – Roaring Mary/The Old Torn Petticoat/The Cotton Mill Song/The Granemore Hare/The Boys of Mullaghbawn/Pulling the Lint. Air – The Melodious Little Fort of Bruff/General Munro/The Load of Kale Plants/O'Meally's Hornpipe. Jigs – Kitty's Bonnet/ The Flax Dresser/The Doffing Mistress/The Maid of Ballydoo/Air – Blind Mary/

Magherafelt Hiring Fair/The Heights of Alma/P. is for Paddy. Reels – Martin Mulhaire's No. 1/Kitty Goes a Milking/Pigeon on the Gate.

12TS210   *The Wide Midland – Songs, Stories and Tunes From the Central Counties*: Various Artists. Dudley Boys/When Shall We Get Married, John?/Slap Bum Tailor/ Swaggering Boney/Black Joke/Stop that Clock/Early in the Morning/When You Get Up in the Morning/Jolly Joe the Collier's Son/Owd Never Could/I Can't Find Brummagem/ Birmingham Jack of All Trades/Nailmaker's Strike/Old Miner/Birmingham Sally/Buffoon/ Staffordshire Hornpipe/Aye For Saturday Night/Aston Villa Supporter (story) – Tom Langley/Motor Trade Workers.

12TS211   *The Phenomenal Bernard Wrigley – Folksongs, Tunes and Drolleries* (with Wilf Darlington). The Molecatcher/The Five Gallon Jar/Mr. Lane's Maggot/The Green Ship/Other Folk's Childer/The Indian Loss/Pay Me the Money Down/Balance a Straw/ Dixie's Dog/The Treadmill Song/Bungereye/Bonny Kate of Aberdeen/Lord Carmarthen's March/The Wassail Song/Gee Whoa, Dobbin/Jack the Horse Courser/The Bonny Bunch of Roses/Haul Away the Bowline/Bobbing Joan/The Ballad of Knocking Nelly.

12TS212   *Welcome To Our Fair*: Oak. Thousands or More/New Rigged Ship – Rig-a-jig-jig/The Lakes of Coolfin/The Nutley Waltz/The Faithful Sailor Boy/Roving Round the County Tyrone/The Scarlet and the Blue/Shepherds Arise/Scan's Polka/Australia/ Cupid's Garden/False, False/Our Good Ship Lies in Harbour/The Bunch of Thyme/The Perfect Cure – The Sweets of May.

12TS213   Test pressing?

12T214   *The Sound of the Cheviots*: The Cheviot Ranters (1972). Circassian Circle – part 1/Rugley Ford/Hesleyside Reel/Redesdale Hornpipe/King of the Fairies/Lads of Whickham/Bugle Horn/Farewell/Jackson's Morning Brush/Northumbrian Waltz/Berwick Fair/Ma Bonny Lad/Keach in the Creel/Morpeth Rant/Banks of Coquet/Rob Roy's Cave/ Kirk's Hornpipe/Cumberland Reel/Quayside Shaver/Geordie's Jig/Corn Rigs/Dunstaburgh Castle/Goodnight and Joy/Bonnie Tyneside/Whittingham Green Lane/Drops of Brandy/ Goswick Kirn/Old Drove Road/Circassian Circle – part 2/Lannigan's Ball/Ellingham Hall.

12TS215   *Trans-Pennine*: Harry Boardman and Dave Hillary. Scarborough Sands/I'll Have a Collier for My Sweetheart/Forty Miles/Tommy Stroo's Ghost/Cowd Stringy Pie/ Tha's Welcome Little Bonny Brid/Nellie o' Bobs o't' Crowtrees/Weaver's Song/Happy Sam/Manchester Canal/T'Auld Wife of Coverdill/Lass o' Dallowgil/My Love, My Love/ Cockfight/Haley Paley/With Henry Hunt We'll Go/Ensilver Song.

12TS216   *Lovely on the Water*: Frankie Armstrong. Tarry Trousers/Green Valley/Low Down in the Broom/Cruel Mother/Crafty Maid's Policy/Maid on the Shore/Frog and the Mouse/Lovely on the Water/Brown Girl/Young Girl Cut Down in Her Prime/Unquiet Grave/Saucy Sailor/Two Sisters.

12TS217   *The Bitter and the Sweet*: Roy Harris. Turpin Hero/Bonnie Green Woods/ Death of Bill Brown/Three Butchers/Ullswater Pack/Poor Owd 'Oss/General Ludd's Triumph/Poverty Knock/Streams of Lovely Nancy/Robin Hood and the Tanner/Royal Oak/Strike the Bell/McCafferty/All Through the Ale.

12T218 *Through Dublin City*: Frank Harte. Rosemary Fair/Johnny Doyle/Dunlavin Green/Spanish Lady/Flower of Magherally/James Connolly/Ship's Carpenter's Wife/Three Weeks We Are Wed/Matt Hyland/Row in the Town/He Rolled Her to the Wall.

12TS219 *Canny Newcassel – Ballads and Songs from Newcastle and Thereabouts*: Various Artists (1972). Canny Newcassel; Sandgate Girl's Lament – Handle, Ross, Anderson, Gilfellon/Miller's Wife of Blaydon – Handle, Ross/Ee Aye, as Cud Hew – Ed Pickford/Three Cows – Pete Elliott with chorus/Billy Boy – Billy Conroy whistle/Bonnie Gateshead Lass – Don Stokoe/My Lad's a Canny Lad – Doreen Henderson/Till the Tide Comes In – Handle, Ross, Anderson; Gilfellon/Silly Galoot – Billy Conroy vocal/Fire on the Quay – Barry Canham with chorus and Handle, Ross/Billy Oliver's Ramble – Barry Canham with Colin Ross (fiddle)/Jowl and Listen – Pete Elliott/Weary Cutter – Pete Elliott/Graveyard Shift – Les Pearson with Ross, Handle/Wylam Away – Colin Ross (Northumbrian pipes)/Footy against the Wall – Tom Gilfellon with Ross, Handle, Anderson/My Old Man's a Dustman – Bruce Elliott/Four and Twenty Bob – Billy Conroy (vocal)/Blaydon Races; Keep Your Feet Still, Geordie Hinny – Handle, Ross, Anderson, Gilfellon.

12TS220 *The Frosty Ploughshare*: Ian Manuel. Drumdelgie/Bogie's Bonnie Belle/Tarves Rant/Lowlands of Holland/Sleepytoon/Moss O' Burreldale/Bonnie Lads that Handle the Plough/Guise o' Tough/Scrankly Black Farmer/Muckin' o' Geordie's Byre/Braes o' Strathblane/Tinker's Wedding/Toon o' Dalry/Erin Go Bragh.

TPSS221 *English Garland Topic Sampler 8*: Various Artists. Roy Harris – Robin Hood and the Tanner/The Bonny Green Woods. The High Level Ranters – The Breakdown/Blanchard Races. Dave and Toni Arthur – Six Jolly Miners/The Lark in the Morning. Anne Briggs – The Snow it Melts the Soonest/The Cuckoo. Peter Bellamy – The Fox Jumps Over the Parson's Gate/The Barley and the Rye. Bernard Wrigley – The Molecatcher/Gee Whoa Dobbin/Jack the Horse Courser. Oak – Thousands or More/Scan's Polkas. Peta Webb – Roving Round the County Tyrone. Tom Gilfellon – The Hexhamshire Lass.

12TS222 *The Cheviot Hills*: The Cheviot Ranters. My Love She's But a Lassie Yet/Caddam Woods/Rose Tree/Sylph/Hermitage/Bryce Anderson/Roxburgh Castle (original)/Sheffield Hornpipe/Mallorca (Northumberland Waltz)/Cheviot Hills/I Have Seen the Rose Blow/Winster Gallop/Teribus/Jimmy Allen/Jack Thompson's Fancy/Newcastle/Nancy/Molly's Fancy/Perfect Cure/Stool of Repentance/Linton Ploughman/Road to the Isles/Roamin' in the Gloamin'/Show Me the Way to go Home/Danish Double Quadrille/Blaydon Races/Keep Your Feet Still Geordie Hinny/Wherever Ye Can Yer Sure tae Find a Geordie.

12TS223 *I Have Wandered in Exile*: Peta Webb with Lucy Farr, Michael Plunkett – fiddle, Reg Hall – melodeon. I Have Wandered in Exile//Oxford City/Moorlough Shore/Blackbird of Sweet Avondale/Backwater Side/Pride of Glencoe/I Am a Poor Girl/Moorlough Mary/Lovely Banks of Lea.

12TS224 *Folk Music of Yugoslavia*.

12TS225 *Songs from Suffolk*: Bob Hart. Cod Banging/Australia/A Broadside (The Female's Captain)/Banks of the Sweet Primroses/What a Funny Little Place to Have One/Bold General Wolfe/Female Cabin Boy/As I Strolled Out to Aylesbury/Scarlet and the Blue/John Barleycorn/Miner's Dream of Home/Young Sailor Cut Down/All Jolly Fellows that Follow the Plough/Underneath her Apron.

12TS226 *The Streets of Glasgow*: Various Artists including Freddy Anderson: Let Glasgow Flourish, etc.

12TS227 *Wild Hills O' Wannie – The Small Pipes of Northumbria*: Billy Pigg, Joe Hutton, Geordie Atkinson: Barrington Hornpipe/Navvy on the Line/Friendly Visit/ Remember Me/Biddy the Bold Wife/Lamb Skinnet/De'il Among the Tailors/Oh Dear What Can the Matter Be? – variations.

12TS228 *The Moon Shone Bright*: The Broadside. Seventeen Come Sunday/Lincolnshire Wedding Song/Bold Grenadier/Gardener and the Ploughman/Free and Easy/Outlandish Knight/Caister Fair/Dick Turpin/Lisbon/American Stranger/Maria Marten/Poacher/ Creeping Jane/Banks of the Sweet Dundee.

12TS229 *English Country Music From East Anglia*: Various Artists (1973). Billy Bennington – Gay Ladies/Dulcie Belle/Yarmouth Hornpipe/On the Green/On Parade/ Slow Step Dance Tune/Jack's the Lad/Red Wing. Oscar Woods – Jig/The Sailor's Hornpipe/ Italian Waltz/Polka/Step Dance Tune/Polka/Oh Joe, The Boat is Going Over. Percy Brown – Oh Joe, The Boat is Going Over/Yarmouth Breakdown/Waltz for the Veleta/ Barn Dance Tune/Sheringham Breakdown/Heel and Toe Polka. Harold Colvill – The Oyster Girl/The Nutting Girl.

12TS230 *The Lark in the Clear Air*: John Doonan – piccolo, whistle, John Wright, etc.

12TS231 *The Folk Music of Greece*.

12TS232 *The Valiant Sailor – Songs and Ballads of Nelson's Navy*: A.L. Lloyd, Roy Harris, Frankie Armstrong, Martyn Wyndham Read, Alistair Anderson, Bobby Campbell. The Banks of the Nile/The Seventeen Bright Stars/Nelson's Death – A.L. Lloyd/Here's the Tender Coming/The Nightingale/The Sailor Laddie/Liberty for the Sailors/The Sailor Boy – Frankie Armstrong, etc.

12TS233 *When the Frost is on the Pumpkin*: Fred Jordan. Six Pretty Maids (The Outlandish Knight)/The Banks of Claudy/Break the News to Mother/Barbara Allen/ Turmot Hoeing/The Horn of the Hunter/When the Frost is on the Pumpkin/The Seeds of Love/The Bonny Bunch of Roses/When Joan's Ale was New/The Volunteer Organist.

12TS234 *Sea Shanties*: Roy Harris, A.L. Lloyd, Ian Manuel, Martyn Wyndham-Read, Bernard Wrigley (1974). Hoorah for the Black Ball Line – Martyn Wyndham-Read and chorus/Old Billy Riley – Roy Harris and chorus/Roll 'er Down the Bay – A.L. Lloyd and chorus/Round the Corner, Sally – Roy Harris and chorus/Haul Away the Bowline – Martyn Wyndham-Read and chorus/The Sailboat 'Malarkey' – A.L. Lloyd and chorus/Bring 'em Down – Roy Harris and chorus/Sally Brown – A.L. Lloyd and chorus/Shallow Brown – Bernard Wrigley and chorus/Bold Riley O – A.L. Lloyd and chorus/Heave Away My Johnny – Bernard Wrigley and chorus/Reuben Ranzo – Martyn Wyndham-Read and chorus/Hilo John Brown – A.L. Lloyd and chorus/Shake Her, Johnny – Roy Harris and chorus/Ho Bowline, Bowline Haul – A.L. Lloyd and chorus/Haul Away for Rosie – Bernard Wrigley and chorus/Blood-Red Roses – Ian Manuel and chorus/Around the Bay of Mexico – A.L. Lloyd and chorus/Goodbye, Fare Ye Well – Roy Harris and chorus.

12T235 *Blackberry Fold*: George Spicer. Blackberry Fold/Cutaway Mike/Oyster Girl/ Faithful Sailor Boy/Three Jolly Boys/Irish Hop Pole Puller/Cunning Cobbler/Folkestone Murder/German Clockmaker/Henry My Son/Coming Home Late/I Wish There Was No Prisons/Searching For Young Lambs/Old Militia Drum.

12TS236 *Ballads, Songs and Recitations – A Lancashire Mon*: Harry Boardman. Lancashire Mon/The Spinner's Tale/Radcliffe Otter Hunt/Victoria Bridge on a Saturday Night/Kitty and Robin/Saddleworth Buck Rabbit/Whoam Brewed/Warrikin Fair/Spinning Shoddy/To the Begging/Beltane Song/Garland/Owdham on a Saturday Night/Nine Times a Night.

12TS237 *Best o't' Bunch*: The Oldham Tinkers (1974). The Rochdale Mashers/Seeing Double/The Pennine Rangers/The Two Jews/A Piecer's Tale/Best o't' Bunch/The Lancashire Toreador/A Cob-Coaling Medley/The Four-Loomed Weaver/John Willie's Ragtime Band/Platt's/Good Time Coming/I Mean to Wait for Jack/Skiing Owdham Style/A Mon Like Thee.

12TS238 *Adieu to Old England*: Shirley Collins (1974). Mistress's Health/Lumps of Plum Pudding/Down By the Seaside/Chiner's Song/Adieu to Old England/Ashen Faggot Wassail/I Sing to a Maiden that is Makeless/Banks of the Mossom/Ram of Berbish Town/Portsmouth/Horkston Grange/Come All you Little Streamers/Spaniards Cry/ Sherborne Jig/One Night as I Lay on my Bed/Death of Nelson/Coronation Jig.

12TS239 *Bonny North Tyne*: Joe Hutton, Billy Atkinson, George Hepple, John Armstrong. John Armstrong – The Rowan Tree/Jock of Hazeldean/Sir Sydney Smith's March/Drink to me Only/Will Yo No Come Back Again, etc.

12T240 *The Boscastle Breakdown – Southern English Country Music* (1974): Walter Bulmer (Norfolk) – recorded 1962; William Hocken (Cornwall) – recorded by the BBC, 1943; Sean Tester; Tintagel and Boscastle Players, etc.

12TS241 *Rough and Wrigley*: Bernard Wrigley. Manchester Recruits/Plastic Pies/Parson in the Peas/Campanero/Strike the Bell/Drop of Good Beer/Saucy Sailor/Free and Easy/ Bertie's Fancy/Collier Brig/First Day at t' Mill/Hand Loom v Power Loom/Along the Rossendale/Old Bill/Constant Billy/Holes in the Road/Old Man and his Wife/Ten Thousand Miles Away/Rigs of London Town.

12TS242 *The Clutha*: Ronnie Alexander. Soor Milk Cairt/Donald Blue/Dell in the Lum/Jigs/Andro and his Cutty Gun/Rigs o' Rye/Johnny Sangster/Wha's Fu/Andrew Ross/Gaberlunzie Man.

12TS243 *Flash Company – Traditional Singers from Suffolk and Essex* incl. Bold Princess Royal/Seventeen Come Sunday/Rap a Tap Tap/Song of the Thrush/Gypsy's Warning/Barbara Allen/Faithful Sailor Boy/Flash Company/Wheel Your Rambulator/Go and Leave Me if You Wish/Ernest Austin: John Barleycorn/Hares on the Mountain/The Knife in the Window.

12T244 *A Garland for Sam*: Sam Larner (1974). Alphabet Song/Merry Month of May/ Napoleon's Dream/London Steamer/Bonny Bunch of Roses/Barbara Allen/The Smacks-man/Lofty Tall Ship/Raking the Hay/Will Watch/The Outlandish Knight/Haisboro' Light Song/Old Bob Ridley-O/The Bold Princess Royal/In Scarboro' Town.

12TS245 *Cheviot Barn Dance*: The Cheviot Ranters. Dashing White Sergeant/Rakes of Mallow/Catherine's Reel/Call of the Pipes/Sweet Maid of Glendaruch/Earl of Mansfield/Nottingham Swing: Marquis o' Lorne/Showman's Fancy/Beggar Boy/Military Two Step: I Do Like to be Beside the Seaside/Here We Are Again/Mademoiselle from Armentiers/Hello, Hello Who's Your Lady Friend?/Swedish Masquerade/Lucky Seven/Toland Dance/Aiken Drum/La Russe/Good Humour/Come Let Us Dance and Sing/Keel Row/There's Nae Much Luck About the House/Castles in the Air/Bridge of Athlone/Pet of the Pipers/Smash the Windows/CircleWaltz/I Belong to Glasgow/Oh Oh Antonio/Peggy O'Beill/Cheviot Rant/Cloudy Crags/Traditional Air/Polka: The Brownieside Polka.

12T246 *French Folk Songs from Corneze*. Collected and recorded by Hugh Shields. 1LP0033141.

12TS247 *The Rose of Britain's Isle*: John Kirkpatrick and Sue Harris. Rose of Britain's Isle/Glorishears/Up in the North/Hunsden House/Whimbleton House/Queen of the May/Old Man Jones/Not for Joe/Weyhill Fair/Milkmaid's Song/Rising Sun/Crown/Sweet Swansea/White Joak/Yellow Joke/Lady and the Soldier/Fireside Polka/Down Sides and up the Middle.

12TS248 *The May Morning Dew*: John Lyons. The Maid on the Shore/The May Morning Dew/Jigs – Morrisons, The Pipe on the Hob, The Tailor Bawn, After Aughtrim, The Boys of Barna-shraide/Erin's Lovely Lea. Reels – The Blackthorn/Un-named/Farmer Michael Hayes/The Lambs on the Green Hills/Fiac an Madrarua/Kitty's Wedding/Farewell, Lovely Mary.

12T249 *The Art of William Kimber*. Haste to the Wedding, Getting Upstairs/Over the Hills to Glory/Haste to the Wedding, Getting Upstairs, Blue Eyed Stranger/Rodney/Rigs of Marlow/Double Set Back/Hunting the Squirrel/Double Lead Through/Over the Hills to Glory/Trunkles/Bean Setting/The 29th of May/Laudnum Bunches/Constant Billy/Country Gardens/Shepherd's Hey/Headington Morris Reel, Soldier's Joy/Jockie to the Fair/Old Mother Oxford/Bacca Pipes, Greensleeves.

12T250 *The Wandering Minstrel*: Seamus Ennis. Wandering Minstrel/Jackson's Morning Brush/Boys of Bluehill/Dunphy's Hornpipe/Glennephin Cuckoo/Littlefair Cannavans/Frieze Britches/Flags of Dublin/Wind that Shakes the Barley/Little Stack of Barley/Cronin's Horpipe/New Demesne/Blackbird/Gillan's Apples/Walls of Liscarroll/Stone in the Field/Molly O'Malone/Kiss the Maid Behind the Barrel/Happy to Meet and Sorry to Part.

12TS251 *The Russell Family of Doolin, Co. Clare*. Campbell's Reel/Heather Breeze/The Traveller/St. Kevins of Glendalough/Potlick/The Peeler's Jacket/Five Mile Chase/Russell's Hornpipe/Fisher's Hornpipe/Poor Little Fisher Boy/Walls of Liscarroll/The Battering Ram/Garret Barry's Reel/Tommy Glenny's Reel/Connemara Stockings/The Westmeath Hunt/When Muskeen went to Bunnan/Tatter Jack Walsh/De'il Among the Tailors/Roscrea Cows/Fair Haired Boy/The Black Haired Lass/Off to California/Give the Girl her Fourpence/Nora Daly.

12TS252 *The Broomfield Wager*: Cyril Poacher. The Broomfield Wager/The Green Bushes/Nancy of Yarmouth/The Maid and the Magpie/The Bog Down in the Valley/

Australia/Joe Moggins/The Black Velvet Band/Flash Company/Plenty of Thyme/The Bonny Bunch of Roses/A Sailor and his True Love/I'm a Young Man from the Country/ The Faithful Sailor Boy/A Broadside/The Nutting Girl.

12T253   *Songs of the Open Road*: Various Artists (1975). Jasper Smith – You Subjects of England/Hartlake Bridge/Thorneymoor Park/The Squire and the Gypsey/While the Yoggar Mush Lays Sleeping. Mrs Haynes – Little Dun Dee/The Young Officer/All Through Mi Rakli/At the Atchin Tan/Erin's Lovely Home. Wiggy Smith – The Oakham Poacher/The Deserter. Joe Jones – The Farmer of Chester/The King was the Keeper. Levi Smith – Georgie/The Haymakers/The Broomdasher/The Game of Cards. Phoebe Smith – Barbara Allen. Bill Ellson – Lavender.

12T254   *When Sheepshearing's Done – Country Songs from Southern England*: Various Artists. Freda Palmer – The Fox and the Grey Goose/The Wandering Girl/The Warwickshire RHA/Oxford City/As I was a' Walking/Up in the North/The Bailiff's Daughter of Islington/William and Mary/Maria Marten. George 'Tom' Newman – All for the Grog/Sing Ovy and Sing Ivy. Bill Whiting – The Broken-down Gentleman/I'm Going to the Woods. Wisdom Smith – The Galloway Man. Bob Blake – When Sheepshearing's Done/The Grey Hawk. Harry Holman – The Life of a Man/Toast. George Spicer – The Thrashing Machine/The Lily White Hand. Bill Dore – Jolly Jarge.

12TS255   *From the North*: Gary and Vera Aspey (1975). From the North/Parting/Coal Picking/Three Foot Seam/Mill Girls Lullaby/King Cotton/Auntie Ketyll/Cum t' thi Tay/ Cradle Song/Roving Navvy/Ship Canal Song/Hailey Go/Tuppence on the Rope/Bit of a Sing.

12TS256   *Champions of Folly*: Roy Harris. Saucy Bold Robber/Bold Lovell/Steepleford Town/Captain Ward/Methody Parson/Caroline and her Young Sailor Bold/Beggar's Song/ When I was a Little Boy/Dragoon's Ride/Cropper Lads/Royal Charter/Topman and the Afterguard/Jovial Hunter/Hard Times of Old England.

12TS257   *Songs of a Donegal Man*: Packie Byrne. John and the Farmer/The Rich Man's Daughter/The Holland Handkerchief/Molly Bawn/The Jolly Ploughboy/Young Alvin/Johnny o' Hazlegreen/Lament to the Moon/The Creel.

12T258   *Sussex Harvest*: Rabbidy Baxter, Bob Blake, Mary Ann Haynes, Harry Upton. Harry Upton – Canadee-I-O/The Freckless Young Girl/The Wreck of 'The Northfleet'/ Poison in a Glass of Wine. Mrs Haynes – The Female Drummer/Poor Leonard/The Old Miser/Riding Down to Portsmouth/Long-a-growing/The Ball of Yarn. Bob Blake – The Basket of Eggs/The Bonny Labouring Boy. Rabbidy Baxter – Will the Weaver.

12T259   *Classics of Irish Piping Vol. 1*: Leo Rowsome. Boil the Breakfast Early/ Heather Breeze/Savourmeen Deelish/Clare's Dragoons/Blackbird/St. Patrick's Day/ Boolavogue/Old Bog Road/Boys of Wexford/Kelly the Boy from Killane/Rights of Man/ Wexford/Dunphy's Hornpipe/Broom/Star of Munster/Milliner's Daughter/Collier's Reel/ The Maid of Tramore/Independent Hornpipe/The Star Hornpipe/Friez Breeches/Tomorrow Morning/Cloone Hornpipe/Cook in the Kitchen/Rakes of Kildare/Sweep's Hornpipe/The Friendly Visit/Jockey to the Fair/My Darling Asleep/Tongues of Fire/Higgin's Hornpipe/ The Queen of May/Fairie's Revels/I Won't Be a Nun/Shandon Bells/Haste, to the Wedding/ Rocky Road to Dublin. See TSCD471.

12TS260   *Up and Awa' with the Laverock*: Lizzie Higgins. Up and Awa' Wi' the Laverock/ Lord Lovat/Soo Sewin' Silk/Lady Mary Ann/MacDonald of Glencoe/Forester/Tammy Toddles/Aul' Roguie Gray/Twa Brothers/Cruel Mother/Lassie Gathering Nuts.

12TS261   *Songs from the Eel's Foot*: Jumbo Brightwell. Flower of London/Derby Miller/ Loss of the Ramillies/Green Mossy Bank of the Lea/Blow the Candle Out/Bold Princess Royal/Newry Town/Indian Lass/Muddley Barracks/False Hearted Knight/Lost Heiress/ Down in the Fields Where the Buttercups Grow/Rumbleaway/Life of a Man.

12T262   *Classics of Irish Piping Volume 2*: William Andrews and Liam Walsh. Portlaw Reel/Faithful Brown Cow/Billy Taylor's Fancy/Garden of Daisies/Bank of the Suir/ Mountain Lark/Dan McCarthy's Fancy/Cliffs of Moher/Saddle the Pony/Yellow John/ Kitty's Rambles/Speed the Plough/Johnny Gorman/Two Single Jigs/May Day/Cuckoo's Nest/Smash the Windows/Rocky Road to Dublin/Bonnie Kate/First House in Connaught/ Munster Buttermilk.

12TS263   *The Singing Molecatcher of Morayshire*: John MacDonald. Sleepytoon/Mains o' Fogieloon/Lord Ronald/Burns Waltz/Dewy Dens o' Yarrow/Bonnie Hoose o' Airlie/ Majuba Hill/Braes o' Balquhidder/Ploughin' Match at Duffus/Haughs o' Cromdale/ Jacobite Waltz/Farewell Tomintoul/Bonnie Lassie Will Ye Gang/My Auntie Jean/Bonnie Udny/Cairgorn Barn Dance/Wandering Shepherd Laddie/Banks of Allan/Ball of Kerrymuir.

12TS264   *The Mountain Streams Where the Moorcocks Crow*: Paddy Tunney. The Mountain Streams Where the Moorcocks Crow/Wee Weaver/Boys of Mullabawn/Old Petticoat/Coinleach Glas an Fhomair/Donall Og/Reaping of the Rushes Green/One Morning in June/Lady Margaret/Inis Dhun Ramha/Old Oak Tree/Drinking Good Whiskey/ Sweet Omagh Town/Green Fields of Canada.

12TS265   *For Pence and Spicy Ale*: The Watersons. Country Life/Swarthfell Rocks/ Barney/Swinton May Song/Bellman/Adieu, Adieu/Apple-Tree Wassailing Song/Sheep-shearing/Three Day Millionaire/King Pharim/T Stands for Thomas/Malpas Wassail Song/ Chickens in the Garden/The Good Old Way. KTSC265 – cassette.

12TS266   *Caledonian Companion – Instrumental Music from Scotland*. Lady Madeline Sinclair/High Road to Linton/White Cockade/Neil Gow's Farewell to Whiskey/Miss Jean Milligan/Muckin' o' Geordie's Byre/Kinnegad Slashers/Bugle Horn/Brig o' Perth/Reel of Tulloch/Forbes Morrison/Ten Pound Fiddle/Smith's a Gallant Fireman/Jenny Dang the Weaver/Bonnie Dundee/Hot Punch/Kenmore's Up and Awa'/J.B. Milne/Lovat Scouts/ Breakdown/Caddam Woods/Polka/Smith's a Gallant Fireman/Soldier's Joy/Kirrie Debbuck/ Sir David Davidson of Cantray/Tam Bain's Lum/Blue Bonnets O'er the Border/Far Frae Scotia's Shore/Alley Crocker/Orange and Blue/Mrs MacLeod of Rasay/Highland Wedding/ Dr. MacDonald/Lady Charlotte Campbell/Mason's Apron/Timour the Tartar.

12TS267   *Northumbrian Country Music*. Morpeth Rant.

12TS268   *The Music of J. Scott Skinner*.

12T269   *You Rambling Boys of Pleasure*: Robert Cinnamond. You Rambling Boys of Pleasure/Van Diemen's Land/You Ribbonmen of Ireland/Rich Shipowner's Daughter/ Napoleon Bonaparte/Weaver/Youghal Harbour/Beggarman/Fly Up, My Cock/I'm A

Rambling Youth/Augalee Heroes/Early in the Spring/Young Willie Reilly/Drowsy Maggie/ Old Man Rocking the Cradle.

12TS270 *The Collier Lad*: Johnnie Handle. Collier Lad/Dust/Durham Big Meetin' Day/Old Man of the Village/New Spotlight/Farewell to the Monty/Stottin' Doon the Waal/Is There Owt Secure/Old Pubs/Decorating/Fearless Mariner/Danny's.

12TS271/2 *The Bonnie Pit Laddie*: The High Level Ranters with Harry Boardman and Dick Gaughan (DLP – 1975). Doon the Waggon Way/Miner's Life/I Wish Pay Friday Would Come/Augengeich Disaster/Collier's Rant/Farewell to the Monty/Putter/Little Chance/My Gaffer's Bait/Coal Owner and the Pitman's Wife/Blackleg Miner/Miners' Lockout/South Medomsley Strike/Durham Lockout/Aa'm Glad the Strike's Done/Collier's Pay Week/I'll Have a Collier/Instrumental Selection/I'll Make Her Fain to Follow Me/ Joyful Days are Coming/Get Her Bo/Stoneman's Song/Hartley Calamity/Bonnie Woodha'/ Banks of the Dee/The Bonnie Pit Laddie (vocal).

12TS273 *Songs and Ballads*: Frankie Armstrong (1975): Little Duke Arthur's Nurse/ Pitmen's Union/Lady Diamond/Lament for the Hull Trawlers/Month of January/Three Drunken Maidens/Jack the Lad/Whore's Lament/Little Musgrave/Collier Lass/Female Drummer.

12TS274 *Down The Long Road*: Bob Davenport.

12TS275 *West Country Melodeon*: Bob Cann. Uncle George's Hornpipe/Tommy Roberts' Hornpipe/Hot Punch/Uncle George's Waltz/Uncle Jim's Waltz/Primrose Polka/Dorsetshire Hornpipe/Kester Rocky Waltz/Family Jig/Woodland Flowers/Ford Farm Reel/Harry Gidley's Waltz/When it's Nighttime in Italy/Climbin' up de Golden Stairs/Lyrinka/ Schottische Hornpipe/Cokey Hornpipe.

12TS276 *For Old Time's Sake*: The Oldham Tinkers. Signora/Eaur Joe's Lad/John Willie's Horse/Barefoot Day's Medley/Lancashire Witches/Come Whoam to thi Childer an' Me/Johnny Bugger/Billy Winker/Bits o' Bromley Stree/The Condemned Cell/The Maypole/For Old Time's Sake. KTSC276 – cassette.

STOP7003 *For Old Time's Sake* c/w *The Lancashire Toreador* (45 – 1975). The Oldham Tinkers.

12TS277 *Will Ye Gang, Love*: Archie Fisher. with Allan Barty and John Tams. O Charlie, O Charlie/Lindsay/The Broom a' the Cowdenknowes/Mally Lee/Will Ye Gang, Love/The Flower of France and England, O/The Laird o' Windy Wa's/Men o' Worth/ Looly, Looly/Dreg Song/Adam Cameron/Blackbirds and Thrushes/The Gallant Ninety Two/The Rovin' Ploughboy.

12TS278 *Cut and Dry Dolly. Collection of Northumbrian Pipe Tunes Featuring Alistair Anderson.* Sunderland Lasses/Lads of Alnwick/All the Night I Lay With Jockie/Peacock Followed the Hen/Jack Layton/Green Breckons/Bob and Jones/Kiss Her Under the Coverlet/Cuckold Came Out of the Amrey/Cuddly Claw'd Her/Holme's Fancy/Stagshaw Bank Fair/Lasses Pass the Brandy/Cut and Dry Dolly/John Fenwick's the Flower Among Them/Over the Border/Pheasant's Dance/Rusty Gully/Keelman Over the Land/I Saw My Love Come Passing By Me/My Laddie Sits O'er Late Up/Shew's the Way to Wallington/ Drops of Brandy.

12T279   *James F. Dickie's Delights*. Cairdin o't/Highland Donald/Francis Sitwell/Hard is my Fate/Good Wife Admit the Wanderer/Dean Brig o' Edinburgh/Glencoe/Trumpet/ Banks/Smith's Waltz/Mulhill's/Laird of Drumblair/Baker Reel/Bonnie Lass o' Bon Accord/ Peterhead Polka/Braes o' Auchtertyre/Leaving the Glen/Miller of Drone/J.F. Dickie's Reel/Bovaglie's Plaid/South of the Grampians/Good Old John/MacPherson's Rant/Madam Frederick/Earl Grey/Whistle o'er the Lave o't/White Cockade.

12T280   *The Strathspey King*: J. Scott Skinner. President – air and variations/Lucania Polka/Freebooter/Tullochgorum/East Neuk of Fife/Allegory/Miller O'Hirn/MacKenzie Fraser/Auld Wheel/Bagpipe Marches/Cameron Highlanders/Inverness Gathering/Celebrated Hornpipes/Eugene Stratton/Banks/Highland Reels Laird o' the Drums/Gavin MacMillan/ Laird of Drumblair/Gladstone's Reel/Bonnie Lass o' Bon Accord/Marquis of Huntly's Farewell/Ten Pound Fiddle/Highland Schottische/No 2 Sandy Cameron Miller o' Hirn/ Glenlivet/Triumph Country Dance/Triumph/Trimour the Tartar/Left Handed Fiddler/Speed the Plough/De'il Among the Tailors/Home Sweet Home/Iron Man Strathspey/Bungalow Reel/Cradle Song/Braes o' Auchtertyre/Athole Highlanders/Glen Grant/Tulchan Lodge/ Parrot/Humorous Pizzicato/Mrs Scott Skinner/MacKenzie Hay/Devil's Elbow.

12TS281   *The Silver Bow – Shetland Fiddlers Vol. 1*: Tom Anderson, Aly Bain. Jack Broke Da Prison Door/Donald Blue/Sleep Soond ida Morning/Lasses Trust in Providence/ Day Dawn/Cross Reel/Shive Her Up/Da Silver Bow/Auld Foola Reel/Wynadepia/Da Slockit Light/Smith o' Couster/Da Grocer/Da Galley Watch/Kair and Knock it Corn/Da Auld Restin' Chair/Hamnavoe Polka/Maggie's Reel/Unst Bridal March/Da Bride is a Bonie Ting/Jack is Yet Alive/Auld Clettenroe/Da Mill/Aoon Da Rooth/Pit Hame Da Borrowed Claes/Wha'll Dance Wi Wattie/Bush Below Da Gairden/Soldier's Joy/Shetland Moods/We'll Stick Da Minister/Taste Da Green/Dean Brig o'Edinburgh/Banks Hornpipe. See TSCD469.

12TS282   *In the Middle of the Tune*: Tom Gilfellon with Martin Carthy, Johnny Handle, Liz and Stefan Sobell (1976). Banks of Red Roses/Boys of Ballysadare/Worker's Song/ Celebrated Working Man/Uncle Albert's Last Heroic Farewell to the World/Lady Ann Montgomery (reel)/Wind that Shakes the Barley/Foxhunter's (reel)/Snow it Melts the Soonest/Bonnie Gateshead Lass/Thomas Friel's Jig/Battering Ram/Two Sisters/Row in the Gutter/Fiery Clockface/Johnny Miner.

12T283   *Holey Ha'penny*: Various Artists. Tom Clough – Holey Ha'penny, Elsie Marley/ The Keel Row. Jim Rutherford – Morpeth Rant. Billy Ballantine – Proudlock's Hornpipe/ Billy Ballantine's Reel/Bonny North Tyne/Mosstrooper's Polka/The Coquet Reel. Ned Pearson – Father's Polka/Schottische/Varsoviana (Old and New)/Highland Laddie/Heel and Toe Polka/The Pin Reel – jig/Cambo March. Joe Hutton – My Lodging is on Cold Ground, Bonnie Dundee/Roxburgh Castle, Devil among the Tailors. Adam Grey – The Roman Wall/Tom Hepple's Polka (The Girl with the Blue Dress On)/The Tow House Polka. Bob Clark – Corn Rigs, The Manchester Hornpipe. Willie Taylor – The Linchope Lope/WillieTaylor's Polka/Nae Good Luck – jig. George Hepple – The Ferry Boat. Tom Hunter and Billy Ballantine – The Gilsland Hornpipe. Jake Hutton, Tom Hunter and Billy Ballantine – The Kielder Shottische. Billy Ballantine and Jimmy Hunter – Schottische/My Lodging's on Cold Ground, Blow the Wind Southerly. John Hepple and George Hepple – Whittingham Green Lane/Ward's Brae/Malorca, Herd on the Hill, Devil among the Tailors.

12TS284   *Beware of the Aberdonian*: The Gaughers. Pete Hall vocal, concertina; Tom Spiers vocal, fiddle; Arthur Watson vocal, whistle, dulcimer, bodhran. Young Jackie/The Cruel Brother/Monymusk Lads/The Keys to the Cellar/Go to Berwick, Johnnie/The Lass o' the Moorland Hills/The Bonny Lass o' Anglesey/Sleep Sound in the Morning/Donald Blue/The Aberdonian/Lochaber No More/The Minister's Sheep/Bogie's Bonnie Belle/The Ewie wi' the Crookit Horn/The Jolly Shepherd/Polly Stewart/The Scranky Black Farmer.

12TS285   *Green Grow the Laurels – Country Singers From the South*: Various Artists. Green Grow the Laurel – Louise Fuller/Rich Lady Gay – Harry Upton/Wexford Town – Mary Ann Haynes/Aylesbury Girl – Jack Goodban/Tree in the Wood – George Tom Newman/I Am a Donkey Driver – Harry Upton/Molecatcher – Louise Fuller/Hopping Down in Kent – Louise Fuller/Shannon Frigate – Jack Goodban/Young Maria – Louise Fuller/Colour of Amber – Mary Ann Haynes/Banks of Sweet Dundee – Harry Upton/Single Life – Harry Upton/Woman's Work is Never Done – Harry Upton.

12T286   *Ye Subjects of England – Traditional Songs from Sussex*: George Maynard. Polly on the Shore/The Sweet Nightingale/Locks and Bolts/Down By the Seaside/Jack the Jolly Tar-O/The Seeds of Love/Shooting Goshen's Cocks Up/William Taylor/Rolling in the Dew/A Sailor in the North Country/The Banks of Claudy/Three Sons of Rogues/The Weaver's Daughter/A Wager, a Wager/The Sun Being Set.

12TS287   *Drops of Brandy*: Sean McAloon and John Rea. Maid in the Meadow/Castlebar Races/Trip to the Cottage/Mountain Lark/Crooked Road to Dublin/Jackson's Drum/Jackson's Mistake/Jackson's Coagy/Blind Mary/Madame Bonaparte/O'Dwyer's Horn-pipes/Crowley's No. 1/Crowley's No. 2/Moloney's/Paddy O'Brien's Jig/First House in Connaught/Copperplate/An Buachaill Caol Dubh/Drops of Brandy/Coil the Hawser/Lord McDonald's/Alexandria's/Higgin's/Sligo Maid/Sheephan's/Wandering Minstrel/Katy is Waiting/Basket of Shamrocks/Tim the Turncoat/Quarrelsome Piper/Old Siege of Valencia/Lark in the Morning.

12T288   *The Last of the Travelling Pipers*: Felix Doran (1976). Mary of Munroe/Green Gates/Dear Irish Boy/Primrose Lass/Rakish Paddy/Rolandstown Churchyard/Ash Plant/Lark in the Morning/Fox Hunt/George White's Favourite/Ivy Leaf/Coolin/Boys of the Lough/Pigeon on the Gate/Miss Monaghan.

12TS289   *The Flowery Vale*: Paddy Tunney. Tis Pretty to be in Ballinderry/Captain Coulson/Ta Me Mo Shui/What Brought the Blood/The Blighted Lover/The Twisting of the Rope/The Blackbird/Old Ardboe/The Old Man Rocking the Cradle/Siubhan Ni Dhuibhir/Dobbin's Flowery Vale/Going to Mass Last Sunday.

12T290   *An Irish Jubilee – Traditional Irish Songs*: Cathal McConnell and Robin Morton.

12TS291   *The Art of the Highland Bagpipe Volume 1*: John Burgess. Compiled in TSCD466 (KTSC291 – cassette). Bundle and Go/Over the Water to Charlie/Cambletown Loch/Joy Go With my Love/Traigh Gruinard/Morag/Bonnie Argyll/The Stirlingshire Militia/The Taking of Beaumont Hamel/Pipe Major John MacDonald's Welcome to South Uist/Delvinside/John Morrison of Assynt House/Salute on the Birth of Rory Mor MacLeod/Colonel Robertson/The 79th Highlander's Farewell to Edinburgh/Major John MacLennan/Leaving Ardtornish/The Geese in the Bog/The Swallowtailed Coat/The

Mallow Men/Pipe Major George S. Allan/Jockey on the Braes of Abernethy/Wee Alec –
Fort William/Paddy Kelly's Stump/The Boys of Bluehill/The Ballachulish Walkabout/
Lord Alexander Kennedy/Tullach Gorum/Mr. MacPherson of Inveran/Duncan Johnstone/
Farewell to Nigg.

12TS292   *Singing Traditions of a Suffolk Family*: The Ling Family. Green Bushes/On
Board the Leicester Castle/Lobster/Died for Love/Little Ball of Yarn/Lakes of Coofin/
Deserter/Little Sweetheart/Jolly Jack the Sailor/Group of Young Squaddies/On the Banks
of the Clyde/Underneath Your Apron/Bonny Bunch of Roses/Nancy of Yarmouth/Man all
Tattered and Torn/Fagin the Cobbler.

12T293   *Davy Stewart*. MacPherson's Rant/Jolly Beggar/Cantering: the 74th Highlander's
Farewell to Edinburgh/Piper's Bonnet/Mrs MacLeod of Rasay/I'm Often Drunk and I'm
Seldom Sober/Taghter Jack Walsh/Connaught Man's Rambles/Overgate/Merchant's Son/
Daft Piper/Boolavogue/Harvest Home/Dowie Dens of Yarrow.

12TS294   *Uilleann Pipes*: Pat Mitchell.

12TS295   *Among the Many Attractions at the Show Will Be a Really High Class Band*:
John Kirkpatrick and Sue Harris. Edgmond Men's Souling Song/Artichokes and
Cauliflowers/Bricklayers/Double Change Sides/Cherry Tree Carol/John of the Greenery
Cheshire Way/Shropshire Lad/I Wish I Wish/Old Sir Simon the King/Adieu to Old
England/Blue Eyed Stranger/Winster Morris Reel/Jim Jones/Blacksmith's Morris/Charlie's
Hornpipe/Cold Blows the Wind/Wilson's Favourite/Shrewsbury Wakes. KTSC295 –
cassette.

12T296   *English Country Music*: Walter and Daisy Bulwer, Billy Cooper, etc. The
Bluebell Polka/The Foggy Dew, The Sailor Cut Down in his Prime/Untitled Polka/Off
She Goes/Red Wing/Believe Me if All Those Endearing Young Charms, Johnny's So
Long at the Fair, The Wild Colonial Boy/Untitled Polka/Jenny Lind Polka, The Girl I
Left Behind Me/Peggy Wood, Where There isn't a Girl About/Washing Day, Old Mrs
Cuddledee, The Cat's Got the Measles/The Waltz Vienna/The Four Hand Reel, Soldier's
Joy/Shepherd's Hey.

12TS297   *Ranting Lads*: The High Level Ranters (1976). Fairly Shot of Her/Wife of
My Own/Dance to your Daddy/Lass Doon on the Quay/Kielder Hunt/Alston Flower
Show/Jane of Biddlestone/Fortune Turns the Wheel/Fenwick of Bywell/Elsie Marley/
Hoop Her and Gird Her/Captain Bover/Here's the Tender Coming/Success to the Fleet/
Proudlock's Hornpipe/Hesleyside Reel/Stanley Market/Marquis of Waterford/Bottle Bank/
Hawk. KTSC297 – cassette.

12TS298   *Airs and Graces*: June Tabor. While Gamekeepers Lie Sleeping/Plains of
Waterloo/Bonny May/Reynardine/The Band Played Waltzing Matilda/Young Waters/Waly
Waly/The Merchant's Son/Queen among the Heather/Pull Down the Lads. KTSC298 –
cassette.

12TS299   *A Taste of Hot Pot*: Gary and Vera Aspey. Eskdale and Ennerdale Hunt Song/
Weepin' and Wailin' Away/Shuttle Kissing Song/Foddered me Yowes/Nightingale/Don't
Get Married Girl/Kids Songs/Coal Hole Cavalry/Morning Stands on Tiptoe.

12TS300   *Crown of Horn*: Martin Carthy. Bedmaking/Locks and Bolts/King Knapperty/

Geordie/Willie's Lady/Virginny/Worcestershire Wedding/Bonnie Lass o'Anglesey/William Taylor the Poacher/Old Tom of Oxford/Palaces of Gold. KTSC300 – cassette.

12TS301   *The Dales of Caledonia*: Ian Manuel. Haughs O' Cromdale/Are Ye Sleeping Maggie?/Young Beichan/Moneymusk Lads/Jamie Raeburn/Gallant Forty Twa/Bonnie Bessie Logan/Merchant's Son and the Beggar Wench/MacCrimmon's Lament/Sweet Kumadie/Overgate/Let Me in This ae Night/Lothian Hairst/Lass of Roch Royal.

12TS302   *Lancashire Sings Again!*: Mary and Harvey Kershaw. Yo're Allus Welcome Here/Gradely Folk/Song of the Knocker-up/Fireleet Fancies/Peigh Fox/Boggart o' Birchenbower/One for the Road/Th' Parson o' Waterhead/Wiff o' Moorlond Air/Love's Labour Lost/Th' Friendship Club/Other Folks' Children/Harkenin' t' Messiah/Toddlin' Whoam.

12T303   *Bound to Be a Row*: Jimmy McBeath. There's Bound to Be a Row/Banks of Inverurie/Ythanside/Erin Go Bragh/Bogie's Bonnie Belle/Cow Wi' the Iron Tail/Arlin's Fine Braes/Bonnie Lass o' Fyvie/Pittenweem Jo/Ye Canna Pit it on tae Sandy/Boston Smuggler/Highland Rorie's Wedding/Magdalen Green/Marin Fair/Roving Baker.

12TS304   *The Travelling Songster*: Phoebe, Minty, Jasper and Levi Smith. Recorded by Mike Yates 1975–76. The Small Bird's Whistle/The Sheepfold/One Penny/The Basket of Eggs/The Pony March/Whistling Rufus/Tuning; Green Bushes/Raking the Hay/The Moon Shines Bright/Father Had a Knife/The Jew's Garden/Step Dance Tunes/Tuning; Sweet William/Johnny Abourne/Died For Love/The Irish Girl/Captain Thunderbold/Jigs and Polkas incl. Cock of the North; Flowers of Edinburgh; The Girl I Left Behind Me/Tuning.

12TS305   *The Men of the Island*: The O'Halloran Brothers. Reels: The Music in the Glen/The Green Fields of America. Jigs: The Lark in the Morning/The Connaughtman's Rambles/The Lowlands of Holland. Barn Dances: Stack of Barley/Johnny, Will You Marry Me? Waltz and Jigs: Martin Byrne's Waltz/A Hundred Pipers/Dingle Regatta/ Granualle. Reels: The Sailor on the Rock/The Maid I Ne'er Forgot. Reel: The Limerick Lasses. Jig: The Lake Shore/The Exile's Return. Reels: The Eel in the Sink/Larry Redigan's/Moorlough Mary. Reels: The Bucks of Oranmore/The Wind that Shakes the Barley.

12TS306   *Irish Fiddle Player*: Jimmy Power (1976). Tommy Pott's Rambling Pitchfork, The Strayaway Child/The Chorus, McKenna's/Jockey to the Fair, Miss Brown's Fancy/ Coleman's Favourite, The Promenade/Dwyer's, The Harvest Home/Jackie Coleman's, The Castle/The Nine Points of Roguery, The Crib of Perches/Whelan's, The Old Lark in the Morning/The Mountain Road/Follow Me Down To Limerick, Hardiman the Fiddler/ Youghal Harbour/The Walls of Liscarrol/The Jug of Punch, The Moving Bogs of Powelsborough/Statia Donnelly's.

12TS307   *Queen Among the Heather*: Belle Stewart. Queen Among the Heather/Here's a Health to all True Lovers/Betsy Belle/Berryfields o' Blair/Soft Country Chief (the Toon o' Dairy)/Whistlin' at the Plough/Bonnie Wee Lassie frae Gourock/Overgate/ Blooming Caroline o' Edinburgh/Busk, Busk, Bonnie Lassie/Late Last Night/Twa Brothers/Leezie Lindsay.

12TS308   *In Sheffield Park*: Frank Hinchcliffe. Pear Tree/Golden Glove/Spotted Cow/ Mary Across the Wild Moor/Nobleman and the Thrasherman/Wilkins and Dinah/Green

Mossy Banks of the Lea/Wild and Wicked Youths/Sheffield Park/Hear the Nightingales Sing/Poor Old Weaver's Daughter/It Hails, It Rains/Nothing Else to Do/Edward/We've Been a While a-Wassailing.

12T309   *Kerry Fiddles – Music from Sliabh Luachra 1*: Padraig O'Keefe, Denis Murphy, Julia Clifford. The Top of Maol, The Humours of Ballydesmond/The Fisherman's, Byrne's Hornpipes/Muckross Abbey, Mulvihill's/Cronin's, The Stack of Barley/O'Donnells Lament/Danny Ab's Slide/The Frieze Breeches, Paudeen O'Rafferty's/Chase Me Charlie, Tom Billy's Favourite/Kennedy's Favourite, The Woman of the House/Apples in Winter, The Maid on the Green, The Thrush in the Straw/The Old Man Rocking the Cradle/The Humours of Galtymore, Callaghan's, The New-Mown Meadows/Calaghan's, The Rights of Man/Johnny When you Die, The Swallow's Tail, Miss MacLeod's.

TSCD309   Reissue of above.

12TS310   *The Star of Munster Trio – Music from Sliabh Luachra 2*: John, Julia and Billy Clifford. Dublin Porter/Mountain Lark/Lark in the Bog/Mountain Road/Paddy Cronin's/Ballydesmond/Knocknabowl/Boil the Breakfast Early/Bunker Hill/Red-haired Boy/Lucy's Reel/Clare Reel/Bill Black's/O'Donovan's/John Mahinney's no. 1/No Name/Grandfather's Thought/Madam, if You Please/Napoleon's Retreat/Connie the Soldier/Humoursof Glen/Palatine's Daughter/Jim Mac's Jig/Cherish the Ladies/Harlequin/Old Bush/Within a Mile of Dublin.

12TS311   *The Humours of Lisheen – Music from Sliabh Luachra 3*: John, Julia and Billy Clifford. Humours of Lisheen/Art O'Keefe's/Tap the Barrel/Jenny Tie the Bonnet/Frisco/Biddy Crowley's Ball/Bold Trainor O/Blue Riband/Up and Away/Callin an ti' Mhoir/Untitled Track/Freddie Kimmel's/Home Brew/Padraig O'Keefe's/Pol Ha'penny/John Mahinney's no. 2/Ducks and the Oats/I Looked East and I Looked West/Worn Torn Petticoat/Taimse I'm Chodladh/Julia Clifford's/Bill the Waiver's/Johnny Cope/John Clifford's/Behind the Bush in the Garden/Going for Water.

12TS312   *Music From Sliabh Luachra 4 – Traditional Flute Solos and Band Music*: Billy Clifford and others. Fermoy Lassies/Honeymoon/Upperchurch Polkas/Jigs/Polkas/Padraig O'Keefe's/Munster/Reel/No Name/Danny Green's Reels/Hollyford Jigs/Flowing Tide/Bracken Brae/Napoleon's Grand March/Top of Maol/Hetty O'Hady's/Milliner's Daughter/Durang's/Bill the Waiver's/Home Brew/Druid's Field/Willie Doherty's/Up on the Waggon/Lilting Banhee/Moycarkey/Byrne's/Charlie Mulvihill's/Muckross Abbey.

12TS313   *Battlefield Band*: The Battlefield Band. Silver Spear/Humours of Tulla/Shipyard Apprentice/Crossing the Minch/Minnie Hynd/Glasgow Gaelic Club/Brisk Young Lad/Birnie Bouzie/Compliments of the Band/A.A. Cameron's Strathspey/Scott Skinner's Compliments to Dr. MacDonald/Bonny Jean/Paddy Fahey's/Joseph's Fancy/Hog's Reel/It Was All for Our Rightful King/Inverness Gathering/Marquis of Huntly's Strathspey/John MacNeil's Reel/Miss Margaret Brown's Favourite/Deserts of Tulloch/Cruel Brother.

12TS314   *Free and Easy*: Kevin Mitchell. Free and Easy/Lurgy Streams/Mickey Dam/Nancy Bell/Boys of Mullaghbawn/Going to Mass Last Sunday/Magherafelt May Fair/Light Horse/Moorlough Shore/Two Strings on a Bow/Sean O'Duibhir/Oul' Grey Man.

12TS315   *Coppers and Brass – Scots and Irish Dance Music on Guitar*: Dick Gaughan. Coppers and Brass/Gander in the Pratie Hole/O'Keefe's/Foxhunter's/Flowing Tide/Fairies

Hornpipe/Oak Tree/Music in the Glen/Planxty Johnson/Gurty's Frolics/Spey in Spate/ Hurricane/Alan McPherson of Mosspark/Jig of Slurs/Thrush in the Storm/Flogging Reel Pipes/Ask my Father/Lads of Laois/Connaught Heifers/Bird in the Bush/Boy in the Gap/ MacMahon's Reel/Strike the Gay Harp/Shores of Lough Gowna/Jack Broke da Prison Door/Donald Blue/Wha'll Dance wi' Wattie.

12TS316   *Old Time Irish Fiddle and Accordion*: Rose Murphy.

12T 317   *Songs and Southern Breeze – Country Singers from Hampshire and Sussex*: Various Artists. Bonnie Bunch of Roses – Noah Gillette/Epsom Races – George Atrill/ Banks of the Mossom; False Lanky – George Fosbury/Cruel Lincoln – Ben Butcher/Silver Pin – Mrs Chapman/Chiner's Song – Frank Bond/God Bless the Master – Frank Bond/ Prickle Holly Bush – Fred Hewitt/Three Maidens a-Milking Did Go – Fred Hewitt/Her Servant Man – Gladys Stone/Rolling in the Dew – Leslie Johnson/Sheffield Park – Ben Butcher/George Collins – Enos White/Streams of Lovely Nancy – Victor Turp Brown/As Broad as I was Walking – Victor Turp Brown/Six Jolly Miners – Victor Turp Brown.

12TS318   *Postcards Home*: Bob Davenport. Byker Hill/Blackleg Miner/Durham Gaol Selection: Gypsy Poacher/Durham Gaol/First Time I Saw Durham City/Ball of Yarn/ Breaking Sticks/Wait till the Work Comes Round/Winter Time is Coming In/Old Changing Ways/When a Man Looks Pale/There's Nae Much Luck About the House/We Plough and Sow/Get Up, Stand Up/Once I Had as a True Love/Lowlands/My Bonnie Lad/Great Little Army March/Unemployed Men Stand on the Corner/McCafferty/I Don't Want to Join the Army/House is Crammed/Good Morning Good Morning/Our Soldiers Went to War/If I Was Fierce/If You Want to Find the Colonel/They Didn't Believe Me/Have You Forgotten Yet/When this Bloody War is Over.

12T319   *Ideal Music*: Bob Smith's Ideal Band (including James Andrews). Eightsome Reel part one/Ashcroft's Reel, Londonderry Air, Breakdown/Argyll and Sutherland Highlanders/Liverpool and Highland Hornpipes/The International/Medley of Popular Waltzes/The Canal Cruise 1 and 2/La Varsovienne/Big Reason Blues/The Boston Two-step/Horseguards Blue/Happy Hours/Woodland Voices/Eightsome Reel part two. Issued 1977.

12T320   *Better than an Orchestra*: Bob Smith's Ideal Band (recorded in London 1930– 31 or Edinburgh *c*.1934. Issued by Topic 1977). Ideal One-Step/James Andrews: The Middy March/Empress Tango/The Red Flag/Wull's Wireless Wails Parts 1 and 2: Flowers of Edinburgh – When You and I were Young, Maggie – Highland Laddie – Orange and Blue – Kafoozalum/Alec Bisset: Medley of Irish Waltzes: The Irish Jaunting Car – Come Back to Erin – Eileen – Alannah/The Ideal Lancers: 1st Fig: Rakes of Mallow – My Love is Like a Red, Red Rose – The Girl I Left Behind Me/2nd Fig: Lass of Gowrie – Kate Dalrymple – Loch Lomond/3rd Fig: Blackthorn Stick – Irish Washerwoman/4th Fig: The Alma (quick march) – Atholl Highlanders – Nora Creina – Biddy the Bowl Wife – Rakes of Kildare – Barren Rocks of Aden/J.B. Andrews (?) and Bob Smith: Dulcimer Tunes from an Old 'National Hall' Favourite parts 1 and 2: The Favourite Hornpipe – Unidentified Barn Dance/I Still Love You – Waltz Hesitation/Heddlestone and Macfarlane: The Call of the Pipes Part 1/Why Worry.

12T321   *Cameron Men – Classic Scots Fiddle Recordings from the 1930s*: Cameron Men. Abercairney Highlanders/Ballochmyle/Speed the Plough/Miss Drummond of Perth/

Maggie Cameron/Favourite/Loch Katrine/Miss Lyall/Loch Leven/Earl Dalhouse/Lady Mary Ramsay/Soldier's Joy/Dashing White Sergeant/My Love She's But a Lassie Yet/ Rose Tree/Original Brechin Bridge/Victoria Hornpipe/Bonnie Anne/Bob Johnston/Auld Lichties/John MacFadyen of Melfort/Brig o' Perth/Earl of Crawford's Reel/Rock and Wee Pickle Tow/Blackthorn Stick/Teviot Brig/Humours of Donnybrook/Rossity Ends/ Smith's a Gallant Fireman/Pretty Peggy/Cumberland Reel/Father O'Flynn/Auld Brig o' Ayr/Wind that Shakes the Barley/Rakes of Kildare/Swallow Tail/Queen's Welcome to Deeside/Drummer/Farewell to Gartly/Stirling Castle/Highland Queen/Forth Brig/Banks of Allan/Craigellachie Brig/Lasses o' Stewarton.

12T322   *Classics of Irish Piping Volume 3*: Leo Rowsome.

12TS323   *Sit Thee Down*: The Oldham Tinkers. The Maid in the Calico Dress/Elsie Bell/Pity Me My Darling/The Talking Dog/To Sarah/Tall Tails Medley/Sit Thee Down/ The Deserter/Poor Little Hauve-Timer/Dad's Medals/Fishing/Jumping Jack/Jim's Medley. KTSC323 – cassette.

12TS324   *Round Rye Bay for More – Traditional Songs from the Sussex Coast*: Johnny Doughty. Herrings' Heads/Wreck of the Northfleet/When I was Single/Golden Vanity/ Saucy Sailor/Baltimore/While Going Round the Cape/Round Rye Bay for More/Spanish Ladies/Sailor's Alphabet/Mermaid Marry Me/I'm Going to be Mother Today/Barbara Allen/ My Boy Billy/Dick Turpin/Let Her Go Back/Rye Harbour Girl/Streets of Port Arthur.

12TS325   *Darby's Farewell – Traditional Songs Played on Flute and Whistle*: Josie McDermott.

12TS326   *The Art of the Highland Bagpipe Vol. 2*: John Burgess.

12TS327   *By Sandbank Fields – Songs and Ballads*: Roy Harris. As I was Going to Banbury/Knight and the Shepherd's Daughter/Baker of Colebrook/Twenty-third of March/ Go From My Window/Think on This (When You Smoke Tobacco)/Dockyard Gate/Lady of Carlisle/Robin Hood and Little John/Sandbank Fields/Spithead Sailor/Unhappy Parting.

12TS328   *Countryside Songs from the South*: Bob Copper. Trooper/Bold Princess Royal/ Farmer from Chester/Mistletoe Bough/Bold Dragoon/Young Johnnie/Parson and the Sucking Pig/Lord Thomas/Squire's Lost Lady/Bold General Wolfe/Dick Turpin/Fox/ Dogs and Ferrets/Fisherman/Rose in June.

12TS329   *Layers*: Chris Foster. Ranter/Coast of Peru/Worcester City/Glastonbury Town/ Lady Maisry/Jack the Sailor Lad/Golden Glove/When a Man's in Love/Buxton Lass/ Flower of Serving Men/Banks of Newfoundland/Black Fox/Low Down in the Broom/ Grey Cock/Pigeon on the Gate/Unicorns/King John and the Abbot of Canterbury/Jump at the Sun/Working Chap/When this Old Hat was New/World Turned Upside Down.

12TS330   *Bonnie Mille Dam*: Clutha. My Apron/Binnie Susie/Farewell Tae Kemper/ Kilworth Hills/High, Jeanie, High/Braes o' Lochie/Terrible Twins/Banks of Allan/Ochitree Walls/Binnorie-o/Logan Water/Neil Gow/Captain MacDuff's Reel/Among the Blue Flowers and the Yellow/False Bride/Maids o' the Black Glen/Back o' the Moon/Donald Willie and his Dog/I Laid a Herrin' in Saut/Mossie and his Mare.

12TS331   *True Hearted Girl*: Lal and Norma Waterson (1978). Young Billy Brown/ Betsy Belle/Beggarman/Welcome Sailor/Meeting is a Pleasure/I Wish I Had Never/

Wealthy Squire/Jenny Storm/Bonnie Light Horseman/Unfortunate Lass/Flowers of the Forest/Grace Darling.

12TS332 *Mike Waterson* (1978). Wensleydale Lad/Brisk Lad/Two Brothers/Man o' War/Charlady's Son/Light Dragoon/Cruel Ship's Carpenter/Bye Bye, Skipper/Tamlin/ Lord Rothschild/Swansea Town/Seven Yellow Gypsies.

12TS333 *Folk Music of Turkey – Anatolian Music.* Reissued as TSCD908?

12TS334 *Wind and Water – Traditional Songs, Ballads and Lilts*: Len Graham. My Parents Reared Me Tenderly/Maggie Picken/Sean O'Duibhir a Ghleanna/County Mayo/ Star of Moville/Green Fields of Amerikay/Western Winds/Paidin O'Raibheartaigh/My Willie O/Daniel O'Connell and his Steam Engine/Rights of Man/One Morning in May/ Knight Templar's Dream.

12TS335 *Memories of Sligo*: Healy-Duffy.

12TS336 *The Watson Family Tradition*.

12TS337 *The Branch Line – Irish Traditional Music from Galway to New York*: Jack and Charlie Coen. Scatter the Mud/Larry Redigan's Jig/Sailor's Cravat/Repeal of the Union/John Conroy's Jig/Peach Blossom/Fiddler's Contest/Jim Conroy's Reel/Pullet/ Redican's Mother/Humours of Kilkenny/Mike Coen's Polka/Branch Line/Have a Drink with Me/Blarney Pilgrim/Two Woodford Flings/Waddling Gander/O'Connell's Jig on Top of Mount Everest/Lads of Laois/Green Groves of Erin/Tongs by the Fire/Spinning Wheel/Whelan's Reel/Jenny Dang the Weaver/Jack Coen's Jig/Paddy O'Brien's Jig.

12TS338 *Traditional Fiddle Music from County Clare*: Vincent Griffin. Fahey's 1 and 2/ Cliffs of Moher/Paddy Ryan's Dream/Mammy's Pet/Martin Rocheford's/Sligo Maid/New Century/Cuckoo/Coleman's/Lord MacDonald's/Ballinasloe Fair/Reefs/McFadden's Favourite/ New Year's In/Youghal Quay/Se Bhfath Mo Bhfuartha (The Cause of My Sorrow)/Lord Gordon's/Dr. Gilbert/Queen of May/Trip to Sligo/Garrett Barry's/Night in Ennis/Maid Behind the Bar/Crowley's/Lady Ann Montgomery/Down the Broom/Gatehouse Maid.

12TS339 *Music from County Leitrim*: Packie Duigan. Shores of Loch Gowna/Rose and the Heather/Devero the Dancer/Connie the Soldier/Tailor's Thimble/Red Haired Lass/ Sean Ryan's Hornpipe/New Found Out Reel/Sporting Paddy/Packie Duigan's Reel/Trip to Athlone/Hag with the Money/Castlebar/Crowley's Reels/Jackie Coleman's Reel/Sailor on the Rock/Bridie Morley/Duigan's Favourite/Kid on the Mountain/Highland Fling/ Mrs. Smullen's Reel/House on the Hill/Duke of Leinster/Dinny Ryan's Reels/Tom Ward's Downfall/Mullaghnavat Reel/Geese in the Bog/Your Jig.

12TS340 *Martin Carthy* – reissue of 1965 Fontana TLS 5269. High Germany/The Trees they do Grow High/Sovay/Ye Mariners All/The Queen of Hearts/Broomfield Hill/ Springhill Mine Disaster/Scarborough Fair/Lovely Joan/The Barley and the Rye/The Wind that Shakes the Barley/The Two Magicians/The Handsome Cabin Boy/And a Beggin' I Will Go. TSCD340 as above, CD reissue.

12TS341 *Second Album*: Martin Carthy. Two Butchers/Ball O'Yarn/Farewell Nancy/ Lord Franklin/Ramblin' Sailor/Lowlands of Holland/Fair Maid on the Shore/Bruton Town/Box on her Head/Newlyn Town/Brave Wolfe/Peggy and the Soldier/Sailor's Life. TSCD341 as above, CD reissue.

12TS342   *Byker Hill*: Martin Carthy with Dave Swarbrick. Man of Burnham Town/ Fowler Jack/Gentleman Soldier/Brigg Fair/Bloody Gardener/Barley Straw/Byker Hill/ Davy Lowston/Our Captain Cried All Hands/Wife of the Soldier/John Barleycorn/Lucy Wan/Bonnie Black Hare.

12TS343   *But Two Came By*: Martin Carthy and Dave Swarbrick – reissue of 1969 Fontana STL 5477. Ship in Distress/Banks of Sweet Primrose/Jack Orion/Matt Hyland/ White Hare/Lord of the Dance/Poor Murdered Woman/Creeping Jane/Streets of Forbes/ Long Lankin/Brass Band Music.

12T344   *Prince Heathen*: Martin Carthy and Dave Swarbrick – reissue of 1970 Fontana STL 5529. Arthur McBride and the Sergeant/Salisbury Plain/Polly on the Shore/The Rainbow/Died for Love/Staines Morris/Reynardine/Seven Yellow Gypsies/Little Musgrave and Lady Barnard/Prince Heathen/The Wren. TSCD344 CD reissue.

12TS345   *Landfall*: Martin Carthy. Here's Adieu to all Judges and Juries/Brown Adam/ O'er the Hills/Cruel Mother/Cold Haily Windy Night/His Name is Andrew/The Bold Poachers/Dust to Dust/The Broomfield Hill/January Man. TSCD344 CD reissue.

12TS346   *Sound, Sound Your Instruments of Joy*: The Watersons. God Bless the Master/ While Shepherds Watch their Flocks by Night/Windham/Heavenly Aeroplane/Christian's Hope/Bitter Withy/Emmanuelle/Idumea/Sound, Sound Your Instruments of Joy/Come All You Faithful Christians/Green Fields/David's Lamentation/Morning Trumpet/Joy, Health, Love and Peace. KTSC346 – cassette.

12TS347   *Highland Fiddle*: Angus Grant. Pipe Major Sam Scott/Portree Bay/Flower O'er the Quern/Mrs H.L. McDonald of Dunach/J.F. MacKenzie/Captain MacDiarmid/ Mo Mhathair/Laura Andrews/Goatherd/Curlew (The)/Millicent's Favourite Hornpipe/ Harvest Home/Stirling Castle/MacKinnon's Reel/Dargai/Kilworth Hills/Loch Maree/ Neil Gow's Lament for His Second Wife/Marquis of Huntly's Farewell/Marquis of Tullibardine/Marquis of Lorne/Minstrel's Favourite Hornpipe/Iain Ghlinn Cuaich/Sean Drochaid/Miss Addy/Lady Montgomery/Da Mirrie Boys of Greenland/Leveneep Head/ Willafjord/Forneth House/Clan MacColl/Cameron's Got His Wife Again/Jock Wilson's Ball.

12TS348   *Unaccompanied*: John Wright. Awake, Awake you Drowsy Sleeper/Four Hand Reel/Murphy's Hornpipe/Gypsy Hornpipe/Henry Martin/Bridget Cruise 2 and 3/Tailor By My Trade/Dornoch Links – The Shepherd's Crook – Lochiel's Awa' to France/Young Charlotte/The Varsoviana/La Valse Vienne/La Schottische Anglaise/L'Angloise/Our Captain Cried All Hands/Ninepins/Saturday Night and Sunday Morning/The Punk's Delight.

12TS349   *Devon Tradition – Various Artists Recorded in a Pub*: Amy Birch, Phoebe Birch, Avice Clarke, Nobby Clarke, Joe Davies, Harold Gill, Charlie Hill, Sophie Isaacs, Henry Mitchmore, Bill Parnell, Bob Penfold, Nelson Penfold, George Roberts, Jim Sanders, Bob Small, Brian Holland, Tom Orchard Snr, Tom Orchard Jnr. Exmoor Ram/ Molecatcher/When I was a Young Man/Tuning/Barbara Allen/Head a Nodding/Thrashing Machine/Sweet Willie/Navvy Boots/Leg o' the Mallard/Royal Comrade/Three Men Went a-Hunting/Farmer in Leicester/Seven Nights Drunk/Remington Greatmeat Pie/Up the Green Meadows/Rattling Irish Boy/Mortal Unlucky Old Chap.

12TS350 *Bob Davenport and The Rakes* (1977). With my Love on the Road/Wild Colonial Boy/Ploughboy Lad/Man in the Moon/Patsy Geary's/Peeler and the Goat/Princess Royal/Lake of Coolfin/Jealous Sailor/Jealous Heart/Keep Your Feet Still Geordie Hinnie/Three Men Went A-Hunting/Country Dance/Three Around Three/Dowie Dens of Yarrow/McCusker's No. 1 (polka)/McCusker's No. 2 (polka)/Jenny Lind/Slievegallion Braes/Star of the County Down/Old Green River.

12TS351 *Folk Music of Norway* (1977). 1LP0129752.

12TS352 *Irish Music in America*: Terry Teahan and Gene Kelly (1977).

12TS353 *The Music of Cape Breton Volume 1 – Gaelic Tradition in Cape Breton* (1978).

12TS354 *The Music of Cape Breton Volume 2 – Cape Breton Scottish Fiddle* (1978).

12TS355 *Shreds and Patches*: John Kirkpatrick and Sue Harris. Waterman's Dance/Gypsy Laddie/Apple Core/Nipper/Tailor and the Louse/Peg Huglestone's Hornpipe/Little Sir William/Game of All Fours/Penny for Them/Whitefryer's Hornpipe/Shreds and Patches/Johnny Sands/Oakham Poachers/Bread and Jam Waltzer/Mr Gubbin's Bicycle.

12TS356 *The Blackbird*: Vera Aspey (1977). Blackbird/Owd Betty Barlow/Ladybird/Maypole Inn/Pit Brow Lassies/My Johnny Was a Shoemaker/Coal Black Faces/Highwayman/Shule Agra/Aggie Bell/Sprig of Thyme.

12TS357 *Music for the Complete Polka Set*: Johnny O'Leary. Murphy's/O'Keefe's/Tarrant's/The Worn Torn Petticoat/Denis O'Keefe's Favourite/The Brosna Slide/The Scartaglen Slide/Padraig O'Keefe's Favourite/If I Had a Wife/No Name/The Gallant Tipperary Boys/Off She Goes.

12TS358 *Music from Sliabh Luachra Vol. 6*: Jackie Daly. Tom Sullivan's/Johnny Leary's/Jim Keefe's/Keefe's/Clog/Tir Na Nog/Callaghan's Hornpipe/Rising Sun/Pope's Toe/Glin Cottage Polkas/Paddy Scully's/Gallant Tipperary/Walsh's/Ballyvourine Polka/Johnny Mickey's/Trip to the Jack's/Where is the Cat/Banks of Sullane/Biddy Martin's/Ger the Rigger/Glenside Cottage/Tdim Gan Airgead/Willy Reilly/Murphy's/Going to the Well for Water.

12T359 *The Bonny Green Tree – Songs of an Irish Traveller*: John Reilly (1978). Adieu Unto All True Lovers/The Raggle Taggle Gypsies/The Well Below the Valley/Tippin' it up to Nancy/Lord Baker/Old Caravee/The Bonny Green Tree/Once there Lived a Captain/Peter Heany/What Put the Blood?/Rozzin Box/The Braes of Strawberries/One Morning I Rambled from Glasgow/The Pride of Clonkeen.

12TS360 *Ashes and Diamonds*: June Tabor. Reynard the Fox/The Devil and Bailiff McGlynn/Streets of Forbes/Lord Maxwell's Last Goodnight/Now I'm Easy/Clerk Saunders/The Earl of Aboyn/Lisbon/The Easter Tree/Cold and Raw/No Man's Land/Flowers of the Forest. KTSC360 – cassette. TSCD360 – CD.

12TS361 *Songs from the Sailing Barges*: Bob A.V. Roberts – vocals, melodeon (1978). The Candlelight Fisherman/The Grey Hawk/Stormy Weather Boys/Waltz with Me/Haul Away Joe/The Oily Rig/The Little Ball of Yarn/The Singing Sailor/Young Collum/The Fish and Chip Shop/While Gamekeepers Lie Sleeping/Windy Old Weather/The London

Waterman/Bob Robert's Waltz/Whiskey Johnny/The Foggy Dew/Bell Bottom Trousers/ The Black Shawl/Little Boy Billee/The Collier Brig/Leave Her Johnny.

12TS362   *Songs from the Irish Tradition*: Mary-Ann Carolan. Bold Doherty/Maid of Ballymore/Bob Riddley/Old Oak Tree/Tinker's Old Budget/Bonnie Light Horseman/In London so Fair/My Father's a Hedger and a Ditcher/Highland Mary/Wedding at Baltray.

12TS363   *Songs Traditional in West Clare*: Tom Lenihan. Paddy's Panacea/Talk of Music at Lenihan's/Wintry Evening/St. James Hospital/Talk of Thady Casey the Dancing Master/Lake of Coolfin/Fair Days in Miltown Malbay/Pat O'Brian/Paddy, the Cockney and the Ass/Straw Boys/Holland Handkerchief/Bobbed Hair/Fair London Town/Garrett Barry and Hurry the Jug.

12T364   *Classic Recordings of Irish Traditional Fiddle Music*: Hugh Gillespie. Dowd's Favourite/McKenna's Farewell/Master Crowley's Reels/Irish Mazurka/Jenny's Welcome to Charlie/Master Crowley's Favourites/Finnea Lassies/Gurren's Castle/Girl that Broke My Heart/Dick Cosgrove's Reels/Farewell to Leitrim/Tom Steele/Jackson's Favourite/ Kips/Paddy Finley's Fancy/Joe O'Connell's Dream/Versevanna/Donegal Traveller/Miss Montgomery/Mountain Stream/Parker's Fancy/Contentment is Wealth/Finley's Jig/Dowd's Number Nine/Jacksons.

12T365   *An Irish Delight*: The Flanagan Bros. Paddy in London/Paddy Ryan's Dream/ Beggarman Song/An Carrowath/Longdance/No Name/My Aunt Jane/Rakes of Mallow/ New Irish Barn Dance/One Step/Irish Boy/Irish Delight/Auld Blackthorn/My Irish Molly O/Old Fashioned Waltz Medley/Highland Fling/Bandy Legged Mule/Sprig of Shillelagh/ Exhibitioned Hornpipe/Blackbird.

12T366   *Early Us*: Dan Sullivan's Shamrock Band – recorded *c*.1934. Dan Sullivan's Hornpipe/Tickling Mary Jane/Rabbit Catcher/Londonderry Hornpipe/Miller's Reel/Duffy the Dancer/Bantry Bay/Billy Hanafin's Reel/Green Grow the Rushes-O/Versouviana Dance/Boil the Kettle Early/Groves Hornpipe/Johnny Will You Marry Me/Blackberry Blossom/Bonnie Kate/I'm Leaving Tipperary/Silver Slipper/Jerry Daly's Hornpipe.

12T367   *John McGettigan and his Irish Minstrels*: John McGettigan. Martha, the Flower of Sweet Strabane/Maid of the Moorlough Shore/Highland Schottische/Turfman from Ardee/Stone Outside Dan Murphy's Door/Medley of Jigs/Erin's Lovely Lee/Shoe the Donkey/Rare Old Irish Whiskey/Rambling Irishman/Medley of Polkas/McGettigan's Jig Medley/Lovely Molly/Medley of Reels/Me Husband's Flannel Shirt/Cutting the Corn in Creeslough Today/Medley of Hornpipes/Star of Donegal.

12TS368   *At the Feis*: John Doonan. Jackie Coleman's Reel/Paddy Cavanagh's/John Brennan's/Any Old Jig will Do/Butterfly/Rodney's Glory/Idle Road/Frost is all Over/ Black Rogue/Spalpeen's Lament/Kesh/Morrison's/Old Joe's/Shannon Breeze/Heathery Breeze/Green Fields of Amerikay/Blackthorn Stick/Hurry the Dance/Rub the Bag/ Blackbird/Spellan the Fiddler/Rights of Man/Irish Washerwoman/Father O'Flynn/Lilting Fisherman.

12TS369   *Songs from County Clare – Lambs on the Green Hills*.

12TS370   *Sheath and Knife*: Gordeanna McCulloch. Yowie Wi the Crookit Horn/There's a Herrin' in the Pan/Sheath and Knife/Jock Since I Ever Saw Yer Face/Chevy Chase/

Captain Wedderburn/The Gallant Weaver/Eence Upon a Time/Caw the Yowes/Bawbie Allen/The Heilan Laddie/Be Kind Tae Yer Nainsel.

12TS371 *Corby Crag*: Alistair Anderson. Hawk Polka/Thrunton Woods/Keelman's Petition/Tipp Staff/La Fille de Lyon/Cotillion des Marionettes/Blake's Hornpipe/President Garfield's Hornpipe/Bonnie Broom Hill/Felton Ionnin/Kirden Fair/Tich Richardson's Favourite/Hey to the Camp/Brosehill/Alistair Anderson's Favourite/Old French/Belfast Hornpipe/Prize Potato/Trip to Carlisle/Corby Crag/Ali Anderson/Henry Atkinson/Blayton Flats/Whittingham Games/James Brown/Derwent Water's Bonnie Lord/Bride's Favourite/ Remember Me/Left Handed Fiddler/Geld Him Lasses, Geld Him/Uncle John/Darkening.

12TS372 *On the Shores of Loch Neagh*: George Hanna and Sarah Anne O'Neill. Brockagh Bae/On Yonder Hill There Sits a Hare/Blackbird of Sweet Avondale/Erin's Lovely Home/Young Edmund in the Lowlands/Kate of Billinamore/Rambler from Clare/ Fair Young Maid in her Father's Garden/John Reilly/Gosford's Fair Demesne/ Carrickmannon Lake/Fisher's Cot.

12TS373 *Irish Music on the Hammer Dulcimer*: John Rea. Whistle o'er the Levet/ Braes of Tullymet/Scudding through the Whins/Bundle and Go/Jug of Punch/Galway Reel/Donny O'Brien's/Ladies of France/Jackson's Trip to Aughrim/Jackson's Return from Dover/Belfast/Rights of Man/Sailor on the Rope/Bonnie Bunch of Roses/Three Sea Captains/Kitty's Fancy/Lady Anne Hope/Boys of Ballycastle/Kinnegad Slashers/ Tenpenny Bit/Plains of Boyle/Jackson's Slippers/Roaring Mary – Stormy Weather/Tim Moloney/Set Dance and Highland/St. Patrick's Day/Duncan Davidson.

12TS374 *Earl Soham Slog – Various Suffolk Traditions*: Fred Whiting, Reg Reeder, Font Whatling, Harkie Nesling. Fred Whiting – Polkas (Harkie's Polkas)/The Earl Soham Slog, Flowers of Edinburgh/The Maid at the Well, The Old Kerry Fiddler, The Priest and His Boots/Hornpipes – The Weaver's, The Bristol Sailorman, Ballinalig in the Morning/ The Hurling Boys ('Old Country Dance'), Jack Tar Hornpipe/Off to California, Will the Waggoner (Gypsy Hornpipe). Reg Reeder – Cat among the Tails, Rakes of Mallow/ Waltz Medley – 1, 2, 3, 4, 5; Jenny Lind; Joe, The Boat is Going Over. Font Whatling – Mick's Tune, Pigeon on the Gate/Polkas/Untitled Tunes/Pigeon on the Gate/ Harkie Nesling – The Sultan's Polka, Untitled Polka/Come and Be My Little Teddy Bear/ Impudence Schottische, Rakes of Mallow, The Barn Dance.

12TS375 *Sing, Say and Play – Various Suffolk Traditions*. Blacksmith's Daughter/ Ratcliffe Highway/Barn Dance/Cock o' the North/London Prentice Boy/Next Tune Tonight/ Turkey in the Straw/Banks of the Nile/Out with my Gun in the Morning/Old Country Waltz/Pigeon on the Gate/Strolling Down to Hastings/Fellow who Played the Trombone/ Sailors Hornpipe Medley/Oak and the Ash/Jolly Tinker/Two Step/Yarmouth Hornpipe/ Parson's Creed (recitation)/Marrowbones/Golden Slippers/Chinaman's Song/Old Brown in the Rose and Crown/Red River Valley/Polka Medley.

12T376 *Melodeon Greats – A Collection of Melodeon Masterpieces* (various dubbings from 78 recordings – reissued and expanded as 601). Peter and Daniel Wyper – Stranger March/Doon the Burn March. Peter Wyper – Silverton Polka/79th Highlanders and Champion/The Dancing Dustman/Lion Quadrilles fig. 4. James Brown – Miss Drummond of Perth/Rose Polka. Fred Cameron – Flowers of Edinburgh, The Old Grey Cat. Peter Latham – The Johnson Hornpipe, Jessie Smith/Shufflin' Samuel/The Laird of Drumblair,

Miss McLeod/Sammie's Schottishe. Pamby Dick – Boston Belles/Stirling Castle, Arthur's Seat, Eugene Stratton. Jack Williams – Queen Mary Waltz.

12TS377   *On Lough Erin's Shore*: Cathal McConnell.

12TS378   *Eston California*: Vin Garbutt. Bantry Bay/Den Toppede Hone/Land of Three Rivers/Gentle Annie/Hornpipes/Belfast/Japanese/Hartlepool Monkey/Tonto McGuire/Ring of Iron/Skibbereen/Their Ulster Peace/Tear the Calico/Providence/Water o' Tyne.

12TS379   *Shetland Folk Fiddling Vol. 2*: Aly Bain and Tom Anderson.

12TS380   *For As Many As Will*: Shirley and Dolly Collins (1978). Lancashire Lass/ Never Again/Lord Allen-Water/The Blacksmith Courted Me/Beggar's Opera Medley/ Can Love Be Control'd by Advice?/O Polly You Might Have Toy'd and Kist/Oh What Pain it is to Part/Miser Thus a Shilling Sees/Youth's the Season Made For Joys/Hither Dear Husband, Turn your Eyes/Lumps of Pudding/German Tune/Gilderoy/Rockley Firs/ Sweet Jenny Jones/Moon Shines Bright/Harvest Home Medley (Peas, Beans, Oats and the Barley)/Mistress's Health/Poor Tom. KTSC380 – cassette.

12TS381   *At the Front*: Battlefield Band. Lady Carmichael/South of the Grampians/ Mickie Ainsworth/Bachelor/Ge Do Theid Mi Do M'leabradh/Battle of Harlaw/Jenny Nettles/Grays of Tongside/Tae the Beggin'/Tamosher/Blackbird and the Thrush/Moray Club/Lang Johnnie More/Brown Milkmaid/Dunnottar Castle/Maid of Glengarrysdale/ Disused Railways/Lady Leroy/Stirling Castle/Earl of Mansfield.

12TS382   *One More Dance and Then*: New Victory Band (1978). Harper's Frolick, Bonny Kate/The Mountain Belle/You Can't Take That on the Train/Charles Lynch's, Cajun Waltz, The Banks of the Dee/Pretty Little Girl from Nowhere/Nellie's First Rag/ Robbie Hopkirk's, Father's/Mrs Grace Bowie, The Hogmanay/Mamie May/Moustache, Corn Riggs/One More Dance and then/Long, Long Trail. KTSC382 – cassette.

12TS383   *Flags of Dublin*: Paddy Glackin – fiddle, Mick Gavin – flute, Michael O'Brien – uilleann pipes.

12TS384   *Gaughan*: Dick Gaughan (1978). Bonnie Jeannie O'Bethelnie/Bonnie Lass Amang the Heather/Crooked Jack/The Recruited Collier/The Pound a Week Rise/My Donald/Willie o' Winsbury/Such a Parcel o' Rogues in a Nation/Gillie Mor.

TSCD384   *Gaughan*: Dick Gaughan (incl. tracks from TS271/2 and 315): Bonnie Jeannie O'Bethelnie/Bonnie Lass Amang the Heather/Alan MacPherson of Mosspark/The Jig of Slurs/Crooked Jack/The Recruited Collier/The Augengeich Disaster/Bonnie Woodha'/ The Pound a Week Rise/Ask My Father – Lads of Laoise – The Connaught Heifers/My Donald/Strike Gay Harp – Shores of Lough Gowna/Willie o' Winsbury/Such a Parcel o' Rogues in a Nation/Jack Broke the Prison Door – Donald Blue – Wha'll Dance Wi' Wattie/Gillie Mor.

12TS385   *Tossin' a Wobbler*: Vin Garbutt. Man of the Earth/Legend of Roseberry/Long Note/Lads of Laois/Le Reel Jeune Marie/Photographic Memory/Yorkshire Volunteer's Farewell to the Good Folks of Stockton/Push about the Jorum/St. Helena's March/ Carrigdhoun/Freemantle Doctor/One-Legged Beggar/They Don't Write 'em Like That Any More.

12TS386   *Bowin' and Scrapin'*: Robin and Barry Dransfield. Rattlin' Roarin' Willie/ Metal Man/Fiddler's Progress/Who Knows Where the Time Goes/My Pagan Love/Sheffield Hornpipe/Pet of the Pipers/Up the Aisle (Swedish Wedding March)/Wedding Song/ Bridie's Wedding/Norwegian Wedding March/Wedding Morris/Sandy Bell's/Obliged to Fiddle/Planxty Oavy/Spanish Cloak/Bushes and Briars/Swedish Air/O'Carolan's Concerto/ Recitation Upon a Gentleman Sitting on a Cremo/Sally Gardens/Conmel Races.

12T387   *Almost a Gentleman*: Billy Bennett (1978). Nell/My Mother Doesn't Know I'm on the Stage/Mandalay/I'll Be Thinking of You/Ogul Mogul – a Kanakanese Love Lyric/No Power on Earth/She Was Poor but She Was Honest/Family Secrets/Please Let Me Sleep on your Doorstep Tonight/Christmas Day in the Cookhouse/Club Raid/Mottoes/ Green Tie on the Little Yellow Dog.

12TS388   *Four in a Bar*: The High Level Ranters. Whinham's Jig/Billy's Jig/Chips and Shavings/Jack's Alive/Dear Tobacco/Town Green Polka/Jenny Bell/Biddlestone Hornpipe/ Last of the Twins/Ruby/Quarrelsome Piper/Rowly Burn/Coates Hornpipe/La Russe/ Whinshield's Hornpipe/Jane's Fancy/Da Road to Houll/Blinkin' Tibbie/Pear Tree/Swalwell Lassies/South Shields Lassies/Moonshine Polka/Quayside/Miss Ward's Reel/Butterclout/ Such a Wife as Willie Had/Willy is a Bonny Lad.

12TS389   *Because It's There*: Martin Carthy (1979). Nothing Rhymed/May Song/ Swaggering Boney/Lord Randal/Long John, Old John and Jackie North/Jolly Tinker/ Lovely Joan/Three Cripples/Siege of Delhi/Nothing Rhymed/Death of Young Andrew. TSCD389 CD reissue.

12TS390   *Tom Ennis and James Morrison*. Money Musk/Johnny Will You Marry Me/ Keel Row/Bags of Spuds/Temple House/Pigeon on the Gate/Job of Journey Work/Girl that Broke my Heart/Galway/Kildare Fancy/New Steam Boat/Books of Oranmore/ Gardener's Daughter/Trip to the Cottage/Limestone Rock/Flowers of Spring/Maid Behind the Bar/Trim the Velvet/Paddy in London/Butcher's March/Sligo Bay/Curlew Hills/Peach Blossoms/Frieze Breeches.

12TS391   *All Things in Common*: Chris Foster. Black Fox/Grey Cock/Pigeon on the Gate/Unicorns/King John and the Abbot of Canterbury/Jump at the Sun/The Working Chap/When this Old Hat was New/The World Turned Upside Down.

12TS392   *A Country Life*: Walter Pardon from Knapton (1982). Raggle Taggle Gypsies/ Peggy Bawn/Bold Princess Royal/One Cold Morning in December/Devil and the Farmer's Wife/An Old Man's Advice/Uncle Walter's Tune/Country Life/Cupid the Ploughboy/ Dandy Man/Jack Hall/I Wish, I Wish/Broomfield Hill/Hungry Army.

12TS393   *The Art of the Highland Bagpipe Vol. 3*: John Burgess. Alexandria Place/ Banks of the Farrar/Struan Robertson/Broadford Bay/Piper's Bonnet/Grey Bob/Mrs William Ross/Corriechoillie Blend/Pap of Glencoe/Campbell of Southall/Braes of Castle Grant/Irish Slow Air/Little House under the Hill/Pibroch/Too Long in this Condition/ Lament for Sir James/MacDonald of the Isles/Slow Air/Malcolm Macpherson Lullaby/ Retreat Marches/Heroes of St. Valerie/Pipe Major/Donald McCloud.

12TS394   *Kentigern*: Kentigern (1979). Cullen Bay – Jig O'Slurs – Seagull/The Corncake/Breton Tunes – Greenwoodside/The Weary Farmers/Pipe Major Donald McLean of Lewis – The Weavers of Newly – Kail and Pudding – Loch Roag/The Iron Horse/The

Last o' Tinkler/Rathven Market – The Conundrum/Gin I Were Shot o' Her/Hebridean Air – The Braes of Tulimet – The Braes of Mellinish/Wild Roving No More/Put Me in the Great Chest – The Three Peaks of South Uist – South Uist.

12TS395 *Travellers Songs – Tunes and Tales of English Gypsies Recorded by Mike Yates.*

12TS396 *You Have Made a Nice Old Mess of It*: Gus Elen. Golden Dustman/E Dunno where 'e are/Mrs Carter/If it Wasn't for the 'Ouses In Between/Me-riah/'Arf a Pint of Ale/Pavement Artist/Wait Till the Work Comes Round/Publican/Coster's Pony/Dick Whittington – a Parody/Nature's Made a Big Mistake/Don't Stop my 'Arf a Pint of Beer/I'm Going to Settle Down/Pretty Little Villa Down at Barking.

12TS397 *Pass the Time – An Anthology of Donegal Fiddling.*

12TS398 *Bundle and Go*: John Doherty. Hudie Gallagher's March/Black Mare of Fanad/March of the Meena Toiten Bull/Kiss the Maid Behind the Bier/The Bargain is Over/21 Highland/Paps of Glencoe/Hare in the Corn/Knights of St Patrick/Dispute at the Crossroads/Roaring Mary – Stormy Weather/Miss Patterson's Slippers/Cat that Kittled in Jamie's Wig/Welcome Home Royal Charlie/Darby Gallagher/Teelin Highland/Heathery Breeze/Monaghan Switch/Black Haired Lass/Paddy's Rambles Through the Park.

12TS399 *That Lancashire Band*: The Oldham Tinkers. Old May Song/John Willie's Performing Newt/Nowt About Nowt/ Captain's Medley/Eawr House – as Was/Oh! That Lancashire Jazz Band/The Lark/John Willie's Grand-Dad/Tribute to Owd Paddy/Old King Coal/Steeple Jack/The Crime Lake Boggart/An Oldham Rugby Medley/McCarthy's Party.

12TS400 *Both Sides Then*: Pete Bellamy. Barbaree/Trees they do Grow High/Lord will Provide/Gallant Frigate Amphitrite/Roving on a Winter's Day/Derry Gaol/Long Time Travelling/Shepherd of the Downs/House Carpenter/When I Die/Edmund in the Lowlands/Around Cape Horn/Turfman from Ardee/Amazing Grace.

12TS401 *After Dawning*: Joe Holmes and Len Graham (1979). Here I Am Amongst You/My Lone Nell/Loughinsholin/Willie Clarke's/Green Grow the Rushes-o/Maid of Mourne Shore/Lovely Glenshesk/Sweet Bann Water/The Girl that Broke My Heart//Gra Mo Chroi/Come Tender Hearted/Hare's Lament/Johnnie and Molly/Dick the Dasher/Parting Glass/Coolfinn – Willie Leonard.

12TS402 *Dookin' for Apples*: Alistair Anderson with Fennig's All Star String Band (1979). Culloden Day/Kaspar's Rant/New Moon/Curds and Cream/Crooked Bawbee/Carrick Hornpipe/Weddings Shoes/Number 28/Highland Reel/West Indian/Stage Hornpipe/Johnson's Hornpipe/White Meadow/Simonside Reel/Wedderburn's Cave/Lookin' for Apples/Mayday/Penicuick Hornpipe/Siver Tassle/Flowers of the Forest/Hold On/Miss Fenwick's Reel/Lads of Leith/Up and Run Away/Whittle Dean Hornpipe/Pet of the Pipers/Bob Johnson's Reel/Miss Soutar of Plains/Great Eastern Reel/Jack's Getting a Wife/New Way of Gettin' Bairns/Carding and Spinning/Polly the Lass. Issued under license from Front Hall Records USA.

12TS403 *Alison McMorland and Peta Webb*. Two Pretty Boys/What Can a Young Lassie/Jogging Up to Claudie/In London So Fair/Convict's Song/Sailing's a Weary Life/

Factory Girl/May Morning Dew/Green Banks of Yarrow/Dowie Dens of Yarrow/Our Ship is Ready.

12TS404   *Stand Easy*: The Battlefield Band. Miss Drummond of Perth/Fiddler's Joy/ Trad. Reels Part 3 and 4/Shetland Fiddler/Seven Braw Gowns/Miss Drummond of Perth's Favourite Scotch Measure/Miss MacLeod's Minuet/My Last Farewell to Stirling/Cuidich'n Righ/I Hae a Herrin' in Salt/My Wife's a Wanton Wee Thing/Banks of Allan/Battle of Falkirk Muir/John D. Burgess/Braemar Gathering/I Hae Nea with I Hae Nae Kin/Miss Lyall/Small Coals for Nailers/Bleaton Gardens/Christ Has My Hart Ay/Joe McGann's Fiddle/Center's Bonnet.

12TS405   *Cilla and Artie*: Cilla Fisher and Artie Trezise. Norland Wind/Beggarman/ What Can a Young Lassie/Fisher Lassies/Generations of Change/Fair Maid of London Town/Wicked Wife/Gypsie Laddie/Blue Bleezin' Blind Drunk/John Grumlie/Jeannie C.

12TS406   *A Bunch of Fives*: Five Hand Reel. I'll Lay You Down/Man from God Knows Where/Maggie Lauder/Satan Will Appear/House of Airlie/Paddy's Green Shamrock/ Land o' the Leal.

12TS407   *Seeing Double*: Gary and Vera Aspey. Seeing Double/My Goodlooking Man/ Miss Tickle Toby/Dowie Dens of Yarrow/Cruise of the Calibar/Hounds and Horn Together/ Bolinder Boatman/Testimony of Patience Kershaw/July Wakes/Knocker Upper Man/ Price of Coal/Coal and Albert Berry.

12TS408   *Facing the Music*: John Kirkpatrick and Sue Harris. John Locke's Polka/ Three Jolly Sheepskins/Kettle Drum/Trip to the Cottage/Hunting the Squirrel/Jack of the Green/Shelter in the Time of Storm/We Shall Be Happy/Millfield/Saturday Night and Sunday Morn/Garrick's Delight/Flaxley Green Dance/Crocker's Reel/Roast Beef/All Flowers in Broome/Rope Waltz/Cheshire's Hornpipe/Black Mary's Hornpipe.

12TS409   *Regrouped*: Boys of the Lough. Star of Munster/Owen Hackett's Jig/King's Favourite/Rocking Chair/Willie O/Bamboo Flute/Albert House/Annalese Bain/Castle/ Mulqueen's/Anac Cuain/Humours of Ballinahinch/Floggin'/I'll Buy Boots for Maggie/ O'Connor's Polka/Moorlough Mary/City of Savannah/Acrobat/Off to California/Da Tushker/Susan Cooper/Millbrae/Jog Along 'till Shearing/Cup of Tea Set.

12TS410   *A Cut Above*: June Tabor and Martin Simpson. Admiral Benbow/Davy Lowston/Flash Company/Number Two Top Seam/Strange Affair/Heather Down on the Moor/Jo Peel/Le Roi Renaud/Riding Down to Portsmouth/Unicorns. TSCD410 CD reissue.

12TS411   *Penguin Eggs*: Nic Jones (1980). Canadee-i-o/The Drowned Lovers/The Humpback Whale/The Little Pot Stove/Courting is a Pleasure/Barrack Street/Planxty Davis/The Flandyke Shore/Farewell to the Gold. TSCD411 CD reissue.

12TS412   *Good Old Way – British Folk Music Today* (1980): Various Artists. Heather Down the Moor – Tabor/Simpson; Lovely Joan – Martin Carthy; Battle of Falkirk Muir – Battlefield; Bonnie Jeannie o' Bethelnie – Dick Gaughan; I'll Buy Boots for Maggie/ O'Connor's Polka – Boys of the Lough; Jack the Sailor – Chris Foster; Crocker's Reel – Kirkpatrick/Harris; The Good Old Ways – Watersons; The Convict's Song – McMoreland/ Webb; The Blarney Stone – Bob Davenport; Canadee-i-o – Nick Jones; Norland Wind – Cilla Fisher and Artie Trezise; Hold On/Miss Fenwick's Reel/Lads of Leith/Up and Run

Away – Alistair Anderson; Paddy's Green Shamrock Shore – Five Hand Reel; Barbaree – Peter Bellamy; Photographic Memory – Vin Garbutt; King Cotton – Gary and Vera Aspey; Harper's Frolick/Bonny Kate – New Victory Band.

12TS413   *Cut and Dry No. 2*: Cut and Dry Band. Barrington Hornpipe/Glen Ain/Wild Hills of Wannies/Swallow's Tail/Jim Hall's Fancy/Breamish/Random Jig/Archie's Fancy/ Little Hennie/Lea Rig/Sir Sydney Smith's March/Mrs Elder/Dr. Whittaker's Hornpipe/ Nancy/Nae Guid Luck Aboot the Hoose/Oh Dear, What Can the Matter Be/East Neuk of Fife/Locomotive/South Shore/Bonnie Woodside/Coffee Bridge.

12TS414   *Tidewave*: Robin Dransfield. Cutty Wren/Barley and the Rye/Fair Maids of February/When it's Night Time in Italy it's Wednesday over Here/Rigs O'Rye/Spencer the Rover/Tidewave/Cadgwith Anthem/I Once had a Dog/Three Muscadets/Mother Nature.

12TS415   *Greenfields*: The Watersons (1981). Stormy Winds/Rosebuds in June/We'll All Go a-Hunting Today/Brave Ploughboy/Sedgefield Fair/Fare Thee Well, Cold Winter/ Young Banker/While Gamekeepers Lie Sleeping/Prickle-holly Bush/Hares in the Old Plantation/Furze Field/I Went to Market/Three Pretty Maidens/Lincolnshire Shepherd. Reissued as TSCD500 (1998).

12TS416   *The Moon's in a Fit: Umps and Dumps* (1980). Up Sides/After You've Got/ Woodland Voices/The Watercress Girl/Maybe She'll Write Me/Rogue's March – Dashing White Sergeant/Marmalade Polka/Underneath her Apron/Lichfield Tattoo/The Willow Tree/Donkey, Jack Donkey – Here it Comes Again/Dark Town Strutter's Ball – Cajun Two Step.

12TS417   *Sidetracks*: Alan Reid and Brian MacNeill. The Gallant Grahams/Sgain S'gur– Farewell to Barra/Atholl Gathering/The Hawk that Swoops on High–Crabs in the Skillet/ Twa Bonnie Maidens/Jig–Sgian Dubh–There's Three Guid Fellows–Leslie's March/Barrat's Privateers/Lady Kilmarnock's Lament/Mr Dundas McQueen's–Mrs Dundas of Arniston– The Highlander's Knee Buckle–The Ardrasar Blacksmith/Henry Martin/The Cove of Cork–Short Life to Stepmother's–Dr Morrison's Seven Thistles.

12TS418   *Sweet Wivelsfield*: Martin Carthy. Originally Deram SML 1111 (1974): Shepherd O Shepherd/Billy Boy/Three Jolly Sneakmen/Trimdon Grange/All of a Row/ Skewbald/Mary Neal/King Henry/John Barleycorn/The Cottage in the Wood.

12TS419   *Handful of Earth*: Dick Gaughan. Erin-Go-Bragh/Now Westlin Winds/Graigie Hill/World Turned Upside Down/The Snows They Melt the Soonest/Lough Erne/First Kiss at Parting/Scojun Waltz/Randers Hopsa/Song for Ireland/Worker's Song/Both Sides of the Tweed. TSCD419 CD reissue.

12TS420   *In the Roar*: Roaring Jelly. Beethoven's Bluebeat/Bucketful of Mud/Maybe it's Just as Well/Irretrievable Breakdown/Cajun Gumbo/Valerie Wilkins/Maracas in Caracas/Dirty Little Stop Out/Thundercloud/Ides of March/Not for the Soul/Christmas in Australia/Bed Bug.

12TS421   *All Buttoned Up*: Hemlock Cock and Bull Band. Donkey Riding–Buffalo Girls/Portobello– Brigham Hornpipes/Berger, Bergere–Bouree–Berrichonne/Tit For Tat/ Princess Amelia's Birthday/Mon Reve–William Irwin's Quickstep/The Cockade–Corn

Riggs–The Twin Sisters/Latrigg Side–The Dorsetshire Hornpipe/Needle Cases/A Trip to Shorts–Lewis Castle/Huzza–Cock and Bull.

12TS422   *In the Tradition*: Boys of the Lough (1981). Out on the Ocean; Padeed O'Rafferty; Isabelle Blackley/Kiss her Under the Coverlet; The Lads of Alnwick/The Road to Cashel; Paddy Kelly's/Lord Gregory/Dark Woman of the Glen/J.O. Forbes Esquire of Corse; The Hawk; Charles Sutherland/Eddie Kelly's; The Greenfields of Glentown/The Eclipse; The Tailor's Twist/Biddy from Sligo/The Sunset/People's/Padraig O'Keefe's; Con Cassidy's/The Sea Apprentice/Miss McDonald/For Ireland I'd Not Tell Her Name (Ar Eirinn ni 'neosfainn ee Hi).

12TS423   *The Piper's Maggot*: Chris Miller and Ken Campbell. Piper's Maggot/Hector the Hero/Left Handed Fiddler/Diggins/Cuddly Clauder/Mally Stewart/When the Tide Comes In/Norwegian Wedding March/Hamburger Polka/Adieu France/Farewell to Gartly/ Danny Deever/Honourable James Ramsay/Speed the Plough/Auld Bougar/Meeting of the Waters/Stool of Repentance/Captain Jimmy Thompson/Heilan' King o' China/Boots of Malin/Dancing Feet.

12TS424   *The Lasses Fashion*: Jock Tamson's Bairns (1982). Lasses Fashion/Robin/ Merry Nicht under the Tummel Brig/Braes o' Balquhidder/Greig's Strathspey/Miss Wharton Duff/Lady Keith's Lament/Gates of Edinburgh/O'er Bogie/Mrs. Gordon's Reel/ Tibbie Fowler/Strathspey: The Shetland Fiddlers Society/Grant's Reel/Gladstone's Reel/ Laird o' Drum/Kempy Kaye/Donald, Willy and his Dog/Peter Mackintosh of Skeabost.

12TS425   *The New High Level Ranters*. Fisherman's Friend/Balck and Grey/Ca' – hawkie/Old Drove Road/Kennedy North/Jim Jones/Tynmouth Volunteer Fire Brigade/ John Peel/Durham Regatta/Little Jeannie/Snows They Melt the Soonest/Yellow Haired Laddie/Glen Coe March/New Song of the Coal/Skipper's Wedding/Duke of Eife/Maggie Lauder.

12TS426   *Out of the Cut*: Martin Carthy (1982). Devil and the Feathery Wife/Reynard the Fox/Song of the Lower Classes/Rufford Park Poachers/Molly Oxford/Rigs of the Time/I Sowed Some Seeds/Friar in the Well/Jack Rowland/Old Horse.

12TS427   *Steel Skies*: Alistair Anderson. First Light/Rhymeside 1/Mountain Stream/ Rhymeside 3/Road to the North/Clennel Street/Franklin River/Air of Maurice Ogg/ Jumping Jack/Green Ginger/Ironbridge/Eynhallow/In Trim/Mount Hooley/Lemington Bank/Kestrel/High Force/Dog Leaps Stairs/Hot Rivets/Seven Gate Road/When the Frosts are Setting In/East Winds/Millstream/Centenary Pack/Rhymeside 2.

12TS428   *Little Innocents*: Vin Garbutt (1983). Royal Blackbird/Fear of Imperfection/ Lynda/Calum More/Coalman/Leslie/Dormanshown Jimmy/If/BlueSunset/Little Innocents.

12TS429

12TS430   *Grinning in Your Face*: Martin Simpson (1983). It Doesn't Matter Anymore/ Little Birdy/First Cut is the Deepest/Roving Gambler/This War May Last for Years/ Masters of War/Green Linnet/Grinning in Your Face/Reuben's Train/Your Cheatin' Heart/ Handsome Molly/Townships Biko/Moonshine.

TSCD430   *The Collection*: Martin Simpson (1992) (from 12TS430/438/446). First Cut is the Deepest/Roving Gambler/This War May Last You for Years/Masters of War/Reuben's

Train/Handsome Molly/Moonshine/Green Linnet/Grinning in your Face/Shawnee Town/ Moth/For Jessica, Sad or High Kicking/No Depression in Heaven/Stillness in Company/ Lakes of Pontartrain/Doney Girl/Essequibo River/Keel Row.

12TS431   *Brass Monkey* (1983).

12TS432   *Abyssinians*: June Tabor. The Month of January/The Scarecrow/One Night as I Lay on My Bed/She Moves Among Men (The Bar Maid's Song)/Lay This Body Down/ A Smiling Shore/The Bonny Boy/I Never Thought My Love Would Leave Me/The Bonny Hind/The Fiddle and the Drum. TSCD432 CD reissue.

12TS433   Not used?

12TS434   *Border Spirit*: The High Level Ranters. Billy's Jig/Gan to the Kye/Border Spirit/Felton Ionnin/Wallington Hall/Foxhunter's/King's Hall/John of Carrick/Bellington Show/Coilsfield House/Thom's March/Canny Shepherd Laddies/Surprise/Kielder Fells/ Billy's Reel.

12TS435   *Fiddle Music from Shetland and Beyond*: Curlew.

12TS436   *Scotch Measure* (1985): Jim and Sylvia Barnes and Andy Lavery. Ythanside/ The Brewer Laddie/The Bonnie Lad that Handles the Plough/Wild Rover/For A' That/ The Laird of Dainty Dounby/The Calton Weaver/The Handweaver and the Factory Maid/ The Twa' Magicians, etc.

12TS437   *When the Wind Blows*: Eric Bogle (1985). When the Wind Blows/Shining River/Birds of a Feather/Hard, Hard Times, etc.

12TS438   *Sad or High Kicking*: Martin Simpson (1986).

12TS439   *The House Band* (1985). War Party/Cawsand Bay/An Erminig Hag An Greskenn/Green Fields of Canada/The Amalgamation/The Pitman's Grievance, etc.

12TS440   *Eyes Closed and Rocking*: Cock 'n' Bull Band (1985): One For Dan/Ridotta Rock, etc.

12TS441   *The Wild West Show*: Bill Caddick. Moses/Superman/Stay on the Line/Dance to the Music of Time/Eights and Aces, etc.

12TS442   *See How It Runs*: Brass Monkey (1986).

12TS443   *Fire in the Glen*: Andy M. Stewart, Phil Cunningham, Manus Lunny.

12TS444   *Out With a Bang* (1986).

12TS445   *Pacific*: The House Band. Pacific/Diamantina Drover/Joy after Sorrow/In at the Deep End/Ol' Man River/Pit Stands Idle/Going Places/For the Sake of Example/ Blazing Ruse.

12TS446   *True Dare or Promise*: Martin and Jessica Simpson (1987). Past Caring/Not the Whiskey Talking/Young Man/Bedlam Boys/Wholly in my Keeping/Rising of the Woman/Man Smart (Woman Smarter)/Essequibo River/Keel Row.

12TS447   *Till the Beasts Returning*: Andrew Cronshaw. TSCD447 The Andrew Cronshaw CD. 'Contains 90% of 447 plus all of Great Dark Water'. Voice of Silence/Wexford

Carol/Andro and his Cutty Gun/Galician Processional/Harry Bloodgood's Famous Jig/ American Boot Dance/Blacksmith/Fingal's Cave/Yowe Came to Our Door/Ships in Distress/St Kilda's Rowing Song/Go to Sea No More/Pandeirada de Entrimo/Gentle Dark Eyed Mary/Empty Places/Dark Haired Youth/Taladh ar Slanair/Freumh as Craobh Taigh Challadair/Wasps in the Woodpile/Turning the Tide/Seana Mheallan/Giullan Nam Bo/Ho Ho Nighean Donn/First of May/Prince of Wales' Jig/Saratoga Hornpipe/An Old Highland Air.

12TS448

12TS449   *Aqaba*: June Tabor. The Old Man's Song/Searching for Lambs/The Banks of Red Roses/Where are You Tonight, I Wonder/Aqaba/Bogies Bonnie Belle/The Reaper/ Verdi Cries/ The Grazier's Daughter/Seven Summers/Mayn Rue Platz/The King of Rome. Original copy also included a free 7" single. TSCD449 CD reissue.

12TS450   *No More to the Dance*: Maddy Prior and June Tabor – Silly Sisters. Blood and Gold – Mohacs/Cakes and Ale/Fine Horseman/How Shall I True Love Know/Hedger and Ditcher/Rosie Anderson/Agincourt Carol – La Route àu Béziers/Somewhere Along the Road/The Barring of the Door/What Will We Do?/Almost Every Circumstance/The Old Miner. TSCD450 CD reissue.

12TS451   *Word of Mouth*: The House Band.

12TS452   *Right of Passage*: Martin Carthy. The Ant and the Grasshopper/Eggs in her Basket/A Stitch in Time/McVeagh/Hommage à Roche Prioux/All in Green/Company Policy/The Banks of the Nile/La Carde Use/Bill Norrie/The Sleepwalker/A Cornish Young Man/The Dominion of the Sword.

12TS453   *Stolen Ground*: John Kirkpatrick and Sue Harris. Arthur McBride/The Juggler/ Clee Hill Tunes/Mother Earth/Black Deer/Must I Be Bound/Mrs. Saggs/The Chickens They Are Crowing/Shepherd's Branie/The Old Miner.

12TS454   *Give Me a Saddle and I'll Trade You a Car*: The Albion Band '89 (1989). Ash on an Old Man's Sleeve/Geoff Collings/Postman's Polka/See Their Mouths to Twisting/ Seven Curses/Cardhouse/Striking for Another Land/Bury My Eyeballs on Top of Boot Hill/Kitty Come Down the Lane/Think it Over/Don't Look at Me/Trip to Cheltenham/ Throw out the Lifeline.

2/TS455/6   *I Never Played to Many Posh Dances*: Scan Tester (Sussex – concertina; double LP compilation 1990).

12TS457   *1990: The Albion Band.* Yellow Dress/The Power and the Glory/Fairford Breakdown/Fossie Shuffle/Rambleaway/The Flood/Nameless Kind of Hell/Adam and Eve/Lock up your Daughters/The Party's Over.

TSCD458   *Plain Capers*: John Kirkpatrick (1992 – originally Free Reed FRR010, 1976). Glorishears/Hammersmith Flyover/Old Molly Oxford/Black Jack/Old Black Joe/ Blue Eyed Stranger/Willow Tree/Brighton Camp/March Past/Bobby and Joan/Monk's March/Fieldtown Professional/Sweet Jenny Jones/Sherbourne Jig/Lumps of Plum Pudding/ Highland Mary/Wheatley Processional/Maid of the Mill/Cuckoo's Nest/William and Nancy/Buffoon/Fool's Jig/Constant Billy.

TSCD459   *The Transports*: Peter Bellamy, Collins, Tabor, Lloyd etc. (1992 – originally Free Reed FRR021/022, double album 1977). Overture/Ballad of Henry and Susannah/ Us Poor Fellows/Robber's Song/Ballad of Henry and Susannah 2/I Once Lived in Service/ Norwich Gaol/Sweet Loving Friendship/Black and Bitter Night/Humane Turnkey/ Plymouth Mail/Green Fields of England/Roll Down/Still and Silent Ocean/Ballad of Henry and Susannah 3, 4 and 5/Convict's Wedding Dance.

TSCD460   *Strict Tempo*: Richard Thompson (1992 CD reissue of 12TS460). New Fangled Flogging Reel – Kerry Reel/Vaillance Polka Militaire – Belfast Polka/Scott Skinner Medley: Glencoe – Scott Skinner's Rockin' Step – Bonny Banchory/Banish Misfortune/ Dundee Hornpipe – Poppy-Leaf Hornpipe/Do It for My Sake/Rockin' in Rhythm/The Random Jig – The Grinder/Will Ye No Cam Back Again – Cam Ye O'er the Stream Charlie – Ye Banks and Braes/Rufty Tufty – Nonsuch à la Mode de France/Andalus – Radio Marrakesh/The Knife Edge.

TSCD461   *Barking Mad*: Four Men and a Dog. Hidden Love/Sheila Coyles/Wee Johnny Set/Wrap It Up/Foxhunters/Waltzing for Dreamers/Reel/Polkas/Swing Set/Short Fat Fanny/ Jigs/The Cruel Father/High on a Mountain/McFadden's Reels.

TSCD462   *For Pence and Spicy Ale*: The Watersons. Reissue of 1975 album plus 3 tracks from Mike Waterson's 1977 solo album and 4 tracks from Lal and Norma Waterson's 'A True Hearted Girl' (1977). Country Life/Swarthfell Rocks/Barney/Swansea Town/ Swinton May Song/Beggar Man/Bellman/Adieu Adieu/Welcome Sailor/Apple Tree Wassail/Seven Yellow Gypsies/Sheepshearing/Three Day Millionaire/King Parim/The Bonny Lighthorsemen/Tam Lyn/T Stands for Thomas/Malpas Wassail/Chickens in the Garden/Grace Darling/The Good Old Way.

TSCD463   *The Real MacColl*: Ewan MacColl compilation 1959–66. Ye Jacobites by Name/Johnny Cope/Cam Ye O'er Fra France/Haughs o' Cromdale/Such a Parcel o' Rogues in a Nation/Farewell to Sicily/Derek Bentley/Johnny Breadiesley/Go Down Ye Murderers/Van Diemen's Land/Minorie/Sheep Crook and Black Dog/The Bramble Briar/ One Night as I Lay on My Bed/The Grey Cock/The Blantyre Explosion/The Gresford Disaster/Four Loom Weaver/Song of the Iron Road/Dirty Old Town.

TSCD464   *Blow the Man Down – Sea Songs and Shanties from 1964 'Farewell Nancy' album plus extra tracks* (1993): Various Artists. Louis Killen – The Wild Goose; Ian Campbell – Lovely Nancy; Ewan MacColl – The Black Ball Line; Cyril Tawney – The Nightingale; Harry H. Corbett – Blow the Man Down; Louis Killen – Heave Away My Johnny; Sam Larner – The Lofty Tall Ship; Ian Campbell – Row Bullies Row; Louis Killen – The Flying Cloud; Cyril Tawney – The Fireship; Bob Davenport – Tom's Gone to Hilo; The Watersons – Greenland Whale Fishery; Louis Killen – The Ship in Distress; Ian Campbell – Lowlands Low; Bob Hart – Cod Banging; Cyril Tawney – One Morning in Spring; Louis Killen – Hilo Johnny Brown; A.L. Lloyd – Bonny Ship the Diamond; Louis Killen – Bold Princess Royal; Bob Davenport – Billy Boy; A.V. 'Bob' Roberts – Windy Old Weather; Cyril Tawney – Bold Benjamin; Ian Campbell – Hog-eyed Man; Louis Killen – Goodbye, Fare Thee Well.

TSCD465   *The Iron Muse – A Panorama of Industrial Folk Music* (reissue). See 12T86 for track listing.

TSCD466 *The King of the Highland Pipers*: John Burgess. Compilation of 12T199 and 12T291.

TSCD467 *The Complete Brass Monkey*: Brass Monkey. Waterman's Hornpipe/Fable of the Wings/The Miller's Three Sons/The Maid and the Palmer/Bad News/Sovay/Tip-Top Hornpipe/Primrose Polka/Jolly Bold Robber/Old Grenadier/George's Son/Da Floo'er o' Taft/The Lass o' Paties Mill/The Handweaver and the Factory Maid/The Rose Lawn Quadrille/Willie the Waterboy/Doctor Fauster's Tumblers/The Night of Trafalgar/Prince William/Riding Down to Portsmouth/Trowie Burn/The Foxhunt.

TSCD468 *Opening Moves*: The Battlefield Band. Silver Spear/Humours of Tulla/ Shipyard Apprentice/Cruel Brother/Ge Do Theid Mid do m'Leadbaidh/Battle of Harlaw/ Jenny Nettles/Grays of Tongside/Tae the Beggin'/Tamosher/Blackbird and the Thrush/ Moray Club/Lang Johnny Moir/Brown Milkmaid/Dunnottar Castle/Maid of Glengarrys-dale/Disused Railway/Lady Leroy/Miss Drummond of Perth/Fiddler's Joy/Traditional Reel/Shetland Fiddler/My Last Farewell to Stirling/Cuidich'n Right/I Hae Laid a Herrin' in Salt/My Wife's a Wanton Wee Thing/Banks of the Allan/Battle of Falkirk Muir/Joe McGann's Fiddle/Center's Bonnet. Compilation.

TSCD469 *The Silver Bow – The Fiddle Music of Shetland*: Tom Anderson and Aly Bain. Jack Broke Da Prison Door/Da Day Dawn/Shive Her Up/Da Silver Bow/Auld Foula Reel/Da Slockit Light/Da Auld Restin' Chair/Unst Bridal March/Jack is Yet Alive/ Da Mill/Pit Haem Da Borrowed Claes/Soldier's Joy/Shetland Moods/Dean Brig/Ferrie Reel/Up an' Doon Da Harbour/The Silvery Voe/If I get a Bonnie Lass/Auld Swaara/ Faroe Rum/Mrs Jamieson's Favourite/All Da Ships Ir Sailin'/Freddie's Tune/The Full Rigged Ship/Naanie an' Betty/Maggie O'Ham/Come Agen Ye're Welcome/Ian S. Robertson. See 12TS281.

TSCD470 *The Folk Collection*: Various Artists. Another Irish Rover – Four Men and a Dog/Carthy's Reel; The Return to Camden Town – Martin Carthy and Dave Swarbrick/ Almost Every Circumstance – Maddy Prior and June Tabor/Oh I Swear – Richard Thompson/Company Policy – Martin Carthy/I Specialise – Gregson and Collister/Party's Over – The Albion Band/Brighton Camp; The March Past – John Kirkpatrick/Good Old Way – The Watersons/Johnny Cope – Ewan MacColl/Battle of Falkirk Muir – Battlefield Band/Reaper – June Tabor/Farewell to the Gold – Nic Jones/Reconcilliation – Ron Kavana/Walsh's Polkas – Patrick Street/Lakes of Ponchartrain – Martin Simpson/Mariano – Robert Earl Keen/Through Moorfields – Andrew Cronshaw/Now Westlin' Winds – Dick Gaughan.

TSCD471 *Classics of Irish Piping Volume 1*: Leo Rowsome. For track listing see 12T259.

TSCD472 *Early Days*: The Watersons (1994). Compilation of vintage Topic recordings. Boston Harbour/The Greenland Whale Fishery/Three Score and Ten/The Broom of Cowdenknowes/King Arthur's Servants/Rap Her to Bank/The Bendigo/The North Country Maid/Brave Wolfe/The Jolly Waggoners/I am a Rover/Fathom the Bowl/Thirty Foot Trailer/The Holmfirth Anthem/Twanky-Dillo/The White Hare of Howden/All for me Grog/The Poacher's Fate/The Tour of the Dales/Willy Went to Westerdale/I'Anson's Racehorse/The Ploughboy/The White Cockade/Ye Noble Spectators/Stow Brow/The Wanton Wife of Castlegate/The Whitby Lad.

TSCD473   *A Short History Of*: John Kirkpatrick (1994). George's Son/Arthur McBride/ Crocker's Reel/Oakham Poachers/Clee Hill Tunes/Jim Jones/Waterman's Dance/The Watercress Girl/Maid of the Mill – Cuckoo's Nest – William and Nancy/Johnny Sands/ Fireside Polka – Down the Side and Up the Middle/Underneath Her Apron/The Buffoon – The Fool's Jig/Old Man Jones/Cheshire Hornpipe/Black Deer/Glorishears/The Old Miner/Constant Billy.

TSCD474   *Her Mantle So Green*: Margaret Barry with Michael Gorman. Reissue of 12T123.

TSCD475   *Waterson:Carthy*: Martin Carthy, Norma Waterson and Eliza Carthy (1994). Bold Doherty/The Light Dragoon/Ye Mariners All/Rags and Tatters – An Moinfeuir/ With Kitty I'll Go/The Grey Cock/When I First Came to Caledonia/Orange in Bloom (the Sherborne Waltz)/The Slave's Lament – Farewell to a Dark Haired Friend/John Hamilton/Sleep On Beloved/Midnight on the Water.

TSCD476   *The Sweet Primeroses*: Shirley Collins reissue of 1964 album plus the *Heroes in Love* EP from 1963. All Things are Quite Silent/Cambridgeshire May Carol/ Spencer the Rover/The Rigs of Time/Polly Vaughan/The Cruel Mother/The Bird in the Bush/The Streets of Derry/The False Bride/Locks and Bolts/Rambleaway/A Blacksmith Courted Me/Brigg Fair/Higher Germanie/George Collins/The Babes in the Wood/Down in Yon Forest/The Magpie's Nest/False True Love/The Sweet Primeroses.

TSCD477   *Ramblin' Jack*: Ramblin' Jack Elliott. CD reissue of vintage Topic recordings (1996). Talking Columbia Blues/Pretty Boy Floyd/Ludlow Massacre/Talking Minor Blues/ Hard Travelling/So Long, It's Been Good to Know You/Talking Dustbowl Blues/1913 Massacre/Rambling Blues/Talking Sailor Blues/San Francisco Blues/Ol Riley/The Boll Weevil/New York Town/Mule Skinner Blues/Dink's Song/It's Hard, Ain't it Hard/All Around the Water Tank/Mother's Not Dead/East Virginia Blues/Danville Girl/Rich and Rambling Boys/Roll On Buddy.

TSCD478   *Once in a Blue Moon*: Lal Waterson and Oliver Knight. At First the Stars/ Eight of the Pelican/Stumbling On/How Can I Leave/Altisidor/Dazed/Phoebe/Cornfield/ Midnight Feast/So Strange is Man/Wilson's Arms/Her White Gown/Some Old Salty.

TSCD479   *The Bird in the Bush*: A.L. Lloyd, Louis Killen, Frankie Armstrong, Norman Kennedy, Dave Swarbrick, Alf Edwards. CD reissue of 12T135 (1966).

TSCD480   *English and Scottish Folk Ballads*: A.L. Lloyd, Ewan MacColl, Anne Briggs, Louis Killen, Norman Kennedy, Mike Waterson.

TSCD481   *The Folk Collection 2*: Various Artists – compilation. Horizonto – Blowzabella; When I First Came to Caledonia – Waterson:Carthy; The Snow It Melts The Soonest – Anne Briggs; Old Grenadier – Brass Monkey; Blood and Gold/Mohacs – Silly Sisters; Both Sides of the Tweed – Dick Gaughan; Da Fields o' Foula/My Love Is a Fair Lad – Tarras; Columbine – Lal Waterson and Oliver Knight; Go Down Ye Murderers – Ewan MacColl; The Sun Is Burning – Ian Campbell Folk Group; Cold, Wet and Rainy Night/The Grand Hornpipe – Eliza Carthy; The Verdant Braes of Skreen – The McPeake Family; The Skewbald – Martin Carthy and Dave Swarbrick; The Hewer – The High Level Ranters; Soldier's Joy – Aly Bain and Tom Anderson; Twa Recruiting Sergeants –

The Exiles; Down by the Seaside – Shirley Collins; Train to Ba – Oliver Knight; Apple Tree Wassail – The Watersons.

TSCD482   *Heat, Light and Sound*: Eliza Carthy (1996). Cold Wet and Rainy Night/The Grand Hornpipe/Cumberland Waltz/Petit Homme/Miss Bowls/What a Beau Your Granny Is/Stone Steps/Ten Thousand Miles/Bacca Pipes/Clerk Saunders/Stamps for the Dog/ Peggy/Blind Fiddler/Lady Barnsley's Fancy/Trip to Cartmel/Hardy's Crow/By Then/ Sheath and Knife/Jacky's Tar.

TSCD483   *Northumberland Forever*: The High Level Ranters. Shew's the Way to Wallington, The Peacock Followed the Hen/The Sandgate Girl's Lament, Elsie Marley/ Bellingham Boat, Lambskinnet/Adam Buckham/Meggy's Foot/The Lads of North Tyne, The Redesdale Hornpipe/The Hexamshire Lass/The Breakdown, The Blanchard Races/ The Lads of Alnwick, Lamshaw's Fancy/Byker Hill/Whinham's Reel, Nancy/Because He Was a Bonny Lad, Salmon Tails Up the Water, Sweet Hesleyside/Dance to You Daddy/ Billy Boy/Nae Guid Luck Aboot the Hoose/Mi' Laddie Sits Ower Kate Up/The Keel Row, Kafoozalum, The Washing Day. Compilation.

TSCD484   *Tommy Armstrong of Tyneside*: Louis Killen, Tom Gilfellon, Johnny Handle, Maureen Craik and Colin Ross. Reissue.

TSCD485   *Deep Lancashire*: Various Artists (The Oldham Tinkers, Harvey and Mary Kershaw, Harry Boardman, Bernard Wrigley, Lee Nicholson, Harry Ogden, Mike Harding, Dave Brooks, Pete Smith). Reissue.

TSCD486   *The Bonnie Pit Laddie*: Various Artists (The High Level Ranters, Harry Boardman, Dick Gaughan). Reissue.

TSCD487   *Northumbrian Small Pipes*: Various Artists.

TSCD488   *Common Tongue*: Waterson:Carthy. Rambleaway/Valentine Waltz/Claudy Banks/Rackabello/Lowlands of Holland/Medley: Grand March in the Battle of Prague – Liverpool Hornpipe – Wellington Hornpipe/Meeting is a Pleasure/Hares in the Old Plantation/Flash Company/Maid Lamenting/American Stranger/French Stroller/Polly's Love/Stars in my Crown.

TSCD489   *Eliza Carthy and the Kings of Calicutt* (1997). Trip/Whirly/Bonaparte's/ Tractor/Mother/Mr Walker/Sea/Sheffield/Fisher/Storyteller.

TSCD490   *Aleyn*: June Tabor (1997). The Great Valerio/I Wonder What's Keeping my True Love, Tonight?/No Good in Love/Bentley and Craig/A Proper Sort of Gardener/The Fiddler/Di Nakht/April Morning/Fair Maid of Islington/Shallow Brown/Johnny O'Bredislee, etc.?

TSCD491   *Life and Limb*: Martin Carthy and Dave Swarbrick. Sovay/The Begging Song/Bows of London/The Pepperpot, Sailing into Walpole's Marsh, Bunker Hill/A Question of Sport/Oh Dear Oh/Carthy's March, The Lemon Tree/Lochmaben Harper/ Byker Hill.

TSCD492   *Skin and Bone*: Martin Carthy and Dave Swarbrick. The Sheepstealer/The Poacher/I Courted a Damsel/Lucy Wan/The Trip We Took Over the Mountain//The Skewbald/The Ride in the Creel/The Brown Girl/Such a War Has Never Been/Perfumes of Arabia/Carthy's Reel, The Return to Camden Town/The New Mown Hay/Clyde's Water/Mrs Bermingham, No 178, Blind Mary.

TSCD493   *Red*: Eliza Carthy (1998). Accordion Song/10,000 Miles/Billy Boy – The Widdow's Wedding/Time in the Son/Stumbling On/Stingo – The Stacking Reel/Greenwood Laddie – Mrs. Capron's Reel – Tune/Walk Away/Adieu, Adieu/Russia (call waiting)/Red Rice.

TSCD494   *Rice*: Eliza Carthy (1998). Blow the Winds – The Game of Draughts/The Snow it Melts the Soonest/Picking Up Sticks – The Old Mole – Felton Lonnin – Kingston Girls/Miller and the Lass/Herring Song/Mons Meg/Tuesday Morning/Haddock and Chips/The Americans have Stolen my True Love Away/Zycanthos Jig – Tommy's Foot – Quebecois/The Sweetness of Mary – Holywell Hornpipe – Swedish/Benjamin Bowmaneer/Commodore Moore – The Black Dance – A Andy O. TSCD493 and TSCD494 also released as a double album TSCD2001.

TSCD495   *Bold Sportsmen All*: Ewan MacColl, A.L. Lloyd, Roy Harris. Reissue combining LP and EP with additional material incl. Roy Harris – The Saucy Bold Robber. Also including: The Sporting Races of Galway/The Bold Gambling Boy/Morrissey and the Russian Sailor/Skewball/Heenan and Sayers, etc.

TSCD496   *English Drinking Songs*: A.L. Lloyd with Alf Edwards and Al Jeffrey. Recordings originally released *c*.1961. The Derby Ram/The Foggy Dew/Maggie May/ When Johnson's Ale Was New/The Butcher and the Chambermaid/A Jug Of Punch/The Parson and the Maid/Three Drunken Horsemen/All for Me Grog/The Drunken Maidens/ Rosin the Beau/The Farmer's Servant/John Barleycorn/A Jug of This.

TSCD497   *Leviathan!*: A.L. Lloyd. Reissue. The Baleana/The Coast of Peru/Greenland Bound/The Weary Whaling Grounds/The Cruel Ship's Carpenter/Off to Sea Once More/ The Twenty Third Of March/The Bonny Ship the Diamond/Talcahuana Girls/Farewell To Tarwathie/Rolling Down to Old Maui/The Greenland Whale Fishery/Paddy and the Whale/The Whaleman's Lament/The Eclipse.

TSCD498   *Along the Coaly Tyne* – Old And New Northumbrian Songs. A reissue taken from 'Northumbrian Garland'; 'Stottin' Doon the Waall'; 'Along the Coaly Tyne'; 'Ranting Lads' (The High Level Ranters): Various Artists.

TSCD499   *Round Cape Horn – Traditional Songs of Sailors, Ships and the Sea*. Various Artists, compiled from deleted albums: Roy Harris, The Watersons, Louis Killen, Peter Bellamy, Cyril Tawney, Frankie Armstrong, A.L. Lloyd, Ewan MacColl.

TSCD500   *Green Fields*: The Watersons: 1998 – reissue from 1981 (see back) plus extra tracks from 'A True Hearted Girl' (Lal and Norma Waterson) and Mike Waterson solo album. We All Go Hunting Today/While the Gamekeepers Lie Sleeping/Hares in the Old Plantation/Rosebud in June/The Brisk Lad, etc.

TSCD501   *Sound and Rumour*: Brass Monkey (1998). The Flash Lad/Morris Tune: The Rose – Trunkles/An Acre of Land/Old Horse/The Heroes of St. Valery/The Charming Maid/The Roving Journeyman/Rodney – When I Was Young – The Quaker/The Old Virginian Lowlands/Auretti's Dutch Skipper – An Adventure at Margate – The Spirit of the Dance/Soldier, Soldier – The Flowers of Edinburgh/The Rambling Comber/Betty Fitchett's Wedding – The German Schottische.

TSCD502 *Chorus from the Gallows*: Ewan MacColl with Peggy Seeger, guitar and banjo – reissue. Derek Bentley/The Black Velvet Band/Jamie Reaburn's Farewell/Johnny O'Breadiesley/Hughie the Graeme/Minorie/The Treadmill Song/Turpin Hero/The Crafty Farmer/McKaffery/Jimmy Wilson/The Lag's Song/Van Diemen's Land/Go Down Ye Murderers.

TSCD503 *Signs of Life*: Martin Carthy (1998). New York Mining Disaster, 1941/ Georgie/Sir Patrick Spens/The Deserter/Heartbreak Hotel/The Bonny Hind/The Wife of Usher's Well/John Parfit/Barbary Ellen/Hong Kong Blues/The Lonesome Death of Hattie Carroll/Prince Heathen/Jim Jones in Botany Bay.

TSCD504 *A Collection*: Anne Briggs. The Recruited Collier/The Doffing Mistres/She Moved Through the Fair/Let No Man Steal Your Thyme/Lowlands/My Bonny Boy/Polly Vaughan/Rosemary Lane/Gathering Rushes in the Month Of May/The Whirly Whorl/ The Stonecutter Boy/Martinmas Time/Blackwater Side/The Snow It Melts The Soonest/ Willie o' Winsbury/Go Your Way/Thorneymoor Woods/The Cuckoo/Reynardine/Young Tambling/Living by the Water/Maa Bonny Lad.

TSCD505 *A Bed of Roses*: Lal Waterson and Oliver Knight. Memories/Foolish One/ Just a Note/Columbine/At First She Starts/Bath Time/Train to Bay/Long Vacation/Party Games/Together/Migrating Bird/Lullaby.

TSCD506 *Rising*: Tarras. Parsons Green/Whiskey Town/Magnadoodle/Oakey Strike Evictions/ Da Fields o' Foula, My Love Is a Fair Lad/Captain Grant/Rising/Be Real/The Happy Salmon/Magpie's Revenge/So Tired/Men Should Wear Their Long Hair Down/ The Long Road Home.

TSCD507 *A True Hearted Girl*: Lal and Norman Waterson. Young Billy Brown/Betsey Belle/The Beggar Man/The Welcome Sailor/Meeting Is a Pleasure/I Wish I Had Never/ The Wealthy Squire/The Pretty Drummer Boy/John Ball/Jenny Storm/The Bonny Light Horseman/The Unfortunate Lass/The Flowers of the Forest/Grace Darling.

TSCD509 *Broken Ground*: Waterson:Carthy. Raggle Taggle Gipsies/The Bay of Biscay/ Sheffield Waltz, Waltz Clog, The Wounded Hussar/The Lion's Den/Fare Thee Well Cold Winter/Rowling Hornpipe, Our Cat Had Kitted, Bleaton Gardens, The Sportsman's Hornpipe/The Forsaken Mermaid/We Poor Labouring Men/The Ditching Carol/Dorrington Lads, Adam a' Bell/The Royal Forester, The Bald Headed End of the Broom.

TSCD510 *A Quiet Eye*: June Tabor. The Gardener/A Place Called England/I Will Put My Ship in Order/I'll Be Seeing You/Out of Winter, Waltzing for Dreamers/Pharaoh/ Must I Be Bound?/The Writing of Tipperary, It's a Long Way to Tipperary/The First Time Ever I Saw Your Face/The Water is Wide, St. Agnes, Jeannie and Jamie.

TSCD511 *Now is the Time for Fishing*: Sam Larner. Now is the Time For Fishing/Up Jumped The Herring/The Dogger Bank/Henry Martin/Butter and Cheese/The Reckless Young Fellow/Blow Away the Morning Dew/All Fours/Green Broom/The Dockyard Gate/No Sir, No Sir/Sealore and Rhymes/The Drowned Lover/The Dolphin/The Bold

Princess Royal/The Ghost Ship/Happy and Delightful/Maids, When You're Young, Never Wed an Old Man/The Wild Rover.

TSCD514   *Walter Pardon*. The Rambling Blade/The Lawyer/The Bold Fisherman/The Dark Eyed Sailor/The Bush of Australia/The Female Drummer/The Bold Princess Royal/ The Banks of Sweet Dundee/The Deserter/The Trees They Do Grow High/Two Jolly Butchers/The Loss of the Ramillies/The Handsome Cabin Boy/The Pretty Ploughboy/ The Cunning Cobbler/The Devil and the Farmer's Wife/The British Man o' War/The Jolly Waggoner/The Rakish Young Fellow.

TSCD515   *Sheila Stewart*. Queen Amongst the Heather/Twa Brothers/False, False/Hatton Woods/Donald's Return to Glencoe/Bogie's Bonnie Belle/The Mill o' Tifty's Annie/Wi' My Dog and Gun/Blackwaterside/Mantle So Green/Blue Blazing Blind Drunk/Willie Leonard/Echo Mocks the Corncrake/Moving on Song/Oxford Tragedy/Love Is the Sweet and Single Life/Convict Song/Here's a Health/The Nobleman's Wedding/The Parting Glass.

TSCD516   *Mike Waterson*. The Wensleydale Lad/The Brisk Lad/The Two Brothers/The Man o' War/The Charlady's Son/The Light Dragoon/The Cruel Ship's Carpenter/Bye Bye Skipper/Sorry the Day I Was Married/The Yorkshire Tup/Tamlyn/Lord Rothschild/ Swansea Town/Seven Yellow Gypsies.

TSCD517   *Rags, Reels and Airs*: Dave Swarbrick with Martin Carthy and Diz Disley; first released in 1967, Polydor 236514. Spanish Ladies Medley/Hens March to the Middens/Bottom of the Punchbowl, The Swallow Tail, Marquis of Tullybardine/Barney Brallaghan, The New Widow Well Married, Paddy Be Aisey/Dill Pickles Rag/Gurty's Frolics/The Blackbird/The Cuckoo's Nest/Lietrum Fancy Medley/Porcupine Rag/ Villafjord, Four Poster Bed/ Staten Island, Jimmy Allen/ The Salamanca Medley/The Teetotallers Medley/Lord Mayo/The Kid on the Mountain/Jolly Tinker, Rags and Tatters/ Father Kelly/Skopje/Sligo Maid.

TSCD600   *Hidden English – A Celebration of English Traditional Music*: Various Artists. Joseph Taylor: Brigg Fair; Bob and Ron Copper: The Sweet Primroses; Walter Bulwer, Billy Cooper, Reg Hall, Daisy Bulwer, Mervyn Plunkett and Russell Wortley: Red Wing Polka; William Kimber: Getting Upstairs – Blue Eyed Stranger; Louis Fuller: Hopping Down in Kent; George 'Pop' Maynard: Polly on the Shore; Billy Bennington: The Pony Trot Polka; Cyril Poacher: The Nutting Girl; Billy Pigg: The Morpeth Rant; Phoebe Smith: Higher Germany; Jasper Smith: Died for Love; Scan Tester, Reg Hall and Daisy Sherlock: Jenny Lind Polka; Bob Hart: Australia; Johnny Doughty: The Golden Vanity; Oscar Woods: Oh, Joe the Boat is Going Over; Harry Cox: The Maid of Australia; Fred Jordan: The Outlandish Knight; Tintagel and Boscastle Players: Boscastle Breakdown; Tom Willett: While Gamekeepers Lie Sleeping; Eely Whent: Two Step; Bob Roberts: The Candlight Fisherman; Sam Larner: The Bold Princess Royal; Bob Cann: Hot Punch/ Uncle's Jug; Joseph Taylor: Lord Bateman.

TSCD601   *Melodeon Greats*. A Collection of Melodeon Masterpieces. Reissue with added tracks (1994). James Brown: Irish Jigs; W.F. Cameron: Flowers of Edinburgh; Peter and Daniel Wyper: Stranger March; James Brown: The Thistle Schottische; William Hannah: Pibroch o' Donald Dhu; James Brown: Miss Drummond Of Perth; Peter Wyper: Silverton Polka; 'Pamby Dick': Boston Bells Barn Dance; James Brown: Irish Jigs; Jack

Williams: Queen Mary Waltz; Peter Leatham: Shufflin' Samuel; Peter Wyper: 79th Highlanders and Champion Marches; Peter Leatham: Hornpipe Medley; James Brown: Rose Polka; Daniel Wyper: Scotch Reels – Roll Her on The Hill/Soldier's Joy/Clean Peastrae/Fairy Dance; 'Pamby Dick': Stirling Castle Strathspey; Peter Wyper: Two Step – The Dancing Dustman; Jack Williams: Bit o' Blarney; Peter Leatham: The Laird o' Drumblair; William Hannah: Duke Of Perth; Peter Leatham: Sammie's Schottische; Peter Wyper: Lion Quadrilles Figure 4; Fred Cameron: Rights of Man Hornpipe; Peter and Daniel Wyper: Doon the Burn March; 'Pamby Dick': Irish Reels.

TSCD602   *Irish Dance Music*. Edited by Reg Hall (1996). A compilation of vintage Irish dance music taken from recordings from the early 1920s to the late 1940s. Frank Quinn – The Westport Chorus. Michael J. Cashin – Jigs – Ginger's Favourite, Bogs of Allen. Tom Morrison and John Reynolds – Sweet Flower of Milltown, The Boys from Knock – Schottische. Michael Coleman – O'Dowd's Favourite Reel Medley. Bart Henry's Traditional Quartet Orchestra – Ah! Surely and the Maid on the Green – Jigs. McKenna and Gaffney – Maids of Galway, Over the Moor to Peggy – Irish Reels. K. Scanlon – Medley of Old Time Fiddling Reels – Bonnie Kate, Swallow's Tail, Molly Brannigan. Michael J. Grogan – Off to California – Hornpipe, Dunphey's Hornpipe. Michael J. Grogan and John Howard – Reels – Drunken Tailor, Teetotaler. George Halpin and M. Stanford – The Maids of Ballinatra – Reel. Flanagan Brothers – Frieze Breetches, The Cook in the Kitchen, Lannigan's Ball – Medley of Irish Jigs. J. Flanagan – Scotch Mary Medley – Irish Reels. McConnell's Four Leaf Shamrocks – Medley of Polkas – Babes in the Wood, Moore's Favourite. The Four Provinces Orchestra – The Pride of Ulster, Maggie Pickens, Cameron's Wife – Fold Dance. Pat Roche's Harp and Shamrock Orchestra – Boys of Blue Hill, Stack o' Wheat – Hornpipe Medley. Erin's Pride Orchestra – Stack of Oats, Shannon Waves – Barn Dances. Frank Lee's Tar Ceilidh Band – Irish Jigs – Kitty's Rambles, The Merry Old Woman, The Humours of Ballinafad. Siamsa Gaedheal Ceilidhe Band – Irish Reel Medley – The High Road to Galway, The Groves Reel, The Salamanca Reel. Ballinakill (Co. Galway) Traditional Dance Players – Carraroe and Lambert's Jigs. Jerry Moloney and Tommy Whyte – The Old Bush Reel. Moate Ceilidhe Band – Reels – The First House in Connaught, The Green Gate. Lough Gill Quartet – Jigs – Mill Pond, Mist on the Meadow. Belhaven Trio – Reels – Ash Plant, The Merry Harriers, The Hut in the Bog. Kincora Ceilidhe Band – Reels – Lasses of Carracastle, Maid of Mt. Kisko, St. Ruth's Bush.

TSCD603   *Paddy in the Smoke – Irish Dance Music from a London Pub* (1997). Reg Hall reissue.

TSCD604   *Past Masters of Irish Dance Music – Irish Piping Anthology*: Various Artists – back catalogue compilation.

TSCD605   *Irish Fiddle Anthology*: Various Artists – back catalogue compilation.

The Voice of the People – the Traditional Music of England, Ireland, Scotland and Wales
TSCD651   *Come Let Us Buy the Licence – Songs of Courtship and Marriage.*

TSCD652   *My Ship Shall Sail the Ocean – Songs of Tempest and Sea Battles, Sailor Lads and Fishermen.*

TSCD653   *O'er His Grave the Grass Grew Green – Tragic Ballads.*

TSCD654   *Farewell, My Own Dear Native Land – Songs of Exile and Emigration.*

TSCD655   *Come All My Lads that Follow the Plough – The Life of Rural Working Men and Women.*

TSCD656   *Tonight I'll Make You My Bride – Ballads of True And False Lovers.*

TSCD657   *First I'm Going to Sing You a Ditty – Rural Fun and Frolics.*

TSCD658   *A Story I'm Just About to Tell – Local Events and National Issues.*

TSCD659   *Rig-a-Jig-Jig – Dance Music of the South of England.*

TSCD660   *Who's That at My Bedroom Window? – Songs of Love and Amorous Encounter.*

TSCD661   *My Father's the King of the Gypsies – Music of English and Welsh Travellers and Gypsies.*

TSCD662   *We've Received Orders to Sail – Jackie Tar at Sea and on Shore.*

TSCD663   *They Ordered Their Pints of Beer and Bottles of Sherry – The Joys and Curse of Drink.*

TSCD664   *Troubles They Are but Few – Dance Tunes and Ditties.*

TSCD665   *As Me and My Love Sat Courting – Songs of Love, Courtship and Marriage.*

TSCD666   *You Lazy Lot of Bone Shakers – Songs and Dance Tunes of Seasonal Events.*

TSCD667   *It Fell on a Day, a Bonny Summer Day – Ballads.*

TSCD668   *To Catch a Fine Buck Was My Delight – Songs of Hunting and Poaching.*

TSCD669   *Ranting and Reeling – Dance Music of the North of England.*

TSCD670   *There Is a Man upon the Farm – Working Men and Women in Song.*

All of the above 20-CD set are compilations of back catalogue material – various artists.

End of series

TSCD700   *The Season Round*: Various Artists – back catalogue compilation. Valley Folk: Come All You True Good Christians; Oak: Shepherds Arise; The Watersons: Here We Come a-Wassailing; The Watersons: Pace Egging Song; The Watersons: The Holly Bears a Berry; Shirley Collins: Cambridgeshire May Carol; The Watersons: Hal-an-Tow; The Valley Folk: Two Brethren; The Watersons: Earlsdon Sword Dance; The Watersons: Harvest Song, We Gets Up in the Morn; The Watersons: Souling Song; The Valley Folk: Cherry Tree Carol; The Watersons: Herod and the Cock; The Valley Folk: The Babe of Bethlehem; The Watersons: Wassail Song; The Watersons: Idumea; The Watersons: Green Fields; Waterson:Carthy: Sleep on Beloved.

TSCD701   *Celtic Voices*: Various Artists.

TSCD702   *Irish Voices*: Various Artists.

TSCD703   *Scottish Voices*: Various Artists.

TSCD704   *Ancient Celtic Roots*: Various Artists. Felix Doran – Mary of Murroe/The Green Gates. Jeannie Robertson – The Gypsy Laddies. John Reilly – The Well Below the Valley. Willie Clancy – The Templehouse/Over the Moor to Maggie. The Exiles – I Will Lay Ye Doon Love. Sean MacDonnachadhe – Mainistra na Buille. Kentigern – Bretton Tunes/Greenwoodside. The Gaughers – The Cruel Brother. Sarah Makem – Barbara Allen. John Doherty – The Dispute at the Crossroads. Ian Manuel – MacCrimmon's Lament. Paddy Tunney – Craigie Hill. James Morrison – The Return of Spring. Joe Heaney – Bean na Leanna. Belle Stewart – Queen Among the Heather. The Clutha – Wha's Fu'. Seamus Ennis – Happy to Meet, Sorry to Part.

TSCD705

TSCD706   *English Originals*: Various Artists. Eliza Carthy and The Kings of Calicutt: Whirly Whorl; Nic Jones: The Flandyke Shore; Brass Monkey: The Flash Lad; June Tabor: April Morning; John Tams: From Where I Lie, Sheep Counting; Anne Briggs: Reynardine; Tarras: Parsons Green; Pop Maynard: Polly on the Shore; Martin Simpson: The Keel Row; Waterson:Carthy: Rambleaway, Valentine Waltz; Sam Larner: The Lofty Tall Ship; Martin Carthy and Dave Swarbrick: Byker Hill; Louis Killen: Young Edwin in the Lowlands; John Kirkpatrick: Sweet Jenny Jones, Sherborne Jig, Sherborne Jig; The Watersons: Sheepshearing; Walter Pardon: Van Diemen's Land; Shirley Collins: A Blacksmith Courted Me; Harry Cox: The Bold Princess Royal; Lal Waterson and Oliver Knight: Some Old Salty.

TSCD707/8   *The Folk Collection*: Various Artists – a double CD reissue of TSCD470 and TSCD481 (see above).

TSCD750   *A Collection*: Martin Carthy. The Trees They Do Grow High/Lord Franklin/ The Bloody Gardener/Poor Murdered Woman/Seven Yellow Gypsies/The Bold Poachers/ Scarborough Fair/Lowlands of Holland/Davy Lowston/Streets of Forbes/Polly on the Shore/Cold Hail Windy Night.

TSCD751   *The Voice of the People – A Selection from the Series*.

TSCD780   *Almost a Gentleman*: Billy Bennett (1978, reissued 1997; tracks 8–12 not previously released): Nell/My Mother Doesn't Know I'm on the Stage/Mandalay/I'll Be Thinking of You/Ogul Mogul – A Kanakanese Love Lyric/No Power on Earth/She Was Poor but She Was Honest/She Was Happier When She Was Poor/The Miser/The Only Girl I Ever Loved/The Charge of the Tight Brigade/Don't Send My Boy to Prison/Family Secrets/Please Let Me Sleep on Your Doorstep Tonight/Christmas Day in the Cookhouse/ The Club Raid/She's Mine/Mottoes/The Green Tie on the Little Yellow Dog.

12TMH781   *Play Another Before You Go*: Various Artists. I'm Henry the Eighth; Cover it Over Quickly Jemima – Harry Champion. The Girls I Left Behind Me, I'll Show You Around Paree – Vesta Tilley; I Wanted a Wife, One of the Bhoys – Mark Sheridan; I May be a Millionaire – Eugene Stratton; Send for John Willie, Playing the Game in the West – George Formby; They're All Single at the Seaside, Molly Malloy – Ella Retford; We All Go the Same Way Home, Play us Another Before you Go – Chas. R. Whittle; Mr and Mrs Smith – Clarice Mayne.

12TMH782   *A Good Blowout for Fourpence*: Various artists.

The Radio Ballads – Ewan MacColl, Peggy Seeger, Charles Parker. Eight programmes first broadcast by BBC Radio between 1958 and 1964.

TSCD801   *The Ballad of John Axton.*

TSCD802   *Song of a Road.*

TSCD803   *Singing the Fishing.*

TSCD804   *The Big Hewer.*

TSCD805   *The Body Blow.*

TSCD806   *On the Edge.*

TSCD807   *The Fight Game.*

TSCD808   *The Travelling People.*

End

TSCD815   *Sweet England*: Shirley Collins. Sweet England/Hares on the Mountain/ Hori-Horo/The Bonny Irish Boy/The Tailor and the Mouse/The Lady and the Swine/ Turpin Hero/The Cuckoo/The Bonny Labouring Boy/The Cherry Tree Carol/Sweet William/Omie Wise/Blackbirds and Thrushes/A Keeper Went Hunting/Polly Vaughan/ Pretty Saro/Barbara Allen/Charlie. Collins' first album, originally released in 1959.

TSCD816

TSCD817

TSCD818   *Fire in the Soul*: Davey Graham. Compiled from 4 late '60s albums plus 'Anji'. No Preacher Blues/The Fakir/Watermelon Man/Money Honey/Fire in My Soul/ Neighbour, Neighbour/Jubilation/Anji/Bad Boy Blues/Tristano/Babe, It Ain't No Lie/ Bruton Town/Jenra/I'm Ready/Buhaina Chant/Hornpie for Harpsichord Played Upon Guitar/Down Along the Cove/Stan's Guitar/Pretty Polly/Oliver/Bulgarian Dance/Blues at Gino's/Sunny Moon for Two/Charlie/Ramblin' Sailor.

TSCD819   *Folk Roots, New Routes*: Davey Graham and Shirley Collins. Originally released 1964, Decca LK4652. Nottamun Town/Proud Maisie/The Cherry Tree Carol/ Blue Monk/Hares on the Mountain/Reynardine/Pretty Saro/Rif Mountain/Jane, Jane/ Love Is Pleasin'/Boll Weevil, Holler/Hori, Horo/Bad Girl/Lord Greggory/Grooveyard/ Dearest Dear.

TSCD820   *Folk Blues and Beyond*: Davey Graham. Originally released 1964, Decca LK4649. Leavin' Blues/Cocaine/Sally Free and Easy/Black Is the Colour of My True Love's Hair/Rock Me Baby/Seven Gypsies/Ballad of the Sad Young Man/Moanin'/Skillet (Good 'n' Greasy)/Ain't Nobody's Business What I Do/Maajun/I Can't Keep from Cryin' Sometimes/Don't Think Twice, It's Alright/My Babe/Goin' Down Slow/Better Git It in You Soul.

Topic World Series
TSCD900

TSCD901   *Music in the World of Islam. The Human Voice and Lutes* (1994). Ex-Tangent?

TSCD902   *Music in the World of Islam. Drums, Reeds and Bagpipes* (1994). Tangent?

TSCD903   *Music in the World of Islam. Strings, Flutes and Trumpets* (1994). Tangent?

TSCD904   *Folk Music of Albania.* Originally 12T154 (1966). Tangent?

TSCD905   *Folk Music of Bulgaria.* Originally 12T107 (1964). Tangent?

TSCD906   *Folk Music of Yugoslavia.* Reissue? (1973). Tangent?

TSCD907   *Folk Music of Greece.* Reissue? (1974). Tangent?

TSCD908   *Folk Music of Turkey.* Originally 12T333 (1977). Tangent?

TSCD909   *Vocal and Instrumental Music of Mongolia.* Originally double LP: 'Vocal Music from Mongolia and ...'. Tangent?

TSCD910   *Music from Ethiopia* (1970). Tangent.

TSCD911   *Music from the Shrines of Ajmer and Mundra* (1970). Tangent.

TSCD912   *Music of the Tartar People.* Tangent.

TSCD913   *Flute and Gamelan Music of West Java.* Reissue (1979). Tangent.

TSCD914   *Gypsy Music of Macedonia and Neighbouring Countries.*

TSCD915   *Instrumental Music from Greece.*

Impact
IMP A 101   *Children's Singing Games.*

IMP A 102   *Southern Freedom Songs.*

IMP A 103   *The Painful Plough.*

IMP A 104   *Room for Company.*

Topic/Free Reed
12TFRS501   *Concertina Workshop*: Alistair Anderson. Dancing Tailor/O'Carolan's Fancy/ Blarney Pilgrim/Barrington Hornpipe/Cliff Hornpipe/Recruited Colliers/Sir Sydney Smith's March/Flannel Jacket/Scholar/Joe Burke's Hornpipe/Fairy Queen/Jenny Lind Polka/One Horned Sheep/Turnpike Side/Sunbeam/Admiral Cole/Derwentwater's Farewell/ Jimmy Allen/Herd on the Hill/King's Favourite/Tipsey Sailor/Aith Rant/Framm upon Him/Da South End/Fateful Head/Randy Wives of Greenlaw/John McNeil's Reel/Kick the World Before You/Come Upstairs With Me/Malt Man Comes on Monday.

12TFRS502   *Clare Concertinas*: Bernard O'Sullivan and Tommy McMahon. Babes in the Wood/Cooraclare Polka/Clare Dragoons/Sandy Groves of Piedmont/Humours of Ennistymon/Old Torn Petticoat/Tommy People's Favourite/Mount Fabus Hunt/Ollie Conway's Selection/Kilrush Races/Clogher Reel/Burren Reel/Bonaparte's Retreat/ Bonaparte's March/Barron's Jig/Jackson's Jig/Miltown Jig/Rodney's Glory/Tommy McMahon's Reel/Over the Waves/Girl I Left Behind Me/Maggie in the Wood/Martin Taltry's Jig/Thomas Friel's Jig/Joe Cunnean's Jig/Sean Ryan's Hornpipe/Danganella Hornpipe/Job of Journey Work/Ash Plant/Maid of Mount Cisco.

12TFRS503   *The Flowing Tide*: Chris Droney. Also listed as 12TS503.

12TFRS504   *Fiddle and Concertina Player*: John Kelly.

12TFRS505   *Irish Traditional Music of County Clare*: Bernard O'Sullivan and Tommy McMahon. I Have a Bonnet Trimmed with Blue/Rakes of Mallow/Farmer Moroney's Reel/Mulvill's Reel/Maud Millar's Reel/Bucks of Oranmore/My Heart's in the Highlands/ Dewdrop/Blooming Meadows/Mullagh Jig/Ballinakill Jig/Merry Sisters/Quilty Reel/Cliff/ Derry Hornpipe/Rose in the Heather/Flowery Mountains/Kiss the Maid Behind the Barrel/Milliner's Daughter/Trip to Durrow/Stack Ryan's Polka/Set Dance/Garden of Daisies/Andy Keone's Jig/Three Sea Captains/Boys of Ballysadare/Five Mile Chase.

12TFRS506   *Irish Traditional Concertina Styles* (1986): Various Artists. King of the Clans/Behind the Bush in Parkhanna/Kit O'Mahoney's/Mountain Road/Reels/Fairy Child/ Argrume Set/Barn Dance/West Along the Road/Morning Dew/Spike Island Lasses/Jenny's Beaver Hat/Drowsie Maggie/Mason's Apron/Sean O'Dwyer's Fling/Kesh Jig/Clare Jig/ Air from Thomas Moor/Fairy Hornpipe/Mrs. O'Dwyer's Fancy/Apples in the Wind.

FRR021/022   *The Transports*. Peter Bellamy et al. (double LP). See TSCD459.

End of Topic/Free Reed collaboration.

String
Traditional and transitional music from the USA, marketed by Topic and supervised by Tony Russell, editor of 'Old Time Music'.

STR801   *Beer Parlor Jive*.

STR802   *Fiddle Tunes from Grayson County, Virginia*: Emmett W. Lundy.

STR805   *Stompin' at the Honky Tonk*: Bar X Cowboys.

Topic/Temple
Topic SP104   'With Spoken Comments by Harry Apton, recorded by Mike Yates.' (1984).

Cassettes
Some cassettes were issued. There is knowledge of: 188; 265; 276; 291; 295; 297; 298; 300; 323; 346; 360; 380; 382. These were distributed in UK by the Selecta Group and were also available by mail order direct from Topic.

Some Topic records were issued on cassette in Ireland only. There is knowledge of: 4T175; 4T177; 4T184; 4T218; 4T230; 4T251. These were distributed in Ireland by Irish Record Factors, Dublin and were also available by mail order direct from Topic.

Bibliography

Anderson, I.A. 'The Editor's Box'. *Folk Roots*, 160 (Oct. 1996).
——. 'The Editor's Box'. *Folk Roots*, 161 (Nov. 1996).
——. 'The Editor's Box'. *Folk Roots*, 162 (Dec. 1996).
Arthur, D. Review of R. Palmer (ed.), *Songs of The Midlands*. In *Folk Music Journal*, 2/4 (1972).
Atkinson, R.F. 'The Philosophy of History'. *History Review*, 13 (Sept. 1992).
Attali, J. *Noise: The Political Economy of Music*. Translated by B. Massumi. Manchester: Manchester University Press, 1977.
Barnard, S. *On the Radio: Music Radio in Britain*. Milton Keynes: Open University Press, 1989.
Barry, P. 'The Part of the Folksinger in the Making of Folk Balladry'. In L. MacEdward and T.P. Coffin (eds), *The Critics and the Ballad*. Carbondale: Southern Illinois University Press, 1961.
Barr, T. 'Guitars and Dance'. *Making Music*, 107 (Feb. 1995).
Baudrillard, J. *The Evil Demons of Images*. Sydney: Power Institute Publications, 1987.
Bellos, Marshall, Pattenden (eds). *The Guide: Festivals '97*. The Guardian/Virgin Megastores (summer 1997).
Benjamin, W. *Illuminations*. Glasgow: Fontana, 1969.
Bluestein, G. *Poplore: Folk and Pop in American Culture*. Amherst: University of Massachusetts, 1994.
Bohlman, P. *The Study of Folk Music in the Modern World*. Bloomington and Indianapolis: Indiana University Press, 1988.
Bourdieu, P. *Distinctions*. Cambridge, Mass.: Harvard University Press, 1984, repr. 2000.
Boyes, G. *The Imagined Village: Culture, Ideology and the English Folk Revival*. Manchester: Manchester University Press, 1993.
Bradley, D. *Understanding Rock and Roll: Popular Music in Britain 1955–1964*. Oxford: Oxford University Press, 1992.
Briggs, A. 'Sleevenotes'. *Classic Anne Briggs: The Complete Topic Recordings*, Fellside FECD78 (1990).
Brocken, M. 'The Tarnished Image'. In M. Talbot (ed.), *The Business of Music*. Liverpool: Liverpool University Press, 2002.
Brown, R. 'Fred Jordan'. *Folk Music Journal*, 6/3 (1992).
Bunzl, M. *Real History: Reflections on Historical Practice*. London: Routledge, 1997.
Bush, A., et al. *Pocket Song Book*. London: Workers' Music Association, 1948.
Cantwell, R. *Ethnomimesis: Folklife and the Representation of Culture*. Chapel Hill and London: University of North Carolina Press, 1993.
Carter, S. 'All Dance and no Song?' *English Dance and Song*, 24/2 (Sept. 1960).
——. 'Editorial'. *English Dance and Song*, 25/1 (Dec. 1961).
——. 'Editorial: Pop Goes the Folk'. *English Dance and Song* (special issue, 1961).
——. 'Going American?' *English Dance and Song* (special issue, 1961).
Chester and District Standard uncredited article. 'Folk Festival's Extra Events'. *Chester and District Standard*, 18 May 2000.

Clarke, D. (ed.). *The Penguin Encyclopedia of Popular Music.* Harmondsworth: Penguin, 1989.

Cohen, S. 'More than the Beatles: Popular Music, Tourism and Urban Regeneration'. Unpublished conference paper, University of Liverpool: Institute of Popular Music, 1997.

Cohn, N. *Awopbopaloobopalopbamboom.* London: Paladin, 1970.

Collinson, F. 'A Review of Folk Song in England'. *Folk Music Journal,* 1/4 (1968), 270–72.

Cook, G. Contributor to sleevenotes. *Classic Anne Briggs: The Complete Topic Recordings,* Fellside FECD78 (1990).

Cook, T. 'What is this Playford Anyway?' *English Dance and Song,* 41/1 (1980).

Cowan, E.J. (ed.). *The People's Past: Scottish Folk, Scottish History.* Edinburgh: Polygon, 1980; 1981.

Crolls, R., and P. Dodd (eds). *Englishness: Politics and Culture 1880–1920.* London: Croom Helm, 1986.

Dalcis, V. 'Homeless Folk Rock', 'Come Write Me Down'. *Folk Roots,* 142 (Apr. 1995).

Dallas, K. 'Lonnie Donegan and Skiffle'. *The History of Rock,* 7 (1982).

——. '1964–74'. In D. Laing and R. Newman (eds), *Thirty Years of the Cambridge Folk Festival.* Ely: Music Maker Books, 1994.

Davies, G. 'Percy Grainger's Folk Music Research in Gloucestershire, Worcestershire and Warwickshire 1907–1909'. *Folk Music Journal,* 6/3 (1992).

De Lisle, T. (ed.). *Lives of the Great Songs.* Harmondsworth: Penguin, 1995.

Debord, G. *La Société du spectacle.* Paris: Buchet-Chastel, 1968.

Denselow, R. 'Folk Rock in Britain', in Laing et al., *The Electric Muse: The Story of Folk into Rock.* London: Methuen, 1975.

——. *When the Music's Over: The Story of Political Pop.* London: Faber and Faber, 1989.

Docherty, T. (ed.). *Postmodernism: A Reader.* London: Harvester Wheatsheaf, 1993.

Douglas, A. 'Owre Thanssynge Day: Parish Dance and Procession in Salisbury'. *Folk Music Journal,* 6/5 (1994).

Douglas, S. 'Is our Tradition Living?' *The Living Tradition,* 10 (Apr.–May 1995).

——. Review of *The Democratic Muse* by Ailie Munro. In *The Living Tradition,* 21 (May–June 1997).

Dundes, A. *The Study of Folklore.* Englewood Cliffs: Prentice Hall, 1965.

Eagleton, T. *Literary Theory: An Introduction.* Oxford: Blackwell, 1983.

Eyerman, R., and A. Jamison. *Music and Social Movements: Mobilizing Traditions in the Twentieth Century.* Cambridge: Cambridge University Press, 1998.

Fairbairn, H. 'Changing Contexts for Traditional Dance Music in Ireland: The Rise of Group Performance Practice'. *Folk Music Journal,* 6/5 (1994).

Finnegan, R. *The Hidden Musicians: Music-Making in an English Town.* Cambridge: Cambridge University Press, 1989.

Fox Strangways, A.H., in collaboration with M. Karpeles. *Cecil Sharp.* London: Oxford University Press, 1933.

Frame, P., with I. Mann, J. Tobler and P. Kendall (eds). *Zig Zag.* Aylesbury: Yeoman Cottage; London: Spicebox; Reading: Prestagate, 1969–77 (issues 1–72).

Freeman, P. 'Freeman in the Fray'. *Taplas,* 64 (June–July 1994).

——. 'Freeman in the Fray'. *Taplas,* 69 (Apr.–May 1995).

Friedman, A.B. (ed.). *The Penguin Book of Folk Ballads of the English-Speaking World.* Harmondsworth: Penguin, 1965, repr. 1982.

Frith, S. 'The Year it all Came Together'. *The History of Rock*, 1 (1982), 4–20.

―― and A. Goodwin (eds). *On Record: Rock, Pop and the Written Word.* London: Routledge, 1990.

Gambaccini, P., T. Rice and J. Rice. *British Hit Singles.* London: GRR Publications, 1989.

Gammon, V. 'Song, Sex, and Society in England, 1600–1850'. *Folk Music Journal*, 4/3 (1982).

――. 'Seeger and MacColl Revisited'. *English Dance and Song*, 45/3 (autumn–winter 1983).

――. 'A.L. Lloyd and History: A Reconsideration of Aspects of "Folk Song in England" and Some of his Other Writings'. In *Singer, Song and Scholar.* Sheffield: Sheffield Academic Press, 1986.

――. 'Crossing Borders'. *Root and Branch 1: A New World* (1999).

Garner, C. *Silver Screens of Wirral.* Merseyside: Countyvise, 1986.

Gillett, C. (ed.). *Rock File 2.* London: Panther, 1974.

―― and S. Frith (eds). *Rock File 3.* London: Panther, 1975.

Goldstein, R. 'The Culture War is Over! We Won! (For Now)'. *Village Voice*, 19 Nov. 1996.

Green, A. *Only a Miner.* Chicago: University of Illinois Press, 1972.

Hamm, C.E. *Putting Popular Music in its Place.* Cambridge: Cambridge University Press, 1995.

Harker, D. *Fakesong: The Manufacture of British 'Folksong' 1700 to the Present Day.* Milton Keynes: Open University Press, 1985.

Hassan, I. and S. (eds). *Innovation/Renovation: New Perspectives on the Humanities.* Madison: University of Wisconsin Press, 1986.

Hatfield, D. 'Spiritual Groundswell?', 'Come Write Me Down'. *Folk Roots*, 142 (Apr. 1995).

Heaney, M. 'With Scarfes and Garters as you Please: An Exploratory Essay in the Economics of the Morris', *Folk Music Journal*, 6/4 (1993).

Hebdige, D. *Subculture: The Meaning of Style.* London: Methuen, 1979.

Herzog, G. 'Musical Typology in Folksong'. *Southern Folklore Quarterly*, 1/2 (1937).

Hexter, J.H. *Reappraisals in History.* London: Longman, 1961.

Heywood, P. 'Editorial'. *The Living Tradition*, 3 (Jan.–Feb. 1994).

――. 'Editorial'. *The Living Tradition*, 14 (Jan.–Feb. 1996).

――. 'Tighten Your Belts!' 'Editorial'. *The Living Tradition*, 15 (Mar.–Apr. 1996).

――. 'Flowers of Edinburgh Wilt!' *The Living Tradition*, 37 (Mar.–Apr. 2000).

Hill, S. *Music-Making in Newcastle.* Unpublished undergraduate dissertation. Liverpool: University of Liverpool, Institute of Popular Music, 1997.

Hille, W. (ed.). *The People's Song Book.* New York: Boni & Gear, 1948.

Hinton, B., and G. Wall. *Ashley Hutchings: The Guv'nor and the Rise of Folk Rock.* London: Helter Skelter Books, 2002.

Hit the Dust uncredited editorial. *Hit the Dust*, 27 (June–Sept. 2000).

Hobsbawm, E.J. *Industry and Empire.* Harmondsworth: Pelican, 1968.

―― and T. Ranger (eds). *The Invention of Tradition.* Cambridge: Cambridge University Press, 1983.

Hoggart, R. *The Uses of Literacy*. Harmondsworth: Pelican, 1957.
—— *A Sort of Clowning: Life and Times Volume 2 1940–1959*. Oxford: Oxford University Press, 1991.
Humphries, P. *Meet on the Ledge*. London: Eel Pie, 1982.
Hunt, K. Contributor to sleevenotes. *Classic Anne Briggs: The Complete Topic Recordings*, Fellside FECD78 (1990).
——. 'The Roots of Modern Folk'. *Record Collector*, 175 (Mar. 1994).
Irwin, C. 'Celtic Overkill'. *Folk Roots*, 150 (Dec. 1995).
Ives, B. *The Burl Ives Songbook*, New York: Ballantine, 1953.
James, S. *The Atlantic Celts: Ancient People or Modern Invention?* London: British Museum Press, 1999.
Jencks, C. *Postmodernism*. London: Academy Editions, 1987.
Jenkins, T. *'Let's Go Dancing': Dance Band Memories of 1930s Liverpool*. Liverpool: Institute of Popular Music, 1994.
Keefe, C. 'A Short History of Luthier Guitars'. Publicity material, 2002.
Kennedy, D. *England's Dances: Folk Dancing Today and Yesterday*. London: G. Bell & Sons, 1949.
——. 'The Director Writes: The Square Dance Comes Back'. *English Dance and Song*, 17/3 (Dec.–Jan. 1952–53).
——. 'Tradition: A Personal Viewpoint'. *Folk Music Journal*, 4/3 (1982).
Kennedy, P. 'British Folk Music on Record'. *Recorded Folk Music: A Review of British and Foreign Folk Music*, 2 (Jan.–Feb. 1959).
—— (ed.). *'Everybody Swing': Square Dance Album 1*. London: Chappell & Co., 1952.
Krezmer, H. 'Sleevenotes'. *David and Marianne Dalmour*, EMI: Columbia 33sx1715 (1965).
Laing, D., with K. Dallas, R. Denselow and R. Shelton. *Electric Muse: The Story of Folk into Rock*. London: Methuen, 1975.
Laing, D., and R. Newman. *Thirty Years of the Cambridge Folk Festival*. Ely: Music Maker, 1994.
Lanza, J. *Elevator Music: A Surreal History of Muzak, Easy Listening and other Moodsong*. London: Quartet, 1994.
Larkin, C. (ed.). *The Guinness Who's Who of Folk Music*. London: Guinness/Square One, 1993.
Leader, B. 'Topic: A People's Label'. *Root & Branch 2: Everbody Swing* (2000).
Lee, K. *Hints to Collectors of Folk Music* (1898). Facsimile in *Root and Branch 1: A New World*. London and Reading: English Folk Dance and Song Society/Unknown Public (1999).
Leslie, P. 'The Music Goes Round'. *Big Bands of the 30s*. London: NEL Flashback, 1971.
Lipsitz, G. *Time Passages: Collective Memory and American Popular Culture*. Minneapolis: University of Minnesota Press, 1990.
Lloyd, A.L. *The Singing Englishman*. London: Workers' Music Association, 1944.
——. *Come all ye Bold Miners*. London: Workers' Music Association, 1952.
——. 'Introduction'. *The Iron Muse: A Panorama of Industrial Folk Song*, Topic Records 12T86 (1963).
——. *Folk Song in England*. London: Lawrence & Wishart, 1967.
——. 'Walk Out, St. George?' *Spin*, 7/1 (1969).

——. 'Towards a Distinction between "Popular" and "Folk": A Bit of History', *Club Folk* (Mar.–Apr. 1970).

Lodge, D. (ed.). *Modern Criticism and Theory*. Harlow: Longman, 1988.

Lomax, J. and A. *Folk Song USA*. New York: Signet, 1947; 1966.

Longly, D. 'The Whole Wide World Record Retailer', 'Come Write Me Down'. *Folk Roots*, 160 (Oct. 1996).

Loveless, Revd K. Review of Karpeles, *Cecil Sharp: His Life and Work*, London: Routledge & Kegan Paul (1967). In *Folk Music Journal*, 1/4 (1968), 268–70.

Mabey, R. *The Pop Process*. London: Hutchinson, 1969.

McAleer, D. *Hit Parade Heroes*. London: Hamlyn, 1993.

MacColl, E. *Journeyman: An Autobiography*. London: Sidgwick & Jackson, 1990.

—— (ed.). *Scotland Sings*. London: Workers' Music Association, 1953.

——. *The Shuttle and Cage: Industrial Folk Ballads*. London: Workers' Music Association, 1954.

McCormick, F. Appraisal of 'Cantometrics: Song and Social Culture'. In *Music Traditions*, 14 (1996), http://members.aol.com/mustrad/.

McGrail, S.'The Harpmakers'. *The Living Tradition*, 37 (Mar.–Apr. 2000).

MacInnes, C. *England, Half English*. London: Chatto & Windus, 1986.

MacKinnon, N. *The British Folk Scene: Musical Performance and Social Identity*. Buckingham: Open University Press, 1993.

McManus, K. *Ceilis, Jigs and Ballads: Irish Music in Liverpool*. Liverpool: Institute of Popular Music, 1994.

Magriel, N. Letter to the Editors of *Sing Out!*, 15/4 (Sept. 1965).

Marcus, G. *Mystery Train*. London: Omnibus, 1976.

Marriott, R. 'Letter to the Editor'. *English Dance and Song*, 45/2 (1983).

Marwick, A. *The Sixties*. Oxford: Oxford University Press, 1998.

Melly, G. *Revolt into Style*. Oxford: Oxford University Press, 1970.

Middleton, R. *Studying Popular Music*. Buckingham: Open University Press, 1990.

Moss, M., with J. Weglarski. 'Meeting the Needs of the Time – An Interview' [with Dick Gaughan]. *Sing Out!*, 30/2 (Apr.–June 1984).

Moulden, J. 'Is our Tradition Living?' *The Living Tradition*, 11 (June–July 1995).

Munro, A. *The Democratic Muse: Folk Music Revival in Scotland*. Aberdeen: Scottish Cultural Press, 1997. Revised and updated edition of *Folk Music Revival in Scotland*, London: Kahn & Averil, 1984.

Murphy, A. 'Why Age shall not Wither an Oxford Rebel: George Butterworth'. *The Times*, 5 Aug. 1996.

Negus, K. *Producing Pop: Culture and Conflict in the Popular Music Industry*. London: Edward Arnold, 1992.

Nuttall, J. *Bomb Culture*. London: Paladin, 1970.

Osgood, R. *American Round Dance Handbook*. Los Angeles: Sets In Order, 1957.

O'Toole, F. 'The Authentic Irish Tradition of Impersonating Elvis'. *Independent on Sunday*, 27 Aug. 1995.

O'Toole, M. 'The 6.5 Special … Oh Boy!' Unpublished University of Liverpool Continuing Education essay (Dec. 1996).

Palmer, R. 'A Begging We Will Go'. *English Dance and Song*, 41/1 (1979).

—— (ed.). *Songs of the Midlands*. London: E.P. Publishing, 1972.

Pegg, B. *Folk: A Portrait of English Traditional Music, Musicians and Customs.* London: Wildwood House, 1976.

Phillips, D. *Music Master Folk Music of the British Isles Catalogue Edition 1.* London: Retail Entertainment Data Publishing, 1994.

Picardie, J. 'The First Time Ever I Saw Your Face'. In T. De Lisle (ed.), *Lives of the Great Songs.* Harmondsworth: Penguin, 1995.

Piepe, J. (ed.). *The Paul Simon Songbook.* London: Pattern, 1995.

Price, S. *Primitive Art in Civilized Places.* Chicago: University of Chicago Press, 1989.

Reeves, J. *The Idiom of the People: Traditional English Verse.* London: William Heinemann, 1958.

Ridgeway, J. 'Folk Rock – From Fairport Forward: A Personal Perspective'. *The Living Tradition*, 6 (July–Aug. 1994).

Robson, J. *Poetry and Jazz.* London: Panther, 1969.

Rogan, J. *Starmakers and Svengalis: The History of British Pop Management.* London: Macdonald/Queen Anne Press, 1988.

Rosselson, L. 'Stand Up, Stand Up For? …'. *Sing Out!*, 24/4 (1975).

Russell, D. *Popular Music in England 1840–1914: A Social History.* Manchester: Manchester University Press, 1987.

Russell, I. (ed.). *Singer, Song and Scholar.* Sheffield: Sheffield Academic Press, 1986.

Sandberg, L., and D. Weissman. *The Folk Music Sourcebook.* New York: Alfred A. Knopf, Inc., 1976.

Savage, J. *England's Dreaming.* London: Faber and Faber, 1992.

Scannell, P., and D. Cardiff. *A Social History of British Broadcasting*, vol. 1: *1922–1939. Serving the Nation.* Oxford: Basil Blackwell, 1991.

Schofield, D. 'A Lancashire Mon'. *Folk Review* (Apr. 1975).

——. Review of Boyes, *The Imagined Village*, in *Folk Music Journal*, 6/4 (1993).

Seabrook, J. 'The Sound of Despair: Review of Folk Song in England'. *New Society*, 272 (14 Dec. 1967).

Selden, R. *The Theory of Criticism: From Plato to the Present.* London: Longman, 1988.

Shank, B. *Dissonant Identities: The Rock 'n' Roll Scene in Austin, Texas.* Middletown, Ct.: Wesleyan University Press, 1988.

Sharp, C. *English Folk Songs: Some Conclusions.* Taunton: Barnicott & Pearce, 1907.

Sharp Collection. 'Letter from Sharp to Mrs Howard 22 December' (1891), at Vaughan Williams Library.

——. 'Musical Herald, 1 December' (1905), at Vaughan Williams Library.

Shepard, L. 'A.L. Lloyd: A Personal View'. In I. Russell (ed.), *Singer, Song and Scholar.* Sheffield: Sheffield Academic Press, 1986.

Shotliff, J. 'Youthquake to Date and Future Proposals'. *Youthquake Information Pack*, Nov. 1994.

Shuker, R. *Understanding Popular Music.* London: Routledge, 1994.

Silber, I. 'News and Notes'. *Sing Out!* 14/6 (Jan. 1964)

Smedley, R. 'A New Society'. *Root and Branch 2: Everybody Swing* (2000).

Smithson, H. 'Come Write Me Down'. *Folk Roots*, 161 (Nov. 1996).

Stephenson, P. *Billy.* London: HarperCollins, 2001.

Stewart, B. *Where is St. George? Pagan Imagery in English Folksong.* Bradford-on-Avon: Moonraker, 1977.

Stewart, S. *On Longing.* Baltimore: Baltimore Press, 1984.

Stradling, R., and M. Hughes. *The English Musical Renaissance 1860–1940: Construction and Deconstruction*. London: Routledge, 1993.

Stump, P. *The Music's all that Matters: A History of Progressive Rock*. London: Quartet Books, 1997.

Sugden, C. 'There are Three Ways of Being "Folk"'. *The Living Tradition*, 20 (Mar.–Apr. 1997).

Susman, W. *Culture as History: The Transformation of American Society in the Twentieth Century*. New York: Pantheon Books, 1984.

Sykes, R. 'The Evolution of Englishness in the English Folksong Revival 1890–1914'. *Folk Music Journal*, 6/4 (1993).

Talbot, M. (ed.). *The Business Of Music*. Liverpool: Liverpool University Press, 2002.

The Topic Record uncredited editorial. 'A Final Word Of Appreciation ...'. *The Topic Record*, 14 (May 1941).

Thompson, E.P. *The Poverty of Theory*. London: Merlin, 1978.

Thompson, F.M.L. 'Social Control in Modern Britain'. *ReFRESH* [*Recent Findings of Research in Economic and Social History*], 5 (Autumn 1987).

———. *The Rise of Respectable Society*. London: Fontana, 1988.

Topic Catalogue uncredited editorial. 'Prologue' (1974).

Topic Press Release uncredited editorial. 'Old Tools Do a New Job' (1956).

Tosh, J. *The Pursuit of History*. London: Longman, 1984.

Upton, E. Review of *Root and Branch* in 'What's Afoot?'. In *Root and Branch* publicity material, English Folk Dance and Song Society (summer 2000).

Vale, V. and J. *Incredibly Strange Music II*. San Francisco: Re/search, 15 (1994).

Vaughan Williams, R. *National Music and Other Essays*. London: Oxford University Press, 1934; 1987.

Wales, T. (ed.). 'Special Issue: Folk Music on Records'. *English Dance and Song*, 31/3 (Autumn 1969).

———. *English Dance and Song*, 40/1 (Spring 1978).

Walser, R. *Running with the Devil: Power, Gender and Madness in Heavy Metal Music*. Middletown, Ct.: Wesleyan University Press, 1993.

Walters, N., and B. Mansfield (eds). *Music Hound Folk: The Essential Album Guide*. Detroit: Visible Ink Press, 1998.

Weskett, A. 'Come Write Me Down'. *Folk Roots*, 150 (Dec. 1995).

Whitcomb, I. *After the Ball*. Harmondsworth: Penguin, 1972.

Williams, R. *Marxism and Literature*. Oxford: Oxford University Press, 1977.

Wilson, P. 'Who Are We? The EFDSS and the Future'. *English Dance and Song*, 62/2 (Summer 2000).

Winter, E. 'Discussion: Topic Folk Song Label', *Sing*, 3/4 (Oct.–Nov. 1956).

———. 'Purists, Popularisers and Tolerators: The Clubs', *Root and Branch 2: Everybody Swing* (2000).

Wood, C. 'No Living Tradition'. *The Living Tradition*, 10 (Apr.–May 1995).

Woods, F. *Folk Revival: The Rediscovery of a National Music*. Poole: Blandford, 1979.

Woolf, A. and C. 'Pity the Downtrodden Landlord'. *Workers' Music Association Sheet Music*, no. 9029 (1944).

Woosnam, D. 'The Tizer Test: The Songs of Ewan MacColl'. *The Living Tradition*, 3 (Jan.–Feb. 1994).

——. 'The National Folk Festival at Sutton Bonnington'. *The Living Tradition*, 6 (July–Aug. 1994).

Yates, M. Review of B. Pegg, *Folk: A Portrait of English Traditional Music, Musicians and Customs* (London, 1976). In *Folk Music Journal*, 3/3 (1977).

——. 'Percy Grainger and the Impact of the Phonograph'. *Folk Music Journal*, 4/3 (1982).

York, P. *Modern Times*. London: Heinemann, 1984.

Young, J. 'Letter to the Editor'. *English Dance and Song*, 45/2 (1983).

Index